AF657412

The Meaning of Nouns

The Meaning of Nouns

Semantic Theory in Classical and Medieval India

Nāmārtha-nirṇaya
of
Kauṇḍabhaṭṭa

translated and annotated
by

Madhav M. Deshpande

D.K.Printworld (P) Ltd.
New Delhi

Cataloging in Publication Data — DK
[Courtesy: D.K. Agencies (P) Ltd. <docinfo@dkagencies.com>]

Kauṇḍa Bhaṭṭa.

[Nāmārtha-nirṇaya. English & Sanskrit]

The meaning of nouns : semantic theory in classical and medieval India = Nāmārtha-nirṇaya of Kauṇḍabaṭṭa/ translated and annotated by Madav M. Deshpande.

x, 296 p., 23 cm.

In Sanskrit; translation, annotations and introductory matter in English.

Reprint. Originally published: Dordrecht : Kluwer Academic Publishers, 1992. (Studies of classical India ; v. 13)

Includes bibliographical references. (p.)

Includes index.

ISBN 8124604312

1. Sanskrit language — Noun. 2. Sanskrit language — Semantics. I. Deshpande, Madhav M. (Madhav Murlidhar), 1946- II. Title. III. Title: Nāmārtha-nirṇaya of Kauṇḍabhaṭṭa.

DDC 491. 255 4 22

ISBN 81-246-0431-2

Published in India in 2007

Reprint from the English language edition: *The Meaning of Nouns* By Madav M. Deshpande

Copyright © 1992 Kluwer Academic Publishers, being a part of Springer Science + Business Media.

This reprint has been authorized by Springer Science + Business Media for publication in India only.

All rights reserved. No part of this publication may be reproduced or transmitted in any form or by any means, electronic or mechanical, including photocopying, recording, or any information storage or retrieval system, without prior written permission of the copyright holder.

Published and printed by:
D.K. Printworld (P) Ltd.
Regd. Office: 'Srikunj', F-52, Bali Nagar
Ramesh Nagar Metro Station
New Delhi-110 015
Phones: (011) 2545 3975; 2546 6019; *Fax*: (011) 2546 5926
E-mail: dkprintworld@vsnl.net
Website: www.dkprintworld.com

Dedicated
with
respect and affection
to
Professor George Cardona

TABLE OF CONTENTS

APPROXIMATE CHRONOLOGY OF INDIAN PHILOSOPHERS

Century	Grammar	Mīmāṃsā	Nyāya-Vaiśeṣika	Other
5th B.C.	Pāṇini			
	Yāska			
4th B.C.	Vyāḍi			
	Vājapyāyana			
3rd B.C.	Kātyāyana			
2nd B.C.	Patañjali	Jaimini	Kaṇāda	
2nd A.D.			Gautama	
4th A.D.		Śabara	Vātsyāyana	
5th A.D.	Bhartṛhari		Praśastapāda	Diṅnāga (B)
6th A.D.			Uddyotakara	
7th A.D.	Vāmana	Kumārila		Dharmakīrti (B)
	Jayāditya	Prabhākara		
		Maṇḍanamiśra		
8th A.D.				Śāntarakṣita (B)
				Kamalaśīla (B)
10th A.D.	Helārāja	Pārthasārathi	Jayantabhaṭṭa	
	Puṇyarāja	Vācaspati	Śrīdhara	
11th A.D.		Someśvara	Udayana	Mammaṭa (P)
		Bhavadeva		
12th A.D.	Kaiyaṭa			
13th A.D.			Gaṅgeśa	
14th A.D.				Viśvanātha-
15th A.D.			Raghunātha	Kavirāja (P)
16th A.D.	Bhaṭṭojī-		Mathurānātha	
	Dīkṣita			
17th A.D.	Haridīkṣita	Gāgābhaṭṭa	Viśvanātha-	Dharmarājā-
	Kauṇḍabhaṭṭa	Khaṇḍadeva	Tarkapañcānana	dhvarīndra (V)
			Jagadīśa	
			Gadādhara	
			Annambhaṭṭa	
			Padmanābhamiśra	
			Rājacūḍāmaṇimakhin	
18th A.D.	Nāgeśabhaṭṭa			

**** B = Buddhism, P = Poetics, V = Vedānta

PREFACE

This book presents a fully revised version of my Ph. D. dissertation which was originally written and completed in Philadelphia in April 1972, and was submitted to the Faculty of the Graduate School of Arts and Sciences of the University of Pennsylvania. I came to Philadelphia as a graduate student in the Department of Oriental Studies of the University of Pennsylvania in September 1968. My earlier academic training was done at Pune in India. I owe my original interest in Sanskrit grammatical tradition to Pt. Vaman Shastri Bhagwat. I studied Sanskrit grammar with him at the Tilak Maharashtra Vidyapeeth, Pune, from the early years of my highschool till I finished my master's degree in Sanskrit at the University of Poona in 1968. Other teachers with whom I studied Sanskrit grammar in my early years include Pt. N.N. Bhide and the late Pt. Narayan Shastri Dikshit. Professor S.D. Joshi of the University of Poona provided the most valuable analytical insights into Sanskrit grammar. I studied with him as part of my coursework for the master's degree in Sanskrit at the University of Poona. I also studied with Professor R.N. Dandekar, Professor G.B. Palsule, and Professor M.A. Mehendale at the University of Poona.

Mostly as a result of efforts and encouragement from Professor S.D. Joshi, I came to the University of Pennsylvania in 1968. Here, my two primary teachers were Professor Ludo Rocher and Professor George Cardona. Besides these, I also studied with Professor Henry Hoenigswald, Professor Paul Thieme, and the late Professor Bimal Krishna Matilal. I owe a great debt to Professor Ludo Rocher who was the chairman of Oriental Studies at Penn, for assisting me in every possible way and for directing me to achieve a synthesis of my eastern training in Sanskrit with the western analytical methods. Most of all I am indebted to Professor George Cardona. With him I learned not just how to read texts in Sanskrit grammar, but essentially how to argue the pros and cons of a complicated argument. It was a most rewarding experience to discuss and argue with Professor Cardona many finer points of Sanskrit grammatical theory and come away with new insights. He read every single line of my original dissertation in its many versions, and made detailed suggestions for improvements.

It has been twenty years since this dissertation was originally written. After 1972, I moved into somewhat different academic areas of Sanskrit linguistics. It was during 1989 that Professor Bimal Krishna Matilal suggested that I should revise my dissertation and publish it in the series *Studies of Classical India* of which he was the editor. I accepted his suggestion and have thoroughly rewritten the original dissertation. It has been bibliographically updated, and I have taken due notice of the many important contributions which have appeared during the last twenty years. I am deeply saddened that Professor Matilal is no longer alive to see this book in print.

I am deeply grateful to the Graduate School of Arts and Sciences of the University of Pennsylvania for providing a four year fellowship which allowed me to complete the original dissertation in a relatively short period. I am equally indebted to my many friends in Philadelphia who helped me in various ways. Last but not least, I would like to thank my wife, Shubhangi, for standing by me and encouraging me all the way.

The person most instrumental in making sure that I write a decent dissertation was after all Professor George Cardona. While I am still responsible for problems and errors in my analysis, the positive merit of the original work is due in large measure to Professor Cardona's watchful eye. Therefore, with great respect and affection, I dedicate this book to him.

Madhav M. Deshpande

April 10, 1992
Ann Arbor, Michigan

INTRODUCTION

A. *ARTHA* "MEANING"

A.1. This book aims at explicating an important Sanskrit text, i.e. Kauṇḍabhaṭṭa's *Nāmārtha-nirṇaya*. The term *nāmārtha* in this title has two components, i.e. *nāman* "name, noun, nominal" and *artha* "meaning." In attempting to comprehend theories developed by Sanskrit grammarians concerning semantics of the various linguistic units, it is absolutely important to understand the terminology of the Sanskrit grammarians in particular, and philosophers in general. While I will use the term "meaning" to render the Sanskrit term *artha,* I must clarify the intended meaning of the term "meaning," and to dissociate this term from some of its uses in the Western philosophical literature which are not relevant in the context of the use of the term *artha* in Sanskrit texts.

A.2. It is not the purpose of this book to go into a full scale comparative study of Indian and Western theories of meaning. Therefore, I shall make reference to Western discussions relating to the notion of meaning only marginally. In the Western literature on the notion of meaning, the term "meaning" is used variously for the notions of sense, reference, denotation, connotation, designatum, intension, and so on. Philosophers agree neither on their terminology, nor on their methods or their analyses. At the outset of our discussion, consider briefly the range of the use of the term "meaning."[1] Wittgenstein separates the signified object from meaning which he explains in terms of the use of words. Quine differentiates the theory of meaning from the theory of reference. Carnap speaks in terms of intension and extension. Frege distinguishes *Bedeutung* "reference" from *Sinn* "sense." John Stuart Mill advocated the distinction between the notions of denotation and connotation of words. All of these various terms have been frequently used in the modern expositions of Sanskrit texts dealing with the notion of meaning to render the Sanskrit term *artha*. However, each of these terms carries a specific significance, and no one of them adequately conveys the idea of *artha*.

A.3. The Sanskrit term *artha* conveys a broad range of meanings conveyed by the term "meaning," though the range of "meaning" in Western literature is not necessarily identical with that of the Sanskrit term *artha*. For instance, while Wittgenstein almost identifies meaning with the use of the word, the Sanskrit term *artha* does not seem to convey such a notion. Sometimes, in the Western literature, meaning of a word is regarded to be the relation of that word with the signified object. The Sanskrit term *artha* does not seem to stand for such a relation. What does then the Sanskrit term *artha* stand for? The

---

[1]For brief surveys of Western theories of meaning, see: Specht (1963: 114), and Staal (1966:305). Also see: Jerzy Pelc (1971: 195ff).

best way to comprehend the meaning of the Sanskrit term *artha* would be to understand it specifically as defined by Indian grammarians and philosophers.

A.4. Following the discussion of the term *artha* by Gadādharabhaṭṭa, it may be said that the term *artha* "meaning" stands for the object or content of a verbal cognition [*śābda-bodha-viṣaya*, cf. **E.4.**] which results from the cognition of a word (*śabda-jñāna*) on the basis of an awareness of the signification function pertaining to that word [*pada-niṣṭha-vṛtti-jñāna*, cf. **E.1.**].[2] Depending upon the kind of signification function (*vṛtti*) involved in the emergence of the verbal cognition, the resulting meaning belongs to a distinct type of meaning. In general terms, one could state the following:

a) If a verbal cognition is generated on the basis of a primary signification function (*śakti* / *abhidhā-vṛtti* / *mukhya-vṛtti*), then the object or content of that verbal cognition is called primary meaning (*śakyārtha* / *vācyārtha* / *abhidheya*).
b) If a verbal cognition is generated on the basis of a secondary signification function (*lakṣaṇā-vṛtti* / *guṇa-vṛtti*), then the object or content of that verbal cognition is called secondary meaning (*lakṣyārtha*).
c) If a verbal cognition is generated on the basis of a suggestive signification function (*vyañjanā-vṛtti*), then the object or content of that verbal cognition is called suggested meaning (*vyaṅgyārtha* / *dhvanitārtha*).
d) If a verbal cognition is generated on the basis of an intentional signification function (*tātparya-vṛtti*), then the object or content of that verbal cognition is called intended meaning (*tātparyārtha*).

A.5. Not all the different schools of Indian philosophy accept all of these different kinds of signification functions for words, and they hold substantially different views on the nature of words, meanings, and the relations between words and meanings. However, the above scheme holds true, in general, for most of the schools. It is a classification of meaning unique to Indian philosophical systems, and one needs to see how Indian notions are significantly different from Western notions.

For instance, the school of Mīmāṃsā believes that the generic property or the class property (*jāti*) such as bull-ness is the sole primary meaning of the word "bull," while the individual object which possesses this generic property, i.e. a particular bull, is only secondarily understood from the word "bull." On the other hand, a school called Kevala-vyakti-vāda argues that the particular individual bull is the sole primary meaning of the word "bull," while the generic property bull-ness is merely a secondary meaning. Let us now examine the definitions of denotation and connotation given by W.P. Alston:[3]

> "W denotes the class C = df. C is the class of all those things of which W can be truly asserted.
> W connotes the property, P = df. The possession of P by something is a necessary and sufficient condition of W being correctly asserted of it."

---

[2] *vṛttyā pada-pratipādya evārtha ity abhidhīyate*, *SV*, p. 4.
[3] W.P. Alston (1964: 16-17).

According to this definition, the word "bull" denotes the class of all individuals of which the word can be truly asserted, and it connotes the property of bull-ness such that possession of bull-ness by something is a necessary and sufficient condition for the word "bull" being truly asserted of it.

It is clear that the Indian concepts of primary meaning and secondary meaning cannot be easily and successfully correlated with Alston's concepts of denotation and connotation. These two concepts, as explained by Alston, do not suggest in any way that one of them is primary in some sense, or that the other is secondary in some sense. Similarly, the Indian concepts of primary and secondary meaning do not carry any guaranty that one of them must be an individual object or a class of objects, while the other must be a property. For instance, the school of Nyāya believes that the primary meaning of a word is an individual object qualified by a generic property (*jāti-viśiṣṭa-vyakti*). This apparently includes both denotation and connotation under primary meaning. The concept of denotation involves the notion of class. In Indian logic and semantics, little is defined in terms of classes. In Indian philosophical discourse, quantification is achieved by using the concept of a limitor or a limiting property [*avacchedaka-dharma*, cf. **E.2.**]. Concepts such as denotation and connotation are rather logical concepts, while concepts in Indian semantics such as primary meaning and secondary meaning are not merely logical notions. They depend upon one's understanding of ontology, epistemology, psychology, and language-learning processes. They also depend upon the specific attitudes and needs of different schools of thought. For example, Mīmāṃsakas must reconcile their linguistic theories with their basic attitudes toward Vedic scriptures and the needs of their system to be able to properly interpret ritual injunctions in Vedic scriptures. Thus the concepts in Indian philosophical texts are best understood in their native environment, and not by being placed blindly in the context of Western logic and semantics.

A.6. In order to understand the specifically Indian connotations of the term *artha* as used in Sanskrit grammatical and philosophical works, it is necessary to examine the use of this term in specific contexts. The two meanings of this term which play a great role in the philosophical contexts are "purpose, goal" and "object." Communication of meaning is the purpose of the use of words and in this sense the term *artha* is used in various places. But at the same time, it also involves the other meaning, i.e. "object." *Artha* refers to the object signified by a word. It often stands for an object in the sense of an element of external reality in a realistic ontology. For instance, Patañjali says:[4]

> "When a word is pronounced, an *artha* 'object' is understood. For example: 'bring a bull,' 'eat yogurt' etc. It is the *artha* that is brought in and it is also the *artha* that is eaten."

Here the term *artha* obviously stands for a tangible object which could be brought in or be eaten, and not just for a concept or a notional object. Patañjali says that the affix *ḍhaK*

---

[4] *śabdenoccaritenārtho gamyate gām ānaya dadhy aśāna iti / artha ānīyate arthaś ca bhujyate /*, *MB*, vol.I., Sec.I., p. 367.

prescribed after *agni* "fire" by rule P.4.2.33 (*agner ḍhak*) can be placed only after the word *agni* and not after the *artha* which is the burning fire.[5]

This connotation of the term *artha* as an external object in terms of a realistic ontology is also found in the schools of Nyāya and Mīmāṃsā. The *Nyāya-bhāṣya* of Vātsyāyana argues that if the relation between a word and its *artha* "meaning" were a natural external relation, there should be real experiences of burning and cutting in one's mouth after hearing words like *agni* "fire" and *asi* "sword."[6] According to both Naiyāyikas and Mīmāṃsakas, generic properties, relations, and qualities are as real as substances which possess them. When a Mīmāṃsaka says that the primary meaning of a word is a generic property, he means that the primary meaning is a real existent entity in his realistic ontology, and not a mere concept or notion. For the Buddhists of Dignāga's tradition, to put it very briefly, a word does not and cannot stand for ultimately real objects. Language cannot describe the real existent entities which exist only for the duration of a moment. Such real momentary entities are beyond perception and description. A word, therefore, always stands for a universal property (*sāmānya*), which for the Buddhist is merely a conceptual construct (*vikalpa / kalpanā*) devoid of any external reality.[7] Thus, while a Mīmāṃsaka and a Buddhist may agree that the primary meaning of a word is only a universal or generic property, this generic property is part of the external reality for the Mīmāṃsaka, while it is a mere concept for the Buddhist.

The tradition of grammarians, beginning with Bhartṛhari, seems to have followed a middle path between the realistic ontologies of Nyāya and Mīmāṃsā and the notional meaning of the Buddhist. As grammarians, these philosophers were not seriously committed to following or defending a definite metaphysical doctrine, and therefore, they finally attempted to develop a distinct view of their own as grammarians and philosophers of language. They used ontological categories as developed by other schools according to their own convenience, without committing to ontological doctrines of those schools.[8] Language is used by everyone; by a realist, by a nominalist, by an idealist, and by the rest of the world. People certainly do seem to understand meanings of words, irrespective of their metaphysical views. Thus the concept of meaning must be closely related to the concept of understanding. Whether or not things are real, people do have ideas or concepts of these things. These ideas or concepts may be Platonic reals, or mere mental constructs, they do form the content of a person's cognitions derived from language. Grammarians thus concluded that *artha* "meaning" as cognized from a word is only a conceptual entity (*bauddhārtha*). Without denying the external reality of objects in the world, Kaiyaṭa says

---

5 *iha ca vyākaraṇe arthe kāryasyāsambhavaḥ / agner ḍhag iti / na śakyate 'ṅgārebhyaḥ paro ḍhak kartum /*, *MB*, Vol.I., Sec.I., p. 367.

6 *na cāyam anumānato 'py upalabhyate - śabdāntike 'rtha iti / ... atrāgny-asi-śabdoccāraṇe pūraṇa-pradāha-pāṭanāni gṛhyeran /*, *NS-B*, p. 116.

7 Stcherbatsky (1930), Vol. II., pp. 405ff. For the Buddhist doctrine of *apoha*, see: Dhirendra Sharma (1970).

8 *asmākaṃ tu śabda-pramāṇakānām padārtha-vicārānādarād yathā-yatham padārtha-kalpanā tairthikaiḥ kṛtā tām āśritya lakṣaṇāṅgāḥ padārthā vyavasthāpyāḥ /*, *VP-H(b)*, p. 396.

that the meaning of a word is only a projection of intellect (*buddhi-pratibhāsa*). Whenever a certain word is heard, a cognition of a certain mental configuration is produced.[9] Nāgeśabhaṭṭa remarks that the external object is not the object of verbal cognition. Only a conceptual or notional entity becomes the content of verbal cognition.[10]

This takes care of expressions like "Pegasus" which are regarded in modern Western discussion on meaning as terms with empty reference. Standard examples offered by Indian philosophers such as *śaśa-śṛṅga* "horn of a rabbit" and *vandhyā-suta* "son of a barren woman," which are also terms with empty reference, become meaningful expressions once the notion of meaning is understood in terms of notional or mental objects. Though there is no horned rabbit on earth, one can still have a concept or an idea of a horn of a rabbit. The fact that this concept does not correspond to external reality does not deprive the expression "horn of a rabbit" of its meaning. For Sanskrit grammarians, the expressions "horn," "rabbit," and "horn of a rabbit" all refer to notional entities or concepts, and the fact that some of these notions do not correspond to external objects makes no difference as far as the meaningfulness of these expressions is concerned. Sanskrit grammarians are thus not concerned with truth functional values of linguistic expressions, and for them the truth of an expression and its meaningfulness are not to be equated.

A.7. Puṇyarāja, the commentator of the *Vākya-padīya*, explains the concept of *artha* in great detail, in all its technical and non-technical aspects. He mentions eighteen different kinds of *arthas*.[11] The term *artha* stands for an external real object (*vastu-mātra*), as well as for the object which is intended to be signified by a word (*abhidheya*). The latter, i.e. meaning in a linguistic sense, could be meaning in a technical context (*śāstrīya*) such as the meaning of an affix or a stem. The meaning intended to be signified may also be meaning as understood by people in actual communication (*laukika*). Then there is a further difference. Meaning may be meaning as intended to be signified by an expression (*abhidheya*), or it could be meaning which is necessarily signified when something else is really intended to be signified (*nāntarīyaka*). Almost everything that is understood from a word on the basis of some kind of signification function is covered by the term *artha* "meaning." It is to be noted again that different systems of Indian philosophy differ with each other whether something is understood from a word on the basis of a signification function of that word (*vṛtti*), or through inference (*anumāna*), or through presumption (*arthāpatti*). If a system claims that something is understood through inference or presumption, then it may not be included in the meaning of that word.

A.8. The scope of the term *artha* is actually not limited in Sanskrit texts to what is usually understood as the domain of semantics in contrast with the domain of syntax. It covers elements such as gender (*liṅga*) and number (*saṃkhyā*). It also covers the

---

[9] *buddhi-pratibhāsaḥ śabdārthaḥ, yadā yadā śabda uccaritas tadā tadā arthākārā buddhir upajāyate /, MB-P*, Vol.I., Sec.I., p. 50.

[10] *bāhyaḥ padārtho na śābda-bodhe viṣayaḥ, kiṃ tu bauddhaḥ /, MB-P-U*, Vol.I., Sec.I., p. 50.

[11] *artho 'ṣṭādaśadhā / tatra vastu-mātram abhidheyaś ca / abhidheyo 'pi dvidhā śāstrīyo laukikaś ca / ..., VP-P*, pp. 170ff. For doubts about Puṇyarāja's authorship, see: Harold Coward and K. Kunjunni Raja (1990: 201).

semantico-syntactic relations (*kāraka*) such as agent-ness (*kartṛtva*) and object-ness (*karmatva*). Tenses such as the present, past, and future, and the moods such as the imperative and optative are traditionally included in the *artha*s signified by a verb root.

Another important aspect of the concept of *artha* "meaning" is revealed in the theory of *dyotyārtha* "co-signified" meaning. There are major controversies regarding this theory. It works in the following way. According to this theory, particles such as *ca* "and" and *vā* "or" do not signify any meaning, if they are used by themselves. In a sense, they do not have any lexical meaning. However, they are said to help other words used in construction with them to signify some special aspects of their meaning.[12] For instance, in the phrase "John and Tom," the meaning of collocation (*samuccaya*) is said to be not directly signified by the word "and." The theory of *dyotyārtha* argues that collocation is a specific meaning of the two words "John" and "Tom," but that these two words are unable to signify this meaning if used by themselves. The word "and" used along with these two words allows them to signify this special meaning of collocation. Thus the word "and" may be said to function as a catalyst, helping other words to signify their own special meanings. In this way, the meaning of collocation may be regarded to be the co-signified meaning (*dyotyārtha*) of the particle "and."

To point to another unusual meaning of the term *artha*, one may refer to the problem of use and mention of words. This is handled in Sanskrit traditions in a peculiar way. According to Sanskrit grammarians, the word itself is also considered to be a part of the meaning it signifies. This aspect of *artha* is totally foreign to Western semantics. We shall have occasion to consider this issue in greater detail.

B. LOGICAL BASIS OF SEMANTIC ANALYSIS

B.1. The Indian grammatical theory as stated explicitly by Bhartṛhari and others claims that ultimately only sentences and sentence-meanings as undivided wholes are real. A sentence or a complete utterance (*vākya*) is the basic unit of actual communication, and sentence-meaning (*vākyārtha*) is the basic unit of meaning that is communicated by one person to another. According to Sanskrit grammarians, these undivided sentences and sentence-meanings are subsequently analysed by theoreticians for explanatory purposes into words and word-meanings. In some sense, these components of sentences and sentence-meanings have a lesser kind of reality. Grammarians argue that such components are useful in theoretical explanations, but have no value in real life linguistic communication. Just as words and word-meanings are abstracted from sentences and sentence-meanings, similarly stems and affixes are abstracted from words, and the meanings of stems and affixes are abstracted from the meanings of words. The wholes are

[12] *dyotakatvaṃ ca sva-samabhivyāhṛta-pada-niṣṭha-vṛtty-udbodhakatvam* /, *PLM*, p. 113.

generally viewed to be more real than the components. The components have only theoretical value. They are useful fictions.

B.2. The method used for abstracting components from wholes is the method of *anvaya-vyatireka*. These terms could be translated respectively by "concurrent occurrence" (*anvaya*) and "concurrent non-occurrence" (*vyatireka*). In commenting on P.1.2.45 (*arthavad a-dhātur a-pratyayaḥ prātipadikam*), Kātyāyana brings up a major philosophical issue. This rule defines a primary nominal stem (*prātipadika*) as a meaningful item which is neither a verb root, nor an affix. The rule thus assumes that nominal stems, verb roots, and affixes are meaningful elements. Kātyāyana begins his discussion by raising an objection: "Meaningfulness [of a nominal stem] cannot be justified, since it is never used by itself."[13] Commenting on this statement of Kātyāyana, Kaiyaṭa points out that in actual linguistic communication only sentences or perhaps whole inflected items are used. One never uses uninflected stems, roots, or affixes by themselves in real linguistic communication. Thus, one may regard whole sentences, or at most whole inflected words to be meaningful, but one may not be able to say that stems, roots, and affixes are equally meaningful.[14] Kātyāyana refutes this objection by saying: "However, [the meaningfulness of uninflected stems] is established on the basis of *anvaya* and *vyatireka*."[15] Patañjali offers a more elaborate account of the analytical method of *anvaya* and *vyatireka*. He says:[16]

> "[The meaningfulness of uninflected stems] is established. How is this done? [This is done] on the basis of concurrent occurrence (*anvaya*) and concurrent non-occurrence (*vyatireka*). What is this concurrent occurrence and concurrent non-occurrence? When one says *vṛkṣas* 'a tree,' one hears an item *vṛkṣa* ending in *a*, and the affix *s*. One also understands some meaning, i.e. something having roots, fruits, leaves etc. and singularity. When someone says *vṛkṣau* 'two trees,' some [part of the earlier] word is lost, some [new part] is added and some [part] continues to occur. [The affix] *s* is lost, [the affix] *au* is added, and the word *vṛkṣa* ending in *a* continues to occur. Similarly, some meaning is lost, some is added, and some continues to occur. [The meaning element of] singularity is lost, [that of] duality is added, and [the meaning element of] something having roots, fruits, leaves etc. continues to occur. Thus, we believe that the meaning

---

13 *arthavattā nopapadyate, kevalenāvacanāt* /, *Vt.* 7 on P.1.2.45, *MB*, Vol.I., Sec.I., p.. 47.

14 *arthavattā vākyasyaiva padasya vā loke prayujyamānasyopapadyate, na tu prakṛti-bhāgasya kevalasya prayogābhāvāt, varṇavad avyavahāryatvāt* /, *MB-P*, Vol.I., Sec.I., p. 47.

15 *siddhaṃ tv anvaya-vyatirekābhyām*, *Vt.* 9 on P.1.2.45, *MB*, Vol.I., Sec.I., p. 47.

16 *siddhaṃ tv anvaya-vyatirekābhyām / siddham etat / katham / anvayād vyatirekāc ca / ko 'sāv anvayo vyatireko vā / iha vṛkṣa ity ukte kaścic chabdaḥ śrūyate vṛkṣa-śabdo 'kārāntaḥ sakāraś ca pratyayaḥ / artho 'pi kaścid gamyate mūla-skandha-phala-palāśavān ekatvaṃ ca / vṛkṣāv ity ukte kaścic chabdo hīyate, kaścid upajāyate, kaścid anvayī / sakāro hīyate, aukāra upajāyate, vṛkṣa-śabo 'kārānto 'nvayī / artho 'pi kaścid dhīyate, kaścid upajāyate, kaścid anvayī / ekatvaṃ hīyate, dvitvam upajāyate, mūla-skandha-phala-palāśavān anvayī / te manyāmahe - yaḥ śabdo hīyate tasyāsāv artho yo hīyate, yaḥ śabda upajāyate tasyāsāv artho yo 'rtha upajāyate, yaḥ śabdo 'nvayī tasyāsāv artho yo 'nvayīti* /, *MB*, Vol.I., Sec.I., p. 47-8.

> which is lost is the meaning of the word which is lost. The meaning which is added is the meaning of the word which is added. The meaning which continues to occur is the meaning of the word which continues to occur."

In the example discussed by Patañjali, there are three linguistic items, i.e. *vṛkṣa, s,* and *au*. Similarly, three meanings are understood, i.e. "something having roots, fruits, leaves etc.," "singularity," and "duality." Let us call the three linguistic items W-1, W-2, and W-3, and the meaning elements M-1, M-2, and M-3 respectively. In the case of the expression *vṛkṣas,* we can locate the pairs [W-1, M-1], [W-2, M-2], and [~W-3, ~M-3]. In the case of *vṛkṣau*, we have the pairs [W-1, M-1], [W-3, M-3], and [~W-2 ~M-2]. We may consider one more example, i.e. *rāmas* (*rāma* + *s*). Here we have the pair [~W-1, ~M-1]. Now we can group these pairs into positive and negative sets:

	Positive	Negative
1.	[W-1, M-1]	[~W-1, ~M-1]
2.	[W-2, M-2]	[~W-2, ~M-2]
3.	[W-3, M-3]	[~W-3, ~M-3]

All these cases are supported by linguistic facts and their analysis. The positive pairs represent concurrent occurrence (*anvaya*) and the negative pairs represent concurrent non-occurrence (*vyatireka*).

B.3. The above analysis shows the logical structure of the *anvaya-vyatireka* method of abstraction. Two items, *x* and *y*, can be said to bear the *anvaya* or concurrent occurrence relation to each other, if they satisfy the condition "*y* occurs, where *x* occurs," and they can be said to bear the *vyatireka* or concurrent non-occurrence relation to each other, if they satisfy the condition "*y* does not occur, where *x* does not occur" or "~*y* occurs, where ~*x* occurs." If two items satisfy these conditions, then they can be said to have a causal relationship. If a word *W* and a meaning *M* satisfy these two conditions, one can say with certainty that *M* is the meaning of *W*. Grammarians use this method to show that a particular linguistic item can be said to have a particular meaning on definite logical grounds. This method establishes a causal relation between an occurrence of a word *W* and a cognition of a meaning *M*, by arguing that when *W* occurs, there is a cognition of *M*, and that when *W* does not occur, there is no cognition of *M*.[17]

B.4. This method of *anvaya-vyatireka* serves as the foundation of linguistic and semantic analysis in the different systems of Indian philosophy, and its explicit formulation goes back to the works of the grammarians Kātyāyana and Patañjali. Different schools of philosophy have applied this method to various different problems and have arrived at varying results.[18] However, the tradition of Sanskrit grammarians beginning with Bhartṛhari believes that the results arrived at by the method of *anvaya-vyatireka* do not represent the real nature of either linguistic items or their meanings. This method, they argue, leads to divisions of linguistic items and meaning items, and that these divisions are

17 Cardona (1967-68: 337, 351-2).

18 *TV(b)*, pp. 276, 950; *MS-B(a)*, Pt.. I., p. 305, and Pt. IV., p. 1205; *TS-D*, pp. 317-321; and *VP-H(P)*, p. 265.

unreal from the point of view of linguistic communication. For Bhartṛhari, there are no divisions in speech acts and communicated meanings. He says that only a person ignorant of the real nature of language believes the divisions of sentences into words, stems, roots, and affixes to be real. Such divisions are useful fictions and have an explanatory value in grammatical theory, but they have no reality in communication.[19] The method of *anvaya-vyatireka* is said to be useful for grammatical deliberations and explanations, though ultimately leading to fictitious divisions of sentences and sentence-meanings.[20] Grammarian-philosophers say that unless and until the whole sentential speech units and the whole sentence-meanings are analysed into some kind of components, however unreal from an ultimate point of view, it would not be possible to initiate an ignorant person into a language.[21] From a theoretical point of view, one can divide up sentences and sentence-meanings into their components, but, in reality, there is no sequence in the cognitions of these different components. The seeming sequence does not exist either in the mind of the speaker or the listener. A sentence-meaning becomes an object or content of a single instance of cognition. Its multifarious qualifications are all integrated into a unity. Such a unified cognitive content is subsequently analysed into unreal divisions and sequences through various theoretical processes.[22]

B.5. Bhartṛhari distinguishes between two kinds of meanings.[23] He uses the terms *apoddhāra-padārtha* and *sthita-lakṣaṇa-padārtha* to refer to these two kinds of meanings. The *sthita-lakṣaṇa-padārtha* refers to meaning as it is actually understood in an instance of linguistic communication. It is of fixed nature and it is a given item which the grammarians cannot alter. Such is the meaning of indivisible sentential utterances. Since the sentential utterances are viewed as being indivisible and fixed in their nature, the meaning understood from these utterances is also fixed and indivisible. Such indivisible sentential utterances and their indivisible meanings subsequently become the starting point for the application of the analytical method of *anvaya-vyatireka*. The meaning elements resulting from the application of the method of *anvaya-vyatireka* are called *apoddhāra-padārtha* "abstracted meanings" or "meanings of abstracted linguistic items." Prior to their abstraction from unified sentence-meanings, such meanings are closely interrelated and integrated with other meanings. Such interrelated and integrated meanings are freed from their interrelations during the process of abstraction. Such abstracted meanings are not

---

19 *śabdasya na vibhāgo 'sti kuto 'rthasya bhaviṣyati / vibhāgaiḥ prakriyā-bhedam avidvān pratipadyate //*, *VP*, II.13.

20 *anvaya-vyatirekau tu vyavahāra-nibandhanam /*, *VP*, II. 12cd.

21 *śāstre padasya prakṛti-pratyayayor anvaya-vyatirekābhyāṃ vinā katham ajño vyutpādyeta /*, *VP-P*, p. 33.

22 *na hi śabdasya kramavatī viramya viramya svārthādiṣu vṛttiḥ sambhavati, sakṛd uccāraṇāt / ... pratipatti-kramo hy ayaṃ śrotur abhidhātur vā na vyavasthitaḥ / sarva-viśeṣaṇa-viśiṣṭaṃ hi vastu ... yaugapadyenaikasyā buddher viṣayatām āpannam ... buddhy-antaraiḥ pravibhajyate /*, *VP-S*, Pt. I., pp. 67-69.

23 *apoddhāra-padārthā ye ye cārthāḥ sthita-lakṣaṇāḥ /*, *VP*, I.24. The *Svopajña* commentary on this verse says: *apoddhāra-padārtho nāmātyanta-saṃsṛṣṭaḥ saṃsargād anumeyena parikalpitena rūpeṇa prakṛta-vivekaḥ sann apoddhriyate / praviviktasya hi tasya vastuno vyavahārātītaṃ rūpam / tat tu sva-pratyayānukāreṇa yathāgamam bhāvanābhyāsavaśād utprekṣayā prāyeṇa vyavasthāpyate / ... so 'yam apoddhāra-padārthaḥ śāstra-vyavahāram anupatati /*, *VP-S*, Pt. I., pp. 57-58.

representative of the actual meanings understood in an act of communication, and hence stand beyond the range of normal usage. Such abstracted meanings are meanings only in a technical or theoretical sense (*śāstrīya*), and they serve the purpose of building explanatory or derivational processes in particular grammatical or philosophical systems. The results of such abstractions depend upon how the method of *anvaya-vyatireka* has been applied in a given system and may differ from tradition to tradition, and from person to person. The aims, attitudes, and presuppositions of a given philosophical system affect the results of abstraction. Thus the same sentential utterances or words could be analysed differently by different schools of thought. Since the analysed elements do not represent the real nature of language, their acceptability or unacceptability depends only upon internal consistency of a particular system. The various theories of nominal meaning under discussion in the work of Kauṇḍabhaṭṭa, translated here, are results of such semantic and linguistic speculation carried out by different schools of Indian thought for over two thousand years.

C. WHAT IS A *NĀMAN* "NOUN, NOMINAL STEM"?

C.1. The term *nāmārtha* "meaning of nouns, nominal stems" involves two factors, a *nāman* "noun, nominal stem" and its *artha* "meaning." So far we have talked about the notion of *artha*. Here, we shall discuss what is meant by the term *nāman* "noun, nominal stem." Starting with the basic reality of whole sentences, their component "parts of speech" are obtained by the process of abstraction (*apoddhāra*) which is based on the method of *anvaya-vyatireka* "concurrent occurrence and concurrent non-occurrence."[24] Just as words are abstracted from whole sentential utterances, so are stems, roots, and affixes abstracted from words.

Original Vedic texts are called *saṃhitā* "continuous, unbroken texts," and these Vedic Saṃhitās were later analysed by ancient scholars into sequences of individual words called *pada-pāṭha*. Works called *Prātiśākhyas* were composed to provide rules of euphonic combinations between words, so that, starting with a word-by-word version given in the *pada-pāṭha*, one could build the *Saṃhitā* version. Somehow the Vedic exegetical traditions came to believe that the word-by-word versions given by the *pada-pāṭha* were more basic and that the *saṃhitā* "continuous, unbroken text" versions were secondarily derived by applying the rules of euphonic combination. On the other hand, the tradition of Sanskrit grammarians argued that the continuous unbroken versions of Vedic texts were the real original versions, and that the word-by-word versions given in the *pada-pāṭha* were secondarily derived by applying the method of abstraction.[25] Historically speaking, the

---

[24] *apoddhṛtyaiva vākyebhyaḥ prakṛti-pratyayādivat* /, *VP*, III.1.1.

[25] *pada-prakṛtiḥ saṃhitā*, *NR*, p. 23. This statement of *Nirukta* is interpreted differently by different systems. The traditions of Vedic exegesis generally interpret this statement to mean that the words are the source for the continuous text (*padāni prakṛtiḥ yasyāḥ sā saṃhitā*). Sanskrit grammarians, on the other hand, interpret this statement to mean that the continuous text is the source for the word-by-word text (*padānām prakṛtiḥ saṃhitā*).

creation of the word-by-word versions of Vedic texts by analysing the continuous Saṃhitā texts marks the beginning of analytical linguistic activity in India. In some instances, the abstracted word-by-word versions also analyse inflected items into stems and affixes, e.g., *rājabhiḥ* > *rāja* + *bhiḥ*. As far as we know, the abstracted word-by-word versions of Vedic texts seem to predate the surviving grammatical texts, and hence may have provided a foundation for the emergence of formal grammatical systems.

C.2. The first systematic linguistic analysis of morphemic units such as stems, affixes, and roots is found in the *Prātiśākhya*s, in Yāska's *Nirukta*, and in Pāṇini's *Aṣṭādhyāyī*. The relative chronology of these texts is still debated by scholars and we shall not get into this debate here. Suffice it to say that the *Prātiśākhya*s as we have them represent texts which have been updated again and again, and hence do contain materials belonging to different periods. It is likely that the same is true of *Nirukta* and *Aṣṭādhyāyī*. The *Nirukta* speaks of four parts of speech (*pada-jātāni*), i.e. *nāman* "noun, nominal stem," *ākhyāta* "verb," *upasarga* "prepositional items prefixed to a verb," and *nipāta* "particle."[26] Here, by the terms *nāman* and *ākhyāta*, Yāska appears to refer to inflected nominal and verbal forms, rather than nominal stems and verb root, though it is possible that by citing inflected items as examples for these categories, he intends to refer to their abstract root and stem forms. Yāska offers semantic definitions of these categories. According to him, a *nāman* "noun, nominal stem" is a word whose principal referent is a *sattva* "an existent, a being, a thing, an entity." It refers to something which already exists. In contrast to this, an *ākhyāta* "verb" refers to *bhāva* "becoming, a fluid action, an action as a process."[27] The same passage also tells us about the etymological values of nominal items and verb roots. According to Yāskan etymologists and the grammarian Śākaṭāyana, every nominal item can be ultimately derived from a verb root. On the other hand, the etymologist Gārgya and some grammarians held that only some, and not all, nominal items can be derived from verb roots, and that there must be some underivable nominal items. Thus, according to a majority of etymologists, every nominal was made up of two or more morphemic items such as a verb root and an affix. The etymological meaning of every nominal must, then, be a combination of the meaning of a verb root and the meaning of an affix. Thus, each nominal item must etymologically refer to an action and something that participates in that action in some way. However, the etymologists were aware of the fact that the etymological meaning of words was not always identical with the conventional meaning of those words in actual usage. This awareness is also shared by many later theorists in Sanskrit traditions. For instance, Viśvanātha, the author of *Sāhitya-darpaṇa*, says that the etymological justification (*vyutpatti-nimitta*) for a given word is different from the reason why a word is actually used in an instance of communication (*pravṛtti-nimitta*).

---

26 *tad yāny etāni catvāri pada-jātāni nāmākhyāte copasarga-nipātāś ca* /, *NR*, p. 23.

27 *tatraitan nāmākhyātayor lakṣaṇam pradiśanti bhāva-pradhānam ākhyātaṃ sattva-pradhānāni nāmāni* /, *NR*, p. 23. Also: *nāmāny ākhyātajānīti nairukta-samayaḥ śākaṭāyanaś ca* / *na sarvāṇīti gārgyo vaiyākaraṇānāṃ caike* /, ibid.

He demonstrates that the word *go* "bull," derived from the verb root *gam* "to go" by adding the affix *-ḍo* etymologically stands for something that goes. However, as Viśvanātha notices, not everything that goes is called *go*, nor would a sleeping bull not be called *go*.[28] The *Ṛk-prātiśākhya* also defines the terms *nāman* and *ākhyāta* in a way analogous to *Nirukta*.[29]

C.3. These early discussions in the *Prātiśākhyas* and *Nirukta* had a substantial impact on the development of later philosophical systems in India. Mīmāṃsakas follow Yāska's lead in defining the term *nāman* by using a semantic characterization. Someśvara in his commentary *Nyāya-sudhā* on Kumārilabhaṭṭa's *Tantra-vārttika* explicitly acknowledges the reliance of Mīmāṃsā upon Yāska's notion that the meaning of nominals is dependent upon the meaning of verbs from which those nominals are derived. According to Someśvara, this opens up a way to interpret nominals by tracing the meanings of verb roots from which they could be derived.[30] Jaimini's *Mīmāṃsā-sūtras* define a *nāman* as a word whose utterance leads to a cognition of the form of an object.[31] Śabara clarifies Jaimini's definition by pointing out that what is understood from a *nāman* is something that lasts for a while after its production and is not destroyed immediately like an action. Action as signified by a verb is fluid and it has no stable existence. On the other hand, the referent of a nominal item is an accomplished, established, and stable existent entity. A *nāman* is a word which signifies either a substance or a quality. By the inclusion of qualities among referents of nominal items, Śabara intends to include adjectives into the category of *nāman*.[32]

C.4. The tradition of Nyāya recognizes the distinctions between an inflected word and its components, i.e. stems, roots, and affixes. The *Nyāya-sūtras* of Gautama define a *pada* "an inflected word" as a group of sounds ending in terminal affixes (*vibhakti*).[33] In his *Nyāya-bhāṣya*, the commentator Vātsyāyana says that terminal affixes (*vibhakti*) are of two types, i.e. case endings which are added after nominal items (*nāmikī*) and finite verb endings which are added after verb roots (*ākhyātikī*). This division of terminal affixes tells us that there are two types of stems, i.e. nominal stems and verb

---

28 In elaborating Gārgya's view that all nominal items are not derived from verbs, *Nirukta* says: *atha cet sarvāṇy ākhyātajāni nāmāni syur yaḥ kaś ca tat karma kuryāt sarvaṃ tat sattvaṃ tathācakṣīran yaḥ kaś cādhvānam aśnuvītāśvaḥ sa vacanīyaḥ syād yat kiñcit tṛndyāt tṛṇaṃ tad athāpi cet sarvāṇy ākhyātajāni nāmāni syur yāvadbhir bhāvaiḥ samprayujyeta tāvadbhyo nāmadheya-pratilambhaḥ syāt tatraivaṃ sthūṇā daraśayā vā sañjanī ca syāt* /, *NR*, I.12. In poetics, Viśvanātha says: *anyad dhi śabdānāṃ vyutpatti-nimittam anyad dhi pravṛtti-nimittam / ... gamer ḍoḥ iti gama-dhātor ḍo-pratyayena vyutpāditasya go-śabdasya śayana-kāle 'pi prayogāt* /, *SD*, p. 9.

29 *nāmākhyātam upasargo nipātaś catvāry āhuḥ pada-jātāni śabdāḥ / tan nāma yenābhidadhāti sattvam, tad ākhyātaṃ yena bhāvaṃ sa-dhātu* //, *RP*, 12.17-19.

30 *niruktād avagato yo dhātvartha-pūrvako nāmārthaḥ / sarvaṃ nāma dhātujam ity artha-kalpanā-dvāraṃ nirukte pradarśitam* /, *TV-NS*, Fasc. III, pp. 225-6.

31 *yeṣām utpattau sve prayoge rūpopalabdhis tāni nāmāni* /, *MS*, 2.1.3.

32 *yeṣāṃ śabdānām uccāraṇotpattau sve 'rthe prayujyamānānāṃ rūpam upalabhyate, yat sakṛd utpannaṃ kālāntaraṃ tiṣṭhati, na kriyā iva utpanna-mātraṃ vinaśyatīty arthaḥ / tāni nāmāni / te dravya-guṇa-śabdāḥ* /, *MS-B(a)*, Pt.I., p. 387.

33 *te vibhakty-antāḥ padam* /, *NS*, 2.2.58.

roots.[34] The later tradition of Nyāya also accepts this two-fold division of stems and inflected items.[35] In contrast with the semantic definitions of *nāman* found in *Prātiśākhyas*, *Nirukta*, and Mīmāṃsā works, definitions found in the works of Naiyāyikas are formal definitions. They do not make a reference to the meaning of nominal stems or verb roots. In offering these formal definitions, Naiyāyikas follow the lead of Sanskrit grammarians. Like Sanskrit grammarians, Naiyāyikas include *upasargas* "prepositional items prefixed to verbs" and *nipātas* "particles" in the category of *nāman*. Naiyāyikas point out that nominal case endings are deleted after items included in the categories of *upasarga* and *nipāta*, and thus these two are simply sub-categories of the larger category of *nāman*.[36] Jagadīśa Bhaṭṭacārya, in his *Śabda-śakti-prakāśikā*, explicitly remarks that the scope of the notion of *nāman* in the Nyāya system is not different from that of the notion of *prātipadika* in Pāṇini's grammar.[37]

C.5. It is believed in the Indian grammatical tradition, that the ancient school of Indra's grammar analysed sentences into their meaningful components, i.e. words, but that it did not distinguish between different categories of words.[38] Pāṇini offers a formal definition of a nominal stem (*prātipadika*), unlike the tradition of *Nirukta* and the *Prātiśākhyas*. Pāṇini's view regarding the etymological status of nominal stems differs from that of Yāska, but seems to come closer to Gārgya's view as reported earlier. Pāṇini believed that while some nominal stems were derived from other more primary units, there were some nominal stems which could not be broken down into their constituents, and hence were essentially underived. Thus, there are two definitions in Pāṇini's grammar to cover the underived and the derived nominal stems. P.1.2.45 (*arthavad a-dhātur a-pratyayaḥ prātipadikam*) says that a [primitive or underived] nominal stem is a meaningful linguistic item which is neither a verb root, nor an affix. This definition presumes that there are three basic types of linguistic items, i.e. nominal stems, verb roots, and affixes. Of these three types, the verb roots are fully listed in the *Dhātu-pāṭha*, which forms an appendix to Pāṇini's grammar. Similarly, affixes are also fully specified by the rules of his grammar. Thus, the remaining category is that of nominal stems. Nominal stems are not fully specified or listed in an appendix to Pāṇini's grammar, but are defined through exclusion of verb roots and affixes. Secondary or derived nominal stems are defined by P.1.2.46 (*kṛt-taddhita-samāsāś ca*). This rule says that formations ending in *kṛt* and *taddhita* affixes and compounds are also nominal stems. The *kṛt* affixes are those affixes which are added to verb roots to derive verbal nouns of various sorts. The *taddhita* affixes are added to nominal stems to derive secondary nouns. Compounds are derived through

---

34 *vibhaktir dvayī, nāmiky ākhyātikī ca /*, *NS-B*, p. 152.

35 *niruktā prakṛtir dvedhā nāma-dhātu-prabhedataḥ /*, *SSP(a)*, p. 68.

36 *upasarga-nipātās tarhi na pada-saṃjñāḥ / lakṣaṇāntaraṃ vācyam iti / śiṣyate ca khalu nāmikyā vibhakter avyayāl lopas tayoḥ pada-saṃjñārtham iti /*, *NS-B*, p. 1 52.

37 *yat pāṇiny-ādi-prabhṛtibhiḥ prātipadikam prakṛtir ity-ādy-uktaṃ tad api nāmno nātiricyate /*, *SSP(a)*, p. 68.

38 *na [nairuktānām] ekam pada-jātaṃ yathārthaḥ padam aindrāṇām iti /*, *NR-B*, p. 35.

combinations of two or more nominal stems. In Pāṇini's grammar, there are only two types of basic stems (*prakṛti*), i.e. *prātipadika* "nominal stem" and *dhātu* "verb root." Only nominal stems can take case endings (i.e. *sup* affixes), and only verb roots can take finite verbal endings (i.e. *tiṅ* affixes). Items ending in these two types of terminal affixes are formally called *padas* "inflected words" by P.1.4.14 (*sup-tiṅ-antam padam*). According to Pāṇini's grammar, only *padas* or inflected words are usable in sentences. In order to get the designation of *pada*, the so-called indeclinable items of Sanskrit vocabulary such as *nipātas* "particles" must in fact receive case endings. For this purpose, these items are included in the class of *prātipadika*. These so-called indeclinable items do take case endings like all other nominal stems, but these case endings are unconditionally deleted after these items by P.2.4.82 (*avyayād āp-supaḥ*). Thus, in Pāṇini's grammar, indeclinable items are those after which case endings are deleted, rather than those which do not take any case endings. Thus, *prātipadika* is only a formal category in Pāṇini's grammar. While Pāṇini assumes these to be meaningful items, there is no further commitment as to the kind of meaning they express.

C.6. While Pāṇini thus stayed away from the semantic definitions of categories like *prātipadika* "nominal stem" and *dhātu* "verb root," his successors returned to the semantic definitions given by Yāska. Patañjali refers to the semantic definitions of these categories, as well as to the four-fold classification of words into *nāman* "nominal stem," *ākhyāta* "verb root," *upasarga* "prepositions prefixed to verbs," and *nipāta* "particles."[39] Patañjali simply replaces the word *sattva* by a more familiar word, i.e. *dravya* "substance." Instead of saying that a nominal signifies a *sattva*, Patañjali says that it signifies a *dravya* "substance" [cf. **D.3.v**]. Sanskrit grammarians care for Pāṇini's two-fold division of stems into nominal stems and verb roots only as far as the derivational procedures in his grammar are concerned. Nāgeśabhaṭṭa attempts to reconcile the fourfold Yāskan division of parts of speech with the twofold division proposed by Pāṇini.[40] However, when it comes to discussing the semantics of words, Sanskrit grammarians generally follow the four-fold division of Yāska, rather than the two-fold division of Pāṇini. Nāgeśabhaṭṭa and Vaidyanātha refuse to accept that indeclinable items (*avyaya*) should be included in the category of *nāman* "nominal stems."[41] Kauṇḍabhaṭṭa and Nāgeśabhaṭṭa separate the *upasargas* "prepositions prefixed to verbs" and *nipātas* "particles" from the category of *nāman* "nominal stem," and treat meanings of these three categories in different sections of their works. In this limited sense, *nāman* includes nouns and adjectives, but excludes prepositions prefixed to verbs and particles. On the whole, Kauṇḍabhaṭṭa's *Nāmārtha-nirṇaya* "Determination of the Meaning of *Nāman*" deals with the meaning of non-adjectival nominals. From a formal point of view, substantives and adjectives form one and

---

39 *catvāri śṛṅgāṇi pada-jātāni nāmākhyātopasarga-nipātāś ca /*, *MB*, Vol.I., Sec.I., p. 30; and *kriyā-pradhānam ākhyātam bhavati / dravya-pradhānaṃ nāma /*, ibid., Vol.II., p. 625.

40 *nāma-śabdena sub-antam ... / upasarga-nipātayoḥ pṛthag upādānaṃ go-balīvarda-nyāyena /*, *MB-P-U*, Vol.I., Sec.I., p. 31.

41 *vastuto 'vyayeṣu nāmatvam eva nety agre vakṣyāmaḥ /*, *LM*, p. 590.

the same class for Sanskrit grammarians, although they do differ in their semantics. At best they are subtypes of the category of *nāman* or *prātipadika*.

D. ONTOLOGY OF POSSIBLE NOMINAL MEANINGS

D.1. The discussion of meaning in Indian grammatical and philosophical systems invariably takes us to a discussion of some sort of ontological categories. Terms like *jāti* "class / class property," *dravya* "substance," *guṇa* "quality," and *kriyā* "action" are used by Pāṇini in his grammar to refer to different kinds of meanings understood from words, though he does not explicitly define or defend an ontological system. It appears that a rudimentary ontological system with some such categories is taken for granted by Pāṇini. It is axiomatic for him, undefined but taken for granted. To the extent it is undefined, we are unable to reconstruct a truly systematic ontology for Pāṇini. However, without such an axiomatic ontological system, Pāṇini would not have been able to describe his semantic categories. Pāṇini does not clearly explain the nature of the meaning of nominals, though we can make some important inferences. His rule P.2.3.46 (*prātipadikārtha-liṅga-parimāṇa-vacana-mātre prathamā*), in its non-traditional but straight forward interpretation, says that the nominative case affix is added to a nominal stem to denote the meaning of the nominal stem (*prātipadikārtha*), gender, and number alone. At the very least, such an interpretation would allow us to distinguish the meaning of a nominal stem (*prātipadikārtha*) from the meaning categories of gender and number. It would seem that these notions were not included in the meaning of the nominal stem itself, but were extraneous to it. Similarly, one might also argue that the *kāraka* categories were also extraneous to the meaning of a nominal stem. Now, one may wonder about what was included in the notion of *prātipadikārtha*. There are numerous kinds of specific meaning categories mentioned in Pāṇini's grammar, and we shall not concern ourselves with those. As far as the so called ontological categories are concerned, Patañjali points out that Pāṇini held both a *dravya* "entity, substance" and *ākṛti* "generic property" as possible meanings signified by a nominal (cf. *ubhayathā hy ācāryeṇa sūtrāṇi praṇītāni / ākṛtim padārthaṃ matvā "jāty-ākhyāyām ekasmin bahuvacanam anyatarasyām" ity ucyate / dravyam padārtham matvā "sarūpāṇām" ity ekaśeṣa ārabhyate /, MB,* Vol.I., Sec.I., p. 44). Without going into an extensive examination of Pāṇini's view, one may point out that he does not use the term *ākṛti*, and that the term *jāti* which he uses in a number of rules refers to a notion of class, rather than to an abstract class or generic property. Similarly, his term for the notion of entity was most probably *sattva*, as can be inferred from rule P.1.4.57 (*cādayo 'sattve*). Besides the term *sattva*, the terms *dravya* [cf. P.5.4.11 (*kim-et-tiṅ-avyaya-ghād āmv a-dravya-prakarṣe*)] and *adhikaraṇa* [cf. P.2.4.13 (*vipratiṣiddhaṃ cānadhikaraṇavāci*)] in his rules also seem to refer to a notion of entity or substance. However, beyond these generalities, it is difficult to reconstruct a more systematic account of Pāṇini's notions. As we move into later periods, we find that the ontological categories come in for a close philosophical examination and numerous alternative ontologies are defined and defended by the various schools of Indian philosophy. In what follows, we shall principally consider the ontological views of Sanskrit grammarians, Naiyāyikas, and Mīmāṃsakas. The ontological views are directly connected to conceptions regarding what one understands from words. The general argument is that linguistic utterances tell us something about real or assumed states of the external world, and hence our conceptions about the structure of the external world are inevitably linked to what we think we understand from linguistic utterances.

To put this in more traditional terms, we can say the following. In an instance of linguistic communication, when one hears a certain word such as *gauḥ* "bull," one is said to understand several different things. As Kumārilabhaṭṭa argues, we cognize seven different meanings or rather entities (*vastūni*) from a word such as *gauḥ* "bull."[42] These are as follows: *jāti* "class property or generic property," *vyakti* "individual or particular object," *sambandha* "relation between the earlier two," *samūha* "collection of these elements," *liṅga* "gender," *kāraka* "semantico-syntactic role of the given object in relation to the production of the activity signified by the verb," and *saṃkhyā* "number." Naiyāyikas argue that *ākṛti* "configuration of the various components of an object" (*avayava-saṃsthāna-viśeṣa*) is different from class property or generic property (*jāti*) and that it is also understood from a nominal stem.[43] Ontological factors such as qualities (*guṇa*) and actions (*kriyā*) are also possible meaning elements understood from a nominal stem. Of these various possible meanings of nominal stems, Kauṇḍabhaṭṭa concentrates only on five meanings in his *Nāmārtha-nirṇaya*, i.e. generic or class property (*jāti*), individual or particular object (*vyakti*), gender (*liṅga*), number (*saṃkhyā*), and the role of the object as a participant in an action (*kāraka*). Kauṇḍabhaṭṭa only deals with these different factors as regards their status as meanings, but takes for granted that the reader knows what these things mean in terms of their ontological or metaphysical status. He does not discuss the ontological nature of these categories. However, in this traditional debate concerning semantics, ontological commitment plays a significant role, and therefore it is important to have a clear idea about the ontological status of these possible meaning elements. In what follows, I shall briefly review the ontological discussions regarding these various elements in the systems of Nyāya, Mīmāṃsā, and Sanskrit grammar. While other systems of philosophy also have their own distinct views regarding these factors, we shall limit ourselves to a consideration of only these three systems, because Kauṇḍabhaṭṭa's work generally does not go beyond a consideration of these three systems. This review of ontological discussions is necessarily brief, and is only aimed at introducing the relevant ontological context of these semantic

---

42 *gaur ity uccarite sapta vastūni pratibhānti naḥ / jātir vyaktiś ca sambandhaḥ samūho liṅga-kārake // saṃkhyā ca saptamī /*, *TV(b)*, p. 267. We should note that very few systems of Indian philosophy treat notions such as *sambandha* "relation" and *samūha* "grouping of various elements" as independent meaning elements.

43 *sā ca [ākṛtir] nānyā sattvāvayavānāṃ tad-avayavānāṃ ca niyatād vyūhād iti /*, *NS-B*, p. 156.

categories, rather than a full scale debate regarding either the history of these discussions, or their viability.

D.2. *JĀTI / ĀKṚTI* "GENERIC PROPERTY / CONFIGURATION"

D.2.i. The terms *jāti* and *ākṛti* appear frequently in Sanskrit texts, and yet their usage differs from text to text. Thus it is necessary to see how each system, or author, uses these terms in a distinct way. Naiyāyikas use both the terms, but with a distinction of meaning. Gautama, in his *Nyāya-sūtra*, distinguishes these two notions in the following way: "*ākṛti* is said to be an indicator [of the existence of] a *jāti*."[44] Here the term *ākṛti* refers to the unique configuration of the different component parts of an object (*avayava-saṃsthāna-viśeṣa*), and it is variously described as "form" or "common structural pattern." The term *jāti* refers to a universal or a generic property or a class property. By observing the particular configuration of an object, one recognizes that that object possesses a certain generic property. In modern terms of logic, one may say that this is how one concludes that an object is a member of a certain class. However, the Naiyāyika ontology asserts the existence of a generic property or a universal, rather than that of a class. The particular configuration of a bull helps us recognize the presence of the generic property of bull-ness in a given entity and ensures membership of that entity in the class of all bulls. However, not all entities have this kind of discernible configuration. On the other hand, Naiyāyikas say that there are cases where a configuration exists without the presence of the related generic property. For instance, a miniature bull made out of clay is said to possess the bull configuration (*gavākṛti*), but does not possess the generic property of bull-ness.

D.2.ii. Gautama, in his *Nyāya-sūtra*, defines *jāti* "universal or generic property" as "[that property of an object which] by its nature produces a uniform cognition [of different objects possessing that property]."[45] According to Vātsyāyana's *Nyāya-bhāṣya* on this definition, a *jāti* "generic property, universal" causes a uniform or identical cognition of different objects and is the reason why so many different objects [possessing that generic property] are not distinguished [in kind] from one another. It causes recurrence of an identical cognition on different occasions. It also helps differentiate one object such as a bull from other objects such as horses, while it removes its difference [of kind] from certain other objects, i.e. other bulls.[46] The term *sāmānya* is also used in Sanskrit literature on many occasions to refer to a *jāti* "generic property, universal." Annambhaṭṭa defines a generic property or universal (*sāmānya, jāti*) as a property which is eternal, single, and is shared by a plurality of objects.[47] If a property is possessed by only one object and none

---

[44] *ākṛtir jāti-liṅgākhyā* /, *NS*, 2.2.68.

[45] *samāna-prasavātmikā jātiḥ* /, *NS*, 2.2.69.

[46] *yā samānām buddhim prasūte bhinneṣv adhikaraṇeṣu, yayā bahūnītaretarato na vyāvarttyante, yo 'rtho 'nekatra pratyayāvṛtti-nimittaṃ, tat sāmānyam / yac ca keṣāñcid abhedaṃ kutaścid bhedaṃ karoti tat sāmānya-viśeṣo jātiḥ* /, *NS-B*, p. 156.

[47] *nityam ekam anekānugataṃ sāmānyam* /, *TS*, pp. 75-76.

other, then it cannot be regarded to be a generic property in the strict Nyāya sense. For instance, according to Nyāya ontology, entities such as ether (*ākāśa*), time (*kāla*), and direction (*dik*) are unique entities. Thus properties such as ether-ness (*ākāśatva*), time-ness (*kālatva*), and direction-ness (*diktva*) are proper only to one single entity each, and hence they cannot be regarded as generic properties in the Nyāya system.[48] On the other hand, properties such as color are shared by many objects, and are yet viewed as being not eternal in the Nyāya system. Hence, such properties are classed separately as qualities (*guṇa*), and are distinguished from generic properties.

D.H.H. Ingalls explains another important point concerning *jāti* in the Nyāya system. He says:[49]

> "In non-Nyāya Sanskrit *jāti* often means a class or genus, but in Nyāya, *jāti* is not the genus itself, but that characteristic by which the genus is recognized in the individual. The *jāti* of a horse is horse-ness. This is not the class of all horses in the sense in which 'class' is used in common speech."

In terms of modern logic, we may call a *jāti* a "class property" whose possession is the necessary and sufficient condition for an object to be included in a class. But we must exclude the empty-class and classes with just one member from consideration. However, this is a mere approximation and not a true characterization of the Nyāya view of *jāti*. The Nyāya conception of *jāti* is not just a logical supposition based on any mathematical conception of class where anything can be a member of a class, and the class property need not be an eternal external entity. The Nyāya notion of *jāti* is often compared to Platonic Ideas.[50] B.K. Matilal (1971: 71) further sharpens the notion of *jāti* in Nyāya:

> "A typical example of a generic property is cowness. Nyāya claims that cowness is real in the sense that apart from cow-individuals there is a separate entity, cowness, which is present or 'manifested' in all cows. Unlike Plato's universals or ideas, cowness, according to Nyāya, is not a denizen of another, more real, world, i.e. not the creative archetype of the existent cows. Cowness is more like an Aristotelian universal which can be predicated of many. Cowness is timeless, i.e. permanent, but is manifested in a cow. If all cows are destroyed, where would cowness go? An Aristotelian can get around this difficulty by resorting to the doctrine of potentiality and actuality. The Nyāya says that cowness is present always and everywhere, but can only be 'manifested' in a cow."

For Naiyāyikas, *jāti* occurs only in substances (*dravya*), qualities (*guṇa*), and actions (*karman*).

---

48 *ākāśa-kāla-diśām ekavyaktikatvād ākāśatvādikaṃ na jātiḥ* /, *KM*, p. 363.

49 Ingalls (1951: 37).

50 "According to the Nyāya teachers, *jāti* is not a class-concept, for a class-concept is subjective, but *jāti* has an objective reality. ... *jāti* thus corresponds to Plato's Ideas." Shastri, A.B. (1939: 156).

D.2.iii. As we move to Mīmāṃsā, we find that the term *ākṛti* is the favorite term for the Mīmāṃsakas, and yet they do not use it in the Nyāya sense of configuration. Kumārilabhaṭṭa clearly states that *jāti* "generic property" of the Naiyāyikas is called *ākṛti* by the Mīmāṃsakas.[51] He argues strenuously to show that *ākṛti* in the Nyāya sense of configuration cannot be regarded to be a word-meaning. It is argued that configuration is not a universal phenomenon. For example, there is no configuration in the case of direction (*dik*), time (*kāla*), soul (*ātman*), mind (*manas*), quality (*guṇa*), and action (*kriyā*). Thus, the Mīmāṃsaka argues that *ākṛti* is a word-meaning in the sense of a generic property, but not in the Nyāya sense of configuration.[52] G.V. Devasthali points out that by and large, the Mīmāṃsā concept of *ākṛti* corresponds to the Nyāya concept of *jāti*,

> "but the expression *ākṛti* would also seem to include the *avayava-saṃsthāna-viśeṣa* or configuration, when we find Śabara declaring, for example, that it is not possible to make a *śyena-vyakti* [= "a hawk-individual"], though a *śyenākṛti* [= "a hawk-configuration"] one may possibly make, so that the text *śyena-citiṃ cinvīta* [= "one should construct a hawk-altar"] becomes plausible only on the assumption that *ākṛti* [= "configuration"] is the exact import of a *śabda* [= "word"]."[53]

In the passage discussed by Devasthali, *ākṛti* stands for something which one could possibly construct or produce. This can only apply to a configuration, and not to a generic property or universal which is supposed to be eternal. Devasthali concludes that apparently the mixed conception of *ākṛti* found in the works of the early Mīmāṃsakas like Śabara has been split up into two notions of *ākṛti* "configuration" and *jāti* "generic property or universal" by Naiyāyikas.[54] It would seem from Devasthali's discussion that Śabara, at least in some places, uses this word in the sense of configuration. On the other hand, the more explicit discussions in the works of Mīmāṃsā authors seem to indicate that they intended to use the term *ākṛti* in the sense of a generic property. M. Biardeau (1964:161-177) tries to show that one cannot say that for Śabara the terms *jāti* and *ākṛti* refer to the same thing. Agreeing with Biardeau's general conclusions, Othmar Gächter (1983: 48) says that for Śabara "*ākṛti* is neither the class (*jāti*) nor the individual (*vyakti*)," and that "it is not clear that the early Mīmāṃsā held the view that the meaning of a word refers to the universal and not to the individual." Francis X. D'sa (1980: 81-93, 151-165) has also discussed this question, and he seems to indicate that a lot of distinctions made by Kumārilabhaṭṭa are implicit in Śabara, though not clearly stated. He also draws our attention to a third party in this evolution. The Vṛttikāra referred to by Śabara seems to hold a position

---

51 *jātim evākṛtim prāhuḥ /*, *SLV*, p. 547.

52 *sarveṣu hi pārthiveṣu gav-ādi-ghaṭādiṣu saṃsthānam bhavet / agni-toya-vāyv-ākāśādīnāṃ tu pārthiva-dravya-parigraha-vaśād ākārānuvṛttiḥ kalpyeta na svātantryeṇa / dik-kālātma-manasāṃ tu guṇa-karmaṇāṃ ca na kathañcid api saṃsthānaṃ sambhavati / ... tasmād etad evābhidheyākṛti-lakṣaṇaṃ nāvayava-racanā-saṃsthānākṛtitvam avakalpate / ... tasya hy upalakṣaṇam ālocyamānaṃ na jāter anyal labhyate, jātir eva hi sāmānyam /*, *TV(b)*, p. 249.

53 Devasthali (1948: 20-21). I have added the translations of Sanskrit terms in square brackets.

54 Devasthali (1948: 20-21).

which is slightly different from that of Śabara. It is clear that the notion of *ākṛti* ranges from abstract to concrete, from configuration to universal in the early works on Mīmāṃsā. D'sa (1980: 92) takes a reverse position as compared to that of Devasthali stated above. D'sa argues that the early Mīmāṃsakas were reacting to the distinctions already made by Naiyāyikas. He says (1980: 92):

> "It might help to remember at the very start that we are here dealing with a topic, speculation on which had been restricted mostly to the grammatical and phenomenal aspects. The Mīmāṃsā, it seems to me, was one of the the pioneers to make a break-through by introducing an epistemological perspective into the discussion. However, the terminology available at the time did influence its thinking and it had to take a stand with regard to it. The Nyāyaḥ, for example, already possessed the terms *jātiḥ, ākṛtiḥ* and *vyaktiḥ*. According to it, *ākṛti* meant the visible form, *jātiḥ* the universal concept and *vyaktiḥ* the concrete individual; and the denotation of a word was understood as connected with all these three. When reacting to the Nyāyaḥ the Mīmāṃsā not only strengthened its own convictions; its clarifications became more articulate. It rejected the Nyāyaḥ position that *jātiḥ, ākṛtiḥ* and *vyaktiḥ* are all denoted by a word; but it took over from the Nyāyaḥ, its understanding of *ākṛtiḥ* as the external form or configuration of the individual of a species. But this was only one aspect of the Mīmāṃsā's understanding of *ākṛtiḥ*. The other more important aspect however was an epistemological one."

D'sa's description of the possible evolution of ideas is somewhat controversial, and he is aware of some of the problems himself (1980: 92). In his discussion, D'sa places unwarranted emphasis on the connection of Mīmāṃsā with Nyāya. There is no evidence that Śabara or the Vṛttikāra are reacting to the three-way distinction made by the *Nyāya-sūtras*. Such a reaction to Nyāya is to be found in the works of Kumārilabhaṭṭa, for whom *ākṛti* is identical with the *jāti* of the Naiyāyikas, rather than with their notion of *ākṛti* as physical configuration. In the work of Śabara on the other hand, there is a much closer relationship with Patañjali's *Mahābhāṣya*. Contrary to D'sa's conclusions, much of the argumentation found in Śabara, including the epistemological concerns, is already anticipated by Kātyāyana and Patañjali, and some of the vagueness in the use of the term *ākṛti* is also due to this connection with the discussions in the grammatical tradition. Recently, Peter Scharf (1990: 354-359) again draws our attention to the unsettled usage of the term *ākṛti* in Śabara's work:

> "Śabara's use of the term *ākṛti* raises some doubts. He does not use the term *jāti* and uses the term *ākṛti* for the property which the individuals of a class have in common. In the *Ākṛtyadhikaraṇa* it is not absolutely clear whether he means the term to refer to an abstract generic property or to a shape. In certain contexts he clearly uses the term *ākṛti* for common

> properties other than a shape, thus implying that he conceives of an *ākṛti* generally as an abstract generic property just as Patañjali does, and just as Vātsyāyana conceives a *jāti*. However, Śabara uses the term *ākṛti* for a shape in another context central to his argument to establish that a generic term denotes a generic property. The success of the argument depends on closely associating, or entirely identifying the two senses of shape and generic property. ... The soundness of his argument depends on identifying the generic property with shape, or at least associating it with shape more closely than a generic property is associated with its own substratum. ... One is forced to concede either that Śabara accepts shape itself as a generic property or that his argument succeeds only by the trick of using the single term *ākṛti* in two different meanings to achieve the appearance of an identity where there is none. If the latter is the case, his argument to establish that a generic term denotes just a generic property fails. On the other hand, if he accepts that shape itself is a class property, the clarity of his concepts must be called into question."

D.2.iv. We shall not go into a detailed examination of the dilemma posed by Peter Scharf. However, we shall distinguish the meaning of the term *ākṛti* as <u>used</u> by Śabara from the meaning which he generally <u>consciously attributes</u> to it. In our view, Śabara takes advantage of the ambiguous usage of the term *ākṛti* found in the earlier works such as Patañjali's *Mahābhāṣya*, and in the course of his debates with his opponents, Śabara is not above using such ambiguities to his own advantage. However, in terms of his own philosophical view of *ākṛti*, it would seem that Kumārilabhaṭṭa is right in identifying Śabara's *ākṛti* with a generic property or a universal. Śabara defines *ākṛti* as a common property shared by different substances, qualities, and actions, and such a definition would certainly not be applicable to shape or configuration.[55] Kumārilabhaṭṭa and Pārthasārathimiśra argue that the term *ākṛti* does not refer to shape or configuration, and that it refers to a generic property or a universal.[56] According to these Mīmāṃsakas, the cognition of an object has two aspects. An object appears to have been differentiated from some other objects, and at the same time it is not differentiated in kind from certain other objects. The *ākṛti* or generic property is the real external property of an object which leads to an object not being differentiated in kind from certain other objects. Though it is not separable from its basis, the individual (*vyakti*), it is admitted as being an ontologically distinct part of external reality. For Kumārilabhaṭṭa, the content of a valid cognition must have a basis (*ālambana*) in external reality, and a generic property or a universal (*ākṛti*) is the external

---

55 *dravya-guṇa-karmaṇāṃ sāmānya-mātram ākṛtiḥ* /, *MS-B(a)*, Pt.I., p. 294.

56 *yady api jātir vyakter atyanta-bhinnā nopalabhyate, tathāpi śabalākāre tasminn upalabhyamāne sāmānya-buddher ālambanam ... ākṛtir itarā vyaktiḥ* /, *TV(b)*, pp. 268-9. Also: *dvy-ākāraiva hi vastuṣu buddhir vyāvṛtty-anugata-rūpā / tatra vilakṣaṇa-buddhy-ālambanaṃ ca vyaktiḥ / sāmānya-buddhy-ālambanaṃ ca sāmānyam / na tad ubhayātiriktaṃ vyakti-mātraṃ nāma kiñcid asti vastuno rūpam* /, *Śāstradīpikā* of Pārthasārathimiśra quoted in a footnote to *MB*, Vol.I., Sec.I., pp. 100-101. Also see: *SLV*, p. 546.

basis for the cognition of uniformity of many different individual objects belonging to a class.[57] According to Mīmāṃsakas, a generic property is directly perceived through the same sense organ which perceives an object, and such cognitions are proofs in themselves of the external existence of entities which appear in the contents of these cognitions.[58] Like the *jāti* of Naiyāyikas, *ākṛti* of Mīmāṃsakas is not just a logical or mathematical class-concept, but is a factor of a realist ontology.

D.2.v. As Peter Scharf (1990: 357) rightly points out: "Śabara's discussion of the denotation of generic terms in the *Ākṛtyadhikaraṇa* borrows considerably from the *Mahābhāṣya*. Śabara both argues against views presented in the *Mahābhāṣya*, and adopts principles and arguments from it. Occasionally he closely paraphrases it." In terms of the development of semantic and philosophical debates with which we are concerned here, the works of the grammarians Kātyāyana and Patañjali are foundational texts. They predate most other philosophical texts available to us, and seem to provide the initial arguments for most important theories of language. Pāṇini himself uses the term *jāti* in a number of his rules, and it seems to refer to the notion of class, rather than to an abstract property like a generic property or a universal. However, commentators on Pāṇini's rules, under the influence of later discussions, seem to take this term to refer to an abstract property, rather than as referring to a class [cf. *MB, MB-P,* and *MB-P-U* on P.1.2.58 (*jāty-ākhyāyām ekasmin bahu-vacanam anyatarasyām*)]. We should note here that the earliest explicit theories concerning the notions of *ākṛti* and *dravya* being the meanings signified by words are those of Vyāḍi and Vājapyāyana. Vājapyāyana proposed that a word signifies an *ākṛti* as its primary meaning, while Vyāḍi proposed that a word signifies an object (*dravya*) as its primary meaning. The views of these two thinkers are cited and debated in the *Vārttika*s of Kātyāyana on P.1.2.64 (*sarūpāṇām eka-śeṣa eka-vibhaktau*) and in Patañjali's *Mahābhāṣya* on these *Vārttika*s. B.K. Matilal (1971: 106ff) has discussed the views of Vyāḍi and Vājapyāyana in detail. Kātyāyana himself seems to prefer the view that words refer to an *ākṛti*, and he extends this doctrine even to phonological contexts, cf. Deshpande (1975, Chapter 2). He proposes that the individual sounds listed in Pāṇini's *Śiva-sūtra*s such as *a-i-u-Ṇ* naturally denote their *ākṛti*s (*MB*, Vol.I., Sec.I., p. 373, on P.1.1.69). While the commentators tend to interpret the term *ākṛti* in these discussions as referring to a *jāti* or generic property, it seems likely that the word refers to a shape or configuration.

In his *Mahābhāṣya*, Patañjali initiates the following discussion: "[We are] talking about a *jāti*. What is a *jāti*? The reply is that a *jāti* is [that which is] recognized on the basis of an *ākṛti*."[59] Hartmut Scharfe compares this statement of Patañjali with the Nyāya definition of *ākṛti* [= *ākṛtir jāti-liṅgākhyā*, cf. **D.2.i**], and on this basis, he concludes that the terms *ākṛti* and *jāti* in the *Mahābhāṣya* are synonymous with their counterparts in the Nyāya

---

57 *bāhyārtha-viṣayatvaṃ ca buddhīnām pratipāditam* /, *SLV*, p. 547.

58 Devasthali (1948: 18).

59 *MB*, Vol.II., pp. 337-8.

system.[60] He renders *ākṛti* by "die Form" and *jāti* by "das Genus," and says: "Die Übersetzung 'Form' für *ākṛti* ist überall möglich."[61] However, Scharfe notes opinions of other scholars who thought that the use of the terms *ākṛti* and *jāti* is highly confused.[62] Otto Strauss and Bruno Liebich held substantially different views in this regard. Strauss translates the term *ākṛti* in the *Mahābhāṣya* by "die Gattung" and says that "*ākṛti* ist synonyme mit *jāti* im Mahābhāṣya und bei Śabarasvāmin."[63] Bruno Liebich renders *ākṛti* by "die Form," and yet identifies it with "Kaṇādas vierte Kategorie *sāmānyam* 'Gemeinsamkeit'."[64] Erich Frauwallner comments: "das Wort die Form (*ākṛti*) bezeichnet."[65] Contrary to earlier studies, Sreekrishna Sarma argues that the word *jāti*, which occurs in the *Mahābhāṣya* more than sixty times, refers to a notion of class, rather than a generic property or a universal as signified by the term *jāti* in Nyāya or by the term *ākṛti* in Mīmāṃsā.[66] On the other hand, Sarma says that the term *ākṛti* in the *Mahābhāṣya* refers to a notion of structural pattern in its permanent as well as non-permanent aspects. In its permanent aspect, Patañjali's *ākṛti* refers to something like a generic property, and is almost the same as the *jāti* for Nyāya, and *ākṛti* for Mīmāṃsā, while in its non-permanent aspect, it is the shape or configuration denoted by the term *ākṛti* in Nyāya. Madeleine Biardeau's conclusions are similar to those of Sreekrishna Sarma.[67] She concludes that by the term *jāti* Patañjali means to refer to a class as defined in terms of some structural pattern, caste, sex, the Vedic branch of learning, etc. It may be a "naturaliste" or a "sociologique" class. She renders *jāti* by "une espèce," "une classe d'êtres distincts," "la categorie d'êtres," "le groupe d'êtres présentant un certain trait commun," etc., and *ākṛti* by "la forme spécifique," "la structure commune à tous les individus d'une même classe," "le patronyme," "un certain trait commun," etc. After an extensive study of the use of the terms *jāti*, *ākṛti*, and *dravya* in Patañjali's *Mahābhāṣya*, Peter Scharf (1990: 353ff) concludes as follows:

> "In his discussions under Pāṇini 1.2.64 and 1.2.58, Patañjali uses the terms *ākṛti* and *jāti* synonymously to mean a generic property, that is, a property wholly present in each of many individuals of a class. He also uses both terms to refer to the class, the aggregate of all the individual objects in which that generic property resides. He uses the term *dravya* to refer to an individual which is part of the class and substratum of the generic property. ... Patañjali recognizes the use of the term *ākṛti* for a shape. He recognizes the role a shape plays in making known the generic property of an object

---

60 Scharfe (1961: 141).
61 Scharfe (1961: 131).
62 Scharfe (1961: 129).
63 Otto Strauss (1927: 135).
64 Bruno Liebich (1923: 212).
65 Frauwallner (1960: 93).
66 Sreekrishna Sarma (1957: 63-65).
67 Madeleine Biardeau (1967: 43-49).

too. However, shape does not enter into his serious discussions of the denotation of a generic term; nor does he use the term *ākṛti* in these discussions to mean shape. Because it is interchanged with the term *jāti* in different contexts, *ākṛti* cannot be understood to mean anything other than a generic property."

D.2.vi. The term *ākṛti* in the *Mahābhāṣya* does range from a generic property to shared form or configuration, while the term *jāti* generally seems to stand for a class in a natural and social sense, rather than for a class property or a generic property. Patañjali speaks of *ākṛti* being not different among different objects belonging to the same class, unbroken when some objects of that class are destroyed, and something which is commonly shared by many objects.[68] On the first *Vārttika* of Kātyāyana on Pāṇini's *Aṣṭādhyāyī* (= *siddhe śabdārtha-sambandhe* ...), Patañjali suggests that this *Vārttika* assumes that the meaning of a word is an *ākṛti*, and therefore it is *nitya* "eternal, permanent." Patañjali says that while the *ākṛti* is permanent, a *dravya* "substance, individual object" is impermanent. From the context of the discussion, it would seem that, in this context, the word *ākṛti* refers to configuration or shape, rather than to a generic property.[69] This seems to be the case from the continuing debate. Patañjali reverses his position and says that one may consider the *ākṛti* to be impermanent and the substance to be permanent. He changes the meaning of the term *dravya* from "individual object" to "substance," and argues that clay possessed with a certain *ākṛti* "shape, configuration" becomes a ball of clay. Then having crushed that *ākṛti*, one can make little pots, and by crushing the *ākṛti* of these little pots, one can make little bowls. With similar other examples, he argues that by crushing the various *ākṛti*s again and again, one can make new objects in such a way that we still have the same *dravya*.[70] In this discussion, the most appropriate way to interpret the term *ākṛti* seems to be to take it to mean shape or configuration which can be crushed without losing the substance (*dravya*). It would not be appropriate to say that one crushes a generic property. Keeping the same sense of the term *ākṛti* as configuration or shape, Patañjali again changes the direction of the argument, and says that the configuration could be considered to be permanent, even though one can crush it to create another object from the same substance, because while we can destroy it in one object, the same configuration can be found in other objects. In order to accomodate this nature of configuration or shape, Patañjali then suggests an alternative view of permanence. He says that one need not argue that only those things are permanent which are unmovable, firm, unchanging, which do not have any decrease, additions, or changes, and which are neither produced, nor grow, nor diminish. One can consider even those things to be

---

68 *yat tarhi bhinneṣv abhinnaṃ chinneṣv acchinnaṃ sa śabdaḥ / nety āha / ākṛtir nāma sā /*, *MB*, Vo.I., Sec.I., p.11.

69 *ākṛtir hi nityā dravyam anityam /*, *MB*, Vol.I., Sec.I., p. 49.

70 *dravyaṃ hi nityam ākṛtir anityā / kathaṃ jñāyate? evaṃ hi dṛśyate loke - mṛt kayācid ākṛtyā yuktā piṇḍo bhavati, piṇḍākṛtim upamṛdya ghaṭikāḥ kriyante, ghaṭikākṛtim upamṛdya kuṇḍikāḥ kriyante / ... ākritir anyā cānyā bhavati dravyam punas tad eva / ākṛty-upamardena dravyam evāvaśiṣyate /*, *MB*, Vol.I., Sec.I., p. 49.

permanent, where in the midst of all kinds of change, the essential nature is not lost. Patañjali says that such is the case with *ākṛti*.[71] In this discussion, it is clear that the term *ākṛti* is used in the sense of shape or configuration which is shared by different objects of the same kind, which can be destroyed without destroying the substance, and which can be viewed to be permanent in the new view of fluid permanence (*pravāha-nityatā*) proposed by Patañjali. While commentators like Kaiyaṭa do seem to interpret some of these passages in such a way that *ākṛti* becomes synonymous with *jāti* "generic property," this is not warranted by the context of the above discussion. This dilemma faced by the commentators Bhartṛhari and Kaiyaṭa is noted by S.D. Joshi and J.A.F Roodbergen (1986: 107, fn. 439). In contrast to the view of these commentators that the term *ākṛti* refers to a generic property, Joshi and Roodbergen correctly translate the term by "shape" (1986: 107).

Patañjali indicates the relationship between *ākṛti* and *jāti* by saying: "*jāti* is grasped on the basis of *ākṛti*."[72] Such a distinction between the notions of *jāti* and *ākṛti* can be best accounted for by taking the word *ākṛti* here to refer to shape or configuration. Madeleine Biardeau says: "le ... individu, par sa naissance, pourra appartenir à la *jāti* 'homme,' ce que nous indique so apparence corporelle -*ākṛti*-."[73] It could possibly be argued that the term *jāti* here stands for a class, and that the term *ākṛti* stands for a generic property, and then Patañjali's statement would mean: the cognition of a generic property residing in an object helps one to recognize the class of which the object is a member. In my view, such an interpretation, while not totally impossible, seems to be unlikely.

D.2.vii. Traditional commentators on the *Mahābhāṣya* generally recognize that the term *ākṛti*, depending upon the context, signifies either a generic property (*jāti*), or a shape or configuration (*saṃsthāna*). Nāgeśabhaṭṭa believes that in the passage cited above, Patañjali uses the term *ākṛti* in a way similar to the use of this term in the Nyāya works to refer to shape or configuration.[74] However, Indian commentators seldom interpret the term *jāti* in the *Mahābhāṣya* as referring to a notion of class, rather than to a generic property or universal. For Nāgeśabhaṭṭa, the term *jāti* in Patañjali has the same meaning as it has in the works of Naiyāyikas and Vaiśeṣikas. A *jāti* is a permanent property which is single and is yet shared by a plurality of objects. Nāgeśabhaṭṭa argues that such a definition equally applies to generic properties such as *brāhmaṇatva* "Brahmin-ness" and *ghaṭatva* "potness."[75] Kaiyaṭa puts forward two explanations for the notion of *jāti*. A *jāti* "generic

---

71 *nityā ākṛtiḥ / kathaṃ na kvacid uparateti kṛtvā sarvatroparatā bhavati / dravyāntarasthā tūpalabhyate / athavā nedam eva nitya-lakṣaṇam - dhruvaṃ kūṭasthaṃ avicāly-anapāyopajana-vikāry-anutpatty-avṛddhy-avyaya-yogi yat tan nityam iti / tad api nityaṃ yasmiṃs tatvaṃ na vihanyate /*, *MB*, Vol.I., Sec.I., pp. 49-50.

72 *ākṛti-grahaṇā jātiḥ /*, *MB*, Vol.II., pp. 337-8.

73 Madeleine Biardeau (1967: 49).

74 *bhāṣye ākṛtiḥ jātiḥ saṃsthānaṃ ca /*, *MB-P-U*, Vol.I., Sec.I., p. 11. Also: *anenaitat-prakaraṇasthākṛti-padasya vyaṅgya-vyañjakobhaya-paratāṃ sūcayati / gautamenāpy uktaṃ 'jāty-ākṛti-vyaktayaḥ padārtha' iti /*, *MB-P-U*, Vol.I., Sec.I., p. 49. This is somewhat comparable to Sreekrishna Sarma's views. See: Sreekrishna Sarma (1957: 63ff). However, Sarma does not treat the term *jāti* in the same way as Nāgeśabhaṭṭa.

75 *vastuto bhinneṣv abhinnaṃ chinneṣv acchinnam iti paspaśā-stha-bhāṣya-bodhitaṃ 'nityatve saty ekatve ca saty anekānugatatvam' eva jāti-lakṣaṇam bhāṣya-sammatam brāhmaṇatva-ghaṭatva-sādhāraṇam /*, *MB-P-U*, Vol.II., p. 339. Actually, the definition cited by Nāgeśabhaṭṭa, i.e. *bhinneṣv abhinnam* etc., is offered by Patañjali as a definition of *ākṛti*. See: *yat tarhi tat bhinneṣv abhinnaṃ chinneṣv acchinnaṃ sāmānya-bhūtaṃ*,

property" could be different from the individual objects in which it resides, and yet it is manifested by those individual objects. On the other hand, a *jāti* may simply refer to individual objects themselves with their distinctions from each other being overlooked.[76] The second interpretation of the term *jāti* comes close to the notion of class, and is similar to the view expressed by Sarma and Biardeau. However, this interpretation of *jāti* as class is not upheld by the tradition of Sanskrit grammarians as their final interpretation.

D.2.viii. Now we shall review the impact of Bhartṛhari's linguistic monism on the interpretation of the notions of *jāti*, *ākṛti*, and *dravya*. Bhartṛhari devotes entire sections of the third *Kāṇḍa* of his *Vākya-padīya* to a detailed discussion of these notions (cf. *Jāti-samuddeśa* and *Dravya-samuddeśa* of the 3rd *Kāṇḍa* of *Vākya-padīya*). Under the influence of Bhartṛhari's ideas, there are two major views found in Kaiyaṭa's commentary on the *Mahābhāṣya*.

[a] On Patañjali's statement that *ākṛti* is impermanent, Kaiyaṭa says that this could be explained even if the term *ākṛti* stands for a generic property (*jāti*). He says that if one accepts the ultimate reality of Brahman, all the so-called permanent generic properties or universals are ultimately unreal and impermenant.[77] It is possible to argue that the real substance (*dravya*) signified by all words is ultimately Brahman, and nothing else. All words signify the same ultimate reality of Brahman, except that each word signifies Brahman as qualified by a different unreal adjunct property.[78] Nāgeśabhaṭṭa explains that these unreal adjuncts are what we normally call generic properties. In this view, generic properties belong to the sphere of cosmic illusion and hence are ultimately unreal and impermanent.[79]

[b] Kaiyaṭa says that Patañjali's statement that *ākṛti* is permanent can be explained by identifying *ākṛti* with *jāti*, or a generic property.[80] This can then be explained further either by taking recourse to permanence of a generic property as detailed in the Nyāya-Vaiśeṣika metaphysics, or by taking recourse to Bhartṛhari's doctrine that pure existence alone is the meaning of all words and this pure existence itself is to be called *jāti*. In his

---

sa śabdaḥ? nety āha, ākṛtir nāma sā /, *MB*, Vol.I., Sec.I., p. 11. However, Nāgeśabhaṭṭa believes that the term *ākṛti* here refers to both a *jāti* "generic property" and *saṃsthāna* "configuration." This allows him to transfer the definition of *ākṛti* to the notion of *jāti*. This is also possibly under the influence of the use of the term *sāmānya* in the Nyāya-Vaiśeṣika literature to refer to *jāti*, rather than to configuration or shape. Compare the wording of *Tarka-saṃgraha* in its definition of *sāmānya* (= *jāti*): *nityam ekam anekānugataṃ sāmānyam*./ *TS*, p. 75-76. This wording compares well with what Nāgeśabhaṭṭa says about the definition of *jāti* intended by Patañjali. For sociological implications of *brāhmaṇatva* as a *jāti*, see: B.K. Matilal (1971: 76).

76 *vyakti-vyatiriktā jātiḥ vyakti-vyaṅgyā* / ... *tyakta-bhedā vyaktaya eva jātiḥ* /, *MB-P*, Vol.I., Sec.II., p. 12.

77 *brahma-darśane ca gotvādi-jāter apy asatyatvād anityatvam* / *MB-P*, Vol.I., Sec.I., p. 47.

78 *dravya-pakṣe 'pi sarva-śabdānām asatyopādhy-avacchinnam brahma-tattvaṃ vācyam iti nityatā* /, *MB-P*, Vol.I., Sec.I., p. 47.

79 *asatyopādhīti* / *jāti-rūpety arthaḥ* / *jātir hi tan-mate āvidyako dharma-viśeṣaḥ* /, *MB-P-U*, Vol.I., Sec.I., p. 47.

80 *arthasyāpi jāti-lakṣaṇasya nityatvam* /, *MB-P*, Vol.I., Sec.I., p. 47.

Vākya-padīya, Bhartṛhari says:[81] "In every existent object, there are two aspects [of which one is] real and [the other is] unreal. Among these [two aspects], the real [aspect] is called *jāti*, while the unreal [aspect] is the individual. [The pure] existence, differentiated into [objects like] bulls etc. on account of the difference in [unreal] adjuncts, is called *jāti*. That [pure existence] is also said to be the meaning of [all] nominals and verb roots. It is eternal. It is the intelligence [*mahat* = *buddhi-tattva* of the Sāṃkhyas]. It is the Self. It is signified by affixes like *-tva* 'ness' and *-taL (= -tā)* 'ness'." Here, Bhartṛhari regards the pure existence to be the *jāti* "generic property" par excellence. It is the ultimate universal comparable to the Platonic Good. It is Brahman. Later grammarians like Bhaṭṭojī Dīkṣita explicitly ascribe this view to Bhartṛhari.[82] As Helārāja explains, in this view of Bhartṛhari, all generic properties are of the nature of pure existence. For instance, the generic property of bull-ness (*gotva*) is the existence of a bull, and the generic property of horse-ness (*aśvatva*) is the existence of a horse.[83]

While both of the views above are found in Bhartṛhari's work, they are opposed to each other, and there is not enough evidence to decide which of these two views is ultimately Bhartṛhari's preferred view. Neither of these two views is seriously entertained by later grammarian-philosophers like Kauṇḍabhaṭṭa and Nāgeśabhaṭṭa in their works on Sanskrit semantics.

D.2.ix. When we look at Kauṇḍabhaṭṭa's *Nāmārtha-nirṇaya*, we find that he uses the terms *jāti* and *ākṛti* as synonyms to refer to the notion of a generic property or a universal, and there is no discussion of *ākṛti* in the sense of configuration. Even as he presents the view of the Naiyāyikas, Kauṇḍabhaṭṭa does not discuss shape or configuration as a possible meaning element. Kauṇḍabhaṭṭa's use of the terms *ākṛti* and *jāti* also needs to be distinguished from the meaning attributed to the term *jāti* by the Naiyāyikas and Mīmāṃsakas. While Kauṇḍabhaṭṭa himself does not clarify this difference, some commentators on his work bring out this important distinction. They explain that the terms *jāti* and *ākṛti* in Kauṇḍabhaṭṭa's view stand for an essential and exclusive property (*a-sādhāraṇa-dharma*) of an object.[84] It is a property which makes an entity what it is. This property necessarily resides in all members of a given class, and only in those members. However, unlike the Naiyāyikas and Mīmāṃsakas, grammarians accept a property to be a *jāti*, even if it resides only in a single entity, if this entity occurs only as a unique single entity in the universe. Thus, properties like ether-ness (*ākāśatva*), time-ness (*kālatva*) etc.

---

[81] *VP*, III, *Jāti-samuddeśa*, verses 32-34; also see: *VP-H(P)*, pp. 40-41.

[82] *jāteś ca brahmātmakatvam uktaṃ hariṇā* /, *SKB(a)*, Vol.I., p. 9.

[83] *tathā hi goḥ sattā gotvam ... evam aśvasya sattā aśvatvam ity ādi vācyam* /, *VP-H(P)*, p. 41.

[84] *jāti-padenātra tat-tat-padārtha-gatāsādhāraṇo dharmo vivakṣito, na tu nityatve saty ekatve ca saty aneka-samavetatva-rūpā jātiḥ / asādhāraṇatvaṃ ca tat-padārthetarāvṛttitve sati tat-padārtha-vṛttitvam / tenākāśatvābhāvatvādīnām aneka-samavetatva-rūpa-jātitvābhāve 'pi nāvyāptiḥ / tat-tat-padārtha-gatāsādhāraṇa-dharmasyaiva śāstre svārtha-śabdena vyavahāraḥ* /, *VBS-S*, p. 216.

are also considered to be *jāti*s by grammarians, even though they reside only in single entities. Finally, a *jāti* for a grammarian like Kauṇḍabhaṭṭa is an "exclusive essential property" rather than a "generic property."

D.2.x. This broad conception of *jāti* is not new to Kauṇḍabhaṭṭa, and it goes back to several other notions. The two related conceptions in the tradition of Sanskrit grammar are those of *svārtha* "the most essential meaning of a word" and *pravṛtti-nimitta* "the property whose possession by an object is the necessary and sufficient condition for the use of a given word to refer to that object." These conceptions are co-extensive with the broad conception of *jāti* as explained earlier. Nāgeśabhaṭṭa argues that the terms *jāti* and *ākṛti* in the works of Patañjali and Kaiyaṭa actually stand for the notion of *pravṛtti-nimitta*.[85] There is another older term which is equivalent to this new interpretation of *jāti*. The term *guṇa* occurs in the works of Kātyāyana and Patañjali in the sense of an essential attribute, and its definition seems to closely correspond to the notion of *pravṛtti-nimitta*. Kātyāyana says: "The affixes *-tva* and *-taL (= tā)* refer to an essential attribute (*guṇa*) of an object, such that the word [to which these items are affixed] refers to a certain object, because of the occurrence of that essential attribute in that object."[86] This is to say that the affix "-ness" added to the word "bull" signifies the *guṇa* "essential attribute" of bull-ness, in such a way that the occurrence of bull-ness in an object is the necessary and sufficient condition for the word "bull" to be used to denote that object. As such, this is a functional or a logical concept, similar to that of denotation as explained by W.P. Alston (1964: 16-17), and there does not seem to be any specific ontological commitment, at least as regards the specific nature of this attribute. Patañjali uses the term *guṇa* to refer to both the attributes of brave-ness (*vīratva*) and man-ness (*puruṣatva*) signified by the words *vīra* "brave" and *puruṣa* "man."[87] Depending upon a particular ontological system, these two properties may differ in their ontological status, and yet, according to grammarians, they are essential attributes in a certain linguistic sense. The word "brave" can be used to refer to an entity *x* , if and only if this *x* possesses the attribute of brave-ness, and the word "man" can be used to refer to an entity *x*, if and only if this *x* possesses the attribute man-ness. Thus, grammarians were concerned primarily with an explanation of language use, and the possible conceptual conditions related to it, and were not committed to defining or defending a particular ontological structure of the world. As a matter of convenience, they used the ontological terminology of other systems of thought, and adjusted it to their own needs, without committing themselves to ontological doctrines of those systems.

---

[85] *jāti-padaṃ ca pravṛtti-nimittopalakṣaṇam* /, *MB-P-U*, Vol.I., Sec.II., p. 512; and *ākṛti-śabdena pravṛtti-nimittam ucyate* /, *MB-P-U*, Vol.I., Sec.II., p. 341.

[86] *siddhaṃ tu yasya guṇasya bhāvād dravye śabda-niveśas tasyābhidhāne tva-talau* /, *Vt.* 5 on P.5.1.119. Also see B.K. Matilal (1971: 101) and (1985: 381).

[87] *anyo hi vīratvaṃ guṇo 'nyo hi puruṣatvam* /, *MB*, Vol.II., p. 538.

D.3. *SATTVA / DRAVYA / VYAKTI* "INDIVIDUAL OBJECT"

D.3.i. Naiyāyikas generally use the term *dravya* to refer to a substance in the context of ontological discussions. There are nine substances according to the late combined school of Nyāya-Vaiśeṣikas: earth (*pṛthivī*), water (*ap*), fire (*tejas*), air (*vāyu*), ether (*ākāśa*), time (*kāla*), direction (*dik*), soul (*ātman*), and mind (*manas*).[88] Substance (*dravya*) is defined in this school as something which possesses the generic property substance-ness (*dravyatva*), or something which serves as a substratum or locus of qualities.[89] The *Vaiśeṣika-sūtras* of Kaṇāda define a substance as: "that which is a substratum or locus of actions and qualities, and is a material [or rather an inherent] cause."[90] The important aspect of the Nyāya-Vaiśeṣika definitions of substance is that a substance is held to be different from its attributes and that it is the substratum which holds those attributes. A substance is not a mere bundle of attributes, without a distinct substratum. In Nyāya discussions regarding meaning, the term *vyakti* occurs more frequently than the term *dravya*. The *Nyāya-sūtras* of Gautama define the notion of *vyakti* as: "a *vyakti* 'individual' is that which is the locus of specific qualities (*guṇa-viśeṣa*) and has a definite or concrete form."[91] According to Vātsyāyana's interpretation, an individual as meant by the term *vyakti* has a perceptible nature, and hence all substances (*dravya*) are not individuals (*vyakti*).[92] An individual, in this view, has specific qualities such as touch, weight, solidity, fluidity etc. and it is of a finite measurement. This excludes substances like ether (*ākāśa*) from being individuals (*vyakti*).

D.3.ii. The peculiarity of the Nyāya view of *vyakti* as espoused by Vātsyāyana needs to be explored further. If a substance such as ether (*ākāśa*) cannot qualify for being included in the category of individual (*vyakti*), does this mean that ether cannot be referred to by a word? Such a question must have haunted the mind of Uddyotakara, who found Vātsyāyana's explanation to be unsatisfactory. He reinterpreted the original *sūtra* of Gautama to extract a different meaning. According to him, the *sūtra* says that the term *vyakti* stands for qualities (*guṇa*), differentiating properties (*viśeṣa*), actions (*kriyā*), and the substance (*dravya*) which is the substratum of these attributes.[93] Qualities such as color (*rūpa*) and substances such as ether (*ākāśa*) which are excluded by Vātsyāyana's interpretation of the term *vyakti* "individual" are thus covered by this new interpretation of Uddyotakara. It would seem that Uddyotakara understands the term *vyakti* in a purely

---

88 *TS*, p. 4.

89 *dravyatva-jātimattvaṃ guṇavattvaṃ vā dravya-sāmānya-lakṣaṇam /*, *TS-D*, pp. 115-117.

90 *kriyā-guṇavat samavāyi-kāraṇam /*, *VS*, 1.1.15.

91 *vyaktir guṇa-viśeṣāśrayo mūrtiḥ /*, *NS*, 2.2.67.

92 *vyajyata iti vyaktir indriya-grāhyeti / na sarvaṃ dravyaṃ vyaktiḥ / yo guṇa-viśeṣāṇāṃ sparśāntānāṃ gurutva-ghanatva-dravatva-saṃskārāṇām avyāpinaḥ parimāṇasyāśrayo yathā-sambhavaṃ tad dravyam mūrtiḥ mūrcchitāvayavattvād iti /*, *NS-B*, p. 115.

93 *sā ca vyaktir yā na jātiḥ, nākṛtis tasyā anena sūtreṇa saṃgrahaḥ / guṇāś ca viśeṣāś ca tad-āśrayaś ca / ... guṇa-viśeṣāśraya-śabdena dravyam ucyate / karmāpi guṇa-viśeṣa-śabdāl labhyate / ... evaṃ caital-lakṣaṇaṃ rūpādy-ākāśādy-anugatam bhavati /*, *Nyāyavārttika*, quoted in *Khadyota* on *NS-B*, pp. 155-6.

linguistic or semantic context, and differentiates it from the strictly ontological term *dravya* "substance." This is what allows him to include under *vyakti* entities which are ontologically diverse. Uddyotakara says that the term *vyakti* covers everything that is not covered by the notions of *jāti* "generic property" and *ākṛti* "configuration." Since, these three categories together cover all types of meaning conveyed by a word in the Nyāya system, Uddyotakara's interpretation covers all ontological categories. However, in the later Nyāya discussions, these issues are not raised again, and the term *vyakti* is used in the general sense of an individual object.

D.3.iii. Mīmāṃsā epistemology and ontology are closely interrelated. Mīmāṃsakas argue that every valid cognition has a basis (*ālambana*) in external reality, and that the occurrence of a cognition of an object is itself a sufficient proof for the external reality of that object.[94] In a cognition of an object (*vastu*), there is a cognition of exclusion (*vyāvṛtti*) of that object from other objects, and also of inclusion of that object in a class of objects, or a cognition of similarity of that object with other objects. Mīmāṃsakas define a *vyakti* as the external basis of the cognition of exclusion (*vyāvṛtti*) of a given object from other objects.[95] In their view, an individual (*vyakti*) and a generic property (*jāti*) are closely related to each other, so that they can be neither separated from each other, nor can they be cognized in isolation from each other.[96]

D.3.iv. In Mīmāṃsā discussions on the theory of meaning, the term *dravya* is not as frequent as the term *vyakti*. Śabara defines *vyakti* as follows: *a-sādhāraṇa-viśeṣā vyaktiḥ*.[97] This definition can be interpreted in two ways:

a) *a-sādhāraṇā viśeṣā eva vyaktiḥ* "the differentiating properties themselves constitute an individual."

b) *a-sādhāraṇā viśeṣā yasyāṃ sā vyaktiḥ* "that which has [or which is the locus of] differentiating properties is the individual."

Both interpretations have been discussed by Kumārilabhaṭṭa in detail.[98] He points out that the term *viśeṣa* "differentiating property" applies to generic properties (*jāti, sāmānya*) as well. With reference to higher level generic properties (*para-sāmānya*), lower level generic properties (*a-para-sāmānya*) can be treated as differentiating properties. For instance, with reference to the higher level generic property of animal-ness (*prāṇitva*), the lower level generic property of man-ness (*naratva*) is a differentiating property. Similarly, the totality of properties in an individual is always different from the totality of properties in any other individual. In this sense, the totality of properties also becomes a differentiating feature of an individual.[99]

---

94 *SLV*, p. 547.

95 See Note 56.

96 See Note 56.

97 *MS-B(a)*, Pt.I., p. 296.

98 *TV(b)*, pp. 250-251.

99 *na caikasyāṃ vyaktau ye samuditā dṛṣṭās ta eva vyakty-antare 'py anyūnānatiriktā dṛśyante / kiñcid utkarṣāpakarṣa-mātreṇa ca sarvatrāsādhāraṇopalakṣaṇa-lābhāt / para-sāmānyāpekṣayā ca sarvāṇy*

The two different interpretations of Śabara's definition of *vyakti* represent two distinct metaphysical notions. Is an individual identical with a bundle of properties without a separate substratum for those properties, or is it different from those properties and serves as their substratum, locus, or receptacle? Ultimately, like Naiyāyikas, Mīmāṃsakas also maintain that an individual (= substance) is different from its properties. Kumārilabhaṭṭa finally says that, according to Śabara, an individual is different from its properties, since he defines it as the locus of generic and differentiating properties.[100]

D.3.v. In Sanskrit grammatical texts, the terms *sattva, dravya* and *vyakti* are used almost as synonyms. Yāska uses the term *sattva* "being, existing entity" to stand for the meaning signified by nouns.[101] In a similar way, Pāṇini says that items such as *ca* "and" are called *nipāta* "particle" when they do not stand for a *sattva*, i.e. they do not refer to an object or entity.[102] On this rule, Patañjali says that the term *sattva* here refers to a *dravya* "object, entity, existent," and offers a Brahman and a Brahman woman as illustrations of entities.[103] While normally one would expect to derive the word *sattva* from the verb root √*as* "to be," Kaiyaṭa says that the word *sattva* can be derived from the root √*sīd* "to sit." With this new etymology, the word *sattva* is interpreted to refer to a locus of generic properties, qualities, and actions, or literally "that in which these attributes sit." Thus, for Kaiyaṭa, the term *sattva* stands for an entity whose form has already been brought into existence (*siddha-rūpaṃ vastu*).[104] However, the term *sattva* is not used as frequently as the terms *dravya* and *vyakti* in the works of later grammarians.

D.3.vi. The most frequent term in early Sanskrit grammatical works is *dravya*. The first serious assertion that a word denotes a *dravya*, and not an *ākṛti*, is ascribed to Vyāḍi, and Vyāḍi's view is discussed in detail by Kātyāyana in his *Vārttikas* on P.1.2.64 (*sarūpāṇām ekaśeṣa eka-vibhaktau*). B.K. Matilal (1971: 106) also discusses Vyāḍi's view in detail. Patañjali discusses the nature of *dravya* in several different places, and these discussions present slightly variant views. One of these views of *dravya* in the *Mahābhāṣya* appears to be similar to the notion of substance espoused by the schools of Nyāya and Mīmāṃsā. Kātyāyana uses the term *adhikaraṇa* "substratum" to refer to a substance.[105] This term literally refers to a locus and in this context it obviously refers to a locus of attributes or properties. Patañjali explains the term *adhikaraṇa* with the term

evāvāntara-sāmānyāni viśeṣa-vyapadeśam prāpnuvanti / saṃghātāvasthāyāṃ ca vyakti-viśeṣaṇatvāt teṣu viśeṣa-śabdaḥ /, *TV(b)*, pp. 250-251.

100 *etac ca vyakter viśeṣāṇām anyatvam upariṣṭād bhāṣyakāro 'pi vakṣyaty eva "yo 'rthaḥ sāmānyasya viśeṣāṇāṃ cāśrayaḥ" sā vyaktir iti /*, *TV(b)*, pp. 250-251.

101 See Note 27.

102 *cādayo 'sattve*, P.1.4.57.

103 *ayaṃ sattva-śabdo 'sty eva dravya-padārthakaḥ / tad yathā - sattvam ayam brāhmaṇaḥ, sattvam iyam brāhmaṇīti /*, *MB*, Vol.I., Sec.II., p. 282.

104 *tatra sīdanty asmin jāti-guṇa-kriyā iti sattvaṃ dravyam ucyate / dravya-śabdena cātra siddha-rūpaṃ vastv abhidhīyate /*, *MB-P*, Vol.I., Sec.II., p. 282.

105 *adhikaraṇa-gatiḥ sāhacaryāt /*, *Vt.* 61 on P.1.2.64.

dravya.[106] While discussing the relationship between a *dravya* and *guṇas* "attributes, qualities," Patañjali offers two alternatives. One of these alternatives is as follows:[107]

> "Substance (*dravya*) is distinct from [qualities (*guṇas*) such as] sound, and it is cognized through inference. ... [Thus], the derivation [of the word *dravya*] is certainly meaningful. The substance (*dravya*) is *guṇa-sandrāva* 'locus or substratum of qualities'."

Kaiyaṭa takes this to be a justification for the view that a substance is the locus of attributes and is different from those attributes (*guṇānām āśrayaḥ*).[108] The commentators, however, point out that this view is not Patañjali's final view, but that this is simply a prima facie view based on naive or common sense beliefs of people, rather than a serious philosophical view.[109]

D.3.vii. The commentators argue that in Patañjali's final judgement, a substance is not truly distinct from its attributes, and that it is a mere aggregate of the attributes. Nāgeśabhaṭṭa suggests that such an aggregate of attributes could be conceptually differentiated from its constituent attributes, and then one could speak of attributes having the substance as their substratum or locus.[110] Such a view of the commentators is based on the following discussions in Patañjali's *Mahābhāṣya*:

a) "The term *avayava* 'part' is synonymous with the term *guṇa* 'attribute.' With respect to what could an attribute be [said to be] a part? With respect to the aggregate [of attributes]."[111]

b) "What is a substance and what are the qualities? The qualities are sound, touch, color, taste, and smell. What remains [apart from these qualities] is the substance. Is a substance different from sound etc., or is it not different? A substance is not different from sound etc. [Apart from these qualities], nothing else is perceived. When an animal is killed and [its various parts are] placed on a hundred leaves, nothing other than sound etc. is perceived."[112]

c) "What do you think of a substance? ... A substance is an aggregate of attributes."[113]

---

106 *ākṛti-sahacarite dravye /*, *MB*, Vol.I., Sec.II., p. 99.

107 *anyac chabdādibhyo dravyam, tat tv anumāna-gamyam / ... anvarthaṃ khalv api nirvacanaṃ - guṇa-sandrāvo dravyam - iti /*, *MB*, Vol.II., p. 539.

108 *MB-P*, Vol.II., p. 539.

109 *tāttvika-bhedābheda-cintā-parihāreṇa loka-prasiddham bhedam āśritya pratyayārtha ācāryeṇa vyava-sthāpitaḥ /*, *MB-P*, Vol.II., p. 539.

110 *samūhasya bheda-kalpanayaiva cāśrayatva-vyavahāro 'pīti bhāvaḥ /*, *MB-P-U*, Vol.II., p. 539.

111 *avayava-śabdo 'yaṃ guṇa-śabdaḥ / ... kaṃ ca praty avayavo guṇaḥ / samudāyam prati /*, *MB*, Vol.II., pp. 562-563.

112 *kim punar dravyam / ke punar guṇāḥ / śabda-sparśa-rūpa-rasa-gandhā guṇāḥ / tato 'nyad dravyam / kim punar anyac chabdādibhyo dravyam, āhosvid ananyat / ... ananyac chabdādibhyo dravyam, na hy anyad upalabhyate / paśoḥ khalv api viśasitasya parṇa-śate nyastasya nānyac chabdādibhya upalabhyate /*, *MB*, Vol.II., p. 539.

113 *dravye ca bhavataḥ kaḥ sampratyayaḥ / ... guṇa-samudāyo dravyam /*, *MB*, Vol.II., p. 299.

Kaiyaṭa identifies the ontological view of substance as an aggregate of qualities expressed in the above passages of the *Mahābhāṣya* as being based on the Sāṃkhya philosophy. According to Sāṃkhyas, the ultimate primal matter (*prakṛti*) is made up of three ultimate constituent elements (*guṇas*), i.e. *sattva, rajas* and *tamas*. The five qualities mentioned by Patañjali are simply evolutes of these three ultimate constituents of primal matter. Kaiyaṭa says that according to Sāṃkhyas all things in the world are simply aggregates of these qualities and elements, and there is no substance over and above these constituent elements.[114] Nāgeśabhaṭṭa in fact believes that it is one and the same Patañjali who wrote the *Yoga-sūtras* and the *Mahābhāṣya*, and hence there are identical views regarding the nature of substance in these two texts.[115] The ontology of the Yoga system is generally similar to that of the Sāṃkhyas.

D.3.viii. Post-Patañjali grammarian-philosophers deal with the concept of substance from the view point of a non-dualistic idealistic ontology with Brahman as being the only ultimately real principle in the universe. Helārāja, commenting on Bhartṛhari's *Vākyapadīya*, speaks of two levels of comprehending the notion of substance, the ultimately real substance (*paramārtha-dravya*) and the phenomenal or conventional substance (*sāṃvyavahārika-dravya*).[116] Grammarians have discussed the notion of substance in both of these aspects.

a) Kaiyaṭa says that Patañjali's statement regarding permanence of substance (*dravya*) against impermanence of generic properties (*ākṛti* = *jāti*) can be explained by equating the substance with Brahman, the ultimate non-dual reality. Brahman, as allegedly limited by unreal adjuncts, i.e. generic properties, is the principal referent for all words. [cf. **D.2.viii.a**]
b) Bhartṛhari says that each entity has a real and an unreal aspect. The real aspect is the generic property which is identical with pure existence (*sattā*). The unreal aspect of an entity is the individual (*vyakti*). [cf. **D.2.viii.b**]

D.3.ix. Over and above these realist and idealist conceptions of substance or individual, grammarians also exhibit a conception of substance which could be said to be purely formal and semantic, and unrelated to any specific ontological commitment. Such a non-ontological semantic notion of *sattva* can be traced as far back as Yāska's *Nirukta*. Yāska states that a nominal denotes a *sattva* "an object, an entity, something that exists," and he further says:[117] "an entity (*sattva*) is referred to by [the pronominal expression] 'this [is so and so]'." Later, the grammarian-philosopher Bhartṛhari interpreted this statement of Yāska as providing a formal definition of an entity. Thus, Bhartṛhari says:[118]

---

114 *tad-[guṇa-]saṃghāta-rūpaṃ ca ghaṭādi / na tu tad-vyatiriktam avayavi dravyam asti iti sāṃkhyānāṃ siddhāntaḥ /, MB-P*, Vol.II., p. 294.

115 *seśvara-sāṃkhyānām ācāryasya patañjaler ity arthaḥ / ... guṇa-samūho dravyam iti patañjalir iti yoga-bhāṣye spaṣṭam /, MB-P-U*, Vol.II., p. 294; also see p. 541. Also see: B.K. Matilal (1985: 387).

116 *dravyaṃ ca dvividham pāramārthikaṃ sāṃvyavahārikaṃ ca /, VP-H(P)*, p. 106.

117 *ada iti sattvānām upadeśaḥ /, NR*, p. 23.

118 *vastūpalakṣaṇaṃ yatra sarva-nāma prayujyate / dravyam ity ucyate so 'rtho bhedyatvena vivakṣitaḥ //, VP*, III, *Bhūyo-dravya-samuddeśa*, verse 3.

"That with reference to which a pronoun indicating an entity is [or rather could be] used, or that which is desired [by the speaker] to be [expressed as] a qualificandum is called an entity." To explain this passage in the *Vākya-padīya*, Helārāja quotes a somewhat altered version of Yāska's statement:[119] "That which is [or rather could be] understood when a pronoun such as 'this' is used is an entity." In short, anything that can be referred to by a pronoun such as "this" is an entity (*dravya, vyakti*) for the purposes of philosophy of language. Grammarians clearly state that there is no particular ontological commitment involved in this conception, and that even generic properties etc. could be regarded to be entities (*dravya, vyakti*) in this sense, if so desired to be referred to by a pronoun, or if they are desired to be expressed as qualified entities.[120] To illustrate this, the action of going signified by the verb form "going" in the sentence "He is going" is not an entity in this formal sense. However, the same action of going signified by the form "going" in "when the going gets tough, [the tough get going]" could be said to be an entity under this view. Actually, this seems to involve a conceptual hypostatization or reification, as described by Yāska in his *Nirukta*,[121] which changes a fluid action as a process into a conceptually frozen action which can be viewed as a concrete (*mūrta*) entity (*sattva-bhūta*). Kaiyaṭa and Nāgeśabhaṭṭa both seem to advocate this non-ontological formal definition of entity:[122]

> "An entity which can be referred to by pronouns such as 'this' and 'that' is a substance (*dravya*)." *MB-P*.
> "[For the purpose of formal grammar], a substance [or rather an entity] is not to be defined as an aggregate of attributes. The above [given formal semantic definition] is the [proper] definition of an entity, useful in this entire system of grammar." *MB-P-U*.

D.4. *LIṄGA* "GENDER"

D.4.i. Gender does not normally figure in the Western discussions of semantics. For centuries, gender has remained a puzzling feature of language for linguists and philosophers. Natural distinctions of physical sex are a matter of reality for the world of living beings. However, genders of words have no necessary relation to physical sex, and deviations of any forced relationship would be too numerous to count. Subramania Iyer refers to such deviations from expected genders in German.[123] In a number of languages, masculine and feminine words are sometimes used to signify members of the opposite sex,

---

119 *etad eva niruktakāreṇāpy uktam - ada iti yat pratīyate tad dravyam iti /*, *VP-H(P)*, pp. 187-188. Compare the statement as quoted by Helārāja with the actual *Nirukta* statement quoted in note 117.

120 *jāty-ādir api viśeṣyatvena ced vivakṣitas tadā dravyam iti /*, *VP-H(P)*, pp. 187-188.

121 *mūrtaṃ sattva-bhūtam [bhāvaṃ] sattva-nāmabhiḥ / vrajyā paktir iti /*, *NR*, p. 42.

122 *idam, tat, iti sarvanāma-pratyavamarśa-yogyaṃ vastu dravyam ity arthaḥ /*, *MB-P*, Vol.II., p. 299; *idaṃ tad iti / na tu guṇa-samūho dravyam ity arthaḥ / idaṃ caitac-chāstra-mātropayogi dravya-lakṣaṇam iti bodhyam /*, *MB-P-U*, Vol.II., p. 299. Also see: B.K. Matilal (1985: 382).

123 Subramania Iyer (1969: 359).

or objects with no physical sex. Similarly, there are neuter words used to signify animate objects with physical sex distinctions. One and the same object is sometimes signified by words with different genders, and the same word in different genders may signify one and the same object. Karl Brugmann argued that the category of gender is entirely superfluous as far as the capacity of language to express thoughts is concerned, and he sides with Sophists like Protagoras who ridiculed the gender distinctions in Greek.[124] Linguists like Herder, Adelung, Jacob Grimm and W. v. Humboldt believed that grammatical gender represents the tendency of the primitive societies to individualize and personify natural objects.[125] However, from the point of view of formal linguistics, Brugmann asserts that grammatical gender does not really signify anything like physical sex, either in literal or figurative sense, but represents only formal morphological distinctions.[126]

D.4.ii. Subramania Iyer rightly points out that the problem of gender in Sanskrit has become more confused since one and the same word, i.e. *liṅga*, stands for linguistic gender and physical sex. This makes a common man inclined to believe that there is a possible relationship between physical sex and linguistic gender.[127] This represents the popular view that linguistic gender is an expression of physical sex (*laukika-liṅga*). In the discussions in the tradition of Sanskrit grammar, such a popular conception is the starting point for the entire debate, and even in the somewhat philosophically sophisticated notions regarding linguistic gender, the influence of the popular view persists. Since the popular conception of linguistic gender as a direct reflection of physical sex distinctions does not work, various technical and philosophical conceptions of gender (*śāstrīya-liṅga*) arose. Some thinkers believed that gender, even in a technical sense, is a property of objects signified by words (*artha-dharma*). Others argued that technical or linguistic gender pertains only to words (*śabda-dharma*) and is not a property of the signified object. There are those who argue that gender, even as a property of the word, is of ontological nature, while others hold, like their modern colleagues in linguistics, that gender pertaining to a word is a purely formal linguistic feature of the word, and that it has nothing to do with the ontological makeup of either words or their meanings. While it is difficult to guess what Pāṇini himself thought about the nature of gender, I have already stated my view that for Pāṇini gender was a meaning category, but it was not included in the meaning of a nominal [cf. **D.1**].

D.4.iii. Patañjali starts the discussion on this topic with a statement of the popular view of linguistic gender being a direct reflection of physical sex. He says:[128]

---

124 Karl Brugmann (1897: 6-7).
125 Karl Brugmann (1897: 7-8).
126 Karl Brugmann (1897: 10).
127 Subramania Iyer (1969: 360).
128 *kim punar loke dṛṣṭvaitad avasīyate - iyaṃ strī, ayam pumān, idaṃ napuṃsakam iti / liṅgam / kim punas tat / stana-keśavatī strī syāl lomaśaḥ puruṣaḥ smṛtaḥ / ubhayor antaraṃ yac ca tad-abhāve napuṃsakam /*, *MB*, Vol.II., p. 289.

> "What is it that people see when they decide that this is a woman, this is a man, and this is something neuter? It is the gender [= sex]. What is that? That individual which has breasts and [long] hair (*keśa*) is a woman, and that which has body hair (*loman*) is a man. That which does not have either of these two distinctions is neuter."

Some commentators interpret the words *keśa* and *loman* as standing for female and male sex organs, and thus define a feminine object as the one with the female sex organ, and the male object as the one with the male sex organ.[129] The upholder of this popular view tries to show that one could speak of inanimate objects as having physical sex-genders by superimposition (*āropa*). Patañjali offers some fascinating speculations on the part of the defender of this popular view:[130]

a) One could say that inanimate objects do not have any actual sex-genders, but that one has a false illusion of the natural sex-gender in an inanimate object. This is like a deer's experience of mirage in a desert, where there is actually no water, or like a person watching the cities of angels in the colorful evening clouds.
b) One could say that inanimate objects are also endowed with real sex-genders, but that the sex-genders of inanimate things are so subtle that they are not readily perceptible, like the slow movement of the sun.
c) The populist may also claim that the sex-genders of inanimate objects exist like well guarded secrets. Since they are like things hidden under a cover, they are not readily perceptible.

Obviously, none of these populist explanations is satisfactory, and finally Patañjali rejects all these explanations and says that a grammarian cannot rely on such a conception of gender as physical sex, and that he must rely on his own technical conception of linguistic gender (*śāstrīya-liṅga*).[131]

D.4.iv. The technical conception of gender as expounded by Patañjali is based on Sāṃkhya-Yoga ontology. As explained earlier [cf. **D.3.vii**], Patañjali's conception of a substance as an aggregate of attributes (*guṇa-samūho dravyam*) is a Sāṃkhya-Yoga conception. Kātyāyana proposes that gender is nothing but *saṃstyāna* and *prasava*.[132] According to the final interpretation offered by Patañjali, these terms refer to actions, and they respectively signify decrease (*styāna* / *apacaya*) and increase (*pravṛtti* / *vṛddhi*) of

---

129 *keśa-śabdasya bhaga-vācakatvād bhagavattvaṃ strītvam, lomaśaḥ puruṣaḥ ity atra lomañ-śabdasya śiśna-vācakatvāt śiśna-vattvam puṃstvam* /, *VBS-S*, p. 226.

130 *asat tu mṛga-tṛṣṇāvad gandharva-nagaraṃ yathā* / *āditya-gativat san na, vastrāntarhitavac ca tat* //, *MB*, Vol.II., pp. 290-291. Also: *VP-H(b)*, pp. 434ff.

131 *tasmān na vaiyākaraṇaiḥ śakyaṃ laukikaṃ liṅgam āsthātum* / *avaśyaṃ kaścit sva-kṛtānta āstheyaḥ* /, *MB*, Vol.I., Sec.I., p. 97, and Vol.II., p. 293.

132 *saṃstyāna-prasavau liṅgam* /, *Vt.* 58 on P.1.2.64.

attributes or qualities (*guṇa*), i.e. sound, touch, color, taste, and smell.[133] The five attributes mentioned by Patañjali are evolutes of the ultimate constituents of the primal matter (*prakṛti*). Commentators are confident that Patañjali is referring to the Sāṃkhya-Yoga philosophy, and also that he himself wrote both the *Mahābhāṣya* and the *Yoga-sūtras*.[134] According to Sāṃkhyas, all objects in the universe are different combinations of the three ultimate attributes of the primal matter. The three attributes, as they constitute different objects, differ in their proportions, and these proportions are continuously changing. Patañjali thus suggests that the masculine gender signified by a word represents an increase of these constituent attributes in a given object. The feminine gender represents a decrease in these constituent attributes in a given object. There is a great debate about what the neuter gender indicates, and we shall review these different conceptions later [cf. **D.4.vi**].

D.4.v. Patañjali says that objects in this world are in a constant flux, and an object either grows or decays, but it never remains stable.[135] The fluctuations of increase and decrease of the constituent primal elements are common to all objects in the world. If all objects in the world have both increase and decrease, or have continuous fluctuations of increase and decrease, then how can there be a definite gender for a given object? Patañjali answers this question by saying that gender depends not so much on the actual ontological state of the constituent primal elements in an object, but upon a speaker's intention, or upon how a speaker wishes to characterize a given object. If the speaker wishes to indicate the increase of primal constituent elements in an object, then he uses a masculine word to refer to that object. If he intends to indicate the decrease of primal constituent elements in an object, then he uses a feminine word to refer to that object. If the speaker wishes to indicate neither increase nor decrease of the primal constituent elements, or if he intends to indicate both, then he uses a neuter word to refer to that object.[136] If genders were so totally dependent upon the intention of a speaker to indicate such changing states of primal constituent elements in an object, then genders of words referring to those objects would change from person to person, and from time to time. To answer such an objection, Kaiyaṭa points out that in this discussion the notion of the intention of a speaker does not refer to the free will of each individual speaker to use any gender for any object or for any

---

133 *iha punar ubhayam bhāva-sādhanaṃ styānam pravṛttiś ca / ... kasya punaḥ styānaṃ strī pravṛttir vā pumān / guṇānām / keṣām / śabda-sparśa-rūpa-rasa-gandhānām /*, *MB*, Vol.I., Sec.I., p. 98, and Vol.II., pp. 293ff. Also see: *styānam apacayaḥ, pravṛttir vṛddhiḥ /*, *MB-P-U*, Vol.I., Sec.I., p. 98.

134 *guṇānāṃ sattva-rajas-tamaḥ-pariṇāma-rūpāṇāṃ śabdādīnām ... /*, *MB-P*, Vol.I., Sec.I., p. 98; *sattva-rajas-tamāṃsi guṇāḥ / tat-pariṇāma-rūpāś ca śabdādayaḥ pañca guṇāḥ ... iti sāṃkhyānāṃ siddhāntaḥ /*, *MB-P*, Vol.II., p. 294; *sāṃkhyānām iti seśvara-sāṃkhyānām ācāryasya patañjaler ity arthaḥ /*, *MB-P-U*, Vol.II., p. 294; *bhāṣye sāṃkhya-matenaiva saṃstyāna-prasavau nirūpitau /*, *LM*, p. 1149.

135 *na hīdaṃ kaścid api svasminn ātmani muhūrtam apy avatiṣṭhate, vardhate yāvad anena vardhitavyam, apacayena vā yujyate / tac cobhayaṃ sarvatra / ... yady ubhayaṃ sarvatra kuto vyavasthā / vivakṣātaḥ / saṃstyāna-vivakṣāyāṃ strī, prasava-vivakṣāyām pumān, ubhayor apy avivakṣāyāṃ napuṃsakam /*, *MB*, Vol.I., Sec.I., p. 98.

136 *ubhaya-vivakṣāyāṃ napuṃsakam /*, *MB*, Vol.II., p. 295.

word, but to the collective intention of the community of speakers which is indicated by the established linguistic usage of that community.[137]

D.4.vi. If the above given explanations seem complicated, the explanations for the use of neuter gender for objects and words seem to have proliferated out of control. Though things in this world are in a constant flux, neuter gender is said to represent the intention of a speaker to indicate the stable condition of the primal constituent elements, to the exclusion of both increase and decrease. This view is expressed in the oft-quoted maxim *sāmānye napuṃsakam*: "neuter gender is used to express a generic condition of the primal constituent elements." This maxim has been explained in several different ways in the Sanskrit grammatical literature. Since these different explanations reflect the changing attitudes of the Sanskrit grammarians, it is worth listing them.

a) As Kauṇḍabhaṭṭa says in **NN.V.2.c.**, neuter gender represents the mere existence (*sthiti*) of primal constituent elements, which is common to increase, decrease, and equillibrium. Kaiyaṭa proposes this view.[138]

b) Some philosophers describe the equillibrium of primal constituent elements in a given object as the meaning of neuter gender.[139]

c) Helārāja, in his commentary on Bhartṛhari's *Vākya-padīya*, offers three explanations for the notion of *sthiti* "constant stable condition" :[140]

c-1) In a stream of evolution, the increase of many consecutive moments could be looked upon as a constant condition. The same could be said about the decreases of many consecutive moments. One could say that such common conditions are represented by neuter gender.

c-2) In both decrease and increase, the common condition is that of change, and one could say that it is this common condition of change that is indicated by neuter gender.

c-3) Every disappearing object is immediately replaced by something else in the continuous evolutionary process. Thus the disappearance of no object is final. One could say that it is this common condition of non-finality of disappearance that is indicated by neuter gender.

d) Mīmāṃsakas interpret Patañjali's view in a different way. Kumārilabhaṭṭa says that, according to Patañjali, masculine, feminine, and neuter genders reflect the conditions of *saṃstyāna, prasava*, and *sthāna*, and Pārthasārathi-miśra explains these three terms as referring to dominance of *rajas, sattva,*

---

137 *loka-vyavahārānusāriṇī vivakṣāśrīyate, na tu prāyoktrī* /, *MB-P*, p. 295. Also: *VP-H(b)*, pp. 437ff.

138 *sthitir napuṃsakaṃ sā ca sarvatra vidyata eveti sthiti-vivakṣāyāṃ siddho napuṃsaka-śabda-prayogaḥ* /, *MB-P*, Vol.I., Sec.I., pp. 105-106; and *sāmānyaṃ hi guṇa-rūpaṃ sthitiḥ* /, *VP-H(b)*, p. 439.

139 *sattva-rajas-tamo-guṇānāṃ sāmyāvasthā napuṃsakatvam* /, *NK*, p. 712.

140 Subramania Iyer (1969: 366-367).

and *tamas*, respectively.[141] However, Pārthasārathimiśra's view has no direct support in the *Mahābhāṣya*.

D.4.vii. All the interpretations of Patañjali's views given above would seem to have one common factor. They all seem to imply that genders are certain ontological characteristics of the objects signified by words, whether these ontological characteristics are true or merely intended by the speaker. Thus, in all the above discussions, genders are viewed as properties of signified objects (*artha-dharma*), and not of words which signify those objects (*śabda-dharma*). On the other hand, Kauṇḍabhaṭṭa says that gender as explained by Patañjali is a property of the signifier word (*śabda-dharma*), and not of the signified object (*artha-dharma*), cf. **NN.V.7.a**. Unfortunately, Kauṇḍabhaṭṭa does not explain how Patañjali's Sāṃkhya-Yoga ontology can be used to account for a view that gender is a property of words, rather than objects. However, commentators on Kauṇḍabhaṭṭa's works do venture a few explanations of such a possibility. The author of the commentary *Prabhā* on Kauṇḍabhaṭṭa's *Vaiyākaraṇa-bhūṣaṇa-sāra* quotes the opinion of his own teacher (*iti guravaḥ*):[142]

> "In fact, both a word and an object are composed of the three primal constituent elements such as *sattva*. It is possible that some elements decrease, while others increase, and thus there is simultaneously increase and decrease [of the primal elements] in one and the same entity. In the case of entities like soul (*ātman*), where there are no constituent elements, there can be nothing like an increase of elements. Yet one could avoid this difficulty by relying on the increase [of elements] in the signifier word [i.e. *ātman* as a masculine word], which is itself composed of the three primal constituent elements."

According to this line of thought, one could say that genders represent the changing conditions of primal constituent elements, not in the signified object, but in the signifier word, since the words are also made up of the same primal constituent elements. Ramanarayan Tripathi ascribes this view to the Nyāya system without offering any textual references.[143]

Nāgeśabhaṭṭa completely disagrees with Kauṇḍabhaṭṭa's interpretation of Patañjali's view of gender, and argues that, according to Patañjali, genders are certain properties of the signified objects (*artha-dharma*), and not of words (*śabda-dharma*).[144] He quotes a

---

141 *saṃstyāna-prasava-sthānair yathā pātañjale mate /*, *SLV*, p. 329; *saṃstyānaṃ rajo-bāhulyaṃ strī-dharmaḥ / prasavaḥ sattva-bāhulyam puṃ-dharmaḥ / sthānaṃ tamo-bāhulyaṃ napuṃsaka-dharma iti /*, *SLV-N*, p. 330.

142 *vastutas tu śabdasyārthasya ca sattvādi-guṇa-trayātmakatayā tatra kasyacid guṇasyopacayaḥ kasyacid apacayaḥ ity evaṃ-rūpasyopacayāpacayasyaikatra sambhavād ātmādi-niravayava-padārtheṣu upacayāder abhāve 'pi tad-vācaka-guṇa-trayātmaka-śabda-gatopacayādim ādāya doṣābhāvāc ceti guravaḥ /*, *VBS-P*, p. 245.

143 Ramanarayan Tripathi (1970: 23).

144 *etena śabda-niṣṭham eva liṅgam ity apāstam / ukta-bhāṣya-virodhāt / ... na hi napuṃsakaṃ nāma śabdo 'stīti svamor iti sūtre bhāṣyāc ca /*, *LM*, pp. 1146-7. Also see: *bhūṣaṇoktiṃ khaṇḍayati, eteneti /*, *LM-KL*, p. 1146. The *Mahābhāṣya* passage quoted by Nāgeśabhaṭṭa occurs in *MB*, Vol.III., p. 28.

statement of Patañjali in support of his interpretation: "Neuter [gender] is certainly not a word." He further points out that Patañjali's view of gender is in agreement with the statement in the *Yoga-bhāṣya*: "According to Patañjali, a substance is an aggregate of attributes," and he cites another statement of Patañjali: "All objects [in this world] have the same constitution [i.e. they are built out of the three primal constituents of matter]."[145] Rejecting Kauṇḍabhaṭṭa's interpretation on these grounds, Nāgeśabhaṭṭa states that a word is called a neuter word for two reasons: a) it signifies a neuter object, and b) it is ultimately identical with the signified neuter object. He ascribes this explanation to Bhartṛhari and Kaiyaṭa.[146]

D.4.viii. Grammarians ascribe an interesting view of gender to Vaiśeṣikas.[147] According to this view, the three genders are distinct generic properties or universals such as masculine-ness, feminine-ness, and neuter-ness, and these generic properties reside in the signified objects, rather than in the words which signify those objects. These genders as generic properties of objects are manifested sometimes by physical features like breasts,[148] or be directly pointed out by words like *strītva* "feminine-ness."[149] Some of Patañjali's own statements seem to point to universal-like features of gender properties: "Feminine-ness (*strītva*) is a single entity."[150] The author of the commentary *Kalā* on Nāgeśabhaṭṭa's *Laghu-mañjūṣā*, says that this view of genders as generic properties is directly supported by the *Mahābhāṣya* and is not opposed to it.[151] These generic properties of gender are neither opposed to each other, nor to other generic properties residing in the object. Every object has all three gender-properties, and yet a word referring to that object expresses only one of them in accordance with one's intention reflecting the established pattern of usage in the community. These generic properties of gender, we are told, are not necessarily reflections of physical sex in any real or imposed sense.

While this view has been ascribed by grammarians to Vaiśeṣikas, very few Vaiśeṣika authors actually discuss the notion of gender. An author named Prasādakṛt, referred to by Padmanābhamiśra in his commentary *Setu* on the *Bhāṣya* of Praśastapāda, seems to have accepted the Sāṃkhyan conception of gender proposed by Patañjali.[152] Padmanābhamiśra himself rejects Patañjali's Sāṃkhyan view of genders, as well as the view that genders are

---

145 *guṇa-samūho dravyam iti patañjalir iti spaṣṭam / tad vakṣyati - sarvāś ca mūrtaya evam-ātmikā - iti / ... etena śabda-niṣṭham eva liṅgam iti navyoktam parāstam /*, *MB-P-U*, Vol.II., p. 294. Here Nāgeśabhaṭṭa seems to refer to Kauṇḍabhaṭṭa's view by calling him a *navya* "a neo-[grammarian]."

146 *napuṃsakārthābhidhāyitvāt tad-abhedāc ca śabdasya napuṃsakatvam iti kaiyaṭa-harī ity anyatra vistaraḥ /*, *LM*, pp. 1146-7.

147 *vaiśeṣikāḥ ... strītva-puṃstva-napuṃsakatva-rūpā liṅgaṃ jātir ity āhuḥ /*, *VP-H(b)*, p. 430, and *vaiśeṣikās tu puṃstvādayo jātayaḥ /*, *LM*, p. 1147. It is possible that Nāgeśabhaṭṭa is simply following Helārāja in ascribing this view to Vaiśeṣikas.

148 *stanādy-upavyañjanā jātiḥ /*, *VP-H(b)*, p. 430; *strītvādīnāṃ stanādy-upavyañjanānāṃ gotvādivat sāmānya-viśeṣatvaṃ darśitam /*, *MB-P*, Vol.II., p. 289.

149 *tad-upavyañjanety atra ... strī-liṅgādi-śabda-pratipādyā vety arthaḥ /*, *PB-S*, pp. 85-6.

150 *eko 'yam arthaḥ strītvaṃ nāma /*, *MB*, Vol.II., pp. 296 and 298.

151 *jāti-svarūpam eva bhāṣyoktam iti na tad-virodho 'pi /*, *LM-KL*, p. 1147.

152 *nanu mahābhāṣya-sammatim puraskṛtyaiva prasāda-kṛtā likhitam puṃstvam upacayaḥ strītvam apacaya iti /*, *PB-S*, p. 84.

generic properties.[153] He points out that even Bhartṛhari who mentions this view does not take it seriously. The properties of gender cannot be generic properties, since they involve the defect of *saṃkara* "cross-connection." Such a cross-connection occurs when two properties of an object are such that the domain of occurrence of one property does not fully contain or include the domain of occurrence of the other property.[154] Mīmāṃsakas also refuse to accept that genders are generic properties.[155] Kaiyaṭa offers further arguments to show why genders cannot be treated as generic properties.[156] The so called generic property of feminine-ness cannot be manifested by a definite shape or configuration, just as the generic property of bull-ness is manifested by a certain common configuration in the object. Different objects such as a bed, a tree, and a city are signified by the feminine words *khaṭvā, śiṃśapā*, and *nagarī*, and yet these objects do not share a common shape or configuration which would manifest the shared generic property of feminine-ness. Bull-ness, a generic property, once explained to an intelligent person can be recognized by him in different instances. However, there is no way to recognize the property of feminine-ness in different objects by recognizing it in a few objects. Thus, finally the view that genders are generic properties (*jāti*) of some sort residing in objects signified by words is rejected by the tradition.

D.4.ix. All the views of gender discussed so far, except Kauṇḍabhaṭṭa's interpretation of Patañjali, hold that gender is a physical or metaphysical property of the object signified by a word (*artha-dharma*), and not of the signifier word (*śabda-dharma*). None of these views seem to be satisfactory, and each would seem to involve some element of sophistry. Kauṇḍabhaṭṭa himself says at some point that just as different accents and vowel lengths differentiate words from one another, similarly genders as properties of words differentiate one word from another [cf. **NN.V.9.a**]. Here, genders are viewed as being properties of words (*śabda-dharma*). However, grammarians do not seem to agree with each other on the nature of gender, even when they regard genders as properties of words.

Helārāja argues that genders cannot be properties of words in the same sense as accents are properties of words. The reason is that one does not feel that the object signified by a word has an accent, because the word has an accent; however, we do feel that the signified

---

153 *api ca bhartṛhari-pariganiteṣu tad-upavyañjanā jātir ity atra na tasya svarasaḥ / ... na ca strītvādir jātiḥ sambhavati, jāti-sāṃkaryāt / strītvasya pṛthivītva-parihāreṇa varuṇa-lokādi-strīṣu sattvāt, pṛthivītvasya strītva-parihāreṇa ghaṭādau sattvāt, bhūtala-varttinīṣu nitambinīṣu dvitaya-sattvāt /*, *PB-S*, pp. 85-7. The argument rejecting the status of genders as generic properties on the basis of *saṃkara* "cross-connection" is interesting. Padmanābhamiśra argues that the property of feminine-ness goes beyond earth-ness, and exists even in the women of the world of Varuṇa which is entirely made out of water. Similarly, earth-ness goes beyond femininity and occurs in pots etc. The earthly women share both femininity and earth-ness. Therefore, femininity cannot be accepted as a generic property.

154 Ingalls (1951: 42).

155 *TV(b)*, pp. 951-2.

156 *na ca gotvādivat saṃsthāna-viśeṣa-vyaṅgyatvaṃ strītvasya yataḥ sāmānya-viśeṣa-rūpatvaṃ syāt / khaṭvā-śiṃśapā-nagary-ādiṣu bhinnatvāt saṃsthānasya / na ca sakṛd ākhyātaṃ strītvaṃ gotvādivat sarveṣu strī-liṅgeṣu vyakty-antareṣu grahītuṃ śakyate /*, *MB-P*, Vol.II., p. 289.

object has a certain gender because the word has a certain gender.[157] Therefore, the *śabda-dharma* view of gender as represented by Kauṇḍabhaṭṭa is not to be confused with Bhartṛhari's view that gender is a *śabda-saṃskāra*. According to Helārāja's explanation, the *śabda-saṃskāra* view of gender holds gender to be the external foundation on the basis of which grammarians accomplish grammatical operations on words. Subramania Iyer believes that this is not Bhartṛhari's final view. According to him, Bhartṛhari's final view is identical with the Sāṃkhyan conception of Patañjali.[158] Different states of the ultimate elements constituting an object form the external foundation on the basis of which grammarians of antiquity could base their grammatical gender assignments. For this reason, these states of ultimate primal elements are regarded to be the *śabda-saṃskāras* "factors which help grammatical processing of words."

D.4.x. According to Nāgeśabhaṭṭa's final view, gender is most certainly a formal property, but it is a formal property of the object, and hence could be recognized as a meaning element. He defines masculine-ness or masculine gender to be the property of an object of being able to be referred to by the masculine pronoun *ayam* "this." Feminine-ness or feminine gender is the property of an object of being able to be referred to by the feminine pronoun *iyam* "this." Neuter-ness or neuter gender is the property of an object of being able to be referred to by the neuter pronoun *idam* "this."[159] In the school of grammar, this is the only formal definition of gender which does not involve any kind of physical or metaphysical commitment concerning the word or the object. But, to me, it is difficult to accept the gender properties as described by Nāgeśabhaṭṭa as true properties of the signified object, and not as properties of the signifier words.

As far as I know, the best and the most modern conception of gender is not found in the tradition of Sanskrit grammar, but in the commentary *Setu* by Padmanābhamiśra on Praśastapāda's *Bhāṣya* on Kaṇāda's *Vaiśeṣika-sūtras*. Padmanābhamiśra says that there is no masculine meaning cognized from a masculine word. Therefore, the masculine gender is not a property of the object. Genders represent merely the systematic differences in the linguistic shapes of words. Differences in word-structures mark different genders. Apart from this perceptible difference in word forms, there is nothing like physical or metaphysical gender. Padmanābhamiśra asserts that this is what is meant by the term *śabda-saṃskāra* used by Bhartṛhari, and that this is also the final view of Bhartṛhari.[160] We are not quite sure if Padmanābhamiśra is correct in interpreting Bhartṛhari's view of *śabda-saṃskāra*. However, his own view is the most commendable conception of gender

---

157 *taṭas taṭī taṭam ity abhinnenāpi śabdenābhinnaṃ vastu tri-liṅgam pratyāyyata iti śabda-saṃskāra-mātraṃ liṅgam āśritaṃ kaiścid, evam api ca bāhyatvenāvasāyāt nodāttādi-dharmavat śabda-dharmatvaṃ liṅgasya, kiṃ tu striyām puṃsi napuṃsaka iti śabdenānvākhyāna-nimitta-bhāva-darśanāt śabda-saṃskāratvam asya /*, *VP-H(b)*, p. 431.

158 Subramania Iyer (1969: 369).

159 *ayam iti vyavahāra-viṣayatvam puṃstvam, iyam iti vyavahāra-viṣayatvaṃ strītvam, idam iti vyavahāra-viṣayatvaṃ klībatvam iti vilakṣaṇaṃ śāstrīyaṃ strī-pun-napuṃsakatvam /*, *PLM*, p. 197.

160 *puṃliṅgādiṣu śabdākāra-bheda-prakārasyaiva prāmāṇikatvenārtha-bhede mānābhāvāt / ata eva bhartṛ-hariṇāpi ... ṣaṭsu pakṣeṣu cāsvarasena śabda-saṃśkāra ity apīti likhitam / ... evaṃ ca puṃstvādi na tattvāntaram iti tattvavin-manoramaṃ tattvam /*, *PB-S*, p. 85.

from the view point of linguistic analysis. Genders simply represent certain systematically distinct classes of linguistic items sharing certain common linguistic features. They offer a convenient device of classifying nominals according to their linguistic behavior. This conception is modern enough to be compared with that of Karl Brugmann (1897: 10).

D.5. *SAṂKHYĀ* "NUMBER"

D.5.i. In **D.1.**, I have expressed my view that Pāṇini did not consider number to be a meaning of a nominal stem, though it was a meaning category for him. Another interesting fact seems to be that Pāṇini uses the term *parimāṇa* to refer to number as a meaning category, while he uses the term *saṃkhyā* to refer to number words like "one" and "two." On the other hand, the commentators take the term *parimāṇa* as referring to a notion of measure, and the terms *vacana* and *saṃkhyā* as referring to a notion of number [cf. commentaries on P.2.3.46 (*prātipadikārtha-liṅga-parimāṇa-vacana-mātre prathamā*)]. We also know little about what Pāṇini thought of number as a possible ontological category.

Praśastapāda, the author of the *Bhāṣya* on the *Vaiśeṣika-sūtras*, defines *saṃkhyā* "number" as: "number is [that which is] the basis of usages such as 'one'."[161] There are two assumptions behind this assertion, a) every instance of cognition has as its content something which is a part of external reality, and b) linguistic usage leads to valid cognitions. Since there is a result, there must be a cause for that result. Since the result is real, the cause must also be real. Uddyotakara wields this realistic argument against objections from Buddhists to the notion of number as an ontological category:[162]

> "[The Buddhist claims that] number does not really exist. ... [The Naiyāyika responds:] The one who says that number does not exist must point out the basis for cognitions of singularity and plurality [of objects]. Why? [This is] because these cognitions of singularity and plurality are undeniable. ... Therefore, that which is the [external] basis of these cognitions is number."

Later Naiyāyikas define number as that which is the exclusive [external] basis of the act of counting.[163]

D.5.ii. Buddhist philosophers argue that linguistic usage is merely a representation of one's conceptual constructions (*vikalpa*), and not of what actually exists out there. For Dignāga and his followers, the reality of what is out there is explained in terms of continually changing states of momentary point instant existents, and such momentary states of what is actually out there are beyond the pale of language. The Buddhists argue that linguistic usage cannot be used as evidence to prove the external existence of what the

---

161 *ekādi-vyavahāra-hetuḥ saṃkhyā /*, *PB*, p. 267.

162 *saṃkhyaiva tāvan nāsti ... / saṃkhyā nāstīti bruvatā ekāneka-pratyayānāṃ ... nimittam upādeyam / kasmāt / ekāneka-pratyayānām apratyākhyeyatvāt / ... tasmād yat tat-pratyaya-nimittaṃ sā saṃkhyeti /*, *NV*, pp. 421-2. The *NV-T* comments: *saṃkhyānām asattvam āśaṅkya nirākaroti /*, *NV-T*, p. 427.

163 *gaṇanā-vyavahārāsādhāraṇa-kāraṇaṃ saṃkhyā /*, *KM*, p. 694.

words seem to refer to. Therefore, for the Buddhists, the usage of number words cannot be used to establish the external ontological reality of numbers[164] Others argued that number cannot be differentiated from its locus, and that it is actually identical with that locus. For these thinkers, any distinction between number and its locus is merely conceptual.[165] There are others who argue that the number one is nothing more than an entity being by itself, while numbers two etc. are simply an entity being in company of other entities. Thus, for these philosophers, number is simply a reflection of a given entity being or not being in company with other entities, and it does not involve any additional ontological commitment.[166]

Vaiśeṣikas and Naiyāyikas hold that number is ontologically different from its locus, i.e. the substance. Vācaspatimiśra says that Uddyotakara has established the ontological distinction between number and substance on the basis of difference in their cognitions.[167] Śrīdhara argues against those who deny this distinction.[168] According to Vaiśeṣikas and Naiyāyikas, number is a quality (*guṇa*) residing in a substance (*dravya*).[169] They argue that a cognition that an object is in company with other objects is different from the cognition of duality etc. Similarly, even for those objects which are in company with other objects, one can have a cognition of singularity. Thus, they argue that it is not the case that one has a cognition of singularity only for those objects which are not in company of other objects.[170] While Mīmāṃsakas agree with Vaiśeṣikas and Naiyāyikas that number is ontologically different from the numbered object, they do not accept number as a quality (*guṇa*) of a substance. Since one can have a cognition that a substance has two or more qualities, it seems that number can be a property of not just substances, but also of qualities and actions, and hence it must be an independent ontological category (*padārthāntara*), distinct from substances, qualities, and actions.[171]

D.5.iii. The view of grammarians as presented by Bhartṛhari and Helārāja is a compromise between the realists and the Buddhists. While these grammarians neither defend or reject the external reality of number, they argue that one must accept number as a necessary semantic postulate to explain linguistic usage. Thus, the concept of number or its psychological reality must be assumed, whether or not one accepts the external reality of number. For Bhartṛhari, every object is spoken of as having a number. In the world, the

---

164 *saṃkhyādīnām asiddhitaḥ* /, *TTS*, verse 681, Vol.I., p. 280.

165 *avyatirikta-dharma-vādinas tu avyatiriktām āśrayāt saṃkhyām manyante* /, *VP-H(b)*, p. 396.

166 *padārtha evāsahāya ekatvaṃ, sa-sahāyaś ca yathā-yogaṃ dvitvādīti sahāya-viraha-tad-yogayor dharmāntaratvābhān na kaścid anyo dravyāt saṃkhyā-lakṣaṇo guṇaḥ* / *iti vyatirikta-saṃkhyābhāvaḥ* /, *VP-H(b)*, p. 395.

167 *pratyaya-bhedāt dravyādibhyaḥ saṃkhyāyā bhedam uktvā* ... /, *NV-T*, p. 428.

168 *yad api dravya-vyatiriktā saṃkhyā na vidyate bhedenāgrahaṇād iti, tad apy ayuktam* /, *PB-K*, p. 270.

169 *vaiśeṣikāṇāṃ dravyāśritā guṇātmikā saṃkhyā* /, *VP-H(b)*, p. 395.

170 *anyo hi sa-sahāyatā-pratyayaḥ, anyaś ca dvau traya ity-ādi-pratyayaḥ* / *sa-sahāyeṣv api caikatva-pratyayo 'stīti na tad-viraha evaikatva-saṃkhyā* /, *VP-H(b)*, p. 395.

171 *mīmāṃsakās tu saṃkhyā guṇādāv api pratīteḥ padārthāntaram eva* /, *NK*, p. 904.

distinction between identity and difference is founded on number.[172] Helārāja comments that the property of number is postulated on the basis of the linguistic usage of unity, duality, and plurality.[173]

Bhartṛhari says:[174]

> "That property [of number] may be [considered to be] different [from the objects] or may be [considered to be] identical with them. [However, this conceptually distinct property] is called *saṃkhyā* 'number' on account of it being the foundation of the difference [in the cognitions of objects]."

Helārāja comments on this verse:[175]

> "The property defined as number may be identical with the numbered objects or it may be different from them. What do we [grammarians] have to do with this fruitless discussion? Here [in grammar], what is proposed to be discussed is the meaning of words, and hence a certain property is postulated as the foundation of the usage of words such as 'one,' 'two,' and 'many.' This kind of linguistic usage cannot be justified on the basis of word-meaning without a distinct property [of number]."

D.5.iv. Several philosophers have pointed out other dimensions of the notion of number. Praśastapāda says that number can have one or more substances as its loci.[176] Depending on the eternal or non-eternal nature of its locus, number can be eternal or non-eternal. Numbers from 'two' onwards are dependent upon number 'one.' Since number is an externally real quality for Vaiśeṣikas, it can be produced or destroyed. Praśastapāda explains that numbers other than 'one' are produced by many 'ones' accompanied by a collective expectancy (*apekṣā-buddhi*).[177] When this collective expectancy dies out, the particular number is also destroyed. A number could also be destroyed by the destruction of its locus. There are some who believe that numbers like 'two' are merely collections of many 'ones,' and are not different entities produced by different 'ones.' Śrīdhara emphatically rejects such a view and argues for production of distinct numbers.[178] All these different alternatives are discussed in detail by the grammarians Bhartṛhari and

---

172 *saṃkhyāvān sattva-bhūto 'rthaḥ sarva evābhidhīyate / bhedābheda-vibhāgo hi loke saṃkhyā-nibandhanaḥ //*, *VP*, III, *Saṃkhyā-samuddeśa*, verse 1.

173 *śabdāc caiko dvau bahava ity-ādi-bhede vyavahāra-hetuḥ kaścid dharmo 'vadhāryate /*, *VP-H(b)*, pp. 395-6.

174 *sa dharmo vyatirikto vā teṣām ātmaiva vā tathā / bheda-hetutvam āśritya saṃkhyeti vyapadiśyate //*, *VP*, III, *Saṃkhyā-samuddeśa*, verse 2.

175 *saṃkhyā-lakṣaṇo dharmas teṣāṃ sattva-bhūtānāṃ saṃkhyeyānām ātmaivābhinna eva vāstu, tebhyo vyatirikto vāstu / kim anena niṣprayojanenāsmābhir vicāreṇa / śabdārthasyeha vicārayitum prakramāt śabdāc caiko dvau bahava ity-ādi-bhede vyavahāra-hetuḥ kaścid dharmo 'vadhāryate / na hi padārtha-mātrād anupādher eṣa vyavahāro ghaṭate /*, *VP-H(b)*, p. 396.

176 *ekādi-vyavahāra-hetuḥ saṃkhyā / sā punar eka-dravyā cāneka-dravyā ca / tatraika-dravyāyāḥ salilādi-paramāṇu-rūpādīnām iva nityānityatva-niṣpattayaḥ /*, *PB*, pp. 267-270.

177 *tasyāḥ khalv ekatvebhyo 'neka-viṣaya-buddhi-sahitebhyo niṣpattir apekṣā-buddhi-vināśād vināśa iti /*, *PB*, p. 272.

178 *tasyā ekatvebhyo niṣpattir eva, na tv ekaika-guṇa-samuccaya-mātram ity arthaḥ /*, *PB-K*, p. 272.

Helārāja, though they themselves do not insist upon a particular ontological view of number.[179]

D.6. *KĀRAKA* "MEANS TO BRING ABOUT AN ACTION"

D.6.i. Pāṇini's system of *kārakas* is an important landmark in the study of syntax. The notion of *kāraka* has attracted the attention of a fairly large number of modern scholars, and hence there is a large modern literature discussing the nature of this system and its problems. For some of the most recent disputations regarding the *kāraka* system, I shall merely refer the reader to the following sample of studies: George Cardona (1967-a, 1970, 1971, and 1974), Madhav M. Deshpande (1979, 1980, and 1991), S.D. Joshi and J.A.F. Roodbergen (1975), Paul Kiparsky (1982), and Bimal Krishna Matilal (1991). These are only some of the studies which go into general issues relating to the nature of the *kāraka* system. As is to be expected, there are major differences of opinion on a number of issues among scholars, and we shall not go into these debates here. In a broad sense, the notion of *kāraka* is illustrated by relations like agent and object, and has directly or indirectly inspired modern notions in case theory, as well as notions of semantic roles, theta-roles, and participant roles. One can get easily carried away and identify Pāṇini's *kārakas* with one of these modern theories. There are indeed similarities, and yet the peculiarly Indian conception needs to be distinguished from the seemingly related western notions. Faddegon considered these *kārakas* to be ideational or logical relations between a noun and a verb.[180] Rosane Rocher identified them as extra-linguistic logical categories.[181] Cardona tries to prove that they are not extra-linguistic,[182] while Staal and Kiparsky have studied the *kāraka* system in comparison with Noam Chomsky's Transformational Grammar and Government and Binding Theory.[183] As mentioned earlier, the *kāraka* system has evoked a great deal of debate in modern times, and I have dealt with it in my own work elsewhere [cf. see the bibliography], and hence we shall not enter into the same modern issues here. Here, we shall focus instead upon the traditional understanding of the *kāraka* system, and its possible ontological implications as explored by Patañjali and others.

To begin our discussion, a *kāraka* is something that helps to bring about an action (*kriyā-janaka*). Modern notions such as case roles, semantic roles, theta roles etc. do not start where Sanskrit grammarians seem to begin. Sanskrit grammarians do not begin their analysis with morphological categories such as case-endings, but with a conception of a prototypical action and the factors which help to bring it about. Among modern terms, the

---

179 Subramania Iyer (1969: 354-8).
180 Faddegon (1936: 19).
181 Rosane Rocher (1966: 115).
182 George Cardona (1967-a: 202).
183 Staal and Kiparsky (1969), and Kiparsky (1982).

term that comes close to capturing this conception is "participant role." However, the literal understanding of the Sanskrit explanation *kriyā-janaka* is more closely related to being a factor which leads to the production of an action, rather than participation in it, and hence one may use a term such as "action-generator" to capture this conception. This is a broad concept. In a sentence such as *rāmaḥ vahninā sthālyām odanam pacati* "Rāma cooks rice in a pot by means of fire," there are the following *kārakas*: agent (*kartṛ*): Rāma, object: (*karman*): rice, instrument (*karaṇa*): fire, and substratum (*adhikaraṇa*): pot. All of these various factors, each in its own way, help to bring about the action signified by the verb, and thus qualify for being called *kārakas* "action-generators."

D.6.ii. Generally, the traditional grammarians speak of six *kārakas*. However, there are many more definitions. The small number of *kāraka* terms are matched with a relatively large number of semantic categories. Thus, each *kāraka* term is matched up with one or more semantic categories. For illustrative purposes, we shall consider the representative definitions for each *kāraka*:

1. P.1.4.54 (*sva-tantraḥ kartā*): "The one who is independent [relative to other *kārakas* in bringing about an action] is termed *kartṛ* 'agent'."
2. P.1.4.49 (*kartur īpsitatamaṃ karma*): "That which the agent most seeks to encompass or reach [with his action] is termed *karman* 'object'."
3. P.1.4.42 (*sādhakatamaṃ karaṇam*): "The means par excellence [for bringing about an action] is termed *karaṇa* 'instrument'."
4. P.1.4.32 (*karmaṇā yam abhipraiti sa sampradānam*): "That for whom [the agent] intends the object [of his action] is termed *sampradāna* 'receiver'."
5. P.1.4.24 (*dhruvam apāye 'pādānam*): "That which is the [relatively] firm point [of departure of something] when departure takes place is termed *apādāna* 'point of departure'."
6. P.1.4.45 (*ādhāro 'dhikaraṇam*): "That which is the substratum [of the agent or of the object of an action] is termed *adhikaraṇa* 'locus'."

As explained earlier, there are several definitions for each *kāraka* term, effectively matching several different semantic categories to a given *kāraka* term. The exact wording of these definitions raises numerous interesting issues, some of which I have dealt with in Deshpande (1991). One important thing to keep in mind is that, strictly speaking, one is not supposed to offer a translation for the *kāraka* terms, since each term is matched with a number of semantic categories. The *kāraka* terms are, thus, labels each subsuming a wider diversity of semantic categories. No unique translation can bring out this semantic diversity subsumed by the *kāraka* terms. The translations offered above are simply given for convenience.

D.6.iii. In each of the above definitions, the formal structure is as follows: "That which is an *x* with reference to an action is termed *y* with reference to that action." Here *x* stands for a semantic element or an empirical fact, while *y* is a grammatical term or designation. If we collect all instances of *x*, we get a wide range of semantic categories or participant roles. Then what is the purpose of the relatively small number of *kāraka* terms to which this wider variety of participant roles is mapped? In Pāṇini's grammar, the semantic roles or participant roles are not directly mapped to morphological items such as case-endings. The *kāraka* terms serve a middle point of this mapping. Participant roles are mapped on to *kāraka* terms by one set of rules, while *kāraka* terms are mapped on to case-endings by another set of rules. A close study of these two sets of rules indicates that Pāṇini needed this intervening category of *kāraka* terms, because there is no one-to-one mapping of semantic roles with morphological categories. We find all sorts of different relationships. Sometimes, the same case-ending is mapped on to more than one *kāraka* term, while sometimes the same *kāraka* term is mapped on to more than one case ending. Thus, *kāraka* terms allow Pāṇini to create a better flow of derivational processes, and in this sense are a technical aid within his system. They are neither purely semantic nor syntactic, but stand midway between semantics and morphology to facilitate the derivational process. With such an understanding of the *kāraka* terms, one can clearly see that they are not ideational, extra-linguistic, or logical categories. They represent an attempt to reclassify semantic and empirical categories to suit the purpose of grammar. The motives behind this reclassification are purely grammatical, and hence one may justifiably call *kāraka*s a set of grammatical categories.

One can see the complexity involved in going from semantics to morphology by looking at a few examples. For instance, P.1.4.43 (*divaḥ karma ca, sādhakatamaṃ karaṇam* continued from 1.4.42) says that the means par excellence in the case of the verb *div* "to play dice" is also termed *karman* "object," in addition to the normal designation *karaṇa* "instrument" by P.1.4.42. Here, the same semantic category or participant role of "means par excellence" is given two alternative *kāraka* terms in the case of the verb *div*. What is the purpose of applying two alternative designations to the same participant role? In Pāṇini's grammar, the assignment of case-endings is not achieved by directly linking them to participant roles, but by linking them to *kāraka* designations alotted to those participant roles. For instance, P.2.3.2 (*karmaṇi dvitīyā, an-abhihite* from P.2.3.1) says that the second triplet of case endings, i.e. the accusative case-endings, is used to signify *karman* "object," if it is not already signified by some other item. This assignment of the second triplet of case-endings rests solely upon the assignment of the grammatical term *karman* to a given participant, and not directly upon the semantic role of that participant. In some cases, a nominal with an accusative case ending may signify something that the agent most seeks to encompass with his action. On the other hand, a nominal item with the same case ending, in connection with the verb *div*, signifies something that is semantically a means-par-excellence. However, in both cases, the same grammatical term *karman* is applicable. Mapping a certain means-par-excellence on to the grammatical term *karman* "object" also allows us, to put it in modern terms, to make it the subject of a passive sentence. Thus, the designation *karman* has a lot to contribute to the grammatical description in Pāṇini's system. Just as one and the same participant role is sometimes matched with more than one grammatical *kāraka* term, we also have examples where the same set of case endings is matched with more than one *kāraka*. For example, P.2.3.18 (*kartṛ-karaṇayos tṛtīyā, an-abhihite* from P.2.3.1) says that the third triplet of case endings is used to signify *kartṛ* "agent" or *karaṇa* "instrument," if not already signified by other elements. Thus, for instance, the agent in a passive sentence and an instrument can have the same case ending.

The above brief description indicates that the *kāraka* system is an attempt by Pāṇini to impose a semi-artificial grammatical reclassification on semantic roles, in order to link these semantic roles to the right morphemic elements, i.e. case endings. A semantic role of the means par excellence can get the grammatical designation *karman* "object" in the case of the verb *div*, and hence one has to admit the purely grammatical purpose involved in adding this intervening layer between semantics and morphology. While the semantic roles and the morphological items are somewhat less negotiable, the intervening layer of *kāraka*s allows a greater degree of theoretical manipulation. It is obvious that Pāṇini felt that this intervening layer added greater theoretical facility to his system. However, in principle, this intervening layer is not truly indispensable, as is demonstrated by the fact that Candragomin in his *Cāndra-vyākaraṇa* actually dispenses with this intervening layer, and links semantic roles directly to morphology, cf. Madhav Deshpande (1979).

D.6.iv. Patañjali discusses the notion of *kāraka* in great detail. He says that if the term *kāraka* is used as a designation (*saṃjñā*), then one must point to its designatum (*saṃjñin*). The designatum of the term *kāraka* is a means of accomplishing an action.[184] However, since Pāṇini does not make such a direct statement, Patañjali argues that the term *kāraka* is an unabbreviated, non-algebraic *mahatī saṃjñā* "long term," and hence it should be understood etymologically. A *kāraka* is that which "does" or "helps to bring about an action," because the word *kāraka* is derived from the root √*kṛ* "to do, to make, to act," with the agentive affix *-aka*.[185] Patañjali distinguishes between an action (*kriyā*) and a *kāraka*, and says that an action is a specific engagement of the *kāraka*s.[186] He often refers to *kāraka*s with the terms *sādhaka* "means" and *nirvartaka* "accomplisher."[187] He also points out that the term *kāraka* is a generic (*sāmānya*) designation, while terms like *adhikaraṇa* "locus" are specific designations. They qualify or specify each other, since they both reside in or apply to the same entity.[188]

D.6.v. In the *Mahābhāṣya*, the discussion of the ontological status of *kāraka*s is very closely connected to views regarding the relationship between a substance and its

---

[184] *kāraka iti saṃjñā-nirdeśaś cet saṃjñino 'pi nirdeśaḥ kartavyaḥ / sādhakaṃ nirvartakaṃ kāraka-saṃjñam bhavatīti vaktavyam /*, *MB*, Vol.I., Sec.II., p. 240.

[185] *kāraka iti mahatī saṃjñā kriyate / ... tatra mahatyāḥ saṃjñāyāḥ karaṇe etat prayojanam - anvartha-saṃjñā yathā vijñāyeta / karotīti kārakam iti /*, *MB*, Vol.I., Sec.II., p. 242.

[186] *na brūmaḥ kārakāṇi kriyeti / kiṃ tarhi / kārakāṇām pravṛtti-viśeṣaḥ kriyeti /*, *MB*, Vol.I., Sec.II., p. 123.

[187] *evaṃ tarhi sāmānya-bhūtā kriyā vartate / tasyāḥ nirvartakaṃ kārakam /*, *MB*, Vol.I., Sec.II., p. 246; *sarvāṇi ca kārakāṇi sādhakāni /*, *MB*, Vol.I., Sec.II., p. 259.

[188] *na hi kārakam ity anenādhikaraṇatvam uktam, adhikaraṇatvam iti vā kārakatvam / ubhau cānyonya-viśeṣakau bhavataḥ / katham / eka-dravya-samavāyāt /*, *MB*, Vol.I., Sec.II., p. 245.

attributes. Patañjali follows the Sāṃkhya doctrine in delineating his conception of substance and attributes. A substance (*dravya*) is an aggregate of properties or attributes (*guṇa*). For Patañjali, the exact ontological status of *kāraka*s is very important. Is a *kāraka* a substance, or is it an attribute of a substance? Patañjali argues both of these alternatives at different places. In some places, he says that a *kāraka* is the object or the substance (*dravya*) itself, and that a substance or an object can be a means of bringing about an action.[189] However, in other places, Patañjali debates these two alternatives. While discussing the question of perceptibility of a *kāraka*, he says:[190]

> "If the means [of bringing about an action] is [a substance defined as] an aggregate of attributes, then this means would be known only through inference. If the means [= substance] were to be different from its attributes, then it would be sometimes directly perceptible, and sometimes not directly perceptible."

This discussion occurs in the context of P.3.2.115 (*parokṣe liṭ*) which says that past perfect affixes are added to a verb to indicate that the action signified by the verb is *parokṣa* "beyond direct perception." Patañjali first argues that an action is always imperceptible, and is accessible only through inference (*kriyā nāmeyam atyantāparadṛṣṭā anumāna-gamyā-śakyā piṇḍībhūtā nidarśayitum*, *MB*, Vol.II., p. 178). If this is the case, then one would have to use past perfect forms alone to the exclusion of all other tenses and moods. Here, Patañjali brings up another alternative. How about if we say that we use past perfect affixes, when the means of action are *parokṣa* "beyond perception." Here one points out that if a substance, as a means of action, is nothing but an aggregate of attributes, then such a substance would always be beyond direct perception, and accessible only to inference, and then one cannot resolve the difficulty raised above. However, if a substance is different from its attributes, then sometimes it may be directly perceived, and sometimes it may be beyond perception. This would account for the occasional use of past perfect forms. Apart from the grammatical context of this discussion, what do we know about Patañjali's ontological views? This particular passage would seem to support an interpretation that, for Patañjali, a substance, as a means of action, is differrent from its attributes, and it is not a mere aggregate of attributes. This causes problems for commentators like Kaiyaṭa who assume that Patañjali actually believes the opposite to be true, and therefore they are forced to offer unconvincing interpretations of the current discussion.[191] In general, however, the commentators are right that Patañjali's view fits the Sāṃkhyan ontology and that he holds a substance to be an aggregate of attributes. The

---

189 *dravyaṃ kriyābhinirvṛttau sādhanatvam upaiti* /, *MB*, Vol.I., p. 92; *sādhanaṃ vai dravyam* /, *MB*, Vol.II., p. 616.

190 *yadi tāvad guṇa-samudāyaḥ sādhanam, sādhanam apy anumāna-gamyam / athānyad guṇebhyaḥ sādhanam, bhavati pratyakṣa-parokṣatāyāṃ sambhavaḥ* /, *MB*, Vol.II., p. 178.

191 *MB-P* and *MB-P-U*, Vol.II., p. 178.

relevance of this discussion to the question of understanding the nature of *kāraka*s is brought out in the following passage of the *Mahābhāṣya*:[192]:

> "Is the means [of bringing about an action (*sādhana* = *kāraka*)] a substance (*dravya*), or is it rather an attribute (*guṇa*)? [The teacher] says that it is an attribute. How is this known? Someone asks a person: 'Where is Devadatta?' That person tells him: 'He is on a tree.' 'On which [tree]?' '[He is on that tree] which stands [here].' That tree first becomes a 'locus,' and later, when expressed by another word, becomes an 'agent.' If the means [of action = *sādhana, kāraka*] were the entity [as a whole], then what is [once] a *karman* 'object' will [always] be a *karman;* what is [once] a *karaṇa* 'instrument' will [always] be a *karaṇa*; and what is [once] an *adhikaraṇa* 'locus' will [always] be an *adhikaraṇa*."

This discussion is understood as implying the following doctrine. A substance or entity has various attributes (*guṇa*) or powers (*śakti*), each of which may work independently to bring about an action in some way, and hence one can say that these attributes or powers are the means of bringing about an action, rather than a substance or an entity as a whole. This allows the same substance or entity to assume different participant roles with respect to different actions. For this reason, the same tree can be an *adhikaraṇa* "locus" in the sentence *asau vṛkṣe* "he is on the tree," and then it can become a *kartṛ* "agent" in the sentence *yas tiṣthati* "[on that tree] which stands." Thus, it would seem fairly certain that, according to Patañjali, a means of bringing about an action is viewed as an attribute of an object and not as the object as a whole. We may also note that the question of whether a substance is itself a simple aggregate of the attributes or is a different entity serving as their substratum is somewhat unrelated to the question of whether a *kāraka* is an entity as a whole or merely an attribute of an entity. However, the discussions in Sanskrit grammatical texts do not make a clear distinction between these issues.

D.6.vi. Bhartṛhari further develops this concept of *kāraka* as an attribute of an entity, rather than an entity as a whole. He generally prefers to use the terms *sāmarthya* or *śakti* to indicate that he views *kāraka*s as being powers or potencies of an object, rather than being mere attributes (*guṇa*). It is the potency of an entity to generate action either in itself, or in some other entity.[193] On this verse, Helārāja comments:[194]

> "The potency (*śakti*) of an entity in bringing about an action is understood as being the means (*sādhana, kāraka*) by Patañjali and others, on the basis

---

192 *kim punar dravyaṃ sādhanam āhosvid guṇaḥ / guṇa ity āha / kathaṃ jñāyate / evaṃ hi kaścit kañcit pṛcchati - kva devadatta - iti / sa tasmāy ācaṣṭe - asau vṛkṣe - iti / - katarasmin - / - yas tiṣṭhati - iti / sa vṛkṣo 'dhikaraṇam bhūtvānyena śabdenābhisambadhyamānaḥ kartā sampadyate / dravye punaḥ sādhane sati yat karma karmaiva syāt, yat karaṇaṃ karaṇam eva, yad adhikaraṇam adhikaraṇam eva /*, *MB*, Vol.I., Sec.II., p. 485.

193 *svāśraye samavetānāṃ tadvad evāśrayāntare / kriyāṇām abhiniṣpattau sāmarthyaṃ sādhanaṃ viduḥ //*, *VP*, III, *Sādhana-samuddeśa*, verse 1.

194 *kriyābhinirvṛttau dravyasya śaktiḥ sādhanam, sādhyate 'nayā kriyeti bhāṣyakāra-prabhṛtayo viduḥ / tathā hi guṇaḥ sādhanam iti bhāṣya uktam / śaktir evādhāra-pāratantryād anyasmāc ca svāśrayasya bhedakatvād guṇa-śabdena uktā /*, *VP-H(p)*, p. 230.

> of the etymology [of the word *sādhana* given as] *sādhyate 'nayā kriyā* 'that by which an action is accomplished.' Thus it is said in the *Mahābhāṣya* that the means [to bring about an action] is an attribute [*guṇa* of an entity, rather than an entity as a whole]. The potency [*śakti* of an entity to bring about an action] is itself referred to by the word *guṇa* 'attribute' [in the *Mahābhāṣya*], since [like any other attribute] it is dependent upon its substratum, and it differentiates its substratum from other [entities]."

Helārāja says that a substance has many potencies, and yet at a given time only one potency is expressed by a word. On the other hand, a substance or an entity as a whole has a unique nature, and hence it cannot be said to assume the role of different *kārakas*. Referring to Patañjali's argument [cf. Note 192] that the same entity assumes different *kāraka* roles in different sentences, and that this behavior indicates that a *kāraka* must be an attribute of an entity, rather than the entity as a whole, Helārāja says that this is the subtle logic for holding that a *kāraka* is a potency of an entity, rather than the entity as a whole.[195] Following Bhartṛhari, all later grammarians interpret Patañjali's term *guṇa* in this context as referring to a potency (*śakti*) of an object.[196]

While grammarians generally seem to interpret *kāraka* as a *śakti* "potency" of an entity, and accept this potency as a kind of *guṇa* "attribute, quality," other philosophical systems have different opinions about the ontological status of a potency. Mīmāṃsakas argue that a potency is, ontologically speaking, not a *guṇa* "quality," but it is an independent ontological category (*padārthāntara*), distinct from other categories like substance, quality, generic property, etc. Naiyāyikas and Vaiśeṣikas, on the other hand, reject this independent status of a potency, and propose that a potency is nothing but a kind of ability to become a cause of something.[197] In response to such ontological controversies, Bhartṛhari and Helārāja say that grammarians do not really care if this potency of an entity to bring about an action is identical with that entity or if it is distinct from that entity. Grammarians consider the linguistic usage to be their supreme form of evidence. The linguistic usage assumes a difference between a potency and the entity in which such a potency resides, and hence, in the view of grammarians, a distinction between these two must be postulated. Again, this discussion brings out the important feature of grammatical notions of meaning. Such notions are semantic postulations for Bhartṛhari. They are the kind of notions which seem to be assumed as axioms when one speaks. As grammarians, Bhartṛhari and his

---

195 *tenāneka-śakter api padārthasya sadaiva tathāvasthāne 'pi kācic chaktiḥ kvacid udbhūtā vivakṣyata iti ghaṭam paśya, ghaṭenodakam ānaya, ghaṭe udakaṃ nidhehīty ādi-karma-karaṇādi-bhāvo niyamenopapadyata iti na kāraka-sāṃkarya-prasaṅgaḥ / dravyasya tv eka-svabhāvatvāt karma-karaṇāditvaṃ nopapadyate iti garbhīkṛteyam atra yuktiḥ śakteḥ sādhanatve boddhavyā /*, *VP-H(p)*, p. 233.

196 For example: *āśritatvāc chaktir evātra guṇa-śabdena vivakṣitā /*, *MB-P*, Vol.I., Sec.II., p. 485; *guṇa-samudāyaḥ śaktīnāṃ samudāyaḥ ity arthaḥ /*, *MB-P*, Vol.II., p. 178.

197 *NK*, pp. 851-2.

commentators argue that they are interested only in exploring these notions as necessary semantic postulates, rather than as ontological categories.[198]

D.6.vii. Later grammarians like Kauṇḍabhaṭṭa and Nāgeśabhaṭṭa continue to support the view of a *kāraka* as a potency of an entity to bring about an action.[199] They have, however, new disputes among themselves. Nāgeśabhaṭṭa ascribes to Bhaṭṭoji Dīkṣita and Kauṇḍabhaṭṭa a view that a *kāraka* is something which is merely related to an action (*kriyānvayi*), and that it need not be something that helps to bring about an action (*kriyā-janaka*). Nāgeśabhaṭṭa disapproves of this view.[200] However, this seems to be a misrepresentation of the view expressed by Bhaṭṭoji Dīkṣita and Kauṇḍabhaṭṭa. Kauṇḍabhaṭṭa says that if something is unrelated to action, then it cannot be a *kāraka,* since Patañjali defines a *kāraka* as that which produces an action (*karoti*).[201] Nāgeśabhaṭṭa seems to have inverted Kauṇḍabhaṭṭa's statement to mean that a *kāraka* is something that is merely related to an action. There is no evidence that Kauṇḍabhaṭṭa opposed the view of a *kāraka* as a potency to produce an action. In fact, Bhaṭṭoji Dīkṣita and Kauṇḍabhaṭṭa both present the view of a *kāraka* as a potency, and adduce arguments in support of such a view.[202]

E. FUNCTIONAL APPARATUS OF A SEMANTIC THEORY

E.1. *VṚTTI / ŚAKTI* "SIGNIFICATION FUNCTION OF WORDS"

E.1.i. In section **A.4.**, the term "signification function" was introduced as a translation of the Sanskrit term *vṛtti*. Literally, the term *vṛtti* stands for occurrence of something. In Sanskrit, we frequently find the following expression: *ayaṃ śabdo 'sminn arthe vartate* "this word occurs in this meaning." This is the same thing as saying that a certain word occurs as a signifier of a certain meaning. Thus, literally the relation between a word and its meaning could be described as an occurrence relation. In semantic terms, this can be safely rendered by the term "signification function." The signification function of a word is also referred to by the term potency (*śakti*) in Sanskrit literature, and this suggests a notion that a signification function is a power or a special ability of a word to function in a certain capacity as a signifier of a certain meaning. It could also be regarded as a function in the terminology of modern logic. The proposition "x signifies y" could be regarded as a diadic function of the form $F(x,y)$, with x and y as variables. Of course, I

---

198 *sa tebhyo vyatirikto vā teṣām ātmaiva vā tathā / vyatirekam upāśritya sādhanatvena kalpyate //*, *VP*, III, *Sādhana-samuddeśa,* verse 15; *nāsmākam atra kaścid graho vyatirekāvyatireka-vāde / śabda-pramāṇakā vayam / yac chabda āha tad asmākam pramāṇam / śabdaś ca padārthānāṃ vyatiriktam eva sādhana-bhāvam pratyāyayati ghaṭasya dṛśi-kriyāyāṃ karma-bhāva iti /*, *VP-H(p)*, p. 243.

199 *kārakaṃ kriyā-janakatva-śaktiḥ /*, *LM*, p. 1193.

200 *kriyānvayitvaṃ kārakatvam iti tu na /*, *LM*, p. 1195; *yat tu dīkṣita-bhūṣaṇakṛd-ādayaḥ kriyānvayitvam kārakatvam ... tat khaṇḍayati /*, *LM-KL*, p. 1195.

201 *tatra ca karotīti yogāśrayaṇāt kriyānanvayino na kārakatvam /*, *VB*, p. 65.

202 *evaṃ cāśrayatvāder eva vācyatve dhruve tad evākhaṇḍaṃ śakti-śabdenocyata iti manasi nidhāya śaktir vibhakty-artha iti saptamī-pañcamyau kāraka-madhye ity-ādau bhāṣyādau vyavahriyate iti tad evābhipretyāha - śaktir eveti /*, *VB*, p. 114.

shall not attempt here to rephrase the concepts in Sanskrit grammar and philosophy in the formulae of modern logic.

According to Naiyāyikas, a word has two signification functions, i.e. *śakti* or *saṃketa* "primary signification function" and *lakṣaṇā* "secondary signification function."[203] Mīmāṃsakas distinguish between three different signification functions, i.e. *abhidhā* "primary signification function," *lakṣaṇā* "secondary signification function," and *gauṇī* "signification function dependent upon qualitative similarity between the primary meaning and the secondary meaning." Other schools generally include the latter two of the above three signification functions under a single category of a secondary signification function (*lakṣaṇā*). The tradition of grammarians as represented by late authors like Nāgeśabhaṭṭa refuses to accept even the secondary signification function as a separate signification function. For them, it is included in the primary signification function. However, they are willing to admit *vyañjanā* "suggestive signification function" as an independent function of words, and in doing so they agree with the tradition of Sanskrit poetics. The tradition of Sanskrit poetics, as represented in works like Mammaṭa's *Kāvya-prakāśa* accepts *abhidhā* "primary signification function," *lakṣaṇā* "secondary signification function," *vyañjanā* "suggestive signification function," and even a fourth function called *tātparya* "intentional signification function." The last one is supposed to provide the listener access to the speaker's intention from a given utterance. This assumes that the first three signification functions of a word may not necessarily convey to the listener the meaning as it is intended by the speaker. Here I shall discuss the primary and the secondary signification functions in some detail, as these two are more relevant to our understanding of Kauṇḍabhaṭṭa's discussion.

E.1.ii. While discussing the notion of a primary signification function, we must consider in detail the following key concepts: *śakti, śakta, śakya, śaktatāvacchedaka,* and *śakyatāvacchedaka*. The first three terms correspond to the notions of a primary signification function, a primary signifier word, and the primary signified meaning. The signification function of a word is said to reside in the signifier word, and the signification function is said to have been described (*nirūpita*) in terms of the signified meaning.

Naiyāyikas define the primary signification function of a word as the significative association, agreement or convention (*saṃketa*) in the form of God's desire that a certain word should signify a certain meaning, or that a certain meaning be signified by a certain word. Thus the primary signification function is a particular desire of God.[204] This primary signification function is a relation of a word to its meaning such that it is conducive to a cognition of that meaning from a cognition of that word.[205] Why is it called a primary signification function? It is primary in the sense that it leads to an immediate cognition of a

---

203 *saṃketo lakṣaṇā cārthe pada-vṛttiḥ* /, *SV*, p. 1; *vṛttir nāma śakti-lakṣaṇānyatara-rūpā* /, *Nyāya-bodhinī* on *TS*, p. 65.

204 *asmāt padād ayam artho boddhavya itīśvarecchā-saṃketaḥ śaktiḥ* /, *TS*, p. 66; *saṃketa eva śaktiḥ* , *TS-D*, p. 316.

205 *artha-smṛty-anukūla-pada-padārtha-sambandhaḥ śaktiḥ* /, *TS-D*, p. 315.

certain meaning from the given word, without the intervention of any other meaning-cognitions.[206] Navya-naiyāyikas say that the primary signification function is a desire, but not necessarily the desire of God. If one believes that the primary signification function is a desire of God, then one cannot account for the meaning of recently developed words. If, however, the primary signification function is just a generic desire, then we can explain the meaning of recently introduced words.[207] Mīmāṃsakas use the term *abhidhā* for the primary signification function, but they differentiate it from the significative convention (*saṃketa*) between a word and its meaning. They argue that the primary signification function of a word is based on the significative convention (*saṃketa*) between a word and its meaning. They also hold that the primary signification function of a word is a functional potency (*śakti*) of a word, and that it is similar to the potency of fire to produce heat. The existence of such potencies of things is inferred on the basis of the observation of their effects. Mīmāṃsakas also argue that such potencies fall into an independent ontological category by themselves, and cannot be subsumed under other categories.[208]

E.1.iii. Among grammarians, there are differences of opinion. According to Bhaṭṭojī Dīkṣita and Kauṇḍabhaṭṭa, the primary signification function of a word is a potency (*śakti, sāmarthya, yogyatā*) of that word to signify a certain meaning, and it is identical with the property of signifier-ness (*bodha-janakatva*) residing in the word.[209] The primary signification function of the word *ghaṭa* is its ability to cause a cognition of the meaning "pot." This potency is natural to a word and it is comparable to the innate ability of sense organs to cause cognitions of objects with which they are in contact. This comparison cited by Bhaṭṭojī Dīkṣita goes back to Bhartṛhari's *Vākya-padīya*. Kauṇḍabhaṭṭa even cites Vedānta works like the *Pañcapādikā-vivaraṇa* to support his view.

Nāgeśabhaṭṭa, the last star in the line of traditional grammarians, fights against all these views. He refutes the view of the Naiyāyikas by pointing out that the primary signification function of a word cannot be a desire, because it is a relation between a word and its meaning. According to the generally accepted notion of a relation (*sambandha*), a relation is different from its two relata (*sambandhin*), is located in both the relata, and it demands the cognition of its loci as being qualified by the relation, or as being possessors of the relation. For instance, the relation of *saṃyoga* "conjunction" between a pot and the ground where it sits is different from the pot and the ground. It resides in both the pot and the ground, and it ensures a cognition of the ground as being the locus of the relation of conjunction described by a pot (*ghaṭa-nirūpita-saṃyogāśrayo bhūtalam*). According to

---

206 *avyavadhānena śabda-janya-pratīty-anukūlā vṛttiḥ śaktiḥ* /, *BC*, p. 74.

207 *navyās tu īśvarecchā na śaktiḥ kiṃ tv icchaiva* / *tenādhunika-saṃketite 'pi śaktir asty evety āhuḥ* /, *KM*, p. 549.

208 *mīmāṃsakās tu abhidhā nāma padārthāntaraṃ saṃketa-grāhyaṃ śaktir ity āhuḥ* /, *NK*, p. 854; *sā ca padārthāntaram iti mīmāṃsakāḥ* /, *TS-D*, p. 315; *BC*, p. 74.

209 *tasmād bodha-janakatvam eva śaktiḥ* / *tac ca bodha-janakatvam indriyādivat* / ... *tathā vivaraṇe 'py uktam "bodha-janana-sāmarthyam eva śabdasyārthena sambandhaḥ" iti* / *evaṃ* ... *śabda-kaustubhe 'py uktam "ghaṭa-bodha-janana-sāmarthyam eva ghaṭādi-padānāṃ śaktiḥ" iti* /, *VB*, p. 191; *vaiyākaraṇās tu bodhakatvam eva śaktiḥ* /, *BC*, p. 74.

Nāgeśabhaṭṭa, this does not hold true in the case of a desire. A desire is not a relation. One does not have a cognition such as "the word *ghaṭa* is a locus of desire," or "the meaning 'pot' is a locus of desire." For this reason, a desire of God or of anyone else is not acceptable as a relation between a word and its meaning.[210]

Nāgeśabhaṭṭa, like Mīmāṃsakas, distinguishes between the primary signification function of a word and the significative convention (*saṃketa*). Quoting the *Yoga-bhāṣya* in his support, he defines the significative convention (*saṃketa*) as the identity between a word and its meaning, based on their mutual superimposition (*adhyāsa*). Such a notion of *saṃketa* is obviously different from notions held by Mīmāṃsakas and Naiyāyikas. He defines the primary signification function of a word as a unique relation between a word and its meaning, i.e. the signifier-signified relation (*vācya-vācaka-bhāva*). He points out that the significative convention between a word and its meaning in the form of their imposed identity is the means for understanding the signifier-signified relation between that word and its meaning.[211] He refers to the view expressed by Bhaṭṭojī Dīkṣita and Kauṇḍabhaṭṭa that the primary signification function of a word is a potency of that word or just its signifierness (*bodhakatā*), and he finally rejects this view.[212]

E.2. *PRAVṚTTI-NIMITTA / ŚAKYATĀVACCHEDAKA*

E.2.i. The term *pravṛtti-nimitta* has been briefly explained in section **D.2.x**. It refers to a property whose possession by an entity is the necessary and sufficient condition for a given word being used to refer to that entity. In Sanskrit grammatical literature, in different contexts, the terms *svārtha, guṇa, jāti,* and *ākṛti* are co-extensive with this term, cf. **D.2.x**. The *Nyāya-kośa* explains this term as referring to something which allows the use of a word to signify a certain meaning, and identifies it with the notion of *śakyatā-vacchedaka*.[213] The term *śakya* stands for the notion of primary meaning. *Śakyatā* thus stands for the property of primary-meaning-ness. The term *avacchedaka* stands for the notion of a limitor or a limiting property. The term *śakyatāvacchedaka* thus stands for the notion of a property which is the limitor of primary-meaning-ness. Sanskrit grammarians borrow this jargon from the tradition of Indian logicians, and hence it is necessary to go into the details of the notion of a limiting property (*avacchedaka-dharma*) in Indian logic,

---

210 *tan na / icchāyāḥ ... sambandhatvāsambhavāt / sambandho hi sambandhi-dvaya-bhinnatve sati dvi-ṣṭhatve ca sati āśrayatayā viśiṣṭa-buddhi-niyāmakaḥ ity abhiyukta-vyavahārāt / ... yathā ghaṭavad bhūtalam ity-ādau saṃyoga-rūpaḥ sambandhaḥ sambandhibhyāṃ bhinno dvi-ṣṭho ghaṭa-nirūpita-saṃyogāśrayo bhūtalam iti viśiṣṭa-buddhi-niyāmakaś ca, nātra tathā ghaṭa-śabda icchāvān, tad-artho vā icchāvān iti vyavahāraḥ /*, *PLM*, p. 37.

211 *tasmāt pada-padārthayoḥ sambandhāntaram eva śaktir vācya-vācaka-bhāvāpara-paryāyā / tad-grāhakaṃ cetaretarādhyāsa-mūlaṃ tādātmyam / tac ca saṃketaḥ / tad uktam pātañjala-bhāṣye "saṃketas tu pada-padārthayor itaretarādhyāsa-rūpaḥ smṛty-ātmako yo 'yaṃ śabdaḥ so 'rthaḥ, yo 'rthaḥ sa śabda iti /*, *LM*, pp. 28-9.

212 *etena bodha-janakatvam eva padānāṃ sambandha ity apāstam /*, *LM*, p. 23; *dīkṣita-bhūṣaṇoktaṃ mataṃ nirācaṣṭe eteneti /*, *LM-KL*, p. 26.

213 *pravṛtti-nimitta-śabdasya vyutpattiḥ pravṛtteḥ śabdānām artha-bodhana-śakter nimittam prayojakam iti / tac ca śakyatāvacchedakatvam bhavatīti jñeyam /*, *NK*, p. 580.

or specifically the terminological usage of the Navya-naiyāyikas. B.K. Matilal (1971: 61) explains the general characteristics of such Navya-nyāya terms:

> "Terms like 'delimitor', 'substratum', and 'property' are used in Navya-nyāya in a sense which is ontologically neutral. A delimitor may be an imposed condition, or an imagined property, or an imagined division of time, or of space, or a real property. In the same way substratum and property (also qualifier and qualificand) are ontologically neutral. A quality like blue color or a generic property (a REAL universal) like cow-ness can be a delimitor, but not all delimitors are real properties in this way. Thus, by using these terms Navya-nyāya philosophers have been able to describe their philosophy of logic without too much commitment to ontology."

E.2.ii. Such limitors or limiting properties (*avacchedaka*) are frequently used in the works of Navya-naiyāyikas to correctly circumscribe given classes of entities. These properties in a way control or limit the membership of a given class of entities. For example, the word *ghaṭa* refers to a pot. A pot is at the same time many things. It is a substance. It has a particular shape or color. It is a substratum of many properties. In a given situation, one may need to specify the particular aspect of pot which makes it relevant in that situation. It could be a pot as a substance, or a pot with a certain color, or a pot with a certain shape, or a pot as a possession of a certain person. Specifying such limiting or controlling properties allows one to make very precise statements which do not undesirably overextend to instances which one does not wish to include under given circumstances.

Consider the following statement: "the stick [of a potter used to turn his wheel] is a cause of the effect, i.e. a pot." Here, the stick has the property *kāraṇatā* "cause-ness," and the pot has the property *kāryatā* "effect-ness." This statement can be generalized to include all [potter's] sticks and all pots by specifying the properties which limit or control the extension of the notions of cause-ness and effect-ness. If one states *dravyatva* "substance-ness" as the limitor of cause-ness, this would indicate that a stick is the cause of a pot by being just a substance, and hence, any substance could have been a cause for this effect. On the other hand, if we specify *daṇḍatva* "stick-ness" as the limitor for cause-ness, this would indicate that, in our judgement, a stick is the cause of a pot because it is a stick, and not just a substance. Similarly, if we state substance-ness as the limitor for effect-ness, this would indicate that a stick is the cause of a pot *qua* substance, and that anything that is a substance would also qualify to be an effect in this case. However, if we specify pot-ness as the limitor of effect-ness, then we include pots *qua* pots in the category of the intended effects. Thus, a modified statement with the addition of appropriate limitors may look like this: *ghaṭatvāvacchinnam prati daṇḍatvāvacchinnaṃ kāraṇam* "an x limited by the property of stick-ness is the cause of a y limited by the property of pot-ness." This amounts to saying that anything which has the property of stick-ness has the potentiality of being the cause of something which has the property of pot-ness. In modern logic, this very result would be achieved in terms of classes and quantification. For instance, we could say:

"For every *y*, such that *y* is a pot, there exists an *x*, such that *x* is a stick, and *x* is the cause of *y*."

For the sake of simplicity, I shall avoid the symbols of modern logic. However, essentially, a similar result is achieved by limitors in Indian logic. The expression "*y* limited by the property of pot-ness" (*ghaṭatvāvacchinna*) in Indian logic actually defines the same class which is defined by the expression "every *y*, such that *y* is a pot" in modern logic. In Indian logic, different quantifications can be achieved by using different limitors. For instance, if we say: "a stick is the cause of a *y*, such that the limitor of effect-ness pertaining to *y* is pot-ness," this means that the effects produced by a stick are only and all pots. The limitor pot-ness allows the inclusion of all and only pots in the class of intended effects, and it excludes all non-pots. It is a different question whether we would wish to make such a statement, but the tools are there to make our statements precise. If we say: "a stick is the cause of *y*, such that the effect-ness pertaining to *y* is limited by effect-ness (*kāryatāvacchinna-kāryatā*)," this would mean that a potter's stick can produce anything that is an effect. This, of course, is not a valid statement. However, one could say following the Naiyāyikas: "God's desire is the cause of *y* such that the effect-ness pertaining to *y* is limited by effect-ness." For a Naiyāyika, this would be a valid statement, since he believes that nothing can be produced in this world without God desiring it. One can also make a realistic statement to indicate that a given potter's stick is the cause of a particular pot. This can be stated by specifying very narrow limitors such as *etad-daṇḍatva-avacchinna-kāraṇatā* "cause-ness limited by this-stick-ness" and *etad-ghaṭatva-avacchinna-kāryatā* "effect-ness limited by this-pot-ness." Another possible traditional way of stating such limitors is to use the following expressions: *etad-daṇḍa-vyaktitva-avacchinna-kāraṇatā* "cause-ness limited by this-stick-particular-ness" and *etad-ghaṭa-vyaktitva-avacchinna-kāryatā* "effect-ness limited by this-pot-particular-ness." This technical jargon of Indian logic is taken over by the tradition of Sanskrit grammarians.

E.2.iii. A *Vārttika* by Kātyāyana discussed in **D.2.x**, is the precursor of the logical concept of *śakyatāvacchedaka*. Kātyāyana says that the affix *-tva* "-ness" applied to a word *W* signifies a property *P*, such that the occurrence of *P* in an entity is the basis for the use of the word *W* to refer to that entity. For instance, the occurrence of the property of bull-ness in an entity is the necessary and sufficient condition for the word "bull" being used to refer to that entity. The particular individual bull referred to by the word "bull" is the primary meaning (*śakya*), and hence it has the property of *śakyatā* "primary-meaning-ness." The property of bull-ness whose occurrence in an entity is the sufficient and necessary condition for the use of the word "bull" to be used to refer to that entity can then be said to be the limitor for the property of primary-meaning-ness. Thus, in this particular case, the property of bull-ness, if specified as the *śakyatāvacchedaka* "limitor of primary-meaning-ness," ensures that the word "bull" can be applied to all those entities which possess the property of bull-ness, i.e. all bulls. In other words, only those entities and all those entities which possess this property are eligible to become the primary meaning of the word "bull," i.e. can be referred to by the word "bull."

E.2.iv. Gadādharabhaṭṭa, a leading Naiyāyika, defines the notion of *pravṛtti-nimitta* or *śakyatāvacchedaka* as follows: "that property, which is itself [a part of] the primary meaning, which resides in something that is also [a part of] the primary meaning, and which appears as the principal qualifier in the cognition of the primary meaning."[214] This definition of a limitor of primary-meaning-ness is directly related to some of the basic doctrines of the Nyāya system. Naiyāyikas hold that the primary meaning of a nominal consists of an individual entity as qualified by a generic property and a particular shape or configuration. Thus, the generic property, such as bull-ness, is itself part of the primary meaning, it resides in another part of the primary meaning, namely in the individual entity, and it is a qualifier of that individual entity in the cognition of the primary meaning. Thus, the generic property of bull-ness can be treated as the *pravṛtti-nimitta* or *śakyatā-vacchedaka* for the word "bull." This is the view of the Naiyāyikas. However, other systems of thought do not necessarily agree with this view of the Naiyāyikas. There are those who believe that the primary meaning for a nominal consists of only the particular individual entity, and yet they accept the generic property as the limitor of primary-meaning-ness (*śakyatāvacchedaka*). In such a view, the limitor of primary-meaning-ness is not part of the primary meaning itself. In **NN.III.10**, Kauṇḍabhaṭṭa discusses these opposing views in detail.

E.2.v. At first glance, the Indian concept of limitor of primary-meaning-ness (*śakyatāvacchedaka, pravṛtti-nimitta*) may seem to be an awkward concept, partly because of its unfamiliar Navya-nyāya English rendering. To help understand its functional value in familiar Western terms, I propose to give a brief account of similar concepts in Western philosophy and logic. However, I do not intend to directly identify any of these with the Indian conception of a limitor of primary-meaning-ness.

Plato argues that general terms like "tree" could be applied to a large number of objects, only if there exist numerically identical entities or Ideas such as tree-ness, shared by each individual of a class.[215] According to the Essentialist theory discussed by Specht, a single name designates all those objects which partake one and the same essence.[216] According to W.P. Alston's explanation of connotation, a word *W* connotes a property *P*, such that its possession by something is a necessary and sufficient condition of *W* being correctly asserted of it.[217] C.I. Lewis speaks of the essential comprehensive character of an object, signified by a word, such that everything having that character is namable by that term, and whatever lacks this character is not so namable. While describing the notion of "sense-

[214] *pravṛtti-nimitte 'pi śakteḥ sattvāt tasyāpi vācyatayā "vācyatve sati vācya-vṛttitve ca sati vācyopasthiti-prakāratvam" iti pravṛtti-nimitta-lakṣaṇe vācyatve satīti viśeṣaṇa-dānam ... upapadyate /*, *SV*, p. 41.

[215] W.P. Alston (1964: 1-2) cites this view from Plato's *Republic*, Chapter X.

[216] Specht (1963: 154).

[217] W.P. Alston (1964: 17).

meaning" as intension, Lewis says that it is a criterion in the mind which enables one to apply or refuse to apply the expression in question in the case of the given things or situations.[218] Describing the view of Realists in formal terms, Michael J. Loux states that a predicate term "F" can be truly affirmed of each of the members of a class (*a* ... *n*), only if each possesses some numerically identical characteristic, F-ness.[219] Eric Buyssens claims that we can freely apply a certain name for any individual showing the characteristics implied by that name.[220]

Though these various conceptions are not identical with each other, there is definitely a common approach going all the way back to Plato. While the ontological assumptions differ from philosopher to philosopher, the semantic or functional assumptions seem to be the same, namely that for a given word to apply to a range of individual entities, those entities must share in some identifiable property implied by that word. The Indian concept of a limitor of primary-meaning-ness is a product of a similar approach. The semantic utility of this concept is quite evident from the fact that systems of Indian philosophy which differ in their ontological perspectives agree on the necessity of some such conception.

E.3. *ŚAKTATĀVACCHEDAKA*

E.3.i. The concept of *śaktatāvacchedaka* is probably unique to Indian philosophy of language. The term *śakta* stands for the primary signifier word, which is the locus of the primary signification function (*śakti*). The primary signifier word (*śakta*) naturally has the property primary-signifier-ness (*śaktatā*). The term *śaktatāvacchedaka* thus refers to a property (*dharma*) which serves as the limitor of primary-signifier-ness pertaining to a word. What does this mean? Just as the term *śakyatāvacchedaka* refers to a property which objects must have in order to be included among the referents of a given word, the term *śaktatāvacchedaka* refers to a property which all instances of a word must possess in order to be able to signify a certain meaning. This particular limitor of primary-signifier-ness is generally taken to be the particular sound sequence (*varṇānupūrvī*) which must characterize all instances of a given word for those instances to signify the same unique meaning. Only by having that specific sound sequence, a word-instance can be recognized as being a token of a certain type.

While the notion of *śaktatāvacchedaka* as a property seems uniquely Indian at first sight, this problem is by no means uniquely Indian, and there is awareness of this dilemma among Western authors. For instance, Bertrand Russell (1940: 22-23) says:

> "The spoken word 'dog' is not a single entity: it is a class of similar movements of the tongue, throat, and larynx. ... The word 'dog' is a universal, just as *dog* is a universal. We say, loosely, that we can utter the

---

218 Lewis (1944: 52-3, 61).

219 Loux (1970: 6-7).

220 Buyssens (1970: 23).

> same word 'dog' on two occasions, but in fact we utter two examples of the same species, just as when we see two dogs we see two examples of the same species. There is no difference of logical status between *dog* and the word 'dog': each is general and exists only in instances."

If the word 'dog' is a species which manifests itself only in its instances, one can legitimately ask as to what regulates the membership of word-instances for this species or class? The Indian tradition came up with the notion of *śaktatāvacchedaka* to answer this same dilemma. While some held a particular sequence of sounds to be the limitor of primary-signifier-ness of a word, others claim the limitor of primary-signifier-ness to be a generic property or a universal, just as the limitor of primary-meaning-ness is a generic property. In this view, just as the object bull has the generic property bull-ness, the word "bull" is said to have the generic property "bull"-ness (*go-śabdatva*) which is shared by all instances of the word "bull."[221] While such a conception seems to add another ontological commitment, grammarians are not particularly bothered by it, since for them all meaning categories are only notional postulations, and the notion of a limitor of primary-signifier-ness, though not strictly speaking a meaning category, is not deemed to be a problem.

E.4. *ŚĀBDA-BODHA* "VERBAL COGNITION"

E.4.i. In section **A.4.**, I introduced the term "verbal cognition" to render the Sanskrit term *śābda-bodha* or *śābda-jñāna*. In general, this term refers to a cognition or a cognitive state, including its contents, resulting directly from a listener's perception of a linguistic expression. It is an instance of cognition (*bodha, jñāna*), directly resulting from a cognition of a verbal expression (*śabda*), and its contents (*viṣaya*) are generally the meaning elements (*artha*). The Naiyāyika author Viśvanātha defines *śābda-bodha* as a cognition [of meaning] which has a cognition of a word (*pada-jñāna*) as its instrumental cause (*karaṇa*).[222] In Sanskrit literature, the term *śābda-bodha* is applied to a meaning cognition resulting from an individual word or a morphemic item, as well as from a complete sentential utterance. Here, we shall be mainly concerned with the verbal cognition of the first type, i.e. verbal cognition produced by individual words. Not every cognition produced by a cognition of a word is a verbal cognition. Viśvanātha specifies that the cognition which is produced by a cognition of a word on the basis of the signification function of that word alone is called a verbal cognition.[223] To defend this position, Viśvanātha provides the following arguments. For Naiyāyikas, the notion of a relation works in the following way. If two items, x and y, are related by a relation R, then a

221 *śaktatāvacchedikāyā varṇa-pada-vākya-niṣṭha-jāteḥ ... /*, *PLM*, p. 76; *yathā ghaṭatvādikaṃ vācyatāvacchedakaṃ tathā ghaṭa-padatvādikaṃ śakyatāvacchedakam /*, *LM-KK*, p. 495.

222 *pada-jñāna-karaṇakaṃ jñānaṃ śābda-bodhaḥ /*, *KM*, p. 419.

223 *vṛttyā pada-janyatvam bodhyam / anyathā ghaṭādi-padāt samavāya-sambandhenākāśa-smaraṇe jāte ākāśasyāpi śābda-bodhopapatteḥ / ... atraiva śakti-jñānasyopayogaḥ / pūrvaṃ śakti-grahābhāve pada-jñāne 'pi tat-sambandhena tat-smaraṇānupapatteḥ / pada-jñānasya hi eka-sambandhi-jñāna-vidhayā padārthopasthākatvam / śaktiś ca padena saha padārthasya sambandhaḥ /*, *KM*, pp. 545-7.

cognition of either x or y, accompanied by an awareness of the relation R between them, leads to a recollection (*smaraṇa*) of the other. In the case of a word like *ghaṭa* "pot," there are two simultaneous relations. The word *ghaṭa*, by being an instance of sound, is, in Nyāya-Vaiśeṣika ontology, a quality (*guṇa*) of ether (*ākāśa*), and, as such, is related to ether through the relation of inherence. Thus, Naiyāyikas argue that a person who has a cognition of the word *ghaṭa*, and is also aware of its inherence relation to ether, will have a recollection of ether. Viśvanātha says that such a recollective cognition of ether, though generated as a result of a cognition of the word *ghaṭa*, is not to be treated as a verbal cognition, since it was not produced on the basis of the awareness of the signification function of that word. Viśvanātha argues that the signification function of a word (*śakti*) is also a relation between the signifier word and the signified meaning. Thus, a person who has a cognition of a word, and is aware of its significative relationship to a certain meaning, has a recollective cognition of that meaning. If a person is unaware of the significative relation of a word to a certain meaning, then even with a cognition of that word, that person will not have a recollective cognition of that meaning. For Naiyāyikas, this is the mechanism of a verbal cognition. It is a special type of recollective cognition.

There are subtle differences within the cognitive processes referred to by the terms *jñāna, graha, bodha, buddhi* etc. For example, the term *śakti-graha* refers to the act of ascertaining the significtion function of a word, and this refers either to a cognitive process of ascertaining or to a cognitive event. On the other hand, the term *śakti-jñāna* refers to the resulting awareness of a signification function, which is not a cognitive event, but a cognitive state which can last for a long period, or can be stored in the form of a mental impression (*saṃskāra*). Generally, the terms *śābda-bodha* or *śābda-buddhi* refer to resulting cognitive states. The cognitive contents of these states are described by Indian philosophers by using a mode of technical paraphrase indicating the relations between the various objects figuring in the contents of a cognition. For a recent discussion of the various dimensions of cognition considered by Indian philosophers, see: B.K. Matilal (1986: 112ff).

E.4.ii. Grammarians also stress the cause-effect relationship (*kārya-kāraṇa-bhāva*) between an awareness of a signification function (*vṛtti-jñāna*) and a verbal cognition. In **A.4.**, I have introduced the term "object or content of a verbal cognition" as a rendition for the Sanskrit expression *śābda-bodha-viṣaya*. The term *viṣaya* refers to the object or content of a cognition, or to that which figures in a cognition. Just as a cognition is said to have a *viṣaya* "object or content", similarly the signification function of a word is also said to have a particular meaning as its object or content. The signification function of a word is said to be ascertained with reference to a certain meaning, and hence that meaning is said to be the object or content of the signification function. There is obviously a very close relation between the object of the signification function and the object of the verbal cognition. We are told that the limitor of object-ness or content-ness is the same in both cases. For example, in the case of the word "pot," the object of its primary signification function is a pot, and the limitor of object-ness with respect to this signification function (*vṛtti-viṣayatāvacchedaka*) is the property of pot-ness. Similarly, the object of the verbal cognition derived from the word "pot" is also a pot. Here too, the limitor of object-ness with respect to this verbal cognition (*śābda-bodha-viṣayatāvacchedaka*) is also pot-ness.

The logical relationship between an awareness of the primary signification function as a causal factor and the cognition of the primary meaning as the effect has been explored further by grammarians and logicians in India. To start with, Nāgeśabhaṭṭa makes the following statement of a causal relationship: "an awareness of a primary signification function with x as its object is the cause of a verbal cognition with x as its object."[224] This is to say that an awareness of a signification function ascertained with respect to x is the cause of a verbal cognition of x. However, this statement relates to x as a particular individual. If the above causal relationship is considered to be valid, then a word such as "pot" will denote only a particular pot. Thus, it is necessary to recognize that the signification function of the word "pot" needs to be ascertained not merely with respect to a particular pot, but with respect to any pot which is a member of the class of all pots. How does one specify such a relationship? In order to achieve a generalized causal relationship, one needs to specify the limitors for object-ness in relation to both the signification function of a word, as well as the verbal cognition generated on the basis of that word. If the object-ness is limited by a property like pot-ness, then all and only those entities which possess pot-ness are included in the class of entities eligible to become objects of the signification function and the verbal cognition. Nāgeśabhaṭṭa therefore offers a revised statement of the causal relationship between a signification function and a verbal cognition:[225]

> "For every instance [of verbal cognition] limited by the property of being a verbal cognition having as its object an entity x limited by the property P, there exists, as its cause, a cognition [of a word] qualified by a signification function described in relation to an entity x limited by the property P."

Here, the expression "an entity x limited by the property P" effectively includes any and all entities which possess P. Therefore, it is possible to account for a situation where the signification function of a word such as "pot" is ascertained with one member of the class of pots, and yet it can lead to a verbal cognition of some other member of that class. An expression such as *ghaṭatvāvacchinna-ghaṭa* "a pot limited by the property of pot-ness" in Indian logic refers to a pot, not as a unique individual entity, but as a member of a class of pots where each member possesses pot-ness. A statement of causal relationship formulated by using such a generalization allows one to state the significative relationship of a word with a particular member of a class, and yet be able to use that word to refer to any other member of that class. Class-membership is controlled by the limiting property P.

---

224 *tad-viṣayaka-śābde tad-viṣayaka-śakti-grahasya kāraṇatvam /*, *LM*, p. 1105.

225 *tad-dharmāvacchinna-viṣayaka-śābda-buddhitvāvacchinnam prati tad-dharmāvacchinna-nirūpita-vṛtti-viśiṣṭa-jñānaṃ hetuḥ /*, *PLM*, p. 27.

E.4.iii. We need to look at the technical vocabulary used by grammarians like Kauṇḍabhaṭṭa and Nāgeśabhaṭṭa in detail, because these grammatical authorities borrow the technical terminology developed by the school of Navya-nyāya. This school had a wide terminological influence on all contemporary schools of thought, even though these other schools did not accept the specific ontological or epistemic doctrines of Navya-naiyāyikas. The terminology developed by Navya-naiyāyikas added a degree of precision to philosophical statements which was not obtained in Sanskrit philosophical literature before this period. We have already explained some of this terminology. However, we need to go into greater details to be able to appreciate the degree of precision achieved by authors like Kauṇḍabhaṭṭa in their works.

Since an awareness of a signification function (*śakti-jñāna*) is a cause (*kāraṇa*) of a verbal cognition (*śābda-bodha*), it has the property of cause-ness (*kāraṇatā*). This cause-ness resides in the awareness of a signification function, and hence the awareness of a signification function is its locus (*āśraya*). This cause-ness is not cause-ness in general, but it is specifically described in reference to a verbal cognition (*śābda-bodha-nirūpita-kāraṇatā*). In plain language, a signification function is not a cause of everything that can be caused, but only of a verbal cognition. Such a fully specified instance of cause-ness, residing in an awareness of a signification function and described in reference to the resulting verbal cognition, must have an appropriately specified limitor (*kāraṇatāvacchedaka*). Such a limitor of cause-ness must be possessed by each and every instance of awareness of a signification function which leads in turn to the cognition of meaning.

Now, what property does an awareness of a signification function have so that it can function as a limitor of cause-ness pertaining to this awareness? Minimally, an awareness of a signification function (*śakti-jñāna*) has the generic property of being an awareness of a signification function, or "awareness-[of-a-signification-function]-ness" (*śakti-jñānatva*). Every instance of an awareness of a signification function obviously must possess this property of awareness-[of-a-signification-function]-ness. However, such a property is too vague as a limiting property to be included in the statement of a binding causal relationship. If the limitor of cause-ness were merely the property of awareness-[of-a-signification-function]-ness, then an awareness of a signification function of any word for any meaning would lead to a verbal cognition of any other meaning. Thus, the limiting property needs to be chosen more carefully. Different schools of Indian philosophy differ on the selection of a limiting property for making such a causal statement.

For instance, the school of Prābhākara Mīmāṃsā argues that an awareness of a signification function of a word ascertained with reference to a generic property alone is sufficient and necessary to produce a verbal cognition of an individual entity qualified by that generic property. Thus, for this school, the limitor of cause-ness pertaining to an awareness of a signification function is the property of *jāti-śakti-jñānatva* "awareness-[of-a-signification-function-ascertained-only-with-reference-to-a-generic-property]-ness." On the other hand, according to Naiyāyikas, an awareness of a signification function ascertained with reference to an individual entity qualified by a generic property (*jāti-viśiṣṭa-vyakti*) alone can be the cause of a verbal cognition of an individual entity qualified by that generic property. Thus, for them, the limitor of cause-ness pertaining to an awareness of a signification function must be specified as the property of *jāti-viśiṣṭa-śakti-jñānatva* "awareness-[of-a-signification-function-ascertained-with-reference-to-an-object-qualified-by-a-generic-property]-ness."

E.4.iv. Similarly, a verbal cognition (*śābda-bodha*) is an effect or result (*kārya*), and hence it must have the property of effect-ness (*kāryatā*). This property of effect-ness resides in the verbal cognition, and hence the verbal cognition serves as the locus of this effect-ness (*śābda-bodha-niṣṭha-kāryatā*). This property of effect-ness resident in a verbal cognition is described in reference to the property of cause-ness resident in an awareness of a signification function (*śakti-jñāna-niṣṭha-kāraṇatā-nirūpita-kāryatā śābda-bodha-niṣṭhā*). Just as there is a limitor for the property of cause-ness (*kāraṇatāvacchedaka*) pertaining to the awareness of a signification function, similarly there must be a limitor for the property of effect-ness (*kāryatāvacchedaka*) pertaining to a verbal cognition.

Again, in general terms, every instance of verbal cognition (*śābda-bodha*) possesses the property of verbal-cognition-ness (*śābda-bodhatva*). Can we specify this property of verbal-cognition-ness as the limitor of effect-ness pertaining to a verbal cognition? Since, every instance of verbal cognition has the generic property of verbal-cognition-ness, such a limitor would mean that from any given instance of awareness of a signification function as a cause, we could have as an effect an instance of verbal cognition, as long as it is an instance of verbal cognition. Obviously, this is too vague a statement, and we must find a more appropriate limitor of effect-ness pertaining to a verbal cognition. Here again, different schools of Indian philosophy respond differently.

For Mīmāṃsakas, the primary verbal cognition is only a cognition of a generic property, and the individual entity which possesses this generic property is not part of primary meaning. Thus, for them, the limitor of effect-ness pertaining to a verbal cognition is the property of *jāti-jñānatva* "cognition-[of-a-generic-property]-ness." For Naiyāyikas, the verbal cognition is always a cognition of an individual qualified by a generic property. Hence, the limitor of effect-ness pertaining to a verbal cognition would be the property of *jāti-viśiṣṭa-vyakti-jñānatva* "cognition-[of-an-individual-qualified-by-a-generic-property]-ness." For those who believe that an individual alone is cognized from a word, the limitor of effect-ness pertaining to a verbal cognition would be the property of *vyakti-jñānatva* "cognition-[of-an-individual]-ness."

Thus, the properties which serve as the limitor of cause-ness (*kāraṇatāvacchedaka*) pertaining to an awareness of a signification function and the limitor of effect-ness (*kāryatāvacchedaka*) pertaining to a verbal cognition do not necessarily correspond to each other. In the schools of Bhāṭṭa-Mīmāṃsā and Nyāya, they do correspond. For the school of Bhāṭṭa-Mīmāṃsā, the limitor of cause-ness (*kāraṇatāvacchedaka*) pertaining to an awareness of a signification function is the property of *jāti-śakti-jñānatva* "awareness-[of-a-signification-function-ascertained-with-respect-to-a-generic-property]-ness," while the limitor of effect-ness (*kāryatāvacchedaka*) pertaining to a verbal cognition is *jāti-jñānatva* "cognition-[of-a-generic-property]-ness." For Naiyāyikas, the limitor of cause-ness (*kāraṇatāvacchedaka*) pertaining to an awareness of a signification function is the property of *jāti-viśiṣṭa-vyakti-śakti-jñānatva* "awareness-[of-a-signification-function-ascertained-with-respect-to-an-individual-qualified-by-a-generic-property]-ness." However, for the school of Prābhākara Mīmāṃsā, the limitor of cause-ness (*kāraṇatāvacchedaka*) pertaining to an awareness of a signification function is the property *jāti-śakti-jñānatva* "awareness-[of-a-signification-function-ascertained-with-respect-to-a-generic-property]-ness," while the limitor of effect-ness (*kāryatāvacchedaka*) pertaining to a verbal cognition is the property *jāti-viśiṣṭa-vyakti-jñānatva* "cognition-[of-an-individual-qualified-by-a-generic-property]-ness." According to this school, even though the signification function of a word is ascertained only with respect to a generic property, the signified meaning consists of an individual qualified by that generic property. In this fashion, different schools of Indian philosophy were able to express their conceptions of causal relationship between the cognition of a word and the cognition of meaning with great precision.

E.5. *LAKṢAṆĀ* "SECONDARY SIGNIFICATION FUNCTION"

E.5.i. Kauṇḍabhaṭṭa's *Nāmārtha-nirṇaya* principally deals with the notion of primary meaning of nominal stems. However, on a few occasions he also refers to the notion of secondary signification function. Just as the primary meaning is called *śakya*, the secondary meaning is called *lakṣya*. Corresponding to the primary signifier word called *śakta*, a word which signifies a certain meaning through its secondary signification function is called *lakṣaka*. The primary meaning and the secondary meaning are not necessarily different entities. The same thing, depending upon how it was signified, can be either a primary meaning or a secondary meaning. The same way, the primary signifier word and the secondary signifier word are the same physical word, but functioning in different capacities. The same word may be called a primary signifier word with respect to its primary meaning, and it may be called a secondary signifier word with respect to its secondary meaning. In general terms, *lakṣaṇā* refers to the secondary signification function, which is described as a relation between the secondary signifier word and the secondary meaning.

E.5.ii. Naiyāyikas define *lakṣaṇā* as the relation of the secondary meaning with the primary meaning, on the basis of the difficulty in justifying the intention behind the utterance.[226] The definition refers to a situation where the primary meaning of an utterance does not appear to make sense in the context of the intention behind the utterance, and hence one looks for a secondary meaning. However, the claim is that the secondary

---

226 *lakṣaṇā śakya-sambandhas tātparyānupapattitaḥ* /, *KM*, p. 588.

meaning is something that is related to the primary meaning in some way or the other. For example, the expression *gaṅgāyāṃ ghoṣaḥ* literally refers to a cowherd-colony on the Ganges. Here, the Naiyāyikas argued that one cannot obviously have a cowherd-colony sitting on top of the river Ganges. This would also go against the intention of the speaker. Thus, there is both a difficulty of justifying the linkage of word-meanings (*anvayā-nupapatti*) and a difficulty of justifying the literal or primary meaning in relation to the intention of the speaker (*tātparyānupapatti*). These interpretive difficulties nudge one to move away from the primary meaning of the expression to a secondary meaning, which is related to that primary meaning. Thus, we understand the expression *gaṅgāyāṃ ghoṣaḥ* to refer to a cowherd-colony on the bank of the river Ganges. Here the secondary meaning "the bank of the river Ganges" is related to the primary meaning "the river Ganges" through the relation of proximity (*sāmīpya*). The relation between the primary meaning and the secondary meaning could be that of proximity (*sāmīpya*), inherence (*samavāya*), conjunction (*saṃyoga*), or shared property (*tāddharmya*). According to the old school of Nyāya, the basis for moving on to the secondary signification function of a word is the difficulty of justifying the linkage of word-meanings (*anvayānupapatti*), while, according to the school of Navya-naiyāyikas, the basis for moving on to the secondary signification function of a word is the difficulty of justifying the primary meaning in relation to the intention of the speaker (*tātparyānupapatti*).[227] The notion of *anvayānupapatti* "difficulty of justifying the linkage of word-meanings" seems to assume a more linear process of understanding meaning from an utterance. The listener first comprehends the primary meaning of words. Then he realizes that the primary meanings do not seem to link up properly to yield an acceptable qualified cognition. Then the listener looks for a related secondary meaning which seems to offer a proper linkage of word meanings. Here, the listener does not presume to know the intention of the speaker. On the other hand, the notion of *tātparyānupapatti* "difficulty of justifying the primary meaning in relation to the [presumed] intention of the speaker" seems to assume that the listener not only has access to the primary or lexical meanings of words, but that he also has access to the speaker's intention from the circumstances.

E.5.iii. The school of Sanskrit poetics also provides a detailed account of the secondary signification function. Sanskrit poetics, for obvious reasons, is more interested in the secondary meaning, and even more so in the suggested meaning of an utterance. This seems natural because the primary meaning is probably the least poetic of all these different meaning varieties. In his *Sāhitya-darpaṇa*, Viśvanātha defines the secondary signification function as follows:[228]

---

227 *anvayānupapattir lakṣaṇā-bījam iti prāñca āhuḥ / tātparyānupapattir eva sarvatra lakṣaṇā-bījam iti navyāḥ prāhuḥ /*, *NK*, p. 698.

228 *mukhyārtha-bādhe tad-yukto yayānyo 'rthaḥ pratīyate / rūḍheḥ prayojanād vāsau lakṣaṇā śaktir arpitā //*, *Sāhitya-darpaṇa* quoted in *NK*, p. 699.

> "That signification function (*śakti*) is called a secondary signification function (*lakṣaṇā*), which involves imposition, and which signifies a meaning which is both different from the primary meaning and is yet related to it, when the primary meaning is contrary (to the context or intention of the speaker). This is done either on the basis of conventional usage, or to achieve some specific communicative purpose."

The last part of this definition refers to two subtypes of secondary signification function. When a word is used in its secondary meaning to achieve a specific purpose, i.e. to imply a specific additional meaning, we get the variety called *prayojanavatī lakṣaṇā*. For example, in the usage *gaṅgāyāṃ ghoṣaḥ* lit. "the cowherd-colony is on the river Ganges," the secondary meaning is that this cowherd-colony is on the bank of the river Ganges. If this is so, then why not explicitly say that it is on the bank of the river Ganges (*gaṅgā-tīre ghoṣaḥ*)? We are told by the philosophers that the purpose in saying that the cowherd-colony is on the river Ganges is to show its intense contact with the holy river Ganges, and thereby imply the holy character of this cowherd-colony.[229] The secondary signification function which is conventionalized through long term usage is called *nirūḍha-lakṣaṇā*. It is like a dead or faded metaphor. Here the primary or the literal meaning is still perceptible, but the so-called secondary meaning is equally conventionalized and carries no special significance. Kumārilabhaṭṭa says that such conventional secondary signification function is almost like the primary signification function.[230] The conventional secondary signification function, we are told, automatically goes into operation like the primary signification function, and one does not need to go through a recognition of the inappropriateness of the primary meaning before reaching the secondary meaning. For Mīmāṃsakas, the word *śukla* "white" primarily signifies only the property (*guṇa*) of white color, but it signifies the white object through this type of conventionalized secondary signification function. It works for some words and does not work for others. For example, it works for color words like *śukla* "white," but does not work for a word like *gandha* "smell." This word cannot be used to refer to the entity which possesses a certain smell. Different schools have further subdivided the secondary signification function into many more types. I shall refer the reader to the excellent discussion of these types by K. Kunjunni Raja.[231]

E.5.iv. Nāgeśabhaṭṭa discusses various definitions of *lakṣaṇā*. He agrees with Navya-naiyāyikas in holding the view that it is the difficulty of justifying the intention (*tātparyānupapatti*) in relation to the primary meaning that leads to the secondary signification function, rather than the difficulty of justifying the linkages of primary meanings (*anvayānupapatti*). He argues that, if it were the difficulty of justifying the

---

229 *iyaṃ ca pāvitryādi-prayojanāpekṣayā pravartamānatvāt* /, *NK*, p. 699.

230 *nirūḍhāḥ lakṣaṇāḥ kāścit sāmarthyād abhidhānavat* / *kriyante sāmprataṃ kāścit kāscin naiva tv aśakti-taḥ* /, *TV(a)*, Pt. I., p. 683.

231 K. Kunjunni Raja (1963: 262).

linkage of primary meanings alone which would lead one to move on to the secondary signification function of words, one could say that in the example *gaṅgāyāṃ ghoṣaḥ*, the word *ghoṣa* denotes an alligator. The cowherd-colony cannot exist in or on the river Ganges, but an alligator can. Thus, switching from the meaning "cowherd-colony" to the meaning "alligator" allows one to have acceptable linkages of meanings, and yet this is so far off as compared to the intention of the speaker.[232] This argument needs some explanation. Naiyāyikas believe that if a linkage of two or more word-meanings creates a possible description of a state of affairs which cannot be true or be possible in terms of known ontology or our knowledge of the world, then the word-meanings are simply not linked. Thus, since it is impossible to situate a cowherd-colony in or on the river Ganges, the respective word-meanings simply cannot be linked. This kind of stand-off in linking primary meanings is then said to be a probable cause leading to secondary signification function. Nāgeśabhaṭṭa seems to be saying that the particular choice of the secondary meaning cannot depend solely upon whether a certain linkage of meanings seems ontologically possible, or possible in terms of our knowledge of the world. One must take into account the likely intention of the speaker.

After the above analysis of the Nyāya view of secondary signification function, Nāgeśabhaṭṭa finally rejects the whole concept of secondary signification function as something different from the primary signification function. Nāgeśabhaṭṭa says that, according to Patañjali, each word has a capacity to signify any possible meaning, provided there is intention of that sort. Therefore, there is no reason to consider some meanings as primary meanings, and others as secondary meanings. Every meaning that a word can signify is a primary meaning. Thus, the category of primary meaning covers what others may include in the category of secondary meaning. However, the primary signification function (*śakti*) is said to be of two types: *prasiddha* "well known" and *a-prasiddha* "not so well known." The primary signification function of the well known type is said to be something which is known even to the dullest person, while the not-so-well-known type is the one which is known only to the sophisticated users of language. Thus, even the dullest person knows that the word *gaṅgāyām* means "on the river Ganges." However, only a sophisticated user can see that this word means "on the bank of the river Ganges" in the expression *gaṅgāyāṃ ghoṣaḥ*.[233] Nāgeśabhaṭṭa's rejection of secondary signification function represents an extreme view, and it is not widely shared by other thinkers.

232 *vastutas tu tātparyānupapatti-pratisandhānam eva tad-bījam / anyathā gaṅgāyāṃ ghoṣa ity-ādau ghoṣādi-pade eva makarādi-lakṣaṇāpattis tāvatāpy anvayānupapatti-parihārāt /*, *PLM*, p. 57.

233 *sati tātparye sarve sarvārtha-vācakā iti bhāṣyāl lakṣaṇāyā abhāvāt / ... śaktir dvi-vidhā / prasiddhā aprasiddhā ca /,.. tatra gaṅgādi-padānām pravāhādau prasiddhā, tīrādau cāprasiddheti kim anupapannam /*, *PLM*, pp. 62-3.

F. *ŚABDA* ITSELF AS *ARTHA*: USE VERSUS MENTION

F.1. Indian Grammarians consider the question of the distinction between the use of a word and its mention to be a part of the semantic theory. Their treatment of this issue is significantly different from the considerations found in Western logic and semantics. For example, discussing the notion of *quotation*, Quine refers to two issues: "use versus mention," and "statements about statements." These are two aspects of the same basic problem, differing only in their magnitude. Quine considers the following three examples:[234]

[1] Boston is populous.
[2] Boston is disyllabic.
[3] 'Boston' is disyllabic.

Quine points out that statements [1] and [3] are true, while statement [2] is false. What is populous is the city of Boston, and what is disyllabic is the place name, the word. Quine comments on these examples:[235]

> "The name of a name or other expression is commonly formed by putting the named expression in single quotation marks; the whole called a *quotation* denotes its interior. In the statement [1], the place-name is used, and in this way the city is mentioned; in [3] a quotation is used, and the place-name is mentioned."

We do not have quotation marks in Sanskrit, but that function is performed by the word *iti*. For instance, the expression *rāmaḥ* refers to a person named Rāma, while the expression *rāmaḥ iti* refers to the word *rāmaḥ*. In this respect the expression *rāmaḥ iti* corresponds to the quotation 'Boston' in Quine's examples. An oft-quoted Sanskrit line says: *rāmeti dvyakṣaraṃ nāma* "the name 'Rāma' is disyllabic." Such a statement is exactly parallel to example [3] cited by Quine.

F.2. In his commentary on P.1.1.44 (*na veti vibhāṣā*), Patañjali discusses the following example:[236]

gaur ity ayam āha "He said: '*gauḥ*'."

Patañjali says that the word *iti* placed after the word *gauḥ* deprives the word *gauḥ* of its normal meaning, i.e. the animal bull. Forced away from its normal meaning, the word thus refers to itself, i.e. to its own word-form. It becomes a name (*saṃjñā*) of the word *gauḥ*. Kaiyaṭa, in his commentary *Pradīpa* on Patañjali's *Mahābhāṣya*, says that the word *iti* leads to the inversion of the meaning of a word.[237] Nāgeśabhaṭṭa explains this notion of

---

234 Quine (1940: 23).

235 Quine (1940: 23).

236 *tad yathā 'gaur ity ayam āha' iti go-śabdād iti-karaṇaḥ prayujyamāno go-śabdaṃ svasmād arthāt pracyāvayati / so 'sau svasmāt padārthāt pracyutaḥ yāsāv artha-padārthakatā tasyāḥ śabda-padārthakaḥ sampadyate /*, *MB*, Vol.I., Sec.I., p. 237.

237 *iti-śabdo 'rtha-viparyāsa-kṛt /*, *MB-P*, Vol.I., Sec.I., p. 237.

inversion of meaning (*padārtha-viparyāsa*) as follows:[238] In the normal usage of a word, a word signifies its meaning as qualified by its own word-form. When a word is normally used in grammar, it signifies its own word-form as qualified by its meaning. If we add *iti* after a word, this normal situation is inverted. In the normal usage, a word followed by *iti* signifies its own word-form as qualified by its meaning. On the other hand, a word followed by *iti* used in grammar signifies its meaning as qualified by its word-form.

F.3. The above explanation given by Nāgeśabhaṭṭa needs further clarification. In his rule P.1.1.68 (*svaṃ rūpaṃ śabdasyāśabda-saṃjñā*), Pāṇini says that, in the system of grammar, a word's own form (*sva-rūpa*) is the designatum (*saṃjñin*) of a word, except when words used in grammar are grammatical designations of linguistic items (*a-śabda-saṃjñā*). For example, P.4.2.33 (*agner ḍhak*) says that the affix *ḍhak* is added after *agni*. In Sanskrit, the word *agni* denotes fire. Does the rule mean to say that an affix is added after fire? Pāṇini says that, in grammar, when he cites words, he means to refer to their word-form. Thus, the affix *ḍhak* is added after the word *agni*, and not after its meaning. However, technical designations of classes of linguistic items always refer to those designated linguistic items rather than to the word-shapes of the used designations. For instance, P.1.1.76 (*vṛddhir yasyācām ādis tad vṛddham*) defines the term *vṛddha* as referring to those linguistic items whose first vowel is either *ā*, *ai*, or *au* (i.e. a *vṛddhi* vowel). Now, P.4.2.114 (*vṛddhāc chaḥ*) prescribes the affix *cha* after *vṛddha*. This does not mean that the affix should be added after the word-form *vṛddha*, but that it should be added after a word-form such as *śālā* "building" which belongs to the class of words designated by the term *vṛddha*.

F.4. Initiating a new debate on this topic, Kātyāyana says that it is not necessary to have an explicit rule like P.1.1.68 (*svaṃ rūpaṃ śabdasyāśabda-saṃjñā*), since the cognition of meaning is always preceded by a cognition of a word.[239] Kātyāyana's argument goes as follows. When a word is uttered, the listener first has a cognition of the word-form, and then he has a cognition of the meaning of that word. One does not go directly to the cognition of meaning by-passing the cognition of the word. Thus, both the word-form and the meaning are cognized by the listener. Since the grammatical operation of affixation is impossible for the meaning of the word, it will be automatically shifted to the word-form. For this reason, Kātyāyana argues that it is not necessary to have a special rule like P.1.1.68. It seems that, in Kātyāyana's opinion, any principles which are available from one's common-sense need not be specifically stated as rules in grammar.

Kātyāyana's comment has wider significance for a philosopher of language. Patañjali explains Kātyāyana's argument as follows.[240] When someone is addressed by a name, and when that person does not fully comprehend that name, he asks: "what did you say,

---

[238] *loke śabda-viśeṣaṇakārtha-pratītiḥ, śāstre 'rtha-viśeṣaṇaka-śabdasya / iti-śabda-samabhivyāhāre viparītam iti viparyāsaḥ /*, *MB-P-U*, Vol.I., Sec.I., p. 237.

[239] *na vā śabda-pūrvako hy arthe sampratyayaḥ /*, *Vt.* 2 on P.1.1.68.

[240] *yo 'pi hy asāv āhūyate nāmnā / nāma ca yadānena nopalabdham bhavati tadā pṛcchati kim bhavān āheti / śabda-pūrvakaś cārthasya pratyayaḥ /*, *MB*, Vol.I., Sec.I., p. 367.

sir?" This experience shows that the cognition of meaning is preceded by the cognition of a word. Bhartṛhari further develops this argument and says that no meaning is cognized from words which are not themselves cognized first. Words, which are not cognized, are unable to signify meaning merely by their existence. Therefore, when the word-form itself is not clearly discerned, one asks: "what did you say?"[241] Helārāja, commenting upon this verse, says that there are three things which are similar in behavior. They are a cognition (*jñāna*), a word (*śabda*), and light (*pradīpa*). These three cause a cognition of an object with a certain power of illumination. However, they illuminate themselves by the same power of illumination. Thus, a word leads to a cognition of meaning, as well as of itself.[242]

With the above explanations, we can say that when a word is *used*, it signifies meaning as qualified by the word-form. However, when a word is *mentioned*, it signifies its own word-form as qualified by its own meaning. Thus, the distinction between use and mention depends upon the intention of the speaker. This intention may be signalled by the use of verbs like "says," "states," etc., or by specific rules such as the one made by Pāṇini, P.1.1.68. The use of quotation marks in English is limited to the written language, though one can certainly say explicitly "I quote."

F.5. There is another set of terminology used in Sanskrit texts to deal with the distinction between use and mention. The terms *anukārya* and *anukaraṇa* refer to notions of "imitated word" and "imitation word," respectively. Pāṇini uses the term *anukaraṇa* in P.1.4.62 (*anukaraṇaṃ cāniti-param*). In short, the imitation is of two kinds, i.e. that of physical non-linguistic sounds (*avyaktānukaraṇa*) and that of articulated linguistic sounds or words (*vyaktānukaraṇa*).[243] In the case of an imitation of a physical sound, such as that of a falling object, the distinction between the imitated sound and the imitation word is quite clear. Here the imitated sound is not a linguistic sound, but a physical sound of the thing falling. On the other hand, the imitation itself is an articulated linguistic word such as *paṭat*. With the addition of the explicit quotation marker *iti*, we can get a usage like *paṭad iti karoti* "he makes the sound *paṭat*." Without the explicit marker *iti*, we get a usage like *paṭa-paṭā-karoti*." It has the same meaning. Pāṇini's rule P.1.4.62 cited earlier deals with the derivation of the latter type of construction. The other type of imitation is that of a linguistic item, and is thus closer to the notions of use and mention. For instance, in the sentence *gaur ity ayam āha* "he said '*gauḥ*'," the expression *gauḥ iti* is an imitation of the word *gauḥ*, which can be used in a sentence like *gaus tiṣṭhati* "here stands a bull." The imitated word refers to a bull (or a cow), while the imitation word refers to the imitated word *gauḥ*.

F.6. We can make some distinction between an imitation word (*anukaraṇa*) and a mentioned word. An imitation word is rather identifiable with a quotation as a whole,

---

241 *viṣayatvam anāpannaiḥ śabdair nārthaḥ prakāśyate / na sattayaiva te 'rthānam agṛhītāḥ prakāśakāḥ // ato 'nirjñāta-rūpatvāt kim āhety abhidhīyate /*, *VP*, I, 56-7.

242 *jñāna-śabda-padīpās trayo hi prakāśā yenaiva prakāśena param prakāśayanti, tenaivātmānam api /*, *VP-H(p)*, p. 125.

243 *VBS-S*, p. 236.

while a mentioned word is in fact identical with an imitated word (*anukārya*) in the aspect of its being the object of imitation. In other words, imitation words (*anukaraṇa*) correspond to quotations, while imitated words (*anukārya*) correspond to contents of quotations. Therefore, I shall not translate the term *anukaraṇa* "an imitation word" with the more common term "a mentioned word."

F.7. Kauṇḍabhaṭṭa exhaustively discusses the topic of imitation words and imitated words [cf. **NN. VII.1-38**]. The discussion of this topic covers almost a third of his work on the meaning of nouns. Is an imitation word identical with the imitated word? How is a word cognized from itself? Is the cognition of word-form a case of direct sensory perception, or does it occur on the basis of a word's primary or secondary signification function? Is an imitation a meaningful word, or does it stand for something which should not be included in the notion of meaning? How does this issue affect the systems of Nyāya and Mīmāṃsā? Which of the alternatives would allow us to interpret Pāṇini's rules in a more efficient way? Kauṇḍabhaṭṭa discusses these and several other questions in his *Nāmārtha-nirṇaya* [cf. **NN.VII.1-38**]. I have elaborate historical and explanatory comments on the translation of these sections. Therefore, to avoid repetition, I shall not duplicate that discussion here.

G. BHAṬṬOJĪ DĪKṢITA AND KAUṆḌABHAṬṬA

G.1. Texts in Pāṇini's school of Sanskrit grammar are generally said to be concerned with two types of grammatical issues, *śabda-prakriyā* "grammatical processing of the word-form" and *artha-prakriyā* "processing of meaning." While some texts are more closely concerned with one or the other of these two modes, most are concerned with both. In terms of discussion of issues related to meaning, we can broadly divide the grammatical tradition into four periods:

Early Period (500-100 B.C.)
Pāṇini, Vyāḍi, Vājapyāyana, Kātyāyana, and Patañjali
Early Middle Period (400-1000 A.D.)
Bhartṛhari, Helārāja, and Puṇyarāja
Late Middle Period (1200 A.D.)
Kaiyaṭa
New Period (1550-1750 A.D.)
Bhaṭṭojī Dīkṣita, Kauṇḍabhaṭṭa, and Nāgeśabhaṭṭa

S.D. Joshi and others have discussed the general questions concerning the dates of Bhaṭṭojī Dīkṣita and Kauṇḍabhaṭṭa, and the known details of their personal lives.[244] It is now commonly held that Bhaṭṭojī Dīkṣita's career ranges from 1560 to 1620 A.D. There are major controversies about his Brahmin sub-caste (cf. *Bhaṭṭoji-dīkṣita-jñāti-viveka*, by

244 S.D. Joshi (1960: Intro, p. vii).. Introductions to *VB*, *VB(M)*, *VB(B)*, and *SM(S)*. For an extensive study of Bhaṭṭojī Dīkṣita's contribution to Sanskrit grammar, see: S.K. Bali (1976).

Vasudev Anant Bambardekar, Bombay 1939), though a majority of scholars accept that he was a Telanga Brahmin. He wrote numerous works on different systems. Four of his works deal with grammar:

Śabda-kaustubha: an extensive commentary on Pāṇini's rules.
Siddhānta-kaumudī: a re-arrangement of Pāṇini's rules with a commentary
Prauḍha-manoramā: an extensive commentary on *Siddhānta-Kaumudī*
Vaiyākaraṇa-matonmajjana: a collection of 76 verses dealing with syntax, semantics, and philosophy of language.

While Bhaṭṭojī Dīkṣita is more widely known for his *Siddhānta-kaumudī*, we are concerned here with his *Vaiyākaraṇa-matonmajjana*. S.D. Joshi discusses the composition of this work in detail.[245] This work is also known by the title *Vaiyākaraṇa-siddhānta-kārikā*. All 76 verses of this text are not composed by Bhaṭṭojī Dīkṣita himself. He borrows verses from Bhartṛhari, Kumārilabhaṭṭa, and Vopadeva. Some of his verses present doctrines which developed long after Bhartṛhari. Joshi comments:[246]

> "It would seem to me, then, that the *Vaiyākaraṇa-matonmajjana* is a collection of useful verses composed by no single author but gathered together by Bhaṭṭojī, who doubtless composed many of them himself, for the instruction of his students."

G.2. Kauṇḍabhaṭṭa was Bhaṭṭojī Dīkṣita's nephew, the son of Raṅgojībhaṭṭa. He studied grammar under Śeṣakṛṣṇa who was also Bhaṭṭojī's teacher, and he refers to his uncle with great respect. Raṅgojībhaṭṭa enjoyed the patronage of king Veṅkaṭappā, a Keladi ruler of Ikkeri in the present state of Karnataka who ruled from 1560 to 1630 A.D. Kauṇḍabhaṭṭa himself refers to king Vīrabhadra, a Keladi ruler, who ruled from 1629 to 1645 A.D. We may safely conclude that Kauṇḍabhaṭṭa lived during the first half of the seventeenth century.[247]

Kauṇḍabhaṭṭa wrote two commentaries on Bhaṭṭojī Dīkṣita's *Vaiyākaraṇa-matonmajjana*. The larger commentary is titled *Vaiyākaraṇa-bhūṣaṇa*, and its abridged version is titled *Vaiyākaraṇa-bhūṣaṇa-sāra*. The shorter work has been popular for a long time and is used in traditional Sanskrit schools in India to this date for instruction in philosophy of grammar. It has been published several times with different commentaries, and several individual sections of the shorter work have appeared separately with translations and commentaries.[248]

---

245 S.D. Joshi (1960: ix ff).

246 S.D. Joshi (1960: xi).

247 S.D. Joshi (1960: vii-ix).

248 S.D. Joshi (1960: xi-xviii). Important editions of both versions are listed in the bibliography. S.D. Joshi's dissertation deals with the *Dhātv-artha-nirṇyaya* section of the shorter version. The same section has appeared with Hindi commentaries by Bhimasen Shastri (1969) and Sudesh Arora (1969). S.D. Joshi (1967) translates the *Sphoṭa-nirṇaya* section of the shorter version. J.A. Gune (1978) translates the *Lakārārtha-nirṇaya* section of the larger version.

I present here a critical translation of the *Nāmārtha-nirṇaya* section of the larger version, i.e. *Vaiyākaraṇa-bhūṣaṇa*. This text was first published in 1899-1900 in the Banaras Sanskrit Series, and was republished in 1915 in the Bombay Sanskrit Series No. LXX. The editor of the second edition, Mr. K.P. Tripathi, edited this text on the basis of the earlier edition, and nine more manuscripts. Tripathi adds some useful notes to this text, though compared to the size and complexity of the text, the notes are somewhat scanty. When I studied and translated *Nāmārtha-nirṇaya* as part of my Ph.D. work at the University of Pennsylvania in 1971-72, only these two editions of the larger text, i.e. *Vaiyākaraṇa-bhūṣaṇa* were available to me, besides several editions of the shorter version. I had to use the commentaries on the shorter version to make sense of the larger version. However, two more editions of the larger work have appeared since my dissertation was completed in 1972. Manudeva Bhattacharya's edition of 1985 does not consult any new manuscripts, but occasionally adds notes in Sanskrit. Vidya Nivas Misra's edition of 1987 cites no new manuscript variants, but adds some useful notes in English. I have consulted all these editions, and found that the text I used as the basis of my translation remains largely unchanged. I have benefitted most from Bimal Krishna Matilal's work (1971, 1985, and 1986), and from Kapil Dev Shastri's editions of Nāgeśabhaṭṭa's *Parama-laghu-mañjūṣā* and *Vaiyākaraṇa-siddhānta-mañjūṣā*. Actually, the publication of Nāgeśabhaṭṭa's larger work, *Vaiyākaraṇa-siddhānta-mañjūṣā* has been a most important recent development. I have also consulted the excellent summary of Kauṇḍabhaṭṭa's works by S.D. Joshi in *The Philosophy of the Grammarians* edited by Harold G. Coward and K. Kunjunni Raja (1990). I have benefitted from all these publications which appeared since I completed my original dissertation in 1972, and I have made use of them in preparing this revised version.

H. KAUṆḌABHAṬṬA'S *NĀMĀRTHA-NIRṆAYA*

H.1. In this book, I have presented a heavily annotated translation of the *Nāmārtha-nirṇaya* ("Determination of the Meaning of Nouns) chapter of Kauṇḍabhaṭṭa's larger work, the *Vaiyākaraṇa-bhūṣaṇa*. This work is an extensive commentary on Bhaṭṭojī Dīkṣita's *Vaiyākaraṇa-matonmajjana* or *Vaiyākaraṇa-siddhānta-kārikā*. The chapter translated here, *Nāmārtha-nirṇaya*, is a commentary on verses 25-27 of Bhaṭṭojī Dīkṣita's work. These verses represent a condensed listing of grammatical doctrines which are then unpacked by Kauṇḍabhaṭṭa's commentary. In verse 25, Bhaṭṭojī lists five alternative views concerning the meaning of nouns. Verses 26 and 27 discuss the question of use and mention of words. Kauṇḍabhaṭṭa elaborates these different views in the same order as they are mentioned by Bhaṭṭojī Dīkṣita.

According to the subject matter of the discussion, I have divided the text of *Nāmārtha-nirṇaya* (= **NN**) into seven major divisions, marked with Roman numarals, **I-VII**. Each division represents a major view concerning the meaning of nouns, and is further subdivided into smaller texts, which are marked with arabic numerals. These smaller texts represent a related group of philosophical arguments. The translation of each of these small text-divisions is further split up into individual arguments, which are marked by letters of the English alphabet. For each text section, I have given a page reference to the Bombay edition. Each translation-section is followed by detailed historical and clarificatory explanations. Each explanation is given the number of the corresponding argument in the translation, e.g. **Explanation [NN.VI.3.b]**.

H.2. Since I have given exhaustive explanations of every argument in this text, containing a historical assessment of the arguments as well as a clarification, I shall not repeat myself by giving here a detailed account of all the arguments for and against different views discussed by Kauṇḍabhaṭṭa. I shall only present very brief descriptions of the contents of the seven sections.

Section I: This section contains a general discussion on the five alternative theories of the meaning of nouns. These five theories are discussed individually in the following sections.

Section II: This section discusses the view that a noun primarily denotes only a generic property. This view was explicitly proposed first by the pre-Kātyāyana philosopher Vājapyāyana, and is later upheld by the school of Mīmāṃsā.

Section III: This section discusses the view that a noun primarily denotes only an individual entity. It does not primarily denote either a generic property alone, or an individual entity qualified by a generic property. This view was upheld first by the pre-Kātyāyana philosopher Vyāḍi, and is later upheld by some Navya-naiyāyikas.

Section IV: This section discusses the view that a noun primarily denotes an individual entity qualified by a generic property. Kauṇḍabhaṭṭa presents two versions of this alternative. According to Naiyāyikas, the primary signification function of a word is ascertained with respect to an individual entity qualified by a generic property, and hence it leads to a verbal cognition of an individual entity qualified by that generic property. According to the second version which is attributed to followers of the Prābhākara school of Mīmāṃsā, the primary signification function of a word is ascertained only with respect to a generic property, and yet it leads to a verbal cognition of an individual entity qualified by that generic property. Kauṇḍabhaṭṭa himself seems to agree with this version.

Section V: This section discusses the view that the primary meaning of a noun also includes gender. Here Kauṇḍabhaṭṭa discusses a number of alternative views of gender and their implications for different schools of philosophy and grammar.

Section VI: This section simply mentions two further alternatives. The first of these says that even number is part of the primary meaning of nouns, and the second adds the notion of *kāraka* to the list of primary meanings.

Section VII: This section discusses the problem of use and mention, or rather the distinction between an imitation word (*anukaraṇa*) and an imitated word (*anukārya*). This is the most exhaustive section of all, and covers more than a third of Kauṇḍabhaṭṭa's discussion of the meaning of nouns.

H.3. In **NN.I.2.a**, Kauṇḍabhaṭṭa says that an individual entity is always a meaning of a noun, rather than the meaning of a case affix. This is also true of a generic property. On the other hand, gender, number, and *kāraka* are sometimes meanings of nouns and sometimes they are meanings of certain affixes. Thus, the apportioning of meanings to stems and affixes depends upon the details of particular examples. Let us say that the letters *P, I, G, N,* and *K,* represent a generic property , an individual entity, gender, number, and *kāraka*, respectively. Thus, the different ways of apportioning meaning between nouns and affixes may be schematically shown as below:

Alternative	Noun-meaning	Affix-meaning
1.	*P*, [*I* secondary]	*G, N, K*
2.	*I*, [*P* secondary]	*G, N, K*
3.	*P, I*	*G, N, K*
4.	*P, I, G*	*N, K*
5.	*P, I, G, N*	*K*
6.	*P, I, G, N, K*	*Ø*

Kauṇḍabhaṭṭa's *Nāmārtha-nirṇaya* refers to these alternative ways of distributing the possible meanings between the noun and the affix. This raises a number of interesting questions. Kauṇḍabhaṭṭa does not discuss the question of why certain other kinds of divisions are not possible. For instance, is it possible to have a case where *P, I,* and *K* are denoted by the noun, while *G* and *N* are denoted by the affix. Mathematically speaking, several other permutations and combinations are possible, and yet Kauṇḍabhaṭṭa lists only some alternatives. Are other alternatives impossible due to some philosophical or practical reason? Alternative 6 listed above also raises some interesting issues. If no meaning is denoted by an affix, what is its function? Kauṇḍabhaṭṭa attempts to answer this question in **NN.I.2.b**. An affix may not have a primary meaning, and yet it need not be meaningless. In traditional terminology, in alternative 6, the affix is not a primary signifier (*vācaka*) of a meaning element such as number, and yet it is said to be a co-signifier (*dyotaka*) of such meaning elements. I have discussed the notion of co-signification in section **A.8**. Such explanations are not new with Kauṇḍabhaṭṭa. They can be traced back to earlier works.[249] However, following Bhartṛhari and Kaiyaṭa, Kauṇḍabhaṭṭa says that this last view (= alternative 6) is not the final view of Patañjali, but is one of the optional views. Bhartṛhari says that all the alternatives mentioned above are mere conceptual constructs of different scholars and that they do not represent the true nature of meaning and its cognition. In a real-life situation of linguistic communication, according to Bhartṛhari, a complete sentential

---

[249] *pañcakaṃ prātipadikārthaḥ / ... vibhaktayas tu kvacid dyotakatvenāpekṣyante /*, *MB-P*, Vol.I., Sec.II., p. 235. Some of these general issues are discussed in the *Mahābhāṣya* on P.1.4.21 (*bahuṣu bahuvacanam*).

utterance signifies a complete sentential meaning. Grammarians subsequently analyse these whole sentences and their undivided whole meanings into theoretical components. There is no communicative reality to these theoretical semantic and morphological divisions.[250] This is Bhartṛhari's view. Nāgeśabhaṭṭa, on the other hand, firmly believes that alternative 6 above is Patañjali's final view. According to him, all meanings are always signified by a nominal stem, and a case-affix is always a mere co-signifier.[251] Such a view is not widely shared by other grammarians, and Kauṇḍabhaṭṭa's view seems to be closer to the view of most of the grammatical tradition.

I. CONCLUSION

I.1. S.D. Joshi says that the author of *Vaiyākaraṇa-bhūṣaṇa* claims no great originality for the semantic doctrines he elucidates.[252] Such a comment may raise some doubts as to why one should choose this work of little originality for such a detailed study. Perhaps, S.D. Joshi is overly pessimistic about his assessment of Kauṇḍabhaṭṭa's contribution. More recent studies of Kauṇḍabhaṭṭa's work seem to present a more upbeat evaluation. For example, V.N. Misra, in his recent edition of the *Vaiyākaraṇa-bhūṣaṇa*, has this to say [*VB(M)*, Intro., p. vi]:

> "Bhaṭṭojī, Kauṇḍabhaṭṭa and Nāgeśa are the three great propounders of an innovation in the Sanskrit grammatical tradition. The new school of grammar called *Navya Vyākaraṇa* is their monumental edifice. ... Within the *Navya Vyākaraṇa* school itself Kauṇḍabhaṭṭa and Nāgeśa hold divergent views on many issues. While Nāgeśa is more versatile and ingeneous in his approach, Kauṇḍabhaṭṭa is more consistent and logical in his contentions. It is for this reason that Kauṇḍabhaṭṭa has built a better integrated theory of language than Nāgeśa. His *Vaiyākaraṇa-bhūṣaṇa* with certain modifications could easily become an unusual model of a prolegomena of a theory of language ..."

Manudeva Bhattacharya [*VB(B)*, Intro. p. 15ff] elaborately discusses the relationship between Kauṇḍabhaṭṭa and Nāgeśabhaṭṭa, and shows that Nāgeśabhaṭṭa has taken over a great deal from his illustrious predecessor, and that Kauṇḍabhaṭṭa alone deserves the title of being the *navya-mata-pratiṣṭhāpaka* "founder of the new school of [grammatical]

---

250 *na hy ete vikalpā laukikāḥ / samudāyārthe hi laukike vyabhicārāt / pañcakaḥ prātipadikārthaś catuṣkas trika iti puruṣa-vikalpādhīna evam-prakāraḥ pakṣa-bhedaḥ /*, *VP-S*, Pt. I., p. 67.

251 *pañcakam prātipadikārtha iti mukhya-pakṣe /*, *MB-P-U*, Vol.I., Sec.II., p. 49; *sa eva pañcaka-pakṣo mukhyaḥ / ... evaṃ ca supāṃ tiṅāṃ ca dyotakatā ity eva bhāṣya-sammatam /*, *MB-P-U*, Vol.I., Sec.II.,, p. 235; *dyotakatva-pakṣa eva tu bhāṣya-sva-rasaḥ /*, *MB-P-U*, Vol.II., p. 280; *idam eva [pañcaka-pakṣa-]darśanaṃ siddhāntina iti bodhyam /*, *MB-P-U*,, Vol.I., Sec.II., p. 323; For a stronger presentation, see: *kārakam api prātipadikārtha iti pañcakam prātipadikārthaḥ / nanv anvaya-vyatirekābhyām pratyayasyaiva tad vācyam iti cet na / dadhi tiṣṭhati, dadhi paśyety ādau kartr-ādi-kāraka-pratīteḥ pratyayaṃ vināpi siddhatvāt / na ca lupta-pratyaya-smaraṇāt tat-pratītir iti vācyam, pratyaya-lopam ajānato 'pi nāmata eva tat-pratīteḥ /*, *PLM*, p. 200.

252 S.D. Joshi (1960), Introduction, pp. xi-xii.

philosophy." In his notes on *Vaiyākaraṇa-bhūṣaṇa*, Bhattacharya shows that Kauṇḍabhaṭṭa was followed not only by Nāgeśabhaṭṭa, but by other later grammatical authorities as well (Ibid., p. 18). The same admiration for Kauṇḍabhaṭṭa is registered recently by Harold Coward and K. Kunjunni Raja (1990: 21):

> "... Bhaṭṭoji is responsible for seventy-four verses on grammar, sometimes referred to as the *Vaiyākaraṇamatonmajjana*, which form the text around which Koṇḍa Bhaṭṭa, the next great figure after Bhaṭṭoji, assembles his magnum opus, the *Vaiyākaraṇabhūṣaṇa* with its *sāra*. Koṇḍa Bhaṭṭa provided in his work of 1630 refutations of rival theories of meaning proposed by other schools, principally the Nyāya and Mīmāṃsā. The work thus stands as the most important treatise after Bhartṛhari's to stem from the Pāṇinian school concerning philosophy as understood for the purpose of this volume [= *The Philosophy of the Grammarians*, edited by Coward and Kunjunni Raja]."

With such high and wide praise of Kauṇḍabhaṭṭa's contribution, I need not be defensive or apologetic about my choice of Kauṇḍabhaṭṭa's *Nāmārtha-nirṇaya,* as I was in my original dissertation. While Kauṇḍabhaṭṭa indeed has his own views, his presentation of opposing views is thorough. Therefore, his work allows us to see the whole wide vista of opinions concerning semantic issues and the entire range of argumentation involved in these debates. Patañjali, Bhartṛhari, and Kumārilabhaṭṭa are the most frequently quoted authors, while a great deal of argumentation is directed against Gaṅgeśa's *Tattva-cintāmaṇi*. Along with a deep understanding of grammatical tradition, Kauṇḍabhaṭṭa exhibits his command of Mīmāṃsā and Navya-nyāya traditions as well.

I.2. I value Kauṇḍabhaṭṭa's work for its comprehensive character, and for its logical and systematic arrangement of arguments. It introduces a new organization of semantic discussions as compared to Bhartṛhari's *Vākya-padīya*. While the third chapter of Bhartṛhari's *Vākya-padīya* discusses semantic issues under section-headings which deal directly with semantic notions such as action (*kriyā*), generic property (*jāti*), individual entity (*vyakti*), gender (*liṅga*) etc., Kauṇḍabhaṭṭa's work shows divisions of morphology as its starting point for discussion of meaning. Chapter-headings in *Vaiyākaraṇa-bhūṣaṇa* follow the pattern of "meaning of *x*," where *x* stands for morphological categories such as *nāman* "noun, nominal stem," *dhātu* "verb root," *lakāra* "endings for tenses and moods," *sup* "case endings," *nipāta* "particle," etc. This shows that Kauṇḍabhaṭṭa had a somewhat different orientation as compared to Bhartṛhari. This new structure for discussing semantics has been followed by Nāgeśabhaṭṭa in his *Parama-laghu-mañjūṣā, Laghu-mañjūṣā,* and *Vaiyākaraṇa-siddhānta-mañjūṣā*. Somewhat similar arrangement is seen in Gāgābhaṭṭa's *Bhāṭṭa-cintāmaṇi*, Jagadīśa Bhaṭṭācārya's *śabda-śakti-prakāśikā*, Khaṇḍa-deva's *Bhāṭṭa-tantra-rahasya* etc. It is perhaps possible to trace the inspiration for this new arrangement for discussion of semantics according to morphological categories to

Gaṅgeśa's *Tattva-cintāmaṇi* and its influence on the subsequent developments in the schools of grammar, Nyāya, and Mīmāṃsā.

I.3. SOME FEATURES OF PHILOSOPHICAL DISCOURSE

Here, I would like to discuss some general features of Kauṇḍabhaṭṭa's philosophical presentation, especially as we look at it from a modern point of view. Kauṇḍabhaṭṭa is representative of his contemporaries and predecessors, and most features of philosophical presentation in his work are shared by many of these authors.

I.3.a. *Acceptance of Alternative Views:*

Kauṇḍabhaṭṭa covers a certain ground in discussing the various alternatives concerning meaning, and yet finally he refuses to take a clear stand in favor of a particular view. In fact he goes in the other direction. He accepts all of the alternative views as possible views. In such an acceptance, there are a number of underlying possible reasons.

a) Kauṇḍabhaṭṭa makes a reference to the Mīmāṃsā doctrine that when there are alternatives of equal strength, one cannot say that one of the alternatives is valid, while others are wrong, cf. **NN.IV.8.** Kauṇḍabhaṭṭa seems to suggest that the alternative views of meaning listed in the beginning of his *Nāmārtha-nirṇaya* are of equal strength, and must be accepted as alternatives.

b) Kauṇḍabhaṭṭa suggests that the alternative views need not be accepted all at once, but one may choose a particular view depending upon the necessity of a particular example at hand (*lakṣyānurodhād vyavasthā*). This seems to suggest a view that one need not look for a fully universal explanation for all linguistic phenomena, and that the diversity and variability built into the fabric of language require different explanations for distinct types of usages, cf. Note 309.

c) Kauṇḍabhaṭṭa is also under the influence of the doctrines advocated by Bhartṛhari. For Bhartṛhari, only the undivided sentences and undivided sentence-meanings have communicative reality. For him, all divisions are unreal, whether they are morphological or semantic, and such divisions, though useful, are simply useful fictions. This being the attitude toward morphological and semantic divisions, there is no reason to argue for one division being superior to some other division. Thus, there is a utilitarian approach to morphological and semantic segmentation. There is no theoretical conviction behind any one particular way of morphological or semantic analysis.

d) Kauṇḍabhaṭṭa also switches his argument from one level to another level, from the communicative level of language to the analytical level of morphology. For a form like *paśunā* he debates the issues with an assumption that there is a nominal stem *paśu-* and an affix *-nā*. Thus, it seems right to debate whether a meaning like gender is signified by the nominal stem or the affix. Both the morphological items are visible, and seem beyond dispute. However, an accusative form such as *dadhi* is cited as a reason to argue that all the five meaning elements are signified by the stem alone, because there is no visible or audible affixal element. Somehow, Kauṇḍabhaṭṭa is unwilling to present an argument on more genuinely Pāṇinian lines and say that here we have a zero allomorph of the accusative affix *-am*, and that this zero is capable of signifying the same meaning as is signified by *-am*. Actually, a non-grammarian user of Sanskrit cannot tell whether the word *vanam* has two components, anymore than knowing the fact that the word *dadhi* has no affix. Ideally, one should either argue at the level of morphological elements, including zero morphs and allomorphs, or one should argue at the level of whole communicative units. Kauṇḍabhaṭṭa seems to be not taking a clear stand on this issue. In contrast with Kauṇḍabhaṭṭa, Nāgeśabhaṭṭa takes a clear stand that all meanings are denoted by the nominal stem, and that the case endings are always co-signifiers. This brings all case-forms, whether with zero affixes or non-zero affixes, to an identical level.

I.3.b. ***Non-separation of different types of discourse***

The debate in Kauṇḍabhaṭṭa's work touches upon arguments which may be roughly divided into three types, ontological, epistemological, and exegetical. Kauṇḍabhaṭṭa moves from one type of argument into another without any indication that he is entering into another realm of issues. In this process, several important distinctions get blurred.

a) ***Ontology versus Epistemology***

In discussing causation of verbal cognition, there are ontological as well as epistemic issues involved in the argument. For example, we can clarify the two issues by making a distinction in our statements:

i) Ontological causation: What must exist out there, in order that we have a certain cognition?

ii) Epistemic causation: What must we know, in order that we have a certain cognition?

When there is a cognition, there may be causal factors which exist that we do not know exist, and there may be things which we know [or believe] to exist, which do not exist out there. For example, the ontological fact, as commonly accepted by Indian philosophers, that sound is a quality of ether may be crucial to our ability to hear a spoken word. Without ether, we will not hear a word. However, it seems to me that one need not know that he hears sounds because sound is a quality of ether. One may be totally innocent of the existence of ether, and yet one may be able to hear sounds because ether exists. Thus, this part of causation is purely ontological, and not epistemic. However, Kauṇḍabhaṭṭa, following illustrious predecessors like Gaṅgeśa, cites as an instance of experience a cognition of ether upon hearing a word. We are told that when one hears a word, he not only has a cognition of meaning, based on the signification function of a word, but one also has a cognition of ether, because a word as an instance of sound is related to its substratum ether through the relation of inherence. Several formulations and reformulations are offered to avoid the inclusion of this cognition of ether in the verbal cognition, cf. **NN.IV.4.d.** This is somewhat similar to the Nyāya notion cited by Kauṇḍabhaṭṭa [cf. **NN.III.12.a.i**] that the word "ether" signifies the meaning "something which is a substratum of sound."

In my personal view, in these instances, philosophers get wrapped up in their own theories and forget that no one outside their philosophical clubs has the faintest notion that sound and ether are connected. Why is there a cognition of ether upon hearing a word? Does it arise because ontologically a word [= sound] is a quality of ether? Does it happen, if and only if, one knows that a word [= sound] is a quality of ether? Does anyone, except a trained Naiyāyika, know that a word [= sound] is a quality of ether? Does a non-Naiyāyika ever have an actual cognition of ether upon hearing a word? Does even a Naiyāyika have a cognition of ether upon hearing a word? Perhaps, given the ontological causation, a Naiyāyika believes that he must have had a cognition of ether, even if he were not aware of it.

One may also mention here that philosophers get wrapped up in their own philosophical doctrines so that they begin citing examples of linguistic usages which no one outside the philosophers' club would consider normal. For instance, in **NN.VII.23.d,** Kauṇḍabhaṭṭa says that whether a property is cognized from a word as a qualificandum or as a qualifier is dependent upon one's knowledge of the speaker's intention, mutual expectancy between words etc. For instance, in the sentence *gaur nityā* lit. "a cow is eternal," we are told that the word *gauḥ,* because of the context of the word *nityā* "eternal," denotes not an individual cow, but the property of cow-ness as the qualificandum or the principal meaning. On the other hand, we are told that in the sentence *gaur anityā* lit. "a cow is non-eternal," the same word *gauḥ* denotes an individual cow. Now, I would argue that no one uses such Sanskrit sentences in any normal communication. Therefore, any statements made about how one deliberately interprets these sentences have actually very little genuine epistemic value.

b) ***Known Cognitive States versus Unknown Cognitive States***

Śabara makes an important statement concerning epistemic processes. He says that when a word is heard, one knows that he has a cognition of an individual object. This experience is *pratyakṣa* "directly perceived." However, one does not know with any direct awareness whether this experience came directly upon hearing a word, or whether it was mediated by a cognition of *ākṛti* "generic property." That process is *apratyakṣa* "not directly accessible to perception," cf. Note 262. I would call this a black-box syndrome. One knows what goes in and what comes out, but one does not know what happens inside this black-box. Śabara says that what happens inside this black-box is decided by further argumentation and analysis. The argument is that one cannot know an object qualified by a property *P*, without first knowing *P*. Thus, since there is a known cognition of an object qualified by *P* upon hearing a word, and since this could not have come about without first having a cognition of *P*, there must have been a cognition of *P*, even though we were never aware of such a cognition. This argument leads to the assumption of cognitions of which one may not be aware, and they must be postulated in order to come up with a chain of causal events which will satisfy our theoretical demands. Here, we in fact had a cognition of an object qualified by *P*, without any prior known cognition of *P*, and then we argue that we could not have had this known cognition of an object qualified by *P*, without having had an unknown cognition of *P*. This presents a very important paradox. However, Kauṇḍabhaṭṭa does not show any awareness of such a paradox involved in these arguments.

c) ***Confusion of Philosophical versus Exegetical Discourse***

While, on the one hand, Kauṇḍabhaṭṭa is locked in debate with Mīmāṃsakas and Naiyāyikas, many of their doctrines, both philosophical and exegetical, have become a matter of common acceptance. Thus, Kauṇḍabhaṭṭa cites a number of Mīmāṃsā doctrines related to the interpretation of Vedic injunctions in support of philosophical conclusions. For example, consider his discussion of whether injunctions like *somena yajeta* "one should sacrifice with Soma," *udbhidā yajeta* "one should sacrifice with Udbhid," and *agniṣṭomena yajeta* "one should sacrifice with Agniṣṭoma." The question, whether one of these is an injunction prescribing an accessory of a sacrifice, or a name of a sacrifice, or whether it is a combined prescription is determined on the basis of a prolonged consideration of the context of that injunction, cf. **NN.VII.19-20**. Such discussions are largely exegetical, and their value for an epistemic theory is not very high, unless of course one is discussing a theory of context, or a theory of discourse. Kauṇḍabhaṭṭa does not separate epistemic questions from exegetical questions in any clear way.

d) ***Tool-box Syndrome***

One often gets a feeling while reading the debate presented by Kauṇḍabhaṭṭa that many participants in this debate, real or straw-men, view things such as the different kinds of signification functions as available tools in a philosopher's tool box. This is especially true in the case of invoking *lakṣaṇā* "secondary signification function" to carry out all kinds of things. If nothing else works, the philosopher invokes *lakṣaṇā*. Because of the exegetical bias of a good deal of Mīmāṃsā discussion, there is a notion of how to get the meaning one needs to get from a particular expression, than how to explain the meaning one would normally understand. Thus, invoking processes like *lakṣaṇā* offers pseudo-epistemic explanations of genuinely exegetical matters. As tools of exegetical deliberation, they lose their true epistemic character.

e) ***Game Syndrome***

A good deal of philosophical presentation in Kauṇḍabhaṭṭa's work, and in a large number of other Indian philosophical works, is filled with what I would call the game syndrome. The debaters are there to win the debate at whatever the cost. Thus, the direction of the argumentation is not always what one might call philosophical, but it is disputational, and all kinds of tricks of debate are used in the course of arguing against one's opponent. The *Nyāya-sūtras* openly discuss these different modes of debate, and not all of them are directed at arriving at the truth. The goal is to win. Therefore, in reading these presentations one needs to be aware of such devices. These various modes of debate have been discussed in detail by B.K. Matilal (1985: 9ff).

These are some of the features of the debate presented in Kauṇḍabhaṭṭa's *Nāmārtha-nirṇaya*. I do not mean to suggest that Kauṇḍabhaṭṭa's work is unique in having these features. In fact, in most respects, Kauṇḍabhaṭṭa is a typical writer, and, therefore, most of the above comments would be applicable to a large number of philosophical works in Sanskrit.

I.4. Using Kauṇḍabhaṭṭa's work as the starting point, I have attempted to trace most of the arguments presented here to their antecedents in those respective systems. The schools of Sanskrit grammar, Mīmāṃsā, and Nyāya, all have a long history full of doctrinal diversity. Over the centuries, these schools vigorously interacted with each other. Similarly, in each school, individual authors pride in showing their individual edge in argumentation. There is no such thing as *the* Indian philosophy of language. Similarly, there is no such thing as *the* view of grammarians, Mīmāṃsakas, or Naiyāyikas. There are multitudes of different opinions on every topic, and each argument needs to be placed in its right historical context. One can also look at the developments which occurred subsequently. For instance, while it is true that a later scholar like Nāgeśabhaṭṭa borrows a great deal from Kauṇḍabhaṭṭa, he also disagrees with Kauṇḍabhaṭṭa on many points. Nāgeśabhaṭṭa himself does not refer to Kauṇḍabhaṭṭa by name while rejecting his views, but commentators on Nāgeśabhaṭṭa's works clarify who he is rejecting. Thus, we can trace a history of argumentation in both directions starting from Kauṇḍabhaṭṭa's vantage point. In my notes on the translation of Kauṇḍabhaṭṭa's *Nāmārtha-nirṇaya*, I have undertaken such a task in a modest way. Through this translation and its explanation, I hope to present a picture of a vibrant period in the history of Indian philosophy of language.

Kauṇḍabhaṭṭa's

Nāmārtha-nirṇaya

SECTION ONE

NN.I.1. (P. 117)

नामार्थानाह् -

"एकं द्विकं त्रिकं चाथ चतुष्कं पञ्चकं तथा ॥
नामार्थ इति सर्वेऽमी पक्षाः शास्त्रे निरूपिताः ॥२५॥"

एकं जातिः । द्विकं जातिव्यक्ती । त्रिकं सलिङ्गे ते । चतुष्कं ससङ्ख्यानि तानि । पञ्चकं सकारकास्ताः ।

Translation [NN.I.1]

[a] [Bhaṭṭojī Dīkṣita] enumerates [the possible alternative views about] meanings of nouns:
"The [primary] meaning of a noun consists of one [element, or a group of] two, three, four, or five [elements]. All these alternative views have been explained in the tradition [of Sanskrit grammar]."

[b] [First view: The primary meaning of a noun consists of] one [element], i.e. a generic property.

[c] [Second view: The primary meaning of a noun consists of] two [elements], i.e. a generic property and an individual entity.

[d] [Third view: The primary meaning of a noun consists of] three [elements], i.e. gender along with the [earlier] two [elements].

[e] [Fourth view: The primary meaning of a noun consists of] four [elements], i.e. number along with those [earlier three elements].

[f] [Fifth view: The primary meaning of a noun consists of] five [elements], i.e. *kāraka* along with those [earlier four elements].

Explanation [NN.I.1.a]: The concepts of a noun or a nominal stem and its meaning are discussed in the Introduction [cf. **A.1-8** and **C.5-6**].

Explanation [NN.I.1.b-f]: In this section, Kauṇḍabhaṭṭa merely lists different alternative views concerning the primary meaning of nouns. However, the listing is not exhaustive enough to cover even his own treatment of the subject. The first view as given in **I.1.b** treats only a generic property as the single element signified by a noun. However, as we see from the text of *Nāmārtha-nirṇaya* [cf. **NN.III.1-12**], this is only one version of this view. The other version of this view is that the meaning of a noun consists of only an individual entity. The listing here is incomplete also in another respect. More than a third of this text deals with the question of use and mention [cf. **NN.VII.1-38**]. Traditionally this is also part of semantics, since the form of a word is considered as a possible meaning under certain circumstances. While translating **NN.I.1.f**, I have retained the Sanskrit term *kāraka*. I have discussed the conception of *kāraka* in the Introduction [cf. **D.6.i-vii**].

NN.I.2. (p. 117)

तत्र पूर्वपूर्वस्य प्रातिपदिकार्थत्वे उत्तरमुत्तरं विभक्त्यर्थो विना द्रव्यम् ।
चरमपक्षे विभक्तिर्द्योतिकैवेति द्रष्टव्यम् ।

Translation [NN.I.2]

[a] Among these [five meaning elements], if certain elements are [considered to be] meanings of a noun [= nominal stem], then the remaining elements are [to be considered to be] meanings of the case endings, excepting the individual entity [which is always a meaning of the noun].

[b] It should be noted that, in the last view, a case ending is merely a co-signifier.

Explanation [NN.I.2.a-b]: According to grammarian-philosophers beginning with Bhartṛhari, the division of sentential utterances and their meanings into constituent units is a mere conceptual construction (*kalpanā*), and yet it is useful in an analytical understanding of language [cf. Introduction, **B.4-5**]. An analysis of the cognition of meaning is said to reveal that there is a definite sequence in one's cognitive reception of different meaning elements. Patañjali says that a man gets up in the morning, finishes his personal matters first, then he works for his intimate friends, and then for his distant relatives. Similarly, a nominal stem first signifies a generic property.[253] Then it signifies an individual which possesses this generic property. Later this individual comes into a relationship with gender and number, and finally it is related to *kāraka*, which requires a relationship to another meaning such as an action. Kaiyaṭa and Nāgeśabhaṭṭa explain the subtle logic behind this statement by Patañjali.[254] A word signifies a generic property before it signifies an individual entity, because it is not possible to know an individual qualified by a property

---

[253] *praty-aṅga-vartī loko lakṣyate / tad yathā / puruṣo 'yam prātar utthāya yāny asya prati-śarīraṃ kāryāṇi tāni tāvat karoti, tataḥ suhṛdām, tataḥ sambandhinām / prātipadikaṃ cāpy upadiṣṭaṃ sāmānya-bhūte 'rthe vartate / sāmānye vartamānasya vyaktir upajāyate / vyaktasya sato liṅga-saṃkhyābhyām anvitasya bāhyenārthena yogo bhavati /*, *MB*, Vol.I., Sec.I., p. 312; *VP-S*, Pt.I., pp. 68-9; *MB-P*, Vol.II., p. 635.

[254] *tatra nāgṛhīta-viśeṣaṇā viśeṣye buddhir ity ādau sāmānyam abhidhīyate / tatas tad-anuraktā dravye pratītiḥ / liṅga-saṃkhyā-śaktīnāṃ cāśrayo dravyam iti tat pūrvam abhidhātavyam / tataḥ saṃkhyāpekṣayā liṅgaṃ samāsannam iti tad abhidhīyate / ... bāhyenārthena ... karmatvādinā ... tad hi kriyāpekṣaṇād bāhyam /*, *MB-P*, Vol.I., Sec.I., p. 312; also see: Ibid., Vol.II., p. 635.

before knowing that property. Therefore, after first knowing a generic property, there follows a cognition of an individual entity qualified by that generic property. This individual entity is the locus of gender and number alike. However, gender is closer to the individual entity as compared to number, and hence it is signified before number. The last element is *kāraka* or the role an entity performs in bringing about a given action. This is the most external element with respect to the individual entity, since this particular characterization of an entity requires the consideration of its relation to an action, an external element. Allocation of certain meaning elements to a nominal stem or to a case ending depends upon the alternative view we choose to accept. This question and the function of a case-affix as a co-signifier (*dyotaka*) have been discussed in detail in the Introduction [cf. **H.3**]. Kauṇḍabhaṭṭa considers all the five views to be of equal importance as possible alternatives.

SECTION TWO

NN.II.1. (p. 117)

तत्र प्रथमपक्ष इत्थमुपपत्तिः । जातिरेव पदार्थो लाघवात् । नानाव्यक्तीनां शक्यत्वे गौरवात् । न च प्रत्येकं व्यक्तिभिः [व्यक्तीनामेकत्वे] विनिगमनाविरहः । एवं व्यक्त्यन्तरे लक्षणायां स्वसमवेतसमवायित्वं संसर्ग इति गौरवम् । जातिशक्तिपक्षे च स्वसमवायित्वं तथेति लाघवात् ।

Translation [NN.II.1]

[a] Among these [five views], the first view is justified on the following grounds.

[b] By the reason of economy [of theoretical assumptions], only a generic property is [held to be] the primary meaning [of a noun]. [This should be the case] by the reason that if different individual entities were primary meanings [of one and the same noun], there would be [unacceptable] prolixity [of theoretical assumptions].

[c] Nor should one claim that there is no decisive way of choosing [between the two alternatives mentioned above] on the ground that each individual entity also has a singularity [of its own, comparable to the singularity of a generic property].

[d] [If one were to accept an individual entity to be the sole primary meaning], in such [a view], there would be [undesirable] prolixity [in resorting to] secondary signification function [of that word to be able to refer to] other individual entities [belonging to the same class]. [This is because, in such a view, one would have to justify the secondary signification function by resorting to a long winding indirect] relation [between the primary meaning (= a certain individual entity) and the secondary meaning (= other individual entities belonging to the same class)]. [The secondary meaning = other individual entities belonging to the same class] is related by inherence to something [i.e. the generic property] which is inherent in [the primary meaning, i.e. the specific initial individual entity].

[e] [On the other hand], there is economy [of assumptions] in the view that the primary signification function [of a noun] is ascertained solely with respect to a generic property. This is because [the relation between a primary meaning, i.e. a generic property, and the secondary meaning, i.e. an individual entity possessing that generic property] is [simply] that of the

secondary meaning [= an individual] being in relation of inherence with [the primary meaning, the generic property].

Explanation [NN.II.1.a]: In the Pāṇinian tradition, the first view that the primary meaning of a noun consists of only one element is presented in two alternatives. Here only one of the two alternatives is presented. Nāgeśabhaṭṭa says that this single meaning element could either be a generic property alone or an individual entity alone.[255] This goes back to Bhartṛhari who says that after the meanings of individual words are abstracted from the initially cognized undivided sentence meaning, one can say that the meaning of all words consists of either a generic property alone or an individual entity alone.[256] Helārāja explains this by saying that, according to Jātivādins, all words primarily denote a generic property alone, while, according to Vyaktivādins, all words primarily denote an individual entity alone.[257] Helārāja's statement is important as a caution, especially when one uses Western terms to refer to Indian semantic theories. For example, Peter M. Scharf's recent (1990) dissertation is titled *The denotation of generic terms in ancient Indian grammar, Nyāya, and Mīmāṃsā*. On the face of it, this wording creates an impression that there are generic terms different from non-generic terms. While this is true for some Indian thinkers in some contexts, theories held by Jātivādins and Vyaktivādins raise global claims about all words. Thus, one would have to say that, for a Jātivādin, all words are generic terms, while, for a Vyaktivādin, all words are non-generic. This is clear from Bhartṛhari and Helārāja [cf. notes 256 and 257].

Patañjali discusses the question of whether Pāṇini was a Jātivādin or a Vyaktivādin. He believes that, according to Pāṇini, both talternatives are valid for different situations.[258] P.1.2.58 (*jāty-ākhyāyām ekasmin bahu-vacanam anyatarasyām*) says: "To denote a *jāti* [= class for Pāṇini, generic property for Patañjali], one may optionally use a plural affix, in the sense of a singular." This rule is taken to support the doctrine that words denote a *jāti* "generic property." P.1.2.64 (*sarūpāṇām eka-śeṣa eka-vibhaktau*) says: "When a number of homophonic nominal stems occur with the same case ending, only one of the homophonic nominal stems is retained [and others are deleted]." This rule is interpreted in the following way. A plural form such as *vṛkṣāḥ* "trees" is grammatically derived from a sequence of many singular forms such as *vṛkṣaś ca vṛkṣaś ca vṛkṣaś ca*. Only one of these stems is retained and a plural affix added after it. For some important comments on the procedure of *eka-śeṣa*, see: B.K. Matilal (1971: 99). This rule is taken to support the view

---

[255] *ekam prātipadikārtha ity asya jāti-vyaktyor madhye 'nyatarad eva tac chakyam ity arthaḥ* /, *LM*, p. 1149.

[256] *padārthānām apoddhāre jātir vā dravyam eva vā* / *padārthau sarva-śabdānāṃ nityāv evopavarṇitau* //, *VP*, III, *Jāti-samuddeśa*, verse 2.

[257] *sarveṣām pada-rūpāṇāṃ jāti-vādi-mate jātir evārtho na dravyam* / *dravya-vādi-mate tu dravyam eva na jātiḥ* /, *VP-H(p)*, p. 8.

[258] *atha dravyam padārtha utākṛtiḥ* / *ubhayam ity āha* / *ubhayathā hy ācāryeṇa sūtrāṇi praṇītāni* / ... *ākṛtim padārtham matvā 'jāty-ākhyāyām ekasmin bahu-vacanam anyatarasyām' ity ucyate* / *dravyam padārtham matvā 'sarūpāṇām' ity eka-śeṣa ārabhyate* /, *MB*, Vol.I., Sec.I., p. 44. One should note here that Patañjali is treating the terms *ākṛti* and *jāti* as synonyms. Pāṇini does not use the term *ākṛti*, and his term *jāti* seems to refer more to a class, than to a generic property. However, Patañjali takes these terms to refer to such an abstract property.

that words primarily denote only a *vyakti* "an individual entity." Grammarians suggest that one chooses between these opposing views depending upon the particular needs of a given grammatical derivation.[259] The view that a generic property alone is the primary meaning of all words is first upheld by the pre-Kātyāyana grammarian Vājapyāyana.[260] This view is later upheld by the Bhāṭṭa school of Mīmāṃsā. Kauṇḍabhaṭṭa follows Mīmāṃsakas in his presentation of this view.

Explanation [NN.II.1.b]: The ontology of a generic property has been discussed in the Introduction [cf. **D.2.i-x**]. The Jātivādin claims that his view has the benefit of economy of assumptions. He argues that, if a generic property alone is the primary meaning of a noun, then one's knowledge of a single relationship between the noun and a given generic property is sufficient to account for verbal cognitions of all individual entities possessing this generic property. On the other hand, if only a single individual entity is the primary meaning of a word, then one would have to assume an infinite number of relationships of one word with all possible individual entities belonging to a class. It is impossible to grasp such an infinite number of relationships, and hence a word would be unable to refer to all individual entities it should be able to refer to. Therefore, it is easier to assume that a noun primarily denotes a generic property.

Explanation [NN.II.1.c]: The reading of this passage as it stands (= *na ca praty-ekaṃ vyaktibhir vinigamanā-virahaḥ*) is difficult to interpret. The two new editions of this text by V.N. Misra and M. Bhattacharya offer neither a new reading, nor indicate that there may be a problem here. The reading of this passage in the shorter version, *VBS*, is probably the correct reading (= *na ca vyaktīnām api praty-ekam ekatvād vinigamanā-virahaḥ*), and I have interpreted the *NN* passage by taking into account the reading as found in the *VBS*.

First Kauṇḍabhaṭṭa presents the view of the Jātivādin, and argues why the view of the Vyaktivādin is not acceptable. Now an objector may say that there is really no way of choosing between these two views. A generic property, shared by a multitude of individual entities, is ontologically speaking a single entity, and hence one claims economy in treating a generic property to be the primary meaning of a noun. But the objector claims that each of the infinite individual entities also has a singularity of its own. Thus, both a generic property as well as a given individual entity have singularity, and hence there is no difference in economy between these two views.

In **NN.II.1.c**, Kauṇḍabhaṭṭa says that this objection should not be raised, and in the following sections, he presents arguments which help one choose between these two alternatives.

Explanation [NN.II.1.d-e]: Kauṇḍabhaṭṭa elaborates the arguments demonstrating economy of assumptions in one view and the lack of economy in the other view. If one

---

259 *pāṇines tūbhayaṃ lakṣyānurodhāt / tat kvacit kiñcid āśrīyate /*, *KS-N*, Vol.I., pp. 42-3.

260 *ākṛty-abhidhānād vaikaṃ vibhaktau vājapyāyanaḥ /*, *Vt.* 38 on P.1.2.64; also see: *MB-P*, Vol.I., Sec.I., pp. 44-5 and *BC*, p. 120. For an analysis of Vājapyāyana's views, see: Matilal (1971: 106ff).

accepts the doctrine of the Jātivādin, then only a generic property is the primary meaning of a noun. How do we then understand individual entities from such a noun? Kauṇḍabhaṭṭa says that one has to accept that the noun signifies (=refers to) individual objects, qualified by the given generic property, through its secondary signification function. Similarly, if one accepts the view of the Vyaktivādin, then a word primarily signifies (= refers to) only a given individual entity. How do we then get this word to signify other individual entities? Kauṇḍabhaṭṭa suggests that even here we must resort to a word's secondary signification function to get it to refer to other individual entities. The prima facie argument now is that if one needs to resort to the secondary signification function of a word to enable it to refer to all individual entities [of a given class], then there is no difference in economy of assumptions.

Kauṇḍabhaṭṭa here [cf. **NN.II.1.d**] points out that, while one does need to resort to a word's secondary signification function in both alternatives, the particulars of these secondary signification functions are different. One has greater economy than the other. The secondary signification function as assumed by the Vyaktivādin has greater prolixity as compared to the secondary signification function as assumed by the Jātivādin [cf. **NN.II.1.e**].

A secondary signification function is thought to be a relation of the primary meaning to the secondary meaning [*sva-śakya-sambandha*]. In the Vyakti-vāda view, the primary meaning of a word is a specific individual entity, while the secondary meaning consists of other individual entities of the same class. The relation between these to, stated in ontological terms, is such that the specific individual entity [= primary meaning] is related by inherence to a generic property, and this generic property is related by inherence to other individual entities [= secondary meaning] belonging to the same class. This is the import of the term *sva-samaveta-samavāyitva*.

Primary Meaning Secondary Meaning
Individual Entity *x* <-----> Generic Property <-----> Other Individual Entities

On the other hand, in the Jāti-vāda view, the primary meaning consists of a generic property alone, and the secondary meaning consists of any individual entity which possesses this generic property. The relation between a generic property and an individual possessing it is that of inherence. Therefore, the relationship between the primary meaning and the secondary meaning is that of a single relation of inherence [*sva-samavāyitva*].

Primary Meaning Secondary Meaning
Generic Property <-----------------------------------> All Individual Entities
belonging to a class

Thus the view of Jāti-vāda is said to involve economy of assumptions. This argument has been discussed in detail by the commentary *Śāṅkarī* on Kauṇḍabhaṭṭa's shorter text, i.e. *Vaiyākaraṇa-bhūṣaṇa-sāra*.[261]

NN.II.2. (p. 117)

किञ्च -

"अन्वयव्यतिरेकाभ्यामेकरूपप्रतीतितः ।
आकृतेः प्रथमज्ञानात्तस्या एवाभिधेयता ॥"

येनापि व्यक्तिर्वाच्याभ्युपेयते तेनापि जातिर्वाच्याभ्युपेयत एव । अन्यथा शुद्धव्यक्तेः शक्यतापत्तेः । तथा चानन्त्याद् व्यभिचाराच्च तत्र शक्तिग्रहानुपपत्तिः ।

Translation [NN.II.2]

[a] Moreover, [the Mīmāṃsakas say]: "It is certain that only a generic property can be a primary meaning, because this is proved -

i) by [using the analytical method of] concurrent occurrence and concurrent non-occurrence;
ii) by the uniform cognition [of meaning from a word in all of its occurrences]; and
iii) by the fact that it [= generic property] is cognized prior [to the cognition of an individual qualified by a generic property]."

[b] Even he [= the Vyaktivādin], who accepts that the primary meaning consists of an individual entity, also accepts a generic property to be part of the primary meaning. Otherwise, a pure individual entity [unqualified by a generic property] would undesirably become the primary meaning.

[c] [In such a view where an unqualified pure individual entity is the primary meaning], it would be impossible to justify the ascertainment of the primary signification function [of a noun], because there is an infinite number of individual entities, and because of the fault of deviation.

Explanation [NN.II.2.a]: The verse quoted here is found in Pārthasārathimiśra's *Śāstra-dīpikā*, and is quoted with a variety of readings in different sources. In *Mīmāṃsā-kośa* [Vol.II., p. 805], the first half of the verse is cited as: *ānantya-vyabhicārābhyām śakty-anekatva-doṣataḥ*. In a footnote to the *Mahābhāṣya* [Vol.I., Sec.II., p. 101], this verse is ascribed to Kumārilabhaṭṭa [cf. *bhaṭṭa-pādair apy uktam*]. However, this verse is not found in the available works of Kumārilabhaṭṭa.

---

261 *VBS-S*, pp. 217-8.

Explanation [NN.II.2.a.i]: The concepts of *anvaya* "concurrent occurrence" and *vyatireka* "concurrent non-occurrence" are discussed in the Introduction [cf. **B.2-4**]. If the generic property is cognized, then an individual qualified by that property can be cognized subsequently. However, if the generic property is not cognized, then one cannot have a subsequent cognition of an individual as qualified by that generic property. Therefore, the generic property must be cognized prior to the cognition of an individual qualified by that generic property. Since, the generic property is thus cognized before the cognition of the individual qualified by that generic property, it alone should be considered to be the primary meaning of a word. Śabara has argued this point at length.[262]

Explanation [NN.II.2.a.ii]: This argument from the *Śāstra-dīpikā* is based on a passage in Kumārilabhaṭṭa's *Tantra-vārttika*.[263] If individual entities, in all their particular colorfulness, were to be the primary meanings of a word, then the verbal cognition derived from a word would be of a different form each time the word is heard. This would have to be the case, because each individual differs from every other individual in some respect. However, in actual experience, the cognition of meaning from a word has a certain uniformity. This uniformity of cognition can be accounted for only by assuming a generic property to be the primary meaning of a word. The same basic argument can also be traced to Kātyāyana and Patañjali, and perhaps to Vājapyāyana, whose version of Jātivāda is discussed at length in the *Mahābhāṣya*.[264]

Explanation [NN.II.2.a.iii]: This argument can also be traced to the works of Śabara and Kumārilabhaṭṭa.[265] When a word such as "bull" is uttered, one cognizes the generic property of bull-ness before cognizing individuals qualified by that generic property. Only after cognizing the generic property, one later cognizes individual entities qualified by that generic property. Thus, for the emergence of a verbal cognition of a generic property, there is no cause other than the cognition of a word. However, the cognition of an individual entity qualified by a generic property can arise only after the cognition of a word and the cognition of a generic property. Considering this cognitive sequence, only a generic property deserves to be included in the primary meaning of a word.

Explanation [NN.II.2.b]: This argument is different from the one in **NN.II.2.a.i.** Naiyāyikas believe that a non-qualificative cognition (*nirvikalpaka-jñāna*) or a cognition of

---

262 *tad etad ātma-pratyakṣaṃ yac chabda uccarite vyaktiḥ pratīyate / kiṃ śabdād utākṛter iti vibhāgo na pratyakṣaḥ / so 'nvaya-vyatirekābhyām avagamyate / antareṇāpi śabdaṃ ya ākṛtim avabudhyeta, avabudhyeta evāsau vyaktim / yas tūccarite 'pi śabde mānasād apacārāt kadācid ākṛtiṃ nopalabheta na jātucid asāv imāṃ vyaktim avagaccheta /*, *MS-B(a)*, Pt.I., p. 305. For the detailed arguments of Śabara in support of Jātivāda, see Peter Scharf (1990).

263 *yadi ca vyaktayo 'bhidheyā bhaveyus tatas tāsāṃ citra-khaṇḍa-muṇḍādi-viśeṣa-svarūpa-grahaṇād vicitrā śabdoccāraṇe buddhiḥ syāt / ekākārā tūtpadyate / tenāpy ākṛtiḥ śabdārtha iti niścīyate /*, *TV(b)*, pp. 272-3.

264 *prakhyāviśeṣāt /*, *Vt*. 39 on P.1.2.64; *na hi gaur ity ukte viśeṣaḥ prakhyāyate śuklā nīlā kapilā kāpotiketi /*, *MB*, Vol.I., Sec.II., pp. 90-1; *avyapavarga-gateś ca /*, *Vt*. 40 on P.1.2.64; *na hi gaur ity ukte vyapavargo gamyate śuklā nīlā kapilā kāpotiketi /*, *MB*, Vol.I., Sec.II., pp. 90-1.

265 *go-śabdoccāraṇe hi pūrvam evāgṛhītāsu vyaktiṣu sāmānyam pratīyate / tad-ākāra-jñānotpatteḥ paścād vyaktayaḥ pratīyante / ataś cākṛti-pratyayasya nimittāntarābhāvāt, vyakti-pratyaye ca pūrva-pratīta-sāmānya-nimittatvād ākṛtiḥ śabdārtha iti vijñāyate /*, *TV(b)*, pp. 272-3.

something not qualified by any property is not useful for any purposeful activity.[266] Therefore, they argue that a word signifies [= refers to] an individual entity qualified by a generic property, and not an individual entity by itself. If the generic property is not included in the primary meaning, and if only an unqualified individual entity is regarded as the primary meaning, it would not serve any purpose.[267] A bull, unqualified by bull-ness, would not even be recognized as a bull, or as a member belonging to the class of bulls. From the cognitive point of view, it would be cognized as a mere something, uncategorized and uncategorizable, and hence of no practical use.

Explanation [NN.II.2.c]: If one accepts the view that an individual alone is the primary meaning, then the intrinsic infinity of individual entities poses a problem. Such an infinity of individuals would lie beyond the range of direct human perception, and hence it would be impossible to ascertain the relation of a word to each and every possible individual entity belonging to a class. Therefore, one can neither accept the theoretical assumption of an infinite number of signification functions for each word in relation to the infinite number of individual entities, nor demonstrate the feasibility of experientially ascertaining all those infinite signification functions. This is the *ānantya* "infinity" argument.

The *vyabhicāra* "deviation" argument goes as follows. To avoid the difficulties pointed out above in the "infinity" argument, one may assume that the primary signification function of a word is ascertained only in relation to a specific individual entity. How do we then account for our experience that we do cognize other individual entities from the same word? Logically speaking, the signification function of a word ascertained with an individual *I* should be able to lead to a verbal cognition of *I* alone and no other individual. Should there be a verbal cognition of an individual other than *I*, even when the signification function of the word is ascertained in relation to *I* alone, this leads to a violation of the postulated cause-effect relationship. Such violations or deviations ultimately lead to the rejection of the postulated causal relationship.[268]

NN.II.3. (p. 117)

एवं चावश्यकत्वात् सैव वाच्यास्तु । एकाकारप्रतीतिश्च शुद्धव्यक्तिवाच्यत्वे न स्यात् । खण्डत्वादेरेव शक्यतावच्छेदकत्वात् । प्रथमत आकृतेरेवोपस्थितेश्च । एवं च नागृहीतविशेषणान्यायेन जातेर्वाच्यत्वावश्यकत्वादास्तां सैवार्थ इति ।

---

266 *na hi svarūpeṇa padārthasya padārthāntarānvayitayā bhānaṃ kaiścit svīkriyate /*, *SV*, p. 200.

267 *nirdharmitāvacchedaka-śābda-bodhasya pravṛtty-ādy-anupayogitayā tat-svīkārāsambhavāt /*, *SV*, p. 200.

268 *ākṛti-vyatirikte 'rthe sambandho nityatāsya ca / na siddhyetām iti jñātvā tad-vācyatvam ihocyate //*, *SLV*, p. 545; *yadi hi ākṛti-vyatiriktā vyaktaya eva sarvatra śabdārthāḥ syus tatas tābhir vyabhicārāt sambandha eva śabdasya na siddhyati / natarāṃ nityatvam / ākṛti-vācyatve tu kvacit tayaiva kvacit tad-viśiṣṭenārthāntareṇa siddhyati śabdasya sambandho nityatā ceti /*, *SLV-N*, p. 545; Also see: *MB-P*, Vol.I., Sec.I., pp. 44-5; *TMT*, Pt.I., p. 135; *BC*, p. 120; *KP*, p. 32; and *LM*, pp. 1105-7.

Translation [NN.II.3]

[a] Thus, by necessity, let the [generic property] be the sole primary meaning [of a noun].

[b] If a pure individual entity [= unqualified by a generic property] were to be the primary meaning, there would not be a uniform verbal cognition [each time the noun is used]. [Such would be the case], because [without the cognition of a generic property] only an individual property such as Khaṇḍa-ness [= particularity pertaining to the specific bull named Khaṇḍa] would be the limitor of primary-meaning-ness [i.e. would regulate eligibility of an entity for inclusion in primary meaning].

[c] [One must finally accept a generic property to be the sole primary meaning], because a generic property is cognized prior [to the cognition of an individual entity qualified by that generic property].

[d] It is necessary to have a generic property included in the primary meaning by the following (cognitive) rule: Without first cognizing the qualifying property, one cannot have a cognition of an entity qualified by that property. Therefore, let it be the sole primary meaning.

Explanation [NN.II.3.a]: To account for a word's ability to refer to all members of a given class, the minimal necessary condition is that one should first have a cognition of the generic property or the class property which regulates membership of this class. If, by this logic, the generic property needs to be cognized before cognizing any individual entity qualified by that generic property, then one need not treat such individual entities to be the primary meaning of a word. This is in accord with the maxim: *ananya-labhyaḥ śabdārthaḥ* "An *x* can be treated as a meaning of a given word *W*, if and only if its cognition is derived solely from *W*." Since, individual entities qualified by a generic property are cognized subsequently on the basis of the cognition of the generic property, and not directly from the word, one cannot consider such individual entities as being part of the primary meaning.

Explanation [NN.II.3.b]: This argument is a further explanation of **NN.II.2.a.ii**. If an unqualified individual were the primary meaning, then each time the verbal cognition would yield a different form. In each instance of verbal cognition, the specificity of a given individual would characterize that individual as it becomes the meaning of a word. This is what is meant by the technical statement that specific properties like Khaṇḍa-ness would become limitors of primary-meaning-ness. For the concept of *śakyatāvacchedaka*, see: Introduction, **[E.2]**. Normally, a generic property functions as the limitor of primary-meaning-ness, i.e. its possession by an individual entity is the necessary and sufficient condition for membership of that entity into the class of entities that a word can refer to. Since, the generic property, functioning as a regulating property, appears as part of the primary meaning, there is a certain uniformity of verbal cognition of each different individual entity. However, if the generic property were not to be cognized, and not to function as a regulating property, then individual entities will be cognized in their particularity, and this would lead to the loss of uniformity of verbal cognition of different individual entities.[269]

Explanation [NN.II.3.c]: This argument is simply a restatement of **NN.II.2.a.iii**.

Explanation [NN.3.d]: This elaborates the argument in **NN.II.3.c**. The elaborate argument occurs in the works of Śabara, Kumārilabhaṭṭa, and several other authors. [270] The maxim quoted by Kauṇḍabhaṭṭa simply says that a cognition of a qualifying property is an essential pre-condition for a cognition of something qualified by that property. Mīmāṃsakas extend this argument to imply that once a word signifies a generic property by its primary signification function, this primary signification function is exhausted or used up and is not capable of further signifying [= referring to] an individual entity qualified by that generic property. The cognition of an individual qualified by the generic property comes on the basis of the secondary signification function of a word. This is the standard argument of the Bhāṭṭa school of Mīmāṃsā.[271]

NN.II.4. (p. 117)

नन्वेवं गां दद्याद् व्रीहीनवहन्तीत्यादिस्थले कथमन्वयः । जातौ तदयोगात् । कथं वा दानकर्मता गोत्वादेरिति चेदत्राक्षेपितव्यक्तौ दानाद्यन्वयः कर्मतापि तस्या एवेत्याहुः । तन्न । प्रत्ययानां प्रकृत्यर्थान्वितेत्यादिव्युत्पत्तेः कर्मत्वान्वयस्यासम्भवात् । उक्तं हि तद्भूताधिकरणे -

"गम्यमानस्य चार्थस्य नैव दृष्टं विशेषणम् ।
शब्दान्तरैर्विभक्त्या वा धूमोऽयं ज्वलतीतिवत् ॥"

Translation [NN.II.4]

[a] [Objection to Jāti-vāda]: If [a generic property is the sole primary meaning], then how to explain the relationship in [sentences like] "one should give a bull (or cow)" and "one husks rice"? [A difficulty arises in interpreting such sentences] because these [acts of giving and husking] cannot be

---

269 *MB*, Vol.I., Sec.II., pp. 90-1; *TV(b)*, pp. 272-3.

270 *gotvaṃ lakṣaṇam bhaviṣyati / yatra gotvaṃ tasyāṃ vyaktāv iti / evaṃ tarhi viśiṣṭā vyaktiḥ pratīyeta / yadi ca viśiṣṭā, pūrvataraṃ viśeṣaṇam avagamyeta / na hy apratīte viśeṣaṇe viśiṣṭaṃ kecana pratyetum arhanti /*, *MS-B(a)*, Pt.I., p. 304; *TV(A)*, Pt.I., pp. 304, 314; *tatra nāgṛhīta-viśeṣaṇā viśeṣye buddhir ity ādau sāmānyam abhidhīyate /*, *MB-P*, Vol.I., Sec.I., p. 312; *viśiṣta-buddhau viśeṣaṇa-jñānasya kāraṇatvāt pūrvaṃ jāty-ādi-jñānam /*, *BSS*, Pt.I., p. 635.

271 *yadi cātrākṛtiḥ pratīyeta śabdena, tadā vyaktir api padārtha iti na śakyate vaktum / kutaḥ / ākṛtir hi vyaktyā nitya-sambaddhā / sambandhinyāṃ ca tasyām avagatāyāṃ sambandhy-antaram avagamyate /*, *MS-B(a)*, Pt.I., p. 305; *jātiś cet pūrvam abhidheyatvenābhyupagatātraiva śabdasyopakṣīṇatvāt na vyakti-vacanatā labhyate / na cākṛti-saṃvedanenāpi vyakti-pratīter anyathāpy upapannatvāt satyāṃ gatāv anekārthatā yujyate 'bhyupagantum / arthāpattyā ca śabdasya vācaka-śaktiḥ kalpyate, sā ca yadā vyakti-pratīter anyathāpy upapannatvāt kṣīṇā, tadā vācaka-śakti-kalpanāyām pramāṇaṃ nāsti / ... anvaya-vyatirekābhyāṃ vyakter aśabdārthatvaṃ niścīyate /*, *TV(b)*, p. 276; also see: *KP*, pp. 44-5.

construed with the generic property [i.e. bull-ness or rice-ness]. How can the generic property of bull-ness be the object of the action of giving?

[b] [Jātivādin's Reply]: If this is the objection, then some say that actions of giving etc. are construed with the individual entity implied [by the inapplicability of such actions to the generic property], and the same [implied individual entity] will bear the relation of being an object [of those actions].

[c] [Vyaktivādin's Response]: That cannot be [accepted]. It is impossible to construe [the affix-meaning] "object-ness" [with the implied individual], due to the following rule: "Affixes signify their meaning as related to the [primary] meaning of stems."

[d] [Vyaktivādin's Response continued]: Also it would not be possible to construe the primary meaning of one word with [the individual entity] implied by another word. For it is said in the *Tadbhūtādhikaraṇa*: "We do not find that a meaning which is implied by a word is qualified either by other words or by a case-ending. For instance, [we cannot say]: 'This smoke is burning'."

Explanation [NN.II.4.a]: This argument is based on the assumption that a cognition of sentence-meaning should directly lead a person to some purposeful activity. The Vyaktivādin claims that his view fares much better in this respect, as compared to the view of the Jātivādin. The specific argument given here can be traced as far back as Kātyāyana's presentation of Vyāḍi's view, and it is elaborated in Mīmāṃsā and Nyāya texts.[272] If one can show that sentences like "bring a bull" and "husk rice" directly lead to purposeful action in a particular view of meaning, then that view must be preferable. If the primary meaning consists of individual entities, then it is easy to explain such sentences, since the activities stipulated in these sentences can be carried out with respect to individual entities, but not with respect to generic properties. One can bring a bull, but not bull-ness. One can husk rice, but not rice-ness. Eternal and immutable generic properties are incompatible with actions. If one were to insist on generic properties being the primary meaning, then these sentences would be comparable to the Nyāya example of semantic incompatibility: "X irrigates with fire."[273]

---

272 *codanāsu ca tasyārambhāt /*, *Vt.* 50 on P.1.2.64; *codanāsu ca tasyārambhāt manyāmahe dravyam abhidhīyata iti /*, *MB*, Vol.I., Sec.II., p. 95; *tad ucyate vyaktiḥ śabdārtha iti / kutaḥ / prayoga-codanābhāvāt / ālambhana-viśasana-prokṣaṇādīnām prayoga-codanā ākṛty-arthe na sambhaveyuḥ /*, *MS-B(a)*, Pt.I., p. 300; *ākṛtir yadi śabdārthaḥ kasya syuḥ prokṣaṇādayaḥ / kena cejyeta na tyāga ākṛter upapadyate // amūrtā hy ākṛtir nityā nāvaghātādi-bhājanī / tad-vidhiḥ pratiṣedho vā tenāsyā nāvakalpate //*, *TV(b)*, pp. 255-6; Also ibid., pp. 257, 262, 269-70; *vaidyāya gāṃ dadātīti dravyasya tyāgo na jāter amūrtatvāt /*, *NS-B*, p. 152. The same argument is presented in Mīmāṃsā texts as a *pūrva-pakṣa* "prima-facie view," while it appears as the *siddhānta-pakṣa* "final view" in Nyāya texts.

273 *agninā siñcatīti vākyaṃ na pramāṇaṃ yogyatā-virahāt /*, *TC*, p. 68.

Explanation [NN.II.4.b]: This is the reply of the Jātivādin. The Jātivādin argues that a word primarily signifies a generic property, and this generic property further implies (*ākṣepa*) the individual entity possessing that generic property. Though the primary meaning of words like "bull," i.e. the generic property of bull-ness, cannot be construed with an action like giving, the implied individual can be construed with such actions. A similar argument can be traced to Patañjali's *Mahābhāṣya*.[274]

Kauṇḍabhaṭṭa says that, according to this view, the implied individual entity becomes the object of actions of giving etc. This is true in referential terms. However, grammarians seem to disagree on whether such a connection can be justified on cognitive grounds. For example, Nāgeśabhaṭṭa says that, according to Kaiyaṭa, only the generic property appears in the contents of a verbal cognition, and that the performance of an action such as giving with respect to the implied individual is only accidental. This suggests that this extension of action to the implied individual is not something that one learns from any signification function of the word, but is a matter perhaps of external inference or presumption. For example, if one is asked to bring fire, he brings it in some container. This container is not requested, and yet must be brought in. Though it is necessary, it is accidental as far as the verbal cognition is concerned.[275] The Naiyāyika author Jagadīśa Bhaṭṭācārya interprets the view of the Mīmāṃsakas in a similar fashion.[276]

However, it appears that Śabara and Kumārilabhaṭṭa have a slightly different view. They accept the generic property as the sole primary meaning, and yet this primary meaning finally becomes a qualifier of the individual entity signified indirectly by the word. Whether the primary meaning is directly construed with the action, or is subordinated to the secondary meaning depends upon the context of the sentence, and one's understanding of the speaker's intention.[277]

Explanation [NN.II.4.c]: In the sentence *gāṃ dadyāt* "one should give a bull (or a cow)," the word *gām* is the accusative singular of the nominal stem *go*, derived by adding the affix *-am* denoting the notion of grammatical object-ness (*karmatva*). We are expected to construe the meaning of the stem with the meaning of the affix. Mīmāṃsakas construe the affix-meaning "object-ness" with the implied meaning of the nominal *go*, i.e. the implied individual, and not with the primary meaning of the word, i.e. the generic property of bull-ness.

The Vyaktivādin rejects this position of the Jātivādin. For this purpose, he brings in a maxim, and interprets it to mean that affixes signify their meaning as related to the primary

---

274 *adhikaraṇa-gatiḥ sāhacaryāt* /, *Vt.* 61 on P.1.2.64; *ākṛtāv ārambhaṇādīnāṃ sambhavo nāstīti kṛtvākṛti-sahacarite dravye ārambhaṇādīni bhaviṣyanti* /, *MB*, Vol.I., Sec.II., p. 99; *sarva evākṛteḥ kriyāyogo 'ntar-bhāvita-dravyāyā eveti dravya-dvāraka eva sampadyate* /, *MB-P*, Vol.I., Sec.II., p. 99.

275 *ākṛtir eva taj-janya-bodhe pradhānam, kriyā tu pātre iva dravya iti bhāvaḥ* /, *MB-P-U*, Vol.I., Sec.II., p. 99.

276 *gām ānayety ādau gotvādi-karmatākatvenaiva ānayanāder anvaya-dhīḥ* / *gavādi-karmatākatvena bodhas tu uttara-kālam ākṣepāt* /, *SSP(a)*, p. 81.

277 *vrīhi-śabda ākṛti-vacanaḥ prayujyate prokṣaṇāśraya-viśeṣaṇāya* / ... *evaṃ ṣaḍ deyā gāvo dakṣiṇā iti dakṣiṇā-dravye* ... *gāva iti ākṛti-vacano viśeṣakaḥ* /, *MS-B(a)*, Pt. VI, p. 2073; also: ibid., Pt. IV, p. 1423,; and *TV(b)*, pp. 276-8.

meaning of the stem, and not just to any meaning of the stem. With the maxim interpreted in this way, the Jātivādin's explanation fails to satisfy this maxim, because the Jātivādin tries to relate the implied meaning of the stem to the meaning of the affix. This criticism of the Jātivādin is attested in Gaṅgeśa's *Tattva-cintāmaṇi*.[278]

Explanation [NN.II.4.d]: This argument of the Vyaktivādin is based on another maxim: *padārthaḥ padārthenānveti, na tu tad-eka-deśena* "The primary meaning of a word is construed with the primary meaning of another word, and not to just a portion of it."[279] For this reason, a sentence such as *ghaṭo nityaḥ* cannot be valid and mean "pot-ness is eternal." The generic property of pot-ness is eternal, but the individual pot is not eternal. The meaning of the word "pot," according to Nyāya, is an individual qualified by pot-ness, and not pot-ness by itself. Therefore, this eternal pot-ness cannot be construed with the primary meaning of the word "eternal." Similarly, the attempt of the Jātivādin to construe the primary meaning of one word with the implied meaning of another word is not acceptable.

Kauṇḍabhaṭṭa interestingly quotes a verse from Kumārilabhaṭṭa's *Śloka-vārttika* as an argument against the view of the Mīmāṃsakas.[280] Pārthasārathimiśra comments that neither the singular in *dhūmaḥ* "[a] smoke," nor the activity of burning signified by the verb *jvalati* "is burning" can be construed with fire, which is not the primary meaning of the word *dhūma* "smoke," but is implied by it. Therefore, the sentence *dhūmo 'yaṃ jvalati* cannot be taken to mean: "this fire is burning."[281] Similarly, says the Vyaktivādin, the Jātivādin cannot construe the implied individual with the action of bringing in the sentence *gām ānaya*. If the primary meaning of this sentence, for the Jātivādin, is "bring bull-ness," it cannot then be taken to mean "bring a bull."

NN.II.5. (p. 117-8)

कश्चाक्षेपपदार्थः । अर्थापत्तिरिति चेन्न । अनुपपत्तिज्ञानमन्तरेणापि गां दद्यादित्यतो बोधदर्शनात् । उक्तदोषानतिरेकाच्च । समानवित्तिवेद्यत्वमिति चेन्न । द्रव्यमित्यादिघटज्ञाने घटत्वभानाभावात् । लक्षणयोपस्थितव्यक्तौ तदन्वयान्नानुपपत्तिरित्यन्ये । तन्न । लक्षणायाः शक्यान्वयानुपपत्तिज्ञानाधीनत्वेनोक्तदोषादिति । अत्र वदन्ति । निरूढलक्षणया जातिव्यक्त्योरभेदाद्वा व्यक्तेर्लाभः । तदुक्तं भट्टैः -

"तेन तल्लक्षितव्यक्तेः क्रियासम्बन्धचोदना ।

---

278 *vayaṃ tu brūmaḥ, vyakter apadārthatve vibhakty-artha-saṃkhyā-karmatvāder vyaktāv ananvayaḥ syāt, sub-vibhaktīnām prakṛty-arthānvita-svārtha-bodhakatvasya vyutpatti-siddhatvāt /*, *TC*, p. 586; Also: *TC*, p. 685; *VV*, p. 71; and *MD*, pp. 77-8.

279 *padārthaḥ padārthenanveti na padārthaika-deśeneti vyutpatteḥ svarūpam / etasyāḥ vyutpatter aṅgīkārād eva ghaṭatve 'bhedena nityānvaya-tātparyakasya 'nityo ghaṭa' iti vākyasya nāpattiḥ / ghaṭatvasya padārthaika-deśatvena tatra nityānvayasya prakṛta-vyutpatti-viruddhatvāt /*, *Jayā* on *VV*, p. 21.

280 *SLV*, p. 858. This verse is sometimes wrongly ascribed to Bhartṛhari, see: *VBS-P*, p. 234.

281 *na hi dhūma ity ekatvaṃ jvalati-kriyā vāgner viśeṣaṇam /*, *SLV-N*, p. 858.

जातिव्यक्त्योरभेदो वा वाक्यार्थेषु विवक्षितः ॥" इति ।

Translation [NN.II.5]

[a] What does the word *ākṣepa* mean?

[b] If [by the word *ākṣepa*] presumption [is meant], then [this interpretation] is not valid. It is observed that there is a verbal cognition from [statements such as] "one should give a bull (or a cow)," even when there is no awareness of any difficulty [of construing the primary meaning]. [Even if one were to accept this view for the sake of argument], one cannot avoid the problems pointed out [earlier].

[c] If [by the word *ākṣepa*, one means that individuals are] cognized by the same cognition [which grasps the generic property], then this [too] is not valid. In the cognition of a pot as a substance, [the generic property] potness is not perceived.

[d] Others think that there is no such difficulty, since these [actions of giving, husking etc.] can be construed with the individual entity cognized through the secondary signification function. This is not valid. This view has the same difficulty as pointed out above. A secondary signification function is dependent upon the realization of the difficulty of construing the primary meaning [and there is no difficulty noticed in construing the meaning of a sentence like "one should give a bull"].

[e] Here some argue that [the cognition of] the individual could be secured either through the conventionalized secondary signification function, or through non-difference between the generic property and the individual.

[f] Thus it is said by [Kumārila]bhaṭṭa: "Therefore, the [Vedic] injunction of performing an action relates to the individual entity ascertained secondarily through that [generic property], or one intends non-difference of a generic property and the individual entity in construing the meaning of a sentence."

Explanation [NN.II.5.a]: This questions the validity of the reply given by the Jātivādin in **NN.II.4.b**, by criticizing the various conceptions of *ākṣepa* "implication."

Explanation [NN.II.5.b]: Presumption (*arthāpatti*) is a kind of necessary assumption. The standard example of presumption in Sanskrit texts is *pīno devadatto divā na bhuṅkte* "Devadatta, who is fat, does not eat during the day."[282] Unless we presume that Devadatta eats at night, we cannot explain his fatness. Similarly, in the view that the term *ākṣepa* refers to presumption, one presumes that actions such as giving and husking relate to individuals qualified by generic properties, since they cannot relate to those generic

---

282 *tatropapādya-jñānenopapādaka-kalpanam arthāpattiḥ / yathā rātri-bhojanena vinā divābhuñjānasya pīnatvam anupapannam /, VPB*, p. 117.

properties themselves. Without such a presumption, one cannot construe the meaning of a sentence such as "one should give a bull."[283]

The essential condition for presumption is that there must be an awareness of the difficulty of justifying the primary meaning.[284] Kauṇḍabhaṭṭa says that, in our common experience, there is no such awareness of the difficulty in understanding the meaning of a sentence like "bring a bull." One comprehends the meaning of such sentences immediately, and hence the Mīmāṃsaka notion of presumption cannot be accepted. Several texts elaborate this argument.[285] Even if one accepts the notion of presumption as the basis for the cognition of an individual entity, still this individual cannot treated as the primary meaning of that word. Hence the difficulty pointed out in **NN.II.4.c-d** still remains unresolved. As it is observed in **Explanation [NN.II.4.cd]**, only a primary meaning of a word can be construed with the meaning of an affix or with the primary meaning of another word.

Explanation [NN.II.5.c]: According to this interpretation, *ākṣepa* refers to the notion of *samāna-saṃvitti-vedyatva.* If two elements, say *x* and *y*, are so closely related that neither of them can be cognized without cognizing the other, then one could say that they are both cognized by the same act of cognition. According to this view, an individual and a generic property are so closely related to each other that one cannot be cognized without cognizing the other. For this reason, the cognition which grasps the generic property also grasps the individual entity. This view has been endorsed by the Prābhākara school of Mīmāṃsā, and by some Vedānta authors like Dharmarāja Adhvarīndra.[286]

Kauṇḍabhaṭṭa argues that this view of *ākṣepa* is equally unacceptable. When somebody looks at a pot, not as a pot, but as a mere substance, one does not cognize the generic property of pot-ness. If the above notion of *ākṣepa* were true, each time one had a cognition of a pot, one would also have a cognition of pot-ness. But, apparently, one can have a cognition of a pot as a substance, without recognizing its generic property of pot-ness.

Other thinkers have offered further arguments against this view of *ākṣepa*. The commentary *Prabhā* on the *Vaiyākaraṇa-bhūṣaṇa-sāra* says that this view of *ākṣepa* is not valid, because when one hears the sentence *gotvam ānaya* "bring bull-ness," one does not have a verbal cognition: "bring an individual possessed of bull-ness."[287] The *Maṇi-darpaṇa* remarks that, in the false cognition of a shell as silver, one cognizes the generic

---

283 *arthāpatter vā tat-siddhiḥ [bhāṭṭa-mate] /*, *TC*, p. 584; *ākṣepād iti - arthāpatti-pramāṇād iti /*, *Nīla-kaṇṭha-prakāśikā* on *TS-D*, p. 317; *ākṣepaś cānumānam arthāpattir vā /*, *SV*, p. 207; and *NK*, pp. 334-5. Kauṇḍabhaṭṭa does not mention the interpretation of *ākṣepa* as inference (*anumāna*). For a detailed treatment of these two views, see: *TC*, pp. 584-7; *SV*, pp. 207ff; *SSP(a)*, pp. 80-2 and 85-6.

284 *ākṣepo 'nupapatti-pratisandhānam /*, *Rāmarudrīya* on *TS-D*, p. 319.

285 *arthāpatter api nāvasaraḥ / anupapatti-jñānam antareṇāpi bodhāt /*, *LM*, p. 1124,; *KM*, p. 570; *TC*, pp. 584ff.

286 *jñeyasya jñāna-vitti-vedyatvavat vyakter api jāti-vitti-vedyatvam anatiprasaṅgāt iti prābhākarāḥ /*, *MD*, p. 77; *jāter vyakti-samāna-saṃvedyatvād iti brūmaḥ /*, *VPB*, p. 94.

287 *gotvam asti iti vākya-janya-pratyaye jāti-viṣayatāyāḥ sattve 'pi gotva-viśiṣṭa-vyakter abodhena vyabhicārāt /*, *VBS-P*, p. 234.

property of silver-ness, but not the individual.[288] Nāgeśabhaṭṭa points out that even if one were to accept this view of *ākṣepa*, the generic property and the individual appearing in the contents of a single cognition would appear as two elements simply added together (*samūhālambana-jñāna*), and there would not emerge a qualificative cognition (*viśiṣṭa-buddhi*).[289] Bhavadeva shows a further difficulty. Acceptance of such a view of *ākṣepa* would force the Prābhākaras to abandon their doctrine that the generic property alone is the primary meaning. It is contradictory to say that the generic property and the individual are both cognized by the same act of cognition, and yet only the generic property is the primary meaning.[290]

Explanation [NN.II.5.d]: This is not an interpretation of the term *ākṣepa*, but a new alternative view. Gaṅgeśa also treats the conception of *lakṣaṇā* "secondary signification function" as an alternative to *ākṣepa*.[291] The notion of a secondary signification function has been explained in the Introduction [cf. **E.5**]. In several passages, Śabara and Kumārila-bhaṭṭa advocate that the generic property is the primary meaning of a word, while individuals are cognized through the secondary signification function.[292]

This view also suffers from the problem that, in actual experience, we do not require to have an awareness of a difficulty in justifying or construing the primary meaning in interpreting simple sentences like "bring a bull." No one is aware of any difficulty, and such an awareness of a difficulty in construing the primary meaning is said to be the basis for moving on to the secondary signification function.[293] For these reasons, it is not proper to claim that a word primarily signifies a generic property and signifies an individual entity through a secondary signification function.

Explanation [NN.II.5.e]: This is a further modification of the view of *lakṣaṇā* presented in **NN.II.5.d**. According to this view, a word signifies only a generic property through its primary signification function, and yet the individuals are cognized through a conventional secondary signification function (*nirūḍha-lakṣaṇā*). This sub-type of secondary signification function has been explained in the Introduction [**E.5.iii**]. This kind of secondary signification function is so deeply entrenched in usage, that it is as good as the primary signification function, and that it does not require any awareness of a difficulty in construing the primary meaning of a word.

---

288 *atra rajatatvam iti bhrame jāti-bhāne 'pi vyakter abhānāt na jāti-vitti-vedyatā vyakteḥ* / , *MD*, p. 77.

289 *kiñ ca gavā vaiśiṣṭyena ca gotvasya samāna-vitti-vedyatve 'pi go-gotva-vaiśiṣṭyānīti samūhālambanam eva syāt, na viśiṣṭa-buddhir ity āhuḥ* / , *LM*, p. 1124.

290 *tathā jāti-vyaktyor eka-saṃvit-saṃvedyatve jātir evābhidheyeti siddhānto 'py anupapannaḥ* / *yato 'bhidhāna-kriyā-janita-jñāna-viṣayatvaṃ khalu vācyatvam* / *tac cākṛter abhyupagamya tasminn eva jñāne vyaktiḥ pratibhāsamānā nābhidhīyata iti citram* / , *TMT*, Pt.I., p. 136.

291 *ata eva na vyakter ākṣepaḥ, kintu lakṣaṇayā* ... / , *TC*, p. 587.

292 *ākṛti-vacanaḥ śabdas tat-sahacaritāṃ vyaktiṃ lakṣayati* / , *MS-B*, quoted in *MK*, Vol.II., p. 780; *vrīhīn prokṣatīti hi vrīhi-jātir nirdiśyate vrīhi-dravya-lakṣaṇārthā* / , *MS-B(a)*, Pt. V, p. 1660; *sāmānādhikaraṇyādi ca lakṣaṇayā kalpyam* / , *TV*, quoted in *MK*, Vol.II., p. 796; *vyakter lakṣaṇayā bodhaḥ* / , *Bhāṭṭa-dīpikā*, quoted in *MK*, Vol.II., p. 806.

293 *vyāptyādi-pratisandhānaṃ vināpi bodhāt* / *etena jāti-śaktasya vyaktau lakṣaṇety apāstam* / , *LM*, p. 1124; *na ca vyaktau lakṣaṇā* / *anupapatti-pratisandhānaṃ vināpi vyakti-bodhāt* / , *KM*, pp. 570-1.

The other alternative is that the generic property and the individual are considered to be non-different from each other. This means that they are conceptually and analytically separable from each other, but they are not separable cognitively or ontologically. Pārthasārathimiśra says that each individual object (*vastu*) has two aspects, i.e. a particular or individual aspect, and a generic aspect. Of these two aspects of an object, the generic aspect is the primary meaning. That which is signified by a word in its generic aspect is also said to be related to an action such as bringing or husking in its particular aspect. The same thing is capable of engaging in an action in its particular aspect.[294] Pārthasārathimiśra mentions both the alternatives, i.e. access to the individual either through a secondary signification function, or through non-difference between a generic property and the individual.

Explanation [NN.II.5.f]: The verse quoted here is not found in the works of Kumārilabhaṭṭa, though Kauṇḍabhaṭṭa seems to ascribe it to him. The verse itself actually speaks of *lakṣaṇā* in generic terms, rather than referring specifically to the sub-type *nirūḍha-lakṣaṇā*. However, Kauṇḍabhaṭṭa takes it to refer to this sub-type. The two views found in this verse can be traced in their general form as far back as Patañjali.[295] It is interesting to note that in explaining the second alternative, Patañjali uses the term *avyatireka* "inseparability," rather than *abheda* "non-difference." Later authors seem to have shifted to the use of the term *abheda*. While the notion of inseparability of a generic property and an individual is more defensible in the context of the present debate, their non-difference would create more problems.

Kauṇḍabhaṭṭa seems to suggest that, for Mīmāṃsakas, a word primarily signifies a generic property, and the individual is understood from the conventional, rather than the simple secondary signification function of a word. However, this is contradicted by the testimony of Śabara and Kumārilabhaṭṭa.[296] Both offer examples of secondary signification function which make it clear that they mean to refer to the simple secondary

---

294 *na hi jātir nāma vyakter arthāntara-bhūtaṃ kim api tattvam / api tu vastv eva hy ekam ubhayātmakaṃ vyāvṛtty-anugata-rūpatayā buddhyate / tatra sāmānyaṃ śabdārthaḥ / ... yac ca sāmānyātmanā śabdena bodhitaṃ tasya kriyā-sambandhaś codyate / śaknoti ca tat kriyāṃ sādhayitum /*, *Śāstra-dīpikā*, quoted in a footnote to *MB* Vol.I., Sec.II., p. 101; Also: *vyakty-ākṛtyor abhedāc ca vyavahāropayogitā /*, *Śāstra-dīpikā*, quoted by Kunjunni Raja (1963: 73).

295 *atheha gaur anubandhyo 'jo 'gnīṣomīya iti katham ākṛtau coditāyāṃ dravye ārambhaṇālambhana-prokṣaṇa-viśasanādīni kriyante iti / ... ākṛtāv ārambhaṇādīnāṃ sambhavo nāstīti kṛtvā ākṛti-sahacarite dravye ārambhaṇādīni kriyante / ... athavā avyatirekād dravyākṛtyoḥ /*, *MB*, Vol.I., Sec.II., p. 386, and Vol.II., p. 370. The first alternative is not strictly speaking that of *lakṣaṇā*, though it is very close to it. On the second alternative, commentators point out that ontologically there is no difference between an individual and a generic property. The difference is made only in our conceptual analysis. *vāstava-bhedābhāvāt, buddhi-parikalpita-bheda-sadbhāvāt /*, *MB-P*, Vol.I., Sec.II., p. 386.

296 *atra gav-ākṛtau dharmaḥ śrūyate / ākṛteḥ padārthatvāt / na ca tatra sambhavati / ato 'sāv ākṛtiḥ sahacāri-piṇḍa-lakṣaṇārthā vijñāyate / yathā gaṅgāyāṃ ghoṣa iti /*, *MS-B(a)*, Pt. IV., pp. 1530-1; *yathaivākṛti-vacanaḥ śabdas tat-sahacaritāṃ vyaktiṃ lakṣayati, tathaiva yaṣṭi-mañcāśvādayaḥ tat-sambaddha-puruṣa-lakṣaṇārthā bhavanti /*, *TV(b)*, p. 318; also p. 1021. Bhavadeva presents a novel interpretation of Kumārilabhaṭṭa's view. He says that Kumārilabhaṭṭa's *lakṣaṇā* is not really a "secondary" signification function, but it is an extension of *abhidhā* "primary" signification function. He says: *ākṛty-abhidhānasyaiva vyakti-paryantatvād eka evāyam ubhayārthābhidhāna-lakṣaṇaḥ śabda-vyāpāraḥ / ... ākṛteḥ sākṣād evābhidhāna-viṣayatvam / ato vyaktir api śabdasyābhidhā-vyāpāra-pratipādyaiva, na tu vyāpārāntara-pratipādyā / anenaivābhiprāyeṇa vārttikakāra-pādair apy uktam - abhidheyāvinābhūta-pratītir lakṣaṇocyate /*, *TMT*, Vol. I., pp. 142-3.

signification function. For instance, an example such as *gaṅgāyāṃ ghoṣaḥ* "the cowherd-colony is on the river Ganges" is not generally considered to be an example of the conventional secondary signification function, but rather that of the simple secondary signification function. They also refer to the notion that one recognizes the difficulty of construing a generic property to the ritual action, and hence moves to the secondary signification function. This would also indicate that they mean to refer to the simple secondary signification function.

It is likely that Kauṇḍabhaṭṭa must have been following some neo-Mīmāṃsaka in making the claim about *nirūḍha-lakṣaṇā*. Such a possibility is strengthened by the fact that a late Mīmāṃsā text, the *Bhāṭṭa-cintāmaṇi*, presents *nirūḍha-lakṣaṇā* as one of the alternative explanations of the term *ākṣepa*, without referring to the simple secondary signification function.[297]

NN.II.6. (p. 118)

नन्वेवं व्यक्तौ संख्याकारकाद्यनन्वयप्रसङ्गः प्रत्ययानामिति व्युत्पत्तेरिति चेन्न । प्रकृत्यर्थत्वं हि वृत्त्या प्रकृत्युपस्थाप्यत्वम् । अन्यथा गङ्गायां घोष इत्यत्र तीरेऽधिकरणत्वान्वयानापत्तेः । तथा च लक्षणयोपस्थितव्यक्तौ तदन्वयो न विरुद्धः ।

Translation [NN.II.6]

[a] [Objection by the Vyaktivādin]: If [the individual is ascertained through the secondary signification function of a word] then there may be a difficulty in construing the [meanings of case-endings such as] number and *kāraka* [with the individual], because of the following maxim: "Affixes signify their meaning as related to the [primary] meaning of their stems."

[b] [Jātivādin's reply]: Such an objection is not valid. The term *prakṛty-artha* "meaning of a stem," [in the maxim you have cited], simply refers to anything that is cognized from a word through its signification function [i.e. *vṛtti*, which includes both the primary and secondary signification functions]. Otherwise, [if this term referred only to primary meaning], one would not be able to construe [the affix-meaning] "locus-ness" with the bank [of the river Ganges, i.e the secondary meaning of the word "Ganges"] in the sentence "there is a cowherd-colony on the Ganges."

[c] Hence, construing these [actions of giving etc.] with the individual ascertained through the secondary signification function is not contrary [to the above maxim].

---

297 *ākṣepo 'rthāpattiḥ samāna-vitti-vedyatvaṃ vā nirūḍha-lakṣaṇā vā* /, *BC*, pp. 120-1.

Explanation [NN.II.6.a]: This is a reiteration of the objection raised in **NN.II.4.c-d** for subsequent rejection, cf. **Explanation [NN.II.4.c-d]**.

Explanation [NN.II.6.b]: According to the Vyaktivādin, the term "meaning of the stem" (*prakṛty-artha*) in the cited maxim refers only to the primary meaning of the nominal stem, and thus creates a problem for the Jātivādin. The Jātivādin rejects this view by pointing out that this term is not limited to just the primary meaning, but is inclusive of all meanings which are understood from a word through its primary and secondary signification functions. Such a wider interpretation, we are told, is necessary to account for all sorts of normal usages with secondary signification function of words. If the wider interpretation of the maxim is accepted, then the objection of the Vyaktivādin is not valid, and one should be able to construe the secondary meaning of the word *go* "individual bull" with the meaning of the accusative affix *-am* "object-ness" (*karmatva*).[298]

Explanation [NN.II.6.c]: It is important to make a clear distinction between implied or inferred (*ākṣepita / anumita*) meaning on the one hand, and the secondary meaning (*lakṣya*) on the other. The first kind of meaning is not signified by a word with its signification function, while the second kind of meaning is signified by a word with its secondary signification function (*lakṣaṇā-vṛtti*). On the basis of this distinction, Kumārilabhaṭṭa and Pārthasārathimiśra refuse to construe the fire inferred from the smoke with the action of burning in a sentence like "this smoke is burning" [cf. **NN.II.4.d**]. They, however, do construe the secondarily signified individual bull with the action of bringing in the sentence "bring a bull." The secondary meaning is secondary, and yet it is a meaning of the word, while fire inferred from smoke is not part of a verbal cognition, and hence not a meaning of the word "smoke."[299]

Naiyāyikas raise other objections against *ākṣepa* "implication" and *lakṣaṇā* "secondary signification function." Gaṅgeśa clearly says that if the individual is cognized through *ākṣepa* "implication," then it is not a word-meaning (*apadārtha*).[300] Naiyāyikas do not say that the secondary meaning of a word cannot be construed with the meaning of an affix or with the meaning of another word. They have other objections against the view that an individual is ascertained through the secondary signification function of a word.

NN.II.7. (p. 118)

नन्वेवं "स्वार्थादन्येन रूपेण ज्ञाते भवति लक्षणा" इति नियमात् कथं घटत्वरूपेणोपस्थिते लक्षणेति चेन्न । एतन्नियमे मानाभावात् । नील-मानयेत्यादौ नीलपदस्य नीलरूपवति लक्षणाभ्युपगमाद् व्यभिचाराच्चेति ।

---

298 Naiyāyikas, however, feel that this interpretation of the term *prakṛty-artha* is too broad. See: *prakṛti-tātparya-viṣaye tad-anvaya-vyutpattau lakṣaṇocchedo gauravaś ca /*, *TC*, p. 586, and *MD*, p. 78.

299 *yad api cārthasya lakṣakatva-pakṣe lakṣyasyāśabdasya vibhakty-arthānanvaya ity uktaṃ tad apy asmin pakṣe tātparyākhya-vṛtti-viṣayatvena śābdatvasya lakṣye 'pi sthāpayiṣyamāṇatvāt akiñcitkaram /*, *MKB*, p. 150.

300 *vyakter apadārthatve vibhakty-artha-saṃkhyā-karmatvāder vyaktāv ananvayaḥ syāt / sub-vibhaktīnām prakṛty-arthānivita-svārtha-bodhakatvasya vyutpatti-siddhatvāt /*, *TC*, p. 586.

तदेतदभिप्रेत्यैव "सवर्णेऽण्ग्रहणमपरिभाष्यमाकृतिग्रहणाद्" इति वार्त्तिकं सङ्गच्छत इति ।

Tranaslation [NN.II.7]

[a] [Objection by the Vyaktivādin]: Since there is a rule, i.e. "the secondary signification function occurs with respect to something which is known in a form different from that of the primary meaning [of a word]," how can [an individual] which has the property of pot-ness be cognized [from the word "pot"] through its secondary signification function?

[b] [Reply by the Jātivādin]: If this [is the objection], then it is not valid, because there is no justification for such a rule. The [so-called] rule is also violated in cases like "bring [a] blue [object]," where the word *nīla* "blue color" is accepted [even by the Vyaktivādin] to have a secondary signification function referring to an object having blue color.

[c] Only with such an interpretation, one can justify the following *Vārttika* [of Kātyāyana]: "In [Pāṇini's rule regarding the procedure of] homogeneous sounds [i.e. P.1.1.69 (*aṇ-udit savarṇasya cāpratyayaḥ*)], the *a-Ṇ* [sounds, i.e. the sounds from *a* in the *Śivasūtra: a-i-u-Ṇ* to the sound *Ṇ* in the *Śivasūtra: la-Ṇ*] need not be included, because the generic properties [of these sounds are supposed to] have been mentioned [in the *Śivasūtras*]."

Explanation [NN.II.7.a]: Kauṇḍabhaṭṭa probably takes over this argument from Gaṅgeśa, who offers it against the view of Maṇḍana that individuals should be regarded as secondary meanings of words.[301] The secondary meaning must have a form different from that of the primary meaning. For example, in the sentence "the cowherd-colony is on the river Ganges," the secondary meaning "the bank of the river Ganges" is different from the primary meaning "the river Ganges." However, an individual bull is not found in any other form except having the generic property of bull-ness. Again, the generic property and the individual have the relation of non-difference (*abheda*) according to Mīmāṃsakas [cf. **Explanation NN.II.5.e**]. Therefore, one cannot have a secondary signification function to refer to an individual which is non-different from the primary meaning, i.e. the generic property. The source of the verse quoted here is not known, but it is often cited by many authors.

Explanation [NN.II.7.b]: The Jātivādin points out that the above quoted rule does not hold true, since there are well known cases of violation. Mīmāṃsakas believe that quality words like *nīla* "blue" primarily signify the respective color qualities, and the individual

---

301 *ucyate / svārthād anyena rūpeṇa jñāte bhavati lakṣaṇā / tīratvena jñāte gaṅgā-padasya / na ceha gotvād anyena rūpeṇa vyakter upasthitiḥ / kiṃ tu gotvenaiva /*, *TC*, p. 587.

objects possessing those color qualities are signified as secondary meanings.[302] It is assumed here that the relation between the color quality and the colored object is that of non-difference (*abheda*), just as the relation between a generic property and the individual possessing that generic property is that of non-difference. If one can accept *lakṣaṇā* in one case, one should accept it in the other. For color quality words, Naiyāyikas accept the notion that colored objects are signified through a secondary signification function.[303] This being the case, the Jātivādin, i.e. the Mīmāṃsaka, argues that there is no reason why one should not accept the same solution for all words.

Explanation [NN.II.7.c]: Here Kauṇḍabhaṭṭa quotes Kātyāyana's *Vārttika* 7 on P.1.1.69. P.1.1.9 (*tulyāsya-prayatnaṃ savarṇam*) says that a sound having in common with another sound a similar oral effort is termed homogeneous with respect to the other sound. P.1.1.69 (*aṇ-udit savarṇasya cāpratyayaḥ*) says that non-affixal sounds denoted by the abbreviation *a-Ṇ*, i.e the sounds included in the *Śivasūtras*: *a-i-u-Ṇ, ṛ-ḷ-K, e-o-Ṅ, ai-au-C, h(a)-y(a)-v(a)-r(a)-Ṭ*, and *l(a)-Ṇ* (excluding the bracketed sounds and sounds represented by upper-case letters), represent both themselves and their homogeneous sounds. We shall not worry about the *udit* sounds at this point. This rule shows that, according to Pāṇini, the *Śivasūtras* are a listing of sound-tokens which basically stand for themselves, rather than for classes of sounds. P.1.1.69, then, endows some of these tokens with the ability to represent classes of homogeneous sounds. This rule is taken to be an indication that, according to Pāṇini, in this context, an individual alone is the primary meaning of a word. Only with such an assumption, we can explain the need to construct P.1.1.69.[304]

Kātyāyana proposes an alternative method to shorten the descriptive procedure. He says: "[The desired morphophonemic procedure] is established by taking the [sound]

---

302 *tathā sāmānādhikaraṇyam api gauḥ śukla ity ādau śukla-padasya guṇa-vācitve lakṣaṇayā, śuklatva-jāti-vācakatve lakṣita-lakṣaṇayopapādanīyam* /, *MKB*, p. 150. This is a significant comment by Khaṇḍadeva. If the word *śukla* has white color as its primary meaning, then the white object becomes its secondary meaning. But if white-color-ness (*śuklatva*) is the primary meaning of the word *śukla*, the the white color is the secondary meaning, and the white object is a still further extension. This final meaning is a second secondary meaning and it is said to have been known by *lakṣita-lakṣaṇā* "secondary extension of a secondary signification function." On another occasion [*MKB*, quoted in *MK*, Vol.II., p. 808], Khaṇḍadeva says that the individual is cognized through *nirūḍha-lakṣaṇā* "conventional secondary signification function." Even Prābhākaras accept this kind of secondary signification function in the case of quality words [*MK*, Vol.I., p. 601]. Grammarians explain quality words in a different way. Patañjali [*MB*, Vol.I., Sec.II., pp. 373, 424] says that a possessive affix *-matUP* is added to the word *śukla* "white color," so that the combination refers to something that has white color. Later this possessive affix is deleted, so that the word *śukla* itself comes to mean "that which has white color." Kumārilabhaṭṭa [*TV(b)*, p. 697] rejects Patañjali's view and supports the acceptance of *nirūḍha-lakṣaṇā*. Prābhākaras say that grammarians' deletion of the possessive affix is just another way to indicate that the quality words signify the individual possessing those qualities through *nirūḍha-lakṣaṇā* [*MK*, Vol.I., pp. 601-2]. For another view, see: B.K. Matilal (1985: 388).

303 *lāghavān nīlādāv eva śaktir nīlādi-viśiṣṭe tu lakṣaṇeti* /, *KM*, p. 560. Naiyāyikas join Mīmāṃsakas in rejecting grammarians' notion of adding and then deleting a possessive affix after color words. See: *atra ca nīlo ghaṭo 'stīty ādau sarvatraiva śābda-bodhāt pūrvaṃ lupta-matub-arthaka-pratyaya-kalpanām apekṣya nīlādi-rūpa-viśiṣṭe nīlādi-padānāṃ lakṣaṇā-kalpanam eva jyāyaḥ* /, *Rāmarudrīya* on *KM*, p. 561.

304 *kevala-vyakti-pakṣe evāṇ-grahaṇasya ... ārambheṇa tasyāpi śāstra-siddhatvāt* /, *VBS-S*, pp. 219-20. For a detailed discussion of this topic, see: Deshpande (1975: 17ff).

genera [or the generic properties of sounds as being mentioned in the *Śivasūtras*]."[305] Patañjali explains this by saying that in the *Śivasūtras*, only the generic properties (or perhaps configurations) of the sounds are mentioned, and that these generic properties (or congfigurations) will cover the whole classes of sounds which possess those generic properties.[306] This is taken to mean that, according to Kātyāyana, words primarily signify generic properties. Kātyāyana clearly says that this is not an explanation of P.1.1.69, but an alternative to it. If one is adopted, the other becomes redundant. If an uttered token of sound is naturally representative of a whole class of sounds, then there is no need to restate the same thing in P.1.1.69.[307] Kātyāyana's statement can be justified only on the assumption of the notion that words naturally signify generic properties, and through these generic properties they secondarily signify individuals which possess those generic properties.[308]

---

305 *ākṛti-grahaṇāt siddham* /, *Vt.* 13 on *Śivasūtra* 1, *MB*, Vol.I., Sec.I., p. 70. For a detailed discussion of Kātyāyana's alternative method and its philosophical and grammatical implications, See: Deshpande (1975: 17ff).

306 *avarṇākṛtir upadiṣṭā sarvam avarṇakulaṃ grahīṣyati* / *tathevarṇākṛtis tathovarṇākṛtiḥ* /, *MB*, Vol.I., Sec.I., p. 70. The term *kula* in *avarṇa-kula* 'family of *a*-sounds' is one of the rare expressions of the notion of class in Sanskrit philosophical literature.

307 For details, see: Cardona (1968: 448) and Deshpande (1975: 17ff).

308 *VBS-S*, p. 219.

SECTION THREE

NN.III.1. (p. 118)

अथवा व्यक्तिमात्रमेकशब्दार्थः । केवलव्यक्तिपक्षस्यापि शास्त्रे बहुशो दर्शनात् । युक्तं चैतत् । व्यवहारेण शक्तिपरिच्छेदकशिरोमणिना व्यक्तावेव तत्परिच्छेदात् । परिच्छिन्नापि लाघवादग्रे बाध्यत इति चेदेवं हि परिच्छिन्नोऽपि कर्मधारयोऽपूर्वकल्पनाभिया बाध्येत इति निषादस्थपत्यधिकरणविरोधः ।

Translation [NN.III.1]

[a] Alternatively, the word "one" [in Bhaṭṭojī Dīkṣita's verse 25] may be taken to mean that only an individual entity [is the primary meaning of a noun]. The view that an individual entity alone is the primary meaning is also seen frequently in grammatical texts.

[b] This is appropriate. By referring to common usage of language, which is the principal means of ascertaining a word's primary signification function, the primary signification function of a word is ascertained with repect to an individual entity alone.

[c] [Objection by the Jātivādin]: Even if [the primary signification function of a word is first] ascertained [with respect to an individual entity alone], it is contradicted later on because of the economy of assumptions [in the other view, i.e. the view that only a generic property is the primary meaning].

[d] [Reply by the Vyaktivādin]: [If the above objection by the Jātivādin were valid, then the Jātivādin, the Mīmāṃsaka, would have to accept the following]: Though [the compound *niṣāda-sthapati* "a *niṣāda* chief" is] ascertained at first to be a Karmadhāraya [i.e. "a chief who is a *niṣāda*"], this conclusion would have to be canceled later on, out of the fear of [additional] assumptions of unforeseen [religious learning on the part of a *niṣāda*, and one would have to adopt a Tatpuruṣa interpretation of the compound to mean "a chief of the *niṣāda*s," who may not be a *niṣāda* himself]. However, such [a cancellation, and adoption of the Tatpuruṣa interpretation] would contradict [what the Mīmāṃsakas themselves say in] the *Niṣāda-sthapaty-adhikaraṇa*.

Explanation [NN.III.1.a]: The exclusive views that only a generic property is the primary meaning and only an individual entity is the primary meaning are possibly traced to

Pāṇini's grammar. P.1.1.69 (*aṇ-udit savarṇasya cāpratyayaḥ*) and P.1.2.64 (*sarūpāṇām ekaśeṣa ekavibhaktau*) are often taken to imply that only an individual entity is the primary meaning of a word [cf. **Explanation (NN.II.7.c)** and **Explanation (NN.II.1.a)**]. However, other rules in Pāṇini's grammar such as P.1.2.58 (*jāty-ākhyāyām ekasmin bahu-vacanam anyatarasyām*) are taken to imply that only a generic property is the primary meaning of a word [cf. **Explanation (NN.II.1.a)**]. The tradition assumes that Pāṇini was philosophically uncommitted and that he used whichever view was convenient for a given purpose.[309] The same attitude about incompatible philosophical alternatives continues into the later grammatical tradition. The tradition is generally unwilling to make any hard and fast ontological commitments, and treats different alternative views simply as convenient devices to be used when needed.

On P.1.2.64, Patañjali refers to Vyāḍi's view that an individual entity (*dravya*) alone is the primary meaning of words.[310] Kaiyaṭa informs us that Vyāḍi did not believe in the very existence of generic properties, so he did not have the option of treating them as part of primary meaning.[311] The *Nyāya-sūtras* and the *Nyāya-bhāṣya* refer to a view which is similar to Vyāḍi's in its insistence on an individual alone as the primary meaning.[312] However, this view does not seem to discount the existence of generic properties.

Kauṇḍabhaṭṭa, moreover, follows here a version of the Kevala-vyakti-vāda which goes by the name of Dravya-vāda in Patañjali's *Mahābhāṣya*. According to this view, an individual alone is the primary meaning of words, and yet generic properties are ontologically admitted and their help is sought to explain the cognition of all individuals belonging to a class.[313] Navya-naiyāyikas like Raghunātha Śiromaṇi uphold a view which is a refined version of the Dravya-vāda in the *Mahābhāṣya*.[314] Kauṇḍabhaṭṭa's presentation of the Kevala-vyakti-vāda is on the lines of Navya-naiyāyikas like Raghunātha Śiromaṇi.

Explanation [NN.III.1.b]: Observation of normal linguistic communication (*vyavahāra*) is unanimously considered to be the most effective means of ascertaining the exact nature of the primary signification function of a word.[315] A child listens to the usage of the elders and then develops ideas about the primary signification function of a word by observing responses. Such observation allows us to correlate certain words with certain individual objects, since these individuals are actually engaged in actions in response to

---

309 *tasmād aśakyam anyatara-pakṣāśrayeṇa lakṣaṇa-praṇayanam iti cet satyam, ata eva lakṣyānurodhāt pakṣa-dvayam apy āśrīyate /*, *SKB(b)*, Pt.I., pp. 22-3.

310 *dravyābhidhānaṃ vyāḍiḥ /*, *Vt.* 48 on P.1.2.64. For a detailed presentation of Vyāḍi's arguments, see: *MB*, Vol.I., Sec.II., pp. 94-5. For a perceptive modern analysis of Vyāḍi's view, see: B.K. Matilal (1971: 106ff).

311 *jāter vṛtti-vikalpākṣamatvenābhāvaṃ manyamāno vyāḍir dravyam eva śabdenābhidhīyata iti manyate /*, *MB-P*, Vol.I., Sec.II., p. 94.

312 *NS*, 2.2.60-61 and *NS-B*, pp. 152-4.

313 *MB-P*, Vol.I., Sec.I., pp. 45, 374; Sec.II., p. 73; *MB-P-U*, Vol.I., Sec.I., pp. 45, 374; Sec.II., pp. 73, 90.

314 *Nīlakaṇṭha-prakāśikā* on *TS-D*, pp. 318-9.

315 *vācya-vācaka-sambandho nācāryair upadiśyate / anyathānupapattyā hi vyavahārāt sa gamyate /*, *TV(b)*, p. 953; also: ibid., pp. 940 and 587; *MS-B(a)*, Pt.I., p. 57; *BC*, p. 74; *TS-D*, pp. 317-21; *SSP(a)*, p. 103; *MB-P*, Vol.II., p. 289.

linguistic usages. Therefore, it is said that one first learns that an individual entity is the primary meaning of a word. The actions which take place in response to linguistic utterances do not seem to be correlated with generic properties.

Explanation [NN.III.1.c]: One may accept the argument of the Vyaktivādin as the initial phase of a process of ascertaining the primary signification function of a word. However, the Jātivādin points out that such an initial judgement in favor of Kevala-vyakti-vāda must be subsequently abandoned, in view of later observations. Presumably the subsequent observation shows that the same word is used to refer to different individuals belonging to the same class, and hence one would need to find a formulation to account for this experience.

Explanation [NN.III.1.d]: The Kevala-vyakti-vādin argues that such a general practice of subsequently canceling something that one has ascertained earlier would lead to rejection of several generally accepted Mīmāṃsā doctrines. The *Niṣāda-sthapaty-adhikaraṇa* section in the *Mīmāṃsā-śūtras* deals with the interpretation of the compound *niṣāda-sthapati* [cf. *MS*, Vol.IV., p. 1386]. The word *sthapati* means "chief," and the word *niṣāda* refers to a tribe of forest-dwelling people of low social rank. The compound *niṣāda-sthapati* could be interpreted in two possible ways:

1. Karmadhāraya compound: *niṣādaś cāsau sthapatiś ca*
   "one who is a *niṣāda* and a chief."
2. Tatpuruṣa compound: *niṣādānāṃ sthapatiḥ*
   "a chief of the *niṣādas*."

We are told that one arrives at the first interpretation simply by understanding the primary meanings of the two words. The second interpretation requires some additional assumptions to explain the necessity for the genitive affix. The Naiyāyikas and the Mīmāṃsakas explain the second interpretation on the basis of a secondary signification function of the word *niṣāda*. The word *niṣāda* itself secondarily signifies the meaning "of the *niṣādas*."[316]

While the Karmadhāraya interpretation thus seems to be easier at first, on second thoughts one realizes that a chief who is a *niṣāda* himself is not included among those who are entitled to perform sacrifices. Neither does he possess the necessary training nor a right to have a sacrificial fire. On the other hand, one who is a chief of the *niṣādas* may not be a *niṣāda* himself. In that case, he may have the necessary training and a right to possess a sacrificial fire. For this practical reason, the Tatpuruṣa interpretation should subsequently cancel the earlier Karmadhāraya interpretation. However, the Mīmāṃsakas do not accept the Tatpuruṣa interpretation and stick to the Karmadhāraya interpretation since it is based on the primary meaning of words [cf. Note 316]. For this reason, a Kevala-vyakti-vādin says that a Mīmāṃsaka cannot say that the primary signification function of a word previously

---

316 *sthapatir niṣādaḥ syāt / niṣāda eva sthapatir bhavitum arhati / kasmāt / śabda-sāmarthyāt / niṣādaṃ hi niṣāda-śabdaḥ śaknoti vaditum śravaṇenaiva / niṣādānāṃ tu sthapatiṃ lakṣaṇayā brūyāt / śruti-lakṣaṇā-viśaye ca śrutir nyāyyā na lakṣaṇā /*, *MS-B(a)*, Pt.IV., pp. 1386-7; also *TV(a)*, Pt. IV, pp. 1386-7.

ascertained with respect to an individual entity is subsequently canceled by other observations. Nāgeśabhaṭṭa, arguing against the Kevala-vyakti-vāda view, says that initially one does ascertain the primary signification function of a word with a specific individual entity, but later, on further observation and analysis, the primary signification function is extended to all the loci of a given generic property.[317] This is somewhat similar to the view of the Mīmāṃsakas.

NN.III.2. (p. 118)

अपि च गां दद्यादित्यत्रानुपपत्तिः । गोत्वादेर्दानाद्यसम्भवात् । शक्य-सम्बन्धरूपलक्षणाया अग्रहात् । व्यक्त्यन्तरे सम्बन्धज्ञानस्य व्यक्त्यन्तर-बोधाहेतुत्वात् । तथात्वे वा हस्तिपकव्यक्त्यन्तरे तत्त्वं धर्मितावच्छेदकी-कृत्यापि हस्तिसम्बन्धग्रहाद्यत्र हस्तिपके स न गृहीतस्तस्यापि हस्तिदर्शने स्मरणापत्तेः ।

Translation [NN.III.2]

[a] Moreover, [if an individual entity were not a primary meaning, then sentences such as] "one should give a bull" would be inexplicable. It is not possible to give [the generic property] of bull-ness.

[b] The secondary signification function, which is of the nature of a relation of the primary meaning [to the secondary meaning], cannot be ascertained [if a generic property is the primary meaning, and if all individuals belonging to a class were to be secondary meanings].

[c] [We will not be able to ascertain the secondary signification function of a word to cover all individuals], because an awareness of a relation with one individual cannot lead to a cognition of another individual.

[d] If it were so [i.e., if an awareness of a relation with one individual were to lead to a cognition of another individual], then [there would be the following problem for the Jātivādin]. [Suppose that] one ascertains the relation of an elephant to a specific elephant-driver, by making his essential property [of specific-elephant-driver-ness] the limitor for [his] being related [to the elephant]. [In this situation, a Jātivādin] would be undesirably forced to accept that, at the sight of the elephant, one remembers a different elephant-driver, whose relation [to the elephant] was never ascertained before.

Explanation [NN.III.2.a]: A Vyaktivādin can easily construe sentences such as "bring a bull" or "one should give a bull," because the word "bull" primarily signifies an

---

[317] *prathamato bālasya yady api viśeṣa-vyaktāv eva śakti-grahas tathāpy āvāpodvāpa-nyāyena vyakty-antare ānayanādi dṛṣṭvā pūrva-jāta-śakti-grahasya jāty-āśraya-mātre vyavasthitir iti tattvam* /, *MB-P-U*, Vol.I., Sec.II., p. 91.

individual animal. On the other hand, if it were to signify only the generic property of bull-ness, these sentences cannot be interpreted in terms of the primary meaning of the word "bull."

Explanation [NN.III.2.b]: The secondary signification function is defined as *śakya-sambandha* "a relation of the primary meaning [to the secondary meaning"], cf. Introduction, **E.5.ii**. If a generic property is the primary meaning, and if its relation with one specific individual is the secondary signification function, then such a secondary signification function is not useful for deriving verbal cognitions of other individuals.

Explanation [NN.III.2.c]: This is an important general principle. Awareness of a relation between x and y, combined with a cognition of x is said to lead to a memory of y. However, under the same circumstances, an awareness of the relation between x and y cannot lead to a memory of z.

Explanation [NN.III.2.d]: This is a continuation of the previous argument. If, for some reason, one were to accept that an awareness of a relation between x and y, combined with a cognition of x, can lead to a memory of z, then there will be all kinds of irregular cognitive experiences. To illustrate this problem, Kauṇḍabhaṭṭa offers an example which is used by many different authors. Suppose that there is an elephant E and a specific elephant-driver D_1. We can caracterize the relation between the two as $R(E, D_1)$. The property of specific-elephant-driver-ness is the limitor of property-possessor-ness (*dharmitāvacchedaka*). Here the term *dharmitāvacchedaka* is used in the sense of *sambandhitāvacchedaka* "limitor of related-ness." In simple language, one is aware of the relation of the elephant E to the elephant-driver D_1, in a very specific way, i.e. we know not only this person as specific person, but we know him as a specific elephant-driver. Normally, our awareness of such a relation, combined with our visual cognition of the elephant E will help us to remember the specific elephant-driver D_1 alone. However, the Vyaktivādin argues that if a Jātivādin thinks that a relation of x to y can help us remember an unrelated z, then, when one sees the elephant E, and when one is aware of his relation with the driver D_1, one may even remember a different driver D_2. Since such a thing does not happen, the Jātivādin must be wrong in his formulation that the relation of the primary meaning [= a generic property] to a secondary meaning [= a specific individual possessing this generic property] is capable of leading to a verbal cognition of other individuals. Nāgeśabhaṭṭa offers this very example against the view of the Vyaktivādin.[318] This example is also commonly used by Navya-naiyāyikas.[319]

---

318 *yat-kiñcid-vyaktau śakti-grahāt ... kiṃ ca hastipaka-vyakty-antare hasti-sambandha-grahād yatra hastipake sa na gṛhītas tasyāpi hasti-darśane smaraṇāpattyā vyakty-antare sambandha-jñānasya vyakty-antara-jñānāhetutvāt* /, *LM*, p. 1105.

319 *SV*, p. 216.

NN.III.3. (pp. 118-9)

सर्वेष्वेव गां नयेत्यादिजातिविशिष्टबोधकवाक्येषु वृत्तिद्वयकल्पनायां गौरवाच्च । युगपद्वृत्तिद्वयविरोधस्यादूषणतापत्तेश्च । अत एव -

"जातेरस्तित्वनास्तित्वे न हि कश्चिद्विवक्षति ।
नित्यत्वाल्लक्षणीयाया व्यक्तेस्ते हि विशेषणे ॥"

इति मण्डनमिश्राः परास्ताः ।

Translation [NN.III.3]

[a] [In the view of the Jātivādin], there is prolixity [of assumptions], since one has to assume the existence of two signification functions [i.e. primary and secondary] in all sentences like "take the bull," which refer to an individual qualified by a generic property.

[b] Simultaneous occurrence of both signification functions [which is generally considered to be a problem] would have to be thought of as being no problem.

[c] For this very reason, the following view of Maṇḍanamiśra is refuted: "Since a generic property is eternal, no one intends to speak of its existence or non-existence. [Existence and non-existence] are qualifications [not of the generic property, but] of the individual entity which is secondarily signified."

Explanation [NN.III.3.a]: According to Mīmāṃsakas, a word primarily signifies a generic property and secondarily refers to an individual possessing that generic property. Thus, almost in every sentence, one would have to invoke both signification functions of the word. Generally, a secondary signification function is supposed to be invoked only occasionally, when the primary signification function somehow does not work. However, the Mīmāṃsā view makes both signification functions equally necessary almost in every sentence. This involves great prolixity, and makes this view unacceptable. In contrast, the version of the Vyaktivāda presented in this section does not require any secondary signification function to explain the meaning of normal sentences. It considers individuals themselves to be the primary meaning.

Explanation [NN.III.3.b]: Kauṇḍabhaṭṭa says that under normal conditions simultaneous occurrence of both primary and secondary signification functions in a single example is considered to be a fault. But Mīmāṃsakas have to accept such a simultaneous occurrence of both signification functions almost in every sentence. This is undesirable. This argument can be traced to Gaṅgeśa's *Tattva-cintāmaṇi*.[320] Gaṅgeśa says that one

320 *nāpi gotva-sambandhini gotva-viśiṣṭe lakṣaṇā, gotve hi na sākṣād dānādy-anvaya iti vyakty-avacchedaka-tayānvaye 'mukhyatvam / lakṣaṇayāpi gotvāvacchinnaiva vyaktiḥ kriyānvayinī pratīyate, na kevalā vyaktir iti gotva-viśiṣṭasya lakṣyatve yugapad-vṛtti-dvaya-virodhaḥ, gotve 'pi vā lakṣaṇā /*, *TC*, p. 587-8.

cannot have a secondary signification function just for the individual, divorced from a generic property. What is involved in actions like bringing or taking is an individual as qualified by a generic property. This being the case, one would have to accept both the signification functions, the primary signification function for the generic property and the secondary signification function for the individual. Both of these functions would have to be functional simultaneously, because when the individual signified secondarily is construed with actions, we expect this individual to be qualified by the generic property which is signified by the primary signification function. Normally, the primary meaning is overridden in moving on to the secondary meaning (*mukhyārtha-bādha*).

This discussion would make one think that simultaneous occurrence of both signification functions is indeed a problem according to Gaṅgeśa. However, some commentators on the *Tattva-cintā-maṇi* thought that it was not a problem according to Gaṅgeśa.[321] Nāgeśabhaṭṭa also believes that such a situation is not necessarily a problem, because sometimes it is necessary to have both signification functions simultaneously. For example, in the sentence *gaṅgāyām mīna-ghoṣau* "a fish and a cowherd-colony are in the Ganges," both the primary and the secondary signification functions of the word *gaṅgāyām* must be taken into account simultaneously. The fish is in the water of the river, and the cowherd-colony is on the bank of the river.[322] I believe that Nāgeśabhaṭṭa has gone a bit too far. Especially, the example *gaṅgāyām mīna-ghoṣau* is unacceptable as a good normal Sanskrit sentence. I cannot think of any Sanskrit author who would actually use such a sentence.

Explanation [NN.III.3.c]: Kauṇḍabhaṭṭa says that, on the basis of reasons given against accepting a secondary signification function, Maṇḍanamiśra's view is automatically refuted. Maṇḍanamiśra evidently believed that while a word primarily signifies a generic property, this generic property being eternal in its nature, no one really intends to refer its existence or non-existence. Therefore, statements involving existence and non-existence must be interpreted on the basis of a secondary signification function of words, and these properties must be understood as being qualifications of the individuals signified secondarily.

When we look at the discussion of Mīmāṃsā views in Nyāya texts[323], we find that Mīmāṃsakas, other than Maṇḍanamiśra, are said to hold a view that individuals are cognized through *ākṣepa* "implication" which can be either an inference (*anumāna*) or presumption (*arthāpatti*). Maṇḍanamiśra is said to have argued that anything cognized through inference or presumption cannot be treated as a word-meaning, and therefore he proposed to treat the individual as something understood through the secondary signification function of a word. This made it into a word-meaning, though secondary.

---

321 *kecit tu maṇi-kṛn-mate vṛtti-dvaya-virodhasyādoṣatvena ... ity āhuḥ* /, *Āloka* on *TC*, p. 673.

322 *yugapad-vṛtti-dvaya-virodho 'py ata eva na doṣāya, dūṣakatā-bījābhāvāc ca / [gaṅgāyām mīna-ghoṣāv ity atra] anvayānupapattyā ca yugapad eva gaṅgātvenaiva nīra-tīrayor upasthitiḥ* /, *LM*, p. 140.

323 *vyakter api bodhaḥ śabdād eva, na tv ākṣepāditaḥ ... lakṣaṇāta eva tad-upapatter iti maṇḍanācārya-matam / tad uktaṃ jāter iti* /, *SV*, pp. 213-4; *TC*, p. 587; *MD*, p. 78. Also see: Note 283.

While this view and the verse are ascribed to Maṇḍanamiśra in Nyāya texts and in the works of Kauṇḍabhaṭṭa and Nāgeśabhaṭṭa, it is not attested in any of Maṇḍanamiśra's extant works. However, it is attested in Kumārilabhaṭṭa's *Śloka-vārttika*.[324] There is no indication that this is Maṇḍanamiśra's view, and not that of Kumārilabhaṭṭa. Actually, Śabara and Kumārilabhaṭṭa show wide support for the view that individuals are cognized through *lakṣaṇā* "secondary signification function" of a word [cf. **Explanation (NN.II.5.d-f)**].

NN.III.4. (p. 119)

जातिव्यक्त्योरभेदाद्दानान्वय इति चेन्न । तथा सति व्यक्तेर्वाच्यत्वमायातमेव । आनन्त्याद्युक्ताकृत्यधिकरणीयदोषतादवस्थ्याच्च । यत्तु तैरुक्तं व्यक्तिर्द्विरूपा सामान्यात्मिका विशेषात्मिकेति । तत्र सामान्यरूपेण वाच्यता न विशेषात्मनेति तन्न । विशेषरूपेणावाच्यताया अस्माभिरपि स्वीकारात् ।

Translation [NN.III.4]

[a] [If the Jātivādin says that, in sentences like "give a bull," the individual bull, which is not the primary meaning], will be construed with [actions of] giving etc. on the basis of non-difference between a generic property [which is a primary meaning] and an individual [which is not a primary meaning], then such an argument is not valid.

[b] If such an argument were valid, the individual does indeed become a primary meaning.

[c] Also, [if individuals were cognized through their non-difference from the generic property, then] the difficulties pointed out in the *Ākṛtyadhikaraṇa*, such as the infinite number [of individuals] etc. remain unresolved.

[d] They [i.e. Mīmāṃsakas] say that an individual has two aspects, i.e. a generic aspect and a specific aspect. [An individual is] a primary meaning [only] in its generic aspect, and not in its specific aspect. That is not valid.

[e] We ourselves [= Vyaktivādins] accept that an individual does not become a primary meaning in its specific aspect.

Explanation [NN.III.4.a]: In **NN.II.5.e-f**, Kauṇḍabhaṭṭa presents the Jātivādin's view that a word primarily signifies only a generic property, and yet actions stipulated in a given sentence can be construed with individuals possessing that generic property, because a generic property and an individual are non-different. This argument is advocated by Pārthasārathimiśra and has a parallel in Patañjali's *Mahābhāṣya* [cf. **Explanation (NN.II.5.e)**].

---

[324] *SLV*, p. 932; also see: *SLV-N*, p. 932. Also K. Kunjunni Raja (1963: 74).

Explanation [NN.III.4.b]: This is a straight-forward argument. If x is a duck and if y is non-different from x, then y must also be a duck. Thus, if a generic property is a primary meaning, and if a generic property is non-different from an individual, then an individual is also a primary meaning. This debate glosses over the distinction between non-difference (*abheda*) versus inseparability (*avyatireka*). Mīmāṃsakas use the term *abheda*, while Patañjali uses the term *avyatireka* [cf. *athavā avyatirekād dravyākṛtyoḥ, MB*, Vol.I., Sec.II., p. 370]. Kauṇḍabhaṭṭa's criticism applies more directly to the notion of non-difference, rather than to the notion of inseparability. This argument is somewhat similar to an argument used by Bhavadeva against the view of Prābhākaras that a generic property and an individual are cognized through one and the same cognitive act [cf. **Explanation (NN.II.5.c)**].

Explanation [NN.III.4.c]: If a generic property and an individual are non-different as claimed by the Jātivādin, then all the problems caused by the infinite number of individuals would apply to the view of the Jātivādin as well. These problems have been discussed by Śabara and Kumārilabhaṭṭa in their commentaries on a section of the *Mīmāṃsā-sūtras* titled *Ākṛtyadhikaraṇa*.[325] The main thrust of this argument is that if individuals were to be the primary meaning of a word, then one would have to assume an infinitie number of primary signification functions corresponding to the infinite number of individuals. If a generic property were non-different from individuals, then the same problem will occur even if a generic property were the primary meaning.

Explanation [NN.III.4.d]: Kauṇḍabhaṭṭa presents the view of Pārthasārathimiśra. This is elaborated in Introduction **D.3.iii** and **Explanation (NN.II.5.e)**.

Explanation [NN.III.4.e]: Kauṇḍabhaṭṭa says that there is no special credit to be given to Mīmāṃsakas. Even a Vyaktivādin does not claim that words primarily signify individuals in their specificity. A word signifies an individual in its generic aspect. This narrows the gap between the Jātivādin and the Vyaktivādin. Where then is the difference between these views? For a Mīmāṃsaka, the generic aspect of an individual is its generic property, and a word primarily signifies this generic property. For the Vyaktivādin, a word signifies an individual in its generic aspect, though it does not signify a generic property. For a Vyaktivādin, though the generic property is not a primary meaning, it is still accepted as a class-marking (*upalakṣaṇa*) or as a limitor of primary meaning-ness (*śakyatā-vacchedaka*), cf. Introduction **E.2.iv**. Kaiyaṭa and Nāgeśabhaṭṭa have explained the doctrine of Vyaktivāda on similar lines.[326]

---

[325] *ākṛtis tu kriyārthatvāt* /, *MS*, 1.3.33; *MS-B(a)*, Pt.I., pp. 302ff; and *TV(a)*, Pt.I., pp. 302ff. For a recent extensive study of the *Ākṛtyadhikaraṇa*, see: Peter Scharf (1990), D'sa (1980), and Gächter (1983).

[326] *vyaktir eva śabdārthaḥ* / *jātis tv aśabdārtho 'py abheda-pratyaya-hetur astīti sarva-vyaktīnām abhedenāśrayaṇād eka-vyakti-nirdeśe 'pi grahaṇaṃ sarva-vyaktīnāṃ siddhyati* /, *MB-P*, Vol.I., Sec.I., p. 374. *sarva-vyaktīnām iti* / *jāti-vaiśiṣṭyena pratyeka-vṛtti-paraspara-bheda-tyāga-pūrvakam abhedenaika-rūpāśrayaṇāt tat-taj-jāty-ākrānta-sarva-vyaktīnāṃ grahaṇaṃ siddhyati* /, *MB-P-U*, Vol.I., Sec.I., p. 374.

NN.III.5. (p. 119)

यत्तु मीमांसकादिभिरप्युक्तम् -

"आनन्त्यव्यभिचाराभ्यां शक्त्यनेकत्वदोषतः ।
सन्देहाच्चरमज्ञानाच्चित्रबुद्धेरभावतः ॥"

केवलव्यक्तेर्वाच्यत्वे तासां बहुत्वाद्गौरवम् । अनन्तव्यक्तीनामेकपदोपस्थित्यभावेन सङ्केतग्रहासम्भवश्च ।

Translation [NN.III.5]

[a] [Objections of the Jātivādin against the Vyaktivādin]: Mīmāṃsakas and others say, "[An individual cannot be a primary meaning], because -

i) [there are] an infinite number [of individuals];
ii) [there would be] a violation [of the primary signification function, if a primary signification function is ascertained only with a specific individual, and yet if there is a cognition of another individual from the word];
iii) there would be the problem of (requiring a) plurality of primary signification functions [for a single word];
iv) there would be a doubt [as to which one among the infinite individuals is the primary meaning of a word in a given context];
v) [the cognition of an individual is] a subsequent cognition [as compared to the cognition of a generic property]; and
vi) there is no varied cognition [of meaning from the same word]."

[b] If an individual alone is the primary meaning, then there is prolixity, because of the plurality of those [individuals].

[c] Since one can never have a cognition of all the infinite individuals from a single word, it would be impossible to ascertain the significatory association [of a given word with its primary meanings].

Explanation [NN.III.5.a]: Sections **NN.III.5-8** introduce objections against the Vyaktivādin raised by Mīmāṃsakas and Ālaṃkārikas. The verse quoted here comes from Pārthasārathimiśra's *Śāstradīpikā*.[327]

Explanation [NN.III.5.a.i]: See: **Explanations (NN.II.1.b; II.2.c; and III.4.c).** Kauṇḍabhaṭṭa again explains this argument in **NN.III.5.b-c**.

Explanation [NN.III.5.a.ii]: See: **Explanation (NN.II.2.c)**. Kauṇḍabhaṭṭa explains it again in **NN.III.6.**

Explanation [NN.III.5.a.iii]: See: **Explanation (NN.II.1.b)**. This is explained again in **NN.III.5.b** and **NN.III.7.a**.

---

327 See: Kunjunni Raja (1963: 73).

Explanation [NN.III.5.a.iv]: A similar argument occurs in **NN.II.1.c**. This argument is again elaborated in **NN.III.7.b**.

Explanation [NN.III.5.a.v]: A converse of this argument occurs in Kumārilabhaṭṭa's *Tantra-vārttika.* He says that a generic property is the primary meaning since it is cognized earlier from the word, before any individuals are cognized.[328] This argument occurs in **NN.II.2.a.iii** and **NN.II.3.c**. Kauṇḍabhaṭṭa again elaborates it in **NN.III.7.c**.

Explanation [NN.III.5.a.vi]: This argument has occurred previously in **NN.II.2.a.ii** and **NN.II.3.b**. It is elaborated again in **NN.III.7.d**.

Explanation [NN.III.5.b]: This is an explanation of **NN.III.5.a.i** and **NN.III.5.a.iii**. The primary signification function of a word is a relation of a word with its primary meaning. It would be necessary to assume a plurality of primary signification functions corresponding to the plurality of individuals, if these individuals were to be the primary meanings of a given word.

NN.III.6. (p. 119)

ननु यत्र क्वचिदेव व्यक्तौ शक्तिग्रहोऽस्तु कारणं शाब्दबोधे त्वगृहीतशक्तिकैव व्यक्तिर्भासत इत्यङ्गीकार्यमिति चेत्तर्हि व्यभिचाराच्छक्तिग्रहः कारणमेव न स्यात् । शक्तिग्रहाविषयस्यापि शाब्दबोधविषयत्वात् । गोपदादश्वादेरपि भानप्रसङ्गश्च ।

Translation [NN.III.6]

[a] [A Vyaktivādin may reformulate his view as follows]. Let the primary signification function of a word ascertained with respect to any specific individual be the cause of a verbal cognition, and then let any other individual figure in the content of the verbal cognition, even though the primary signification function is not ascertained with respect to it.

[b] [The Jātivādin rejects this formulation]. If one were to accept such a formulation, then due to the violation [of the previously ascertained primary signification function], one's awareness of such a primary signification function will no longer be treated as the cause [of a verbal cognition]. [There would be a violation of the proposed causal relationship] because [an individual] which is not known while ascertaining the primary signification function [of a word] would appear in the content of a verbal cognition.

[c] [If such violations were to be tolerated], one would be forced to accept that there can be a cognition of a horse from the word "bull."

---

[328] *pūrvaṃ sāmānya-vijñānāt ... go-śabdoccāraṇe hi pūrvam evāgṛhītāsu vyaktiṣu sāmānyam pratīyate / tad-ākāra-jñānotpatteḥ paścād vyaktayaḥ pratīyante / TV(a)*, Pt.I., p. 314.

Explanation [NN.III.6.a]: A cause is defined by Naiyāyikas as that which invariably exists prior to the production of the effect.[329]

A Vyaktivādin reformulates his argument to claim that the primary signification function of a word is ascertained only with respect to a specific individual, say I_1, and that this becomes the cause of a verbal cognition of some other individual, say I_2. Thus, the Vyaktivādin argues that the primary signification function of a word need not be ascertained with reference to all individuals.

Explanation [NN.III.6.b]: The Jātivādin points out that this formulation involves a violation of the postulated causal relationship. The primary signification function of a word ascertained with respect to a given individual can cause a verbal cognition of that individual alone. If there is a meaning cognition of an individual, such that the primary signification function of a word was never ascertained with respect to it, then there is a violation. Hence, the previously ascertained signification function will not be treated as a cause. This explains the argument of deviation or violation in more general terms. If the primary signification function of a word *W* is ascertained with respect to a specific meaning *M*, then that word *W* can lead to a meaning cognition of *M*, and *M* alone. If such is the case, then there is no deviation. However, if something other than *M* appears in the meaning cognition, then there is a violation. Nāgeśabhaṭṭa also presents this argument.[330]

Explanation [NN.III.6.c]: The reformulation of the Vyaktivādin leads to some very awkward conclusions. If the primary signification function of a word, ascertained with respect to a given individual, can lead to a verbal cognition of some other individual, then one could even have a verbal cognition of a horse from the word "bull." Nāgeśabhaṭṭa also presents this argument.[331]

NN.III.7. (p. 119)

शक्तेः पदार्थान्तररूपत्वात्तस्याश्च ससम्बन्धिकपदार्थस्य सम्बन्धिभेदेन भिन्नत्वात्तत्तद्व्यक्तिभेदेन भेदप्रसङ्गाच्च । गोपदादियं सा वेति सन्देह-प्रसङ्गाच्च । चरमं व्यक्त्युपस्थितेश्च । गोपदात् खण्डत्वादिरूपेण बोध-प्रसङ्गाच्चेति ।

Translation [NN.III.7]

[a] [Objections against the Vyaktivādin continued]. Since the primary signification function is a distinct [ontological] category, and since a thing [invariably] related to its relatum is [ontologically] differentiated with each

---

329 *kārya-niyata-pūrva-vṛtti kāraṇam /*, *TS*, p. 36; also: *TS-D*, pp. 225-6, and *NK*, pp. 224-7.

330 *tad-viṣayaka-śābde tad-viṣayaka-śakti-grahasya kāraṇatvābhyupagame tatra vyabhicāraś ca /*, *LM*, p. 1105.

331 *yat-kiñcid-vyaktau śakti-grahāt tad-aviṣaya-vyakty-antarasyāpi śābde bhāne go-padād aśvasyāpi bhānāpattiḥ /*, *LM*, p. 1105.

different relatum, a primary signification function would have to be [ontologically] differentiated with each distinct individual.

[b] [If an individual alone is the primary meaning, then] one will be faced with a doubt as to which of the many different individuals is cognized [in a given context] from the word "bull."

[c] [An individual cannot become a primary meaning], since it is cognized subsequently.

[d] [If an individual alone were the primary meaning], one would have to accept that [individuals] would be cognized from a word like "bull" with all their specific properties like *khaṇḍa*-ness [i.e. the specific property pertaining to a bull named Khaṇḍa].

Explanation [NN.III.7.a]: According to Mīmāṃsakas, a primary signification function of a word is a potency (*śakti*). In Mīmāṃsā ontology, such potencies are ontologically different from all other categories, and hence represent additional ontological categories. Thus, a theory which populates the world with fewer such additional ontological commitments is a better theory. A Mīmāṃsaka fears that the Vyaktivādin's view would lead to an addition of an infinite number of such potencies to one's ontology. The ontological commitment involved in a signification function has been discussed in Introduction **E.1.ii**. With this new ontological commitment, the analysis of the relationship between a word and its meaning changes to some extent. Now there are three things to worry about, i.e. a word, its meaning, and the relationship between the two. In the world of Mīmāṃsa, all these three things are independent ontological existents. The primary signification function or the potency of a word is an externally existent entity which is invariably related to the word and its meaning.

As a general principle, if an item x is invariably related to some other item, and that its existence itself is a dependent or relative existence, then x as related to y and x as related to z must be differentiated from each other, if y and z are different from each other. Similarly a primary signification function related to an individual I_1 must be differentiated from a primary signification function related to an individual I_2. Thus, with respect to each numerically different I, there must be an ontologically different primary signification function. By this logic, ultimately there must be an infinite number of primary signification functions for each word corresponding to the infinite number of individuals. With so many distinct signification functions, each ontologically distinct from all others, the world would be too crowded. For a Mīmāṃsaka, a generic property is the primary meaning, and the total number of generic properties being smaller than that of the infinite variety of individuals, the number of signification functions to be postulated would be relatively very small.

Explanation [NN.III.7.b]: Since, for the Vyaktivādin, a word primarily signifies an individual, and since there are infinite individuals, one will always be in doubt as to which one of them is the primary meaning in a given context. In fact, this argument can be raised against the Jātivāda, or any other view for that matter.

Explanation [NN.III.7.c]: This explains the argument in **NN.III.5.a.v.** Cf. **Explanations** on **NN.II.2.a.iii, NN.II.3.c,** and **NN.III.5.a.v.**

Explanation [NN.III.7.d]: While explaining Vājapyāyana's view, Patañjali says that when the word "cow" is used, no distinctions such as white, black, or brown are realized by the listener.[332] Also see: **Explanation [NN.II.3.b].**

NN.III.8. (p. 119)

यदपि काव्यप्रकाशकारेणोक्तम् - "गौः शुक्लश्चलो डित्थ इत्यादीनां जाति-
गुणक्रियासंज्ञाशब्दत्वेन विषयविभागः शुद्धव्यक्तिवाच्यत्वे न स्याद्" इति ।

Translation [NN.III.8]

[a] The author of the *Kāvya-prakāśa* also says: If a word were to signify [only] a pure individual [i.e. = an individual unqualified by any property], then it would not be possible to classify words like *gauḥ* "bull," *śuklaḥ* "white," *calaḥ* "moving," and *ḍitthaḥ* "with the name Dittha" into the four categories of words denoting *jāti* "generic property," *guṇa* "quality," *kriyā* "action," and *saṃjñā* "name," respectively.

Explanation [NN.III.8.a]: Mammaṭa introduces two alternative views in his *Kāvya-prakāśa*, i.e. *upādhi-vāda* and *jāti-vāda*. The first view holds that a word primarily signifies an attribute (*upādhi*). The term attribute covers all qualifying properties like generic properties (*jāti*), qualities (*guṇa*), actions (*kriyā*), and designations (*saṃjñā*). While these things are ontologically different from each other, they are qualifications of entities, and as such are class-properties. The second view is that of *jātivāda*, a doctrine identical with that of Mīmāṃsakas, which holds that all words primarily signify only generic properties. Mammaṭa discusses the doctrine of Vyaktivāda, and offers the arguments of infinity of individuals and violation of causal relations to reject it. He then offers the argument presented here by Kauṇḍabhaṭṭa.[333] If words were to signify a pure individual, devoid of any of the four attributes, then we will not be able to classify them into the four categories mentioned above. Nāgeśabhaṭṭa offers a further argument.[334] If all words, including the four examples cited by Mammaṭa, were to denote pure individuals, devoid of

332 See Note 264.

333 *saṃketitaś caturbhedo jāty-ādir jātir eva vā / yady apy artha-kriyā-kāritayā pravṛtti-nivṛtti-yogyā vyaktir eva, tathāpy ānantyād vyabhicārāc ca tatra saṃketaḥ kartuṃ na yujyate iti /, gauḥ śuklaś calo ḍittha ity ādīnāṃ viṣaya-vibhāgo na prāpnotīti ca tad-upādhāv eva saṃketaḥ /, KP*, pp. 32-3.

334 *kiṃ ca sarveṣāṃ śabdānāṃ vyakti-mātra-bodhakatve gauḥ śuklaś calo ḍittha ity eṣāṃ saha-prayogānupapattiḥ /, LM*, p. 1105.

any properties, then all these words would be completely synonymous, and as such one would not be able to use them together in one utterance.

NN.III.9. (p. 119)

तच्चिन्त्यम् । येन रूपेणोपस्थिते शक्तिग्रहस्तेन रूपेण पदार्थोपस्थितिः । स च धर्मोऽशक्योऽपि तदवच्छेदकत्वात् पदात् स्मृतः शाब्दबोधे भासते । अतो जातिप्रकारकबोधजनकस्तदवच्छिन्नशक्तिमान् वा जातिशब्द इति व्यवस्थावशान्न कश्चिद्दोषः । उक्तं च भट्टपादैररुणाधिकरणे -

"आनन्त्येऽपि हि भावानामेकं कृत्वोपलक्षणम् ।
शब्दः सुकरसम्बन्धो न च व्यभिचरिष्यति ॥" इति ।

Translation [NN.III.9]

[a] That [i.e. all the above arguments against the Vyaktivādin] is dubious.

[b] [The Vyaktivādin reasserts his view]. The meaning is cognized from a word only in that form in which it was known while ascertaining the primary signification function [of that word].

[c] That property [= specific form of meaning, attribute of an individual] is not a primary meaning [itself], and yet it is the limitor of [primary-meaning-ness]. A word leads to a recollection of such a property, and then that property appears in the verbal cognition.

[d] Thus, one can have a [fourfold] classification of words [as mentioned by Mammaṭa, even in the view of Vyaktivāda, by defining these categories in the following way]. [For example], a *jāti-śabda* "a generic word" is a word which can cause a cognition [of an individual] qualified by a generic property, or a word whose primary signification function is limited by a generic property. Then there is no difficulty.

[e] Thus, it is said by the honorable [Kumārila]-bhaṭṭa in *Aruṇādhikaraṇa*: "Though there is an infinite number of individual existents, it is easy to establish the relationship of a word [to an infinite number of entities] by selecting a single marking property. [The word whose relation is ascertained in this manner] will not deviate."

Explanation [NN.III.9.a]: This is a reference to objections in sections **NN.III. 5-8**. Beginning with this section, the doctrine of Vyaktivāda is defended against these objections. The objector argues in the following way. If the primary signification function of a word is ascertained with reference to an unqualified individual x, then such a signification function will lead to a verbal cognition of the individual x, and x alone. In response to this, the Vyaktivādin presents his reformulated view.

If the primary signification function of a word is ascertained with respect to some individual *x*, such that every *x* is invariably marked by a property *P*, then this primary signification function can lead to a verbal cognition of any *x* marked by *P*. This reformulation involves a generalization of the targeted primary meaning from a specific individual entitiy to a class of individual entities marked by the possession of a certain unique property. While the primary signification function of a word is not ascertained directly with respect to such a property, its marking function is accepted as a condition. Nāgeśabhaṭṭa further refines this argument.[335]

Explanation [NN.III.9.b]: This is a response to the objection raised in **NN.III.6.b**.

Explanation [NN.III.9.c]: Though this admission of a limitor or a marking property helps to generalize the target class of a primary signification function, the primary signification function is, according to this formulation, not ascertained with respect to such a property. For instance, the primary signification function of the word "bull" is said to be ascertained with respect to some individual bull, and not with respect to the generic property bull-ness. However, the generic property bull-ness is accepted as the limitor of primary-meaning-ness with respect to the word "bull." Possession of bull-ness is the necessary and sufficient condition for inclusion in the targeted class of primary meaning.

The Vyaktivādin makes some finer distinctions. Though the word does not signify a generic property as its primary meaning, the generic property is remembered when one hears the word. The signification function of a word is ascertained with respect to an individual as a locus of the limiting property, and an individual appears in the content of the verbal cognition as a locus of that limiting property.[336] In this option, it is not necessary to say that the limitor of primary-meaning-ness is also a primary meaning.[337]

Explanation [NN.III.9.d]: This resolves the difficulty raised in **NN.III.8.a**. A word primarily signifies an individual alone, and yet one can explain the classification of words into four categories, i.e. generic words, quality words, action words, and proper names.

According to the Jātivādin, all words are generic words, since they all primarily signify generic properties. According to the Vyaktivādin's new reformulation, a generic word is that word which produces a verbal cognition of an individual qualified by a generic property, or a word whose primary signification function is limited by a generic property.

In the true blue version of Jātivāda, one cannot get a fourfold classification of words, since all words signify generic properties as their primary meanings. All words become generic words. However, in the modified version called Upādhivāda, as presented by Mammaṭa, a word primarily signifies only an attribute, which may be a generic property, a

[335] *tad-dharmāvacchinna-viṣayaka-śābda-buddhitvāvacchinnam prati tad-dharmāvacchinna-nirūpita-vṛtti-viśiṣṭa-jñānaṃ hetuḥ* /, *PLM*, p. 27.

[336] *yathā ca śakti-grahe śakyatāvacchedakānugatīkṛta-sakala-vyakti-bhānam evaṃ śābda-bodhe 'pi tad-anugatī-kṛta-sakala-vyakti-bhānam* /, *LM*, p. 1108.

[337] *etena śakyatāvacchedake 'pi śaktir ity apāstam* /, *LM*, p. 1108; *tatra [śakyatāvacchedake] tu na śaktir iti mañjūṣāyām pratipāditam* /, *MB-P-U*, Vol.I., Sec.I., p. 45, and also see: ibid., Sec.II., p. 93.

quality, an action, or a name. Thus, there can be a fourfold classification of words.[338] The Vyaktivādin reformulation takes care of the fourfold classification by admitting all four types of attributes as properties which could limit the primary signification function or primary-meaning-ness, and appear in the verbal cognition as qualifiers of the individual.

Explanation [NN.III.9.e]: The verse quoted by Kauṇḍabhaṭṭa is attested in Kumārilabhaṭṭa's *Tantra-vārttika*.[339] In the verse cited here, Kumārilabhaṭṭa is explaining the view of Vyaktivāda. He says that one could have a primary signification function of a word ascertained with respect to some individual marked with an indicatory qualifier. Then the word can signify any individual marked with that indicatory qualifier. The primary signification function does not deviate in signifying different individuals, since it is not ascertained with respect to a specific individual marked by its specific property, but with respect to an arbitrary individual marked with a class property.

Actually, this argument is subsequently rejected by Mīmāṃsakas. They argue that one must first cognize the property which one wishes to function as an indicatory qualifier, before it can actually function in that capacity. However, if it is first cognized, then it becomes the primary meaning of the word.[340]

Kauṇḍabhaṭṭa interprets the term *upalakṣaṇa* "indicatory qualifier" as a synonym for the term *śakyatāvacchedaka* "limitor of primary-meaning-ness." On the other hand, Navya-naiyāyikas make a distinction between these two notions. They refuse to accept a generic property to be an indicatory qualifier (*upalakṣaṇa*), but they are ready to accept it as the limitor of primary-meaning-ness (*śakyatāvacchedaka*). For instance, Gadādhara says that if the generic property of pot-ness is just an indicatory qualifier (*upalakṣaṇa*) of individual pots, then there are other properties of these individual pots which could as well become indicatory qualifiers. In that case, one cannot say why one always has a uniform verbal cognition from that word. If the generic property is the limitor of primary-meaning-ness, these difficulties would not arise.[341]

---

338 *MB-P*, Vol.I., Sec.I., pp. 44-5; *BC*, p. 120; *KP*, pp. 32-7.

339 *TV(a)*, Pt.II., p. 678. The term *upalakṣaṇa* is used in philosophical texts in a variety of meanings. Matilal (1968: 118) translates this term with "adventitious qualifier" and "indicatory qualifier." The standard example of this type is: "Devadatta's house is the one where the crow is sitting," or "the moon is in the branch of the tree," where the crow and the branch are "indicatory qualifiers." See: *NK*, pp. 170ff. Nāgeśabhaṭṭa on several occasions identifies *upalakṣaṇa* with *śakyatāvacchedaka* "limitor of primary-meaning-ness." See: *upalakṣaṇa-bhāveneti / śakyatāvacchedakatvenety arthaḥ /*, *MB-P-U*, Vol.I., Sec.I., p. 45; Sec.II., p. 93. Kauṇḍabhaṭṭa also interprets the term *upalakṣaṇa* in the sense of *śakyatāvacchedaka*.

340 *gotvaṃ lakṣaṇam bhaviṣyatīti / yatra gotvaṃ tasyāṃ vyaktāv iti / tarhi viśiṣṭā vyaktiḥ pratīyeta / yadi ca viśiṣṭā, pūrvataran viśeṣaṇam avagamyeta /*, *MS-B(a)*, Pt.I., p. 304; *na hy anabhidhāya gotvam upalakṣaṇaṃ go-vyaktāv eva prayoga-vyavasthā labhyate / tac ced abhihitaṃ siddham ākṛtir vācyeti /*, *TV(b)*, p. 275.

341 *ghaṭādi-padasya padārthatāvacchedakībhūta-ghaṭatvādi-viśiṣṭa eva śaktiḥ, na tu ghaṭatvopalakṣite / ghaṭatvāder upalakṣaṇatve tasya dravyatva-kambu-grīvādimattvādy-aviśeṣeṇa ghaṭādi-padāt kambu-grīvādi-mattvādinā na bodho 'pi tu ghaṭatvādinaiveti niyamānupapatteḥ /*, *SV*, p. 40. Occasionally, Nāgeśabhaṭṭa also follows Gadādhara's view of *upalakṣaṇa*, that it is neither *śakya* nor *śakyatāvacchedaka*. See: *MB-P-U*, Vol.I., Sec.II., p. 73. Contrast this with Nāgeśabhaṭṭa's other statements cited in Note 339.

NN.III.10. (p. 119)

एवं चाव्यापकस्यापि व्यापकतावच्छेदकत्ववद्, अलक्ष्यस्य च न्यायनये लक्ष्यतावच्छेदकत्ववद्, अकारणत्वेऽपि कारणतावच्छेदकत्ववद् अशक्यत्वेऽपि शक्यतावच्छेदकत्वं सम्भवत्येव ।

Translation [NN.III.10]

[a] [The Vyaktivādin defends his new formulation]. Thus it is certainly possible that something [i.e. a generic property or an attribute] can be a limitor of primary-meaning-ness, though it is not a primary meaning itself. This is similar to the following [views which are widely accepted].

[b] That which is not a pervader itself, can yet become a limitor of pervader-ness.

[c] In the Nyāya system, that which is not a secondary meaning itself, can yet become a limitor of secondary-meaning-ness.

[d] That which is not a cause by itself, can yet become a limitor of cause-ness.

Explanation [NN.III.10.a]: Here, Kauṇḍabhaṭṭa presents a view which is upheld by some Navya-naiyāyikas.[342] As stated in **Explanation [NN.III.1.a]**, the *Nyāya-sūtras* and the *Nyāya-bhāṣya* do not endorse the doctrine of Kevala-vyakti-vāda, but adopt a view that a word primarily signifies both an individual and a generic property, i.e. the doctrine of Viśiṣṭa-vyakti-vāda. This is the view accepted by the majority of Naiyāyikas.[343] However, Raghunātha Śiromaṇi seems to be the first one to adopt the revised formulation presented here by Kauṇḍabhaṭṭa.[344] This view has been rejected by the later Naiyāyika authors like Gadādharabhaṭṭa and Rājacūḍāmaṇimakhin, who uphold the Viśiṣṭa-śakti-vāda view of the old school.[345]

According to the usual Nyāya definition of a limitor of primary-meaning-ness [cf. Introduction **E.2.iv**], this property is a part of the primary meaning, and then it resides in the individual and qualifies it. However, the Vyaktivāda as advocated by Raghunātha Śiromaṇi sought to change this conception. In this view, the generic property functioning as the limitor of primary-meaning-ness is not a primary meaning itself.[346]

Explanation [NN.III.10.b]: In the relation of invariable concomitance (*vyāpti*) between fire and smoke, fire is the pervader (*vyāpaka*) and smoke is the pervaded (*vyāpya*)

---

342 *[navyās tu] lakṣyatāvacchedatva-graha-mātreṇa lakṣyatāvacchedakasya yathā śābda-bodhe bhānam, tathā śakyatāvacchedakatva-graha-mātreṇa śakyatāvacchedakasyāpi śābda-bodhe bhānaṃ sambhavatīti śakyatāvacchedake na śaktiḥ kalpanīyeti vadanti* /, *Nīlakaṇṭha-prakāśikā* on *TS-D*, p. 318.

343 *TC*, pp. 577-8, and 589-91; *NM*, Pt.I., pp. 296-7; *TS-D*, pp. 320-1; *SSP(b)*, pp. 17ff; *SV*, p. 41; and *KM*, pp. 576ff.

344 *padārthāṃśe ghaṭatvādi-dharmasya śābda-bodha-prakāratāyāṃ tat-pada-śakyatāvacchedakatvam eva prayojakam / ... iti śakyatāvacchedake śaktiṃ dūṣayatā dīdhiti-kṛtā pratyakṣa-maṇi-dīdhiti-pradarśita-matam* /, *SV*, p. 61, and *MD*, p. 80.

345 *SV*, p. 62, and *MD*, p. 80.

346 *śakyatāvacchedakatvaṃ tu śakyatvāghaṭitam eveti bhāvaḥ* /, *VBS-K*, p. 443, and *LM*, pp. 1108-9.

term. Where there is smoke, there is fire. However, there can be fire without smoke. The property of fire-ness residing in the pervader, fire, is the limitor of pervader-ness (*vyāpakatāvacchedaka*). It is the special property of the pervader by virtue of which the pervader pervades something. It is the fire-ness of fire, rather than some other property such as its color or its substance-ness, which makes it the pervader of smoke. However, fire-ness itself cannot be treated to be the pervader, since it does not fit the definition of a pervader. We cannot say that where there is smoke, there is fire-ness. There is no fire-ness in the mountain, which has smoke. Thus, a property such as fire-ness can be a limitor of pervader-ness, without being a pervader.

In the technical jargon of Navya-nyāya,[347] a pervader (*vyāpaka*) is defined as: *tat-samānādhikaraṇātyantābhāva-pratiyogitānavacchedaka-dharmavattvam*. This could be explained as: The item x pervades y, if x has a property which is not a limitor of counter-positive-ness to a constant absence in the locus of y. The limitor of pervader-ness (*vyāpakatāvacchedaka*) is defined as: *tadvan-niṣṭhātyantābhāva-pratiyogitānavacchedaka-tvam*. This could be explained as: If x pervades y, then the limitor of pervader-ness pertaining to x, is a property which does not limit the counter-positive-ness to a constant absence residing in the locus of y. With this technical jargon, it is possible to explain why fire-ness is a limitor of pervader-ness, but not a pervader itself.

Fire-ness is not a pervader of smoke, since it does possess a property [i.e. fire-ness-ness], which is a limitor of the counter-positive-ness to the constant absence [of fire-ness] in the locus of smoke [e.g. the mountain]. However, fire-ness is a limitor of pervader-ness of fire with respect to smoke, since it is a property which does not limit the counter-positive-ness to a constant absence [of fire] in the locus of smoke [e.g. the mountain].

This technical explanation of why fire-ness can be a limitor of pervader-ness, but not be a pervader itself was suggested to me in a personal communication by my Nyāya teacher from Pune, Paṇḍita Kavīśvara Śāstrī. The English rendering is of course my own.

Explanation [NN.III.10.c]: In the standard example of secondary signification function, i.e. *gaṅgāyāṃ ghoṣaḥ* "there is a cowherd-colony on the Ganges," the word "Ganges" secondarily signifies the bank of Ganges. The generic property bank-ness is the limitor of secondary-meaning-ness (*lakṣyatāvacchedaka*). In simple terms, the bank of Ganges becomes the secondary meaning by being a river-bank, rather than being just a stretch of land, or because it has a certain color or smell.

In the Nyāya view, a secondary signification function is a relation of a primary meaning with the secondary meaning. The relation of the Ganges with its bank is that of conjunction (*saṃyoga*), while the relation between Ganges and bank-ness of the bank is a complex relation of inherence with something connected through conjunction (*saṃyukta-samavāya*). The Ganges is related to its bank through conjunction, and the bank is related to bank-ness through inherence. Therefore, it is not possible to relate the Ganges to both the bank and

[347] D.H.H. Ingalls (1951: p. 147), and *NK*, p. 829.

bank-ness through the same relation. Either we must assume two different secondary signification functions, or one should say that bank-ness is cognized simply because it is a limitor of secondary-meaning-ness pertaining to the bank. Naiyāyikas choose the second alternative.[348]

Kauṇḍabhaṭṭa specifically attributes this view to Naiyāyikas. The schools of Sanskrit Poetics and Mīmāṃsā are said to believe that bank-ness, which is the limitor of secondary-meaning-ness is also a secondary meaning itself.[349]

In adducing this argument to support the view on the limitor of primary-meaning-ness, Kauṇḍabhaṭṭa is explaining the position of Raghunātha alone. Gadādhara and others do accept that there is no secondary signification function with respect to the limitor of secondary-meaning-ness. However, they reject Raghunātha Śiromaṇi's view that there is no primary signification function for the limitor of primary-meaning-ness.[350]

The terms *lakṣya* and *lakṣyatāvacchedaka* also occur in another meaning in Navya-nyāya, i.e. definiendum and limitor of definiendum-ness respectively, cf. B.K. Matilal (1985: 170ff). This meaning is not intended in this context.

Explanation [NN.III.10.d]: The relation between a potter's stick (*daṇḍa*) and a pot (*ghaṭa*) is a cause-effect relation. The stick fits in the definition of a cause. The property stick-ness residing in the stick is the limitor of cause-ness (*kāraṇatāvacchedaka*). In simple terms, a stick becomes a cause of a pot, by being a stick, rather than by being a substance, or by having a certain color or some other property. At the same time, stick-ness itself is not a cause of the pot. A cause must be an invariable antecedent of the effect and also be unconditional or indispensable (*an-anyathā-siddha*).[351] The property of stick-ness is conditional (*anyathā-siddha*) with respect to a pot, and hence it is not a cause of a pot.[352] Thus, that which is not a cause itself can be the limitor of cause-ness. B.K. Matilal (1985: 290) discusses the notion of *ananyathāsiddha* as follows:

> "Thus, it was felt in Navya-nyāya that the criterion of invariable sequence was not enough for distinguishing causal conditions of a particular effect. For example, the production of a pot is preceded invariably not simply by the potter's wheel, but also by the color and circularity of the potter's wheel. But the color of the wheel is immaterial and irrelevant to the production of the pot. To exclude such irrelevant items from being considered as causes

---

348 *lakṣaṇā-sthale hi lakṣya-lakṣyatāvacchedakayor naikā lakṣaṇā sambhavati / tīre saṃyogasya, tīratve saṃyukta-samavāyasya lakṣaṇātvāt / atas tatrāgatyā tīra-smṛtau lakṣaṇā, tīratva-smṛtau lakṣaṇā-graha-prakāratvam iti niyāmaka-dvayaṃ kalpyate /*, *MD*, p. 80, also pp. 91-2; *LM-KL* (p. 119) explicitly attributes this view to Dīdhitikāra, Raghunātha Śiromaṇi.

349 *lakṣyatāvacchedake 'pi lakṣaṇā bhavaty eva /*, *LM*, p. 117. *LM-KL* (p. 119) attributes this view to Mīmāṃsakas. *VBS-K* (p. 443) says that even the Ālaṃkārikas hold the same view: *ālaṃkārikādi-naye tu lakṣya-tāvacchedake 'pi lakṣaṇā asty eva /*.

350 *SV*, pp. 61-2; *MD*, p. 80. Harinātha Tarkasiddhānta Bhaṭṭācārya, in his *SV-V* (p. 56), says that Dīdhitikāra's view is the right view, and that it cannot be refuted even by the gods!

351 Matilal (1968: 130) and (1985: pp. 290-294).

352 *daṇḍatvādīnām anyathā-siddhatvena ghaṭam prati akāraṇatve 'pi kāraṇatāvacchedakatvam /*, *VBS-P*, p. 233. Also: *NK*, pp. 41-43; *TS-D*, pp. 225-6, and *KM*, pp. 206-8.

> of the particular effect in question, such Navya-nyāya authors as Śaśadhara and Gaṅgeśa introduced the notion of what they called *ananyathāsiddhatva* 'unconditionality.' The invariable presence of the color of the wheel before the pot is produced is conditioned by the presence of the wheel itself, and hence, it need not be taken into account while we consider the relevant (causal) conditions for the effect in question."

The property of stick-ness (*daṇḍatva*) being eternal would precede and follow the production of any effect, and hence is not particularly relevant, while the presence of a potter's stick before the production of a pot is very directly relevant. The property of stick-ness is conditioned by the presence of the stick, and is not independently relevant.

NN.III.11. (pp. 119-120)

तत्प्रकारकभानमपि [सम्भवति] । हस्तिमात्रादौ हस्तिपकादिसम्बन्धग्रहणात्तद्रूपेणोपस्थितिवत् ससम्बन्धिकपदार्थमात्र एव सम्बन्धग्रहणस्य विशिष्टोपस्थापकत्वात् ।

Translation [NN.III.11]

[a] It is also possible to have a [verbal] cognition [of an individual] qualified by that [generic property, without having the primary signification function of a word ascertained with respect to that generic property].

[b] [This is like the following example]. If the relation of an elephant driver is ascertained with respect to elephants in general [i.e. any individual qualified by elephant-ness], then from the [awareness of such a relation], one can have a recollection of [an individual elephant] qualified by the [generic property of elephant-ness at the sight of the elephant driver].

[c] [The above cognitive episode is possible] on the ground that only the awareness of a relation of [of some *x*] which is invariably linked to something [e.g. *P*], is the cause of a cognition of [some *x*] qualified [by *P*].

Explanation [NN.III.11.a]: A generic property is not a primary meaning, and yet it is the limitor of primary-meaning-ness. The signification function ascertained with respect to some individual qualified by a generic property causes a verbal cognition of any individual as qualified by that generic property. The primary signification function of a word, according to this view, is not ascertained with respect to the generic property, but the generic property does figure in the primary meaning cognition as a qualifier. It does not, however, have the status of primary meaning.

Explanation [NN.III.11.b]: This is a difficult and a somewhat ambiguous passage. The word *mātra* in *hasti-mātra* can literally mean either inclusion of all instances (*kārtsnya*) or restriction to only the elephants (*avadhāraṇa*). Perhaps, the notion of a limiting property (*avacchedaka*) achieves both of these results at once. An individual, specified as being the locus of a generic property refers to all individuals which possess that generic property, and to only those individuals which possess that generic property.

Here, one has ascertained the relation of an elephant driver with some unspecified elephant. The expression *hasti-mātra* may be interpreted in the following way. We know that this driver is related to some elephant. We do not know the identity of this animal beyond the fact that this animal is an elephant. It is an elephant, and none other than an elephant, but we do not know which elephant. Here, the property of elephant-ness is not directly a party to the relation, but is a limitor of relatum-ness (*sambandhitāvacchedaka*). If such a relation is ascertained, then, at the sight of the driver, one has a recollection of an elephant, i.e. some individual qualified by elephant-ness.

Gadādhara offers this example in support of Prābhākaras. He says:[353] "Though one has not ascertained a relation [of a driver] with respect to [the property of] elephant-ness, which is the limitor of relatum-ness [pertaining to an elephant], when there is a recollection of an elephant, on the basis of a reminder in the form of a cognition of the driver related to an elephant, the [property of] elephant-ness also figures in the cognition of the recollected elephant as its qualifier."

Explanation [NN.III.11.c]: This explains the general principle behind the example given in the last section. This general principle can be explained as follows:

If one ascertains the relation of x to y, $R(x,y)$, then an awareness of this relation $R(x,y)$, aided by a cognition of x, can cause a recollection of y. This relation $R(x,y)$ is a specific relation in the sense that it is ascertained with respect to a specific individual y, and can cause a recollection of only that individual y. Here y is not a variable, but a constant, a specific individual in its specific aspect.

However, suppose that one ascertains the relation of x with some y, $R(x,y)$, such that every y is invariably qualified by a property P. Then, an awareness of this relation, though it is not ascertained with respect to the property P, leads to a recollective cognition of some y *qua* a locus of P, or some y qualified by P. The invariable qualifier of y, i.e. P, figures in the recollective cognition of y as a qualifier. Similar statements are found in the works of Nāgeśabhaṭṭa.[354] He explains this process as follows:

If x is related to y, such that y qualifies x, then x is the qualificandum (*viśeṣya*) in the cognition of the relation, $R(x,y)$. Since x is the qualificandum, it has the property of qualificandum-ness (*viśeṣyatva*). It is this qualificandum-ness of x, with respect to its relation with y, that regulates or exacts (*niyāmaka*) the cognition of the relatum x, each time the co-relatum y is cognized. In this case, the property of x-ness is the limitor

[353] *sambandhitāvacchedaka-hastitvādi-sambandhāgrahe 'pi hasty-ādi-sambandhi-hastipakādi-jñānātmakod-bodhaka-balād hasty-ādi-smaraṇe hastitvādeḥ prakāratayā bhānāt /*, *SV*, p. 216. Kauṇḍabhaṭṭa and Gadādhara both offer the same argument. However, in Gadādhara, this argument occurs in support of Prābhākaras, and not in support of the Vyaktivāda.

[354] *sambandha-graha-viśeṣyatvasya sambandhi-bhāna-niyāmakatvavat tad-avacchedakatvasya dharma-bhāna-niyāmakatvam /*, *LM*, p. 1108.

(*avacchedaka*) of qualificandum-ness pertaining to *x* (i.e. *sambandha-graha-viśeṣyatā-vacchedaka*). It is this kind of limitor-ness pertaining to *x*-ness, which assures the cognition of *x*-ness as a qualifier of *x*, each time *x* is cognized.

Similarity between this explanation of the general principle and the example of a driver and the elephant in the last section is obvious. Similarly, the primary signification function of the word "bull" is its relation with its primary meaning. This relation is ascertained with some individual bull *qua* a locus of bull-ness. This is the same as saying that the relation of the word "bull" is ascertained with some *x*, such that every *x* is qualified by bull-ness. The relation is not ascertained directly with bull-ness, but bull-ness figures in the meaning cognition as a qualifier, without being a primary meaning.

NN.III.12. (p. 120)

न्यायनयेऽप्याकाशादिपदानां शब्दाश्रयत्वविशिष्टेऽशक्तत्वस्वीकारात् तस्माच्छब्दाश्रयत्वरूपेण, गङ्गायां घोष इत्यादौ तीरत्वादिना, दण्डाद् घटत्वेन, घटाद् दण्डत्वेन चोपस्थित्यर्थं तथानियमावश्यकत्वादिति सुधीभिरूह्यम् ।

Translation [NN.III.12]

[a] Scholars should realize that such a principle [as given in the previous section] is necessary to account for the following:

i) [The above principle is necessary] to account for a [verbal] cognition [of ether] qualified by the property of being a locus of sound from a word such as "ether." This is necessary, because even the Nyāya school does not accept that the word "ether" has its primary signification function ascertained with respect to [ether] qualified by the property of being a locus of sound.

ii) [The principle is necessary] to account for a [verbal] cognition [of the river-bank] qualified by the property of bank-ness from a construction like "there is a cowherd-colony on the Ganges."

iii) [The principle is necessary] to account for a recollection [of a pot] qualified by pot-ness from a [correlatum, i.e.] a potter's stick.

iv) [The principle is necessary] to account for a recollection [of a stick] qualified by stick-ness from a [correlatum, i.e.] a pot.

Explanation [NN.III.12.a]: The general principle defended in this section is as follows: "If the relation of x with some y, $R(x,y)$, is ascertained, such that every y is qualified by a certain property P, then, given a cognition of x, the previously ascertained relation $R(x,y)$ can produce a recollection of some y qualified by P." The following arguments are meant to show that this principle is needed not only to defend the doctrine of

Vyaktivāda as described in this section, but to account for several notions commonly accepted in the Nyāya system.

Explanation [NN.III.12.a.i]: Ether (*ākāśa*) is a unique substance, and hence the property of ether-ness (*ākāśatva*) is a unique property having only one locus. For this reason, it is not a generic property according to Naiyāyikas [cf. Introduction **D.2.ii**]. Ether-ness is identical with locus-ness (*āśrayatva*) with respect to sound, and this is a distinctive property of ether.[355] The old school of Nyāya accepts this nature of ether-ness, but it does not accept that the word "ether" primarily signifies ether as qualified by this sort of locus-ness. The word is said to signify unqualified ether, and its locus-ness with respect to sound is only an indicatory qualifier (*upalakṣaṇa*).[356] On the other hand, the Navya-naiyāyika Raghunātha Śiromaṇi treats locus-ness with respect to sound to be the limitor of primary-meaning-ness pertaining to ether. Such a limitor is not a primary-meaning itself, but it is said to have been cognized from a word and appears as a limitor or qualifier of the primary meaning. Therefore, locus-ness with respect to sound is certainly cognized from the word "ether" as a qualifier of ether, and yet it is not a primary meaning. Raghunātha Śiromaṇi argues that the word "ether" is not different from the word "bull" in its behavior, though the ontological status of ether-ness is different from that of bull-ness.[357] Gaṅgeśa himself seems to hold a similar view, and this is reported by Nāgeśabhaṭṭa.[358] This is the view which is presented by Kauṇḍabhaṭṭa as the view of Naiyāyikas. This is different from the old school of Nyāya, and it is also rejected by later Naiyāyikas like Gadādhara and Jagadīśa.[359]

Explanation [NN.III.12.a.ii]: According to the Nyāya school, the secondary signification function of a word is not ascertained with respect to the limitor of secondary-meaning-ness (*lakṣyatāvacchedaka*), and yet it is cognized from a word as a qualifier of the secondary meaning, just by virtue of being a limitor of secondary-meaning-ness [cf. **Explanation (NN.III.10.c)**]. The relation of the primary meaning, the river Ganges, is ascertained with the bank of the river, the secondary meaning, such that this river-bank is always qualified by bank-ness. Hence, in the cognition of secondary meaning, it is said that bank-ness figures in as a qualifier, though it is not a secondary meaning itself.

Explanation [NN.III.12.a.iii]: A potter's stick (*daṇḍa*) is a cause (*kāraṇa*), while a pot (*ghaṭa*) is an effect (*kārya*). The generic property of pot-ness (*ghaṭatva*) is the limitor

---

355 *ākāśa-kāla-diśām eka-vyaktikatvād ākāśatvādikaṃ na jātiḥ, kiṃ tu ākāśatvaṃ śabdāśrayatvam /*, *KM*, p. 363.

356 *śabdāśrayatvasyākāśa-pada-vācyatvam anaṅgīkartṛbhiḥ prācīnair ākāśa-padād ākāśāṃśe tad-upasthāpyāprakāraka-śābda-buddher evopagamāt /*, *SV*, p. 65; *ākāśa-pade tu niravacchinnaiva śaktiḥ / vyaktīnām ānantyābhāvenānugamaka-dharmānapekṣaṇāt /*, *Tarka-prakāśa*, *NK*, p. 855; *ākāśādi-pade na dharme śaktiḥ /*, *BC*, p. 120.

357 *śabdāśrayatvasyāpy ākāśa-pada-vācyatvam āvaśyakam ity abhipretyaiva dīdhiti-kṛtā ... gotvādinā śabdāśrayatvasyāviśeṣaṃ vyutpādya, prakāśastha-pravṛtti-nimitta-lakṣaṇe vācyatva-viśeṣaṇopādānaṃ dūṣitam eva / pratyakṣa-maṇi-dīdhitau ca padārthāṃśe gotvādeḥ prakāratāyāṃ śakyatāvacchedakatāyāḥ prayojakatvam upagamya śakyatāvacchedake śaktir dūṣitaiva /*, *SV*, p. 67.

358 *ata eva "ākāśa-padasya śabdāśrayatve śakty-abhāve 'pi tatas tad-rūpeṇa bodhaḥ / tad-viśiṣṭa-viṣayaka-sambandha-grahasya tad-viśiṣṭa-viṣayaka-jñāna-hetutvāt" iti maṇi-kṛtoktam /*, *LM*, p. 1109.

359 *SV*, p. 65ff; *SSP(b)*, p. 25.

of effect-ness (*kāryatāvacchedaka*). There is a cause-effect relation between a potter's stick and a pot, such that, every pot is necessarily qualified by pot-ness. There is no cause-effect relation between a stick and pot-ness. Still such a relation is said to cause a recollective cognition of a pot qualified by pot-ness, when one sees the other correlatum, the stick. Pot-ness is said to figure in the recollective cognition as a qualifier, just by being either a limitor of effectness (*kāryatāvacchedaka*) or by being a limitor of relatum-ness (*sambandhitā-vacchedaka*). This example is also cited by Nāgeśabhaṭṭa.[360]

Explanation [NN.III.12.a.iv]: With the above given cause-effect relation between a potter's stick and a pot, one can also go in the reverse cognitive experience. When one sees the relatum pot, one is reminded of the correlatum stick. The cause-effect relation is not ascertained with stick-ness, but with a stick, such that each potter's stick is qualified by stick-ness. The property of stick-ness is still to be accepted as the limitor of cause-ness (*kāraṇatāvacchedaka*) or as the limitor of relatum-ness (*sambandhitāvacchedaka*). Though it is not directly a part of the relation ascertained between the stick and the pot, it still figures in the recollective cognition of a stick as its qualifier just by being a limitor of the above type. This example is also cited by Nāgeśabhaṭṭa.[361]

360 *ata eva daṇḍād ghaṭatvena ghaṭasyopasthitiḥ* /, *LM*, p. 1108.
361 *ghaṭāc ca daṇḍatvena daṇḍasyopasthitiḥ* /, *LM*, p. 1108.

SECTION FOUR

NN.IV.1. (p. 120)

द्विकमिति । जातिव्यक्तीत्यर्थः । अयं भावः । जातिविशिष्टा व्यक्तिः शब्दार्थः । सङ्केतस्य बोधकत्वस्य वा विशिष्ट एव ग्रहात् ।

Translation [NN.IV.1]

[a] [The primary meaning of a noun consists of] two elements, i.e. a generic property and an individual entity.

[b] That is to say, an individual qualified by a generic property is the primary meaning of a word, because the significatory association (*saṃketa*) or the signifier-ness [of a word] is ascertained only with respect to [an individual entity] qualified [by a generic property].

Explanation [NN.IV.1.a]: According to this view, the primary signification function of a word is ascertained not only with respect to an individual entity or a generic property, but with respect to both. Both the elements figure in the cognitive content and are regarded as primary meanings.

Śabara and Kumārilabhaṭṭa refer to certain other theoretically possible views.[362] One of these views holds that the primary meaning consists of a generic property qualified by an individual, while the other view holds that the primary meaning consists of the sum of an individual and a generic property. Patañjali informs us that, according to Pāṇini, both the elements could be primary meanings, but only one at a time [cf. **Explanation (NN.II.1.a)** and **Explanation (NN.III.1.a)**]. However, Nāgeśabhaṭṭa says that occasionally Pāṇini accepts both elements as primary meanings at the same time.[363] According to the Nyāya school, the primary meaning consists of an individual entity, a generic property, and the shape or configuration of that entity.[364] Most of the later Naiyāyikas neglect *ākṛti* "configuration," and some of them interpret this term in the *Nyāya-sūtras* to mean the relation between an individual entity and a generic property.[365] Most of them say that an individual qualified by a generic property is the primary meaning.[366]

---

362 *nanu vyakti-viśiṣṭāyām ākṛtau vartate |*, *MS-B(a)*, Pt.I., p. 317; *TV(b)*, p. 276. Also: *kiṃ jātir eva śabdārtho vyaktir evāthavobhayam | kiṃ vikalpo 'tha sambandhaḥ samudāyo nirūpyatām ||*, *TV(b)*, p. 267.

363 *atra sūtre prātipadikārthaśabdena pravṛtti-nimittaṃ tad-āśrayaś ca ity etāvan-mātraṃ gṛhyate |*, *BSS*, Vol.II., p. 790; *LSR*, p. 612.

364 *vyakty-ākṛti-jātayas tu padārthaḥ |*, *NS*, 2.2.66; *NS-B*, pp. 154-5; *TC*, pp. 589-91; *MD*, p. 79; *SSP(b)*, pp. 26-7; *SV*, p. 215.

365 *sautram ākṛti-padaṃ na saṃsthāna-paraṃ kiṃ tu karaṇa-vyutpattyākāra-nirūpakārthakaṃ jāti-vyaktyoḥ saṃsarga-param eva | anyathā samavāyāder api sambandha-vidhayā gav-ādi-pada-śakyatvena tad-anuktyā muner nyūnatāpatteḥ | kvācitkas tu jāti-saṃsthānābhyāṃ gavāder avagamo gav-ādi-padasya jāty-ākṛti-viśiṣṭe śakti-bhrameṇa lakṣaṇayā vā sampādya iti punar nyāya-rahasye 'smad-guru-caraṇāḥ |*, *SSP(b)*, pp.

However, as it will be made clear in the subsequent discussion, the *dvika* view described by Kauṇḍabhaṭṭa is not the view of Naiyāyikas, but that of Prābhākara Mīmāṃsakas. This is a significant deviation, and this has been criticized by Nāgeśabhaṭṭa.

Explanation [NN.IV.1.b]: This is just a plain initial statement. The primary signification function of a word, according to this view, is ascertained only with respect to an individual entity qualified by a generic property. Kauṇḍabhaṭṭa mentions two alternative views on the nature of primary signification function. It may be the same as *saṃketa* "significatory association," or *bodhakatva* "signifier-ness." These views have been discussed in the Introduction [cf. **E.1.ii-iii**].

A child listens to a sentence such as "bring a bull," and finds that a certain object is brought in, in response to this utterance. From this observation, the child learns to associate the word "bull" with the object that is brought in. Such an observation is possible only with individual objects qualified by some properties, but is not possible with either an unqualified individual, or with properties alone. Thus, it is natural to assume that the primary meaning consists of an individual qualified by a generic property.[367]

The *Nyāya-sūtras* refute the Kevala-vyakti-vāda and adopt the Viśiṣṭa-vyakti-vāda. Vātsyāyana explains that the word "cow" in "that cow is sitting" does not refer to just any *x*, but only to an *x* qualified by the generic property of cow-ness.[368]

NN.IV.2 (p. 120)

घटत्वप्रकारकघटविशेष्यकबोधे घटशक्तिज्ञानत्वेन कारणतेत्यपि न । द्रव्यादिपदानामप्येवमापत्तौ घटपदाद् द्रव्यत्वप्रकारकबोधप्रसङ्गात् । न च द्रव्यपदोपस्थितित्वेनापि तत्र हेतुत्वमिति वाच्यम् । तत्पर्यायान्तरात्तथा-बोधानापत्तेः ।

Translation [NN.IV.2]

[a] [Objection by the Kevala-vyakti-vādin]: The awareness of a primary signification function [ascertained] with respect to [an individual] pot leads to a [meaning] cognition of the [individual] pot as its qualificandum and [the generic property] pot-ness as its qualifier.

[b] [Reply by the Viśiṣṭa-vyakti-vādin]: One should not say this, for the following reason. If the same [rule] were to apply to words like

---

26-7. This is a reference to the Nyāya text *Nyāya-rahasya* composed by the teacher of Jagadīśa Bhaṭṭācārya. The author goes to the extent of saying that the occasional cognition of *ākṛti* "configuration" from a word should be explained by taking recourse to *śakti-bhrama* "misconstrued signification function, or an apparent signification function" or *lakṣaṇā* "secondary signification function."

366 *TS-D*, p. 321; *BC*, p. 121.

367 *gām ānayety ādau vṛddha-vyavahāreṇa sarvatrānayanāder vyaktāv eva sambhavena jāti-viśiṣṭa-vyaktāv eva śakti-kalpanāt* /, *TS-D*, pp. 317-321.

368 *na, tad-anavasthānāt* /, *NS*, 2.2.61; *na vyaktiḥ padārthaḥ* / *kasmāt* / *anavasthānāt* / *yā gaus tiṣṭhati, yā gaur niṣaṇṇeti na dravya-mātram aviśiṣṭaṃ jātyā vinābhidhīyate* / *kiṃ tarhi* / *jāti-viśiṣṭam* /, *NS-B*, p. 154.

"substance," one would be forced to concede that there could be a [meaning] cognition [of an individual pot] with substance-ness as [its] qualifier, from the word "pot."

[c] [The Kevala-vyakti-vādin responds]: Only a cognition generated by the word "substance" can cause that kind of a meaning cognition [of an individual qualified by substance-ness].

[d] [The Viśiṣṭa-vyakti-vādin responds]: One should not say that, [because, if this were true], there would be no [cognition of an individual qualified by substance-ness] even from a synonym [of the word "substance"].

Explanation [NN.IV.2.a]: This is an objection raised by the Kevala-vyakti-vādin. The objector implies that the view of the Viśiṣṭa-vyakti-vādin involves prolixity of assumptions. The objector says that it is not necessary to have the primary signification function of a word ascertained with respect to an individual qualified by a generic property, since the primary signification function ascertained with respect to an individual alone would be sufficient to lead to a meaning cognition of an individual qualified by a generic property.

Explanation [NN.IV.2.b]: The Viśiṣṭa-vyakti-vādin refutes the above contention of the Kevala-vyakti-vādin. If the primary signification function of a word ascertained with respect to an individual alone is sufficient to cause a meaning cognition of an individual qualified by a property P, then the same signification function could cause a meaning cognition of that individual as qualified by a property Q, assuming that both P and Q are properties of the given individual.

For instance, a pot is a substance besides being a pot, and hence has both properties, i.e. pot-ness and substance-ness. If the primary signification function of the word "pot" ascertained with respect to an individual alone were to lead to a meaning cognition of a pot qualified by pot-ness, the same primary signification function could as well lead to a meaning cognition of a pot qualified by substance-ness. Similarly, the word "substance" could lead to a meaning cognition of an individual pot qualified by pot-ness.

If the primary signification function is ascertained only with respect to an individual, then any property of that individual can be treated as an indicatory qualifier (*upalakṣaṇa*). Such being the case, the word "pot" may lead to a meaning cognition of an individual pot qualified by any one of its many properties.

On the other hand, if one claims that the primary signification function of a word is ascertained with respect to an individual qualified by a generic property, then that generic property is not a mere indicatory qualifier, but it is the limitor of primary-meaning-ness (*śakyatāvacchedaka*). Then, as a rule, the word "pot," with its primary signification function ascertained with respect to an individual pot qualified by the generic property of pot-ness would lead to a meaning cognition of an individual pot qualified by pot-ness, and not a pot qualified by some other property.[369]

Explanation [NN.IV.2.c]: The Kevala-vyakti-vādin modifies his argument to avoid this objection. He now claims that there should be an additional condition in the causal relationship. The primary signification function of a word like "pot" is ascertained only with respect to an unqualified individual, and yet a meaning cognition generated specifically by the word "pot" has for its content an individual qualified by pot-ness. Similarly, only a cognition derived from the word "substance" would have for its content an individual qualified by substance-ness. Thus, an additional factor of "being derived from a given word *x*" should be added to the statement of causal conditions for a meaning cognition of an individual qualified by the property *x*-ness.

Explanation [NN.IV.2.d]: This reformulation of the Kevala-vyakti-vādin is rejected by the Viśiṣṭa-vyakti-vādin. If the above reformulation were valid, then one would have a meaning cognition of an individual qualified by substance-ness from the word "substance," but one would not have the same meaning cognition from a synonym of the word "substance" (*dravya*), such as *vastu*. While both words refer to the same thing, they are different words, and as such, according to the above reformulation, cannot lead to the an identical meaning cognition.

NN.IV.3. (p. 120)
नापि द्रव्यत्वार्थकपदज्ञानत्वेन हेतुता । द्रव्यादिपदानामतथात्वेन ततोऽपि तथाबोधानापत्तेः ।

Translation [NN.IV.3]:

[a] [The Kevala-vyakti-vādin reformulates his causal statement by saying that] the cognition of a word which signifies [the generic property of] substance-ness is the cause [of a meaning cognition of an individual qualified by substance-ness].

[b] [The Viśiṣṭa-vyakti-vādin rejects the above claim by saying that, in the view of Kevala-vyakti-vāda] even words like "substance" are not like that [i.e. they do not signify the generic property of substance-ness], and, therefore, one cannot have a [meaning] cognition of that kind [i.e. of an individual qualified by substance-ness] even from those [words].

Explanation [NN.IV.3.a]: This modification of the statement of the causal relationship is meant to overcome the defect pointed out in **NN.IV.2.d**. The Kevala-vyakti-vādin says that one can indeed have a meaning cognition of an individual qualified by substance-ness from the awareness of the primary signification function of a word

---

369 *SV*, p. 40. This passage is cited in Note 341. Also see: *VBS-K*, p. 444.

ascertained only with respect to an individual, not only from the word "substance," but also from its synonyms. To achieve this goal, it is proposed that one include a separate causal condition: "there must be a cognition of a word which signifies substance-ness." It is assumed that the word "substance," and its synonyms signify substance-ness. Hence, it is claimed that one can have a meaning cognition of an individual qualified by substance-ness from any of these synonymous expressions.

Explanation [NN.IV.3.b]: The Viśiṣṭa-vyakti-vādin points out that the above formulation is inappropriate. According to the Kevala-vyakti-vādin, words do not primarily denote any generic properties, and hence it cannot be claimed that the word "substance" signifies substance-ness. If even the word "substance" does not signify substance-ness, none of its synonyms can signify it either. Such being the case, one cannot assert the above reformulation, because it assumes that words do signify generic properties. One cannot be a Kevala-vyakti-vādin, and yet claim that words principally signify generic properties. This is a self-contradiction.

NN.IV.4. (p. 120)

न च पदज्ञानस्य सम्बन्धिज्ञानत्वेन हेतुता । तत्र च येन रूपेणोपस्थितयोः सम्बन्धग्रहस्तेन रूपेणोपस्थापकत्वनियमाद्गवादिपदानां गोत्वरूपेणोपस्थिते तद्ग्रहाद्गोत्वाद्यंशे शक्त्यग्रहेऽपि तेनैव रूपेणोपस्थितिर्नान्यथेति वाच्यम् । पदान्नियमेनोपस्थितावपि गोत्वादेः शाब्दे विषयत्वासम्भवात् । तदंशे शक्त्यभावात् । अन्यथा गोपदस्य शक्तिग्रहसमये गोत्वस्येव धर्मान्तरस्याप्युपस्थितौ शाब्दबोधे भानप्रसङ्गः । घटादिपदादुपस्थितस्याकाशादेरपि शाब्देऽन्वयापत्तेश्चेति ।

Translation [NN.IV.4]

[a] [The Kevala-vyakti-vādin reformulates his view]: A cognition of a word causes [a meaning cognition], by being a cognition of one relatum [of the relation between a word and its meaning]. As a rule, the awareness of a relation causes a cognition of [its relata] only in that form in which they were perceived while ascertaining the relation. Therefore, there is no primary signification function of the word "bull" ascertained [directly] with respect to the generic property of bull-ness, and [yet] this word can cause a cognition of [an individual] qualified by bull-ness. This is because the primary signification function of a word like "bull" is ascertained with respect to an individual, which [as it happens, is always] perceived as being qualified by the property of bull-ness.

[b] [Rejection of this reformulation by the Viśiṣṭa-vyakti-vādin]: One should not say this, for the following reason. Though an invariable cognition of

bull-ness might thus result from words like "bull," a property so cognized cannot be treated as a legitimate content of the [meaning] cognition. This is because there is no primary signification function ascertained [directly] with respect to it.

[c] Otherwise there would be the following problem. While ascertaining the primary signification function of the word "bull," there may be an [associated] cognition of some other property, just as [there is an associated cognition of] bull-ness. Then, one would have to accept a meaning cognition of that property from the word ["bull"], though the primary signification function of the word is not ascertained [directly] with respect to it. Such a property would also [have to] be [accepted as being part of] the content of the [meaning] cognition [derived from the word].

[d] For instance, [there may be an associated] cognition of ether from the word "pot," and then, one would have to accept that this [ether] is also connected with the verbal cognition [derived from the word "pot"].

Explanation [NN.IV.4.a]: This is the standard argument given by the Kevala-vyakti-vādin, cf. **Explanation [NN.III.9.b-c]**.

Explanation [NN.IV.4.b]: If one accepts the argument in the last section, one may have to accept that there is a cognition of an individual qualified by bull-ness, from the word "bull", even though the primary signification function of the word "bull" is not directly ascertained with respect to the property of bull-ness. However, there is a distinction made between a mere cognition and a meaning cognition. The element of bull-ness cognized in the above fashion will not qualify for being treated as a meaning element, since there is no primary signification function with respect to this element. The cognition of bull-ness in the above mentioned circumstances will only be an accidental or associative cognition, and not a meaning cognition.

Explanation [NN.IV.4.c]: If the associative cognition of bull-ness from the word "bull" is to be treated as a meaning cognition, then any other associative cognitions resulting from the same word would also qualify for inclusion in the meaning cognition. Since there are many different elements associated with a bull-individual and with the word "bull," one can think of a number of different associative cognitions, and all of them would have to be treated as meaning cognitions.

Explanation [NN.IV.4.d]: Kauṇḍabhaṭṭa illustrates the above counter-argument by referring to the associative cognition of ether from a word. According to Nyāya ontology, sound is considered to be a quality (*guṇa*) of ether (*ākāśa*), and as such there is a relation of inherence (*samavāya*) between the two. A word being essentially nothing but sounds is also invariably linked to ether through inherence. Thus, when one hears a word, there is said to be an associative cognition of ether on the basis of the inherence relation. If an associative cognition were to be treated as a meaning cognition, one would have to consider ether as a meaning understood from every word. This being unacceptable, we cannot accept an associative cognition as a kind of meaning cognition. Also see: **Explanations** on **NN.III.9.c, III.100.a,** and **III.11.a-c**.

NN.IV.5. (p. 120)

तस्माद्विशिष्टं शक्यम् । एकमिति पक्षस्य चैकमेवान्तर्भाव्य कार्यकारणभाव इत्यभिप्रायः । तथा हि घट इत्येतादृशबोधे घटत्वशक्तिज्ञानत्वेन कारणता । लाघवात् । न तु घटत्वविशिष्टशक्तिज्ञानत्वेन । शक्तिज्ञानकारणत्वे वैशिष्ट्यघटयोरवच्छेदकत्वमपेक्ष्य घटत्वमात्रस्यैव तत्त्वौचित्यात् । तथा च त्वया तत्कारणतायामवच्छेदकतया घटस्तद्वैशिष्ट्यं चाधिकं प्रवेश्यत इति गौरवम् ।

Translation [NN.IV.5]

[a] [The Viśiṣṭa-vyakti-vādin now states his view]. Therefore, [an individual entity] qualified [by a generic property] is the primary meaning.

[b] The first view that [the primary meaning of a word is only a] single [element] is to be understood to mean that the causal relation [between the awareness of the primary signification function and a meaning cognition] is [established] on the basis of the inclusion of only one [element, i.e. a generic property].

[c] Thus, on the grounds of economy [of assumptions], the awareness of a primary signification function [of a word ascertained] with respect to potness [alone] is regarded to be the cause of a meaning cognition of a pot [i.e. an individual qualified by pot-ness].

[d] The awareness of a primary signification function [of a word ascertained] with respect to an individual qualified by pot-ness need not be required [as the cause of a meaning cognition of an individual qualified by pot-ness, as is done by Naiyāyikas]. It is appropriate to hold pot-ness alone to be the limitor of cause-ness pertaining to the awareness of a primary signification function, rather than accepting an individual pot and the relation of qualification [by pot-ness] to be [additional] limitors [of that cause-ness].

[e] [Criticism of the view of Naiyāyikas]: Thus, your introduction of an individual pot and the relation of qualification [by pot-ness] as additional limitors of cause-ness pertaining to the [awareness of a primary signification function] involves prolixity [of assumptions].

Explanation [NN.IV.5.a]: The view presented by Kauṇḍabhaṭṭa here is in agreement with the view upheld by the school of Prābhākara Mīmāṃsā. Kauṇḍabhaṭṭa agrees with

Naiyāyikas only as far as the nature of the cognized meaning is concerned, i.e. the primary meaning is an individual qualified by a generic property. However, he disagrees with them about the nature of the primary signification function. For Kauṇḍabhaṭṭa, the primary signification function of a word is ascertained with respect to only a generic property. For Naiyāyikas, the primary signification function of a word is ascertained with respect to an individual, a generic property, and the relation of qualification between the two.

Explanation [NN.IV.5.b]: Kauṇḍabhaṭṭa attempts to interpret the first view listed by Bhaṭṭojī Dīkṣita to suit this purpose. The first view says that the primary meaning consists of only one element. Kauṇḍabhaṭṭa interprets this to mean that the primary signification function of a word is ascertained only with respect to a single element, i.e. the generic property, and not that there is only one element in the cognized meaning.

Explanation [NN.IV.5.c-d]: Kauṇḍabhaṭṭa and Naiyāyikas agree on the notion that the primary meaning consists of an individual qualified by a generic property. However, they differently conceive the cause-effect relation between a primary signification function and the meaning cognition. The awareness of a primary signification function leads to a meaning cognition. Thus, this awareness has the property of cause-ness. For Kauṇḍabhaṭṭa, this cause-ness is limited by only the generic property belonging to the individual. This is to say that it is essential to have the primary signification function of a word ascertained with respect to a generic property in order to have a meaning cognition of an individual qualified by that generic property. This statement of causality is said to have economy of assumptions, because there is only one limitor of cause-ness.

Explanation [NN.IV.5.e]: The view rejected here as containing prolixity of assumptions is the view of Naiyāyikas. For Naiyāyikas, the primary signification function of a word must be ascertained with respect to an individual, a generic property, and the relation of qualification between them. Thus, all these three elements must be accepted as limitors of cause-ness for the awareness of a primary signification function, so that it can lead to a meaning cognition of an individual qualified by a generic property.[370] For Naiyāyikas, the position defended here by Kauṇḍabhaṭṭa involves a contradiction, and Jagadīśa explicitly rejects such a view.[371] Even Nāgeśabhaṭṭa sides with Naiyāyikas in explaining the *dvika* view. He specifically points out that the primary signification function of a word must be ascertained with both the qualificandum and the qualifier, or with the individual entity and the generic property.[372]

---

370 *ara vadanti, tad-viśiṣṭe śaktir ity asya tad-dharma-tad-vaiśiṣṭya-tad-āśrayeṣu triṣv eva śaktir ity arthaḥ* /, *SV*, p. 41; also: *TS-D*, p. 318, and *Nīlakaṇṭha-prakāśikā* on *TS-D*, p. 318.

371 *jāti-mātre hi saṃketād vyakter bhānaṃ suduṣkaram* /, *SSP(a)*, pp. 79-80.

372 *atra ca viśeṣaṇa-viśeṣyayor ubhayor api śaktiḥ* /, *LM*, p. 1107.

NN.IV.6. (p. 120)

अयं च जातिशक्तिवादो गुरूणामपि सम्मतः । अन्यथा केवलजातावेव शक्त्यभ्युपगमे कार्यान्विते पदशक्तिवादस्तेषां न सिद्ध्येत् । व्यक्तीनामेव कार्यान्वितत्वात् ।

Translation [NN.IV.6]

[a] This doctrine of the primary signification function [of a word ascertained only] with respect to a generic property [causing a cognition of an individual qualified by a generic property] is acceptable even to Prābhākaras.

[b] Otherwise, if they were to accept that the primary signification function of a word is grasped only with respect to a generic property, [and also that it leads to a meaning cognition of only a generic property], then they will not be able to establish their doctrine that the primary signification function of a word is [ascertained] with respect to something that is involved in an action. Only individuals are involved in actions.

Explanation [NN.IV.6.a]: This is a clear statement of source by Kauṇḍabhaṭṭa. It seems that, for some unknown reason, he himself also preferred this view of Prābhākaras, over the view of Naiyāyikas. Nāgeśabhaṭṭa subsequently disagrees with Kauṇḍabhaṭṭa and rejects this view.[373]

According to Prābhākaras, the awareness of a primary signification function ascertained with respect to only a generic property causes a meaning cognition of an individual qualified by that generic property. It is accepted in this school that the primary signification function of a word relates differently to an individual and to a generic property. The primary signification function bound with respect to an individual causes a cognition of that individual by the very existence of such a signification function [*svarūpa-satī*], and one need not be explicitly aware of it [*na tu jñātā*]. However, the primary signification function as bound with respect to a generic property must be known, and only through its awareness it leads to a meaning cognition of an individual qualified by a generic property.

According to Prābhākaras, this involves economy of assumptions. First a generic property is cognized from a word, but the cognition which comprehends the generic property also automatically comprehends the individual [*samāna-saṃvitti-vedyatva*, cf. **Explanation (NN.II.5.c)**], because a generic property is ontologically inseparable from its locus, the individual. This view is called Kubja-śakti-vāda. With respect to the cognition of the individual, the primary signification function is said to be "humpback, deformed." It is inactive or invalid, since its cognition is deemed to be not essential for a meaning

---

[373] *yat tu jāti-pakṣe 'pi gav-ādi-padānām ubhayatra śaktiḥ / śakti-graha-kārya-kāraṇa-bhāve ca jāti-prakārakatvasyaiva niveśaḥ / na tu vyakti-viśeṣyakatvasya / ata eva vyakty-aṃśe kubjā śaktiḥ / tad-aṃśe taj-jñānānapekṣaṇāt / etāvataiva jātau śaktir iti vyavahāraḥ / iti tada api na / gauravāt /*, *LM*, p. 1121; *bhūṣaṇkārādy-uktiṃ khaṇḍayati yat tv ity ādinā /*, *LM-KL*, p. 1120.

cognition of an individual qualified by a generic property. Thus, Prābhākaras believe that it is not necessary to be explicitly aware of the primary signification function of a word with respect to an individual to be able to a have a meaning cognition of an individual, and this is the economy of assumptions.[374]

Explanation [NN.IV.6.b]: Prābhākaras have a special theory of meaning. It depends upon a specific analysis of language-leaning. If a child first hears a sentence such as "the book is blue," then it is hard for him to guess its meaning, or its relation to the objective reality. On the other hand, if someone says, "bring a cow," and the child watches someone bring a cow, then he can correlate the words he heard with the objects involved in the observed action, with relative ease. Thus, Prābhākaras claim that all words signify things as they are involved in some actions (*kāryānvita*).[375] Only individual entities participate in actions, while the eternal generic properties cannot. Since an individual is cognized by the same cognition which cognizes a generic property, there is no difficulty in the view of Prābhākaras in linking the perceived meaning with actions.[376] Kauṇḍabhaṭṭa seems to prefer this view. However, it has been strongly attacked by Bhāṭṭa Mīmāṃsakas, Navya-naiyāyikas, and later grammarians like Nāgeśabhaṭṭa.[377]

NN.IV.7. (p. 120-1)

यत्तु घटत्वशक्तिज्ञानत्वेन घट इत्येतादृशबोधे कारणतायां घटोऽस्तीत्यत्रेव घटत्वमस्तीत्यत्रापि तथाबोधापत्तिरिति विशिष्टशक्तिज्ञानत्वेन हेतुतेति । तत्तुच्छम् । घटत्वप्रकारकघटविशेष्यकशाब्दबोधं प्रति घटत्वांशेऽन्याप्रकारकघटत्वशक्तिज्ञानत्वेन हेतुताभ्युपगमात् । तत्र शुद्धस्याभिलापासम्भवाद् घटत्वशब्देनाभिधानं कृतम् । अत एव घटत्वशक्तिज्ञानत्वेन हेतुत्वमते घटत्वत्वप्रवेशाद्गौरवमिति प्रत्युक्तम् । वस्तुतो निरवच्छिन्नप्रकारतासम्बन्धेन घटत्वविशिष्टशक्तिज्ञानत्वेनैव तत्र हेतुत्वम् । घटत्वमस्तीत्यत्र च घटत्वं प्रकार इति न दोषः ।

---

374 *evaṃ ca jāti-śaktatvena jñātam padaṃ jāti-viśiṣṭasya smārakam anubhāvakaṃ ceti / ... evaṃ ca jāti-vyakti-jñāna-janakatvād ubhayatrāpi śaktiḥ / jāty-aṃśe sā jñātā, vyakty-aṃśe svarūpasatī hetur lāghavād iti kubja-śakti-vādaḥ / ... vyakteḥ śakyatve 'pi vyakti-śakti-jñāna-janita-jñāna-viṣayatvalakṣaṇaṃ vācyatvaṃ nāsti / ... vyakteḥ śakyatve 'pi vyakti-śakti-jñānaṃ na kāraṇaṃ, vyakti-śakti-jñānatvaṃ nāvacchedakam iti lāghavam /*, *TC*, pp. 566-7; also: Ibid., pp. 570, 588-9; *NRM*, p. 120; *MK*, Vol.I., p. 490; *TMT*, Pt.I., p. 135; *SV*, p. 204.

375 *prābhākarās tu kāryānvite padānāṃ śaktiḥ /*, *BC*, p. 82; also: *Nṛsiṃha-prakāśikā* on *TS-D*, p. 327.

376 *evaṃ ca ghaṭādi-padāni ghaṭatvādi-jāti-smaraṇa-dvārā ghaṭādeḥ kāryānvayānubhava-janakāni /*, *BC*, p. 82.

377 *nānubhava-janana-sāmarthyam īśvara-saṃketo vā vṛtti-rūpā śaktiḥ, api tu padārthāntaram eva / sā ca jātāv eva kalpyate, na tu vyakty-ādāv iti na tatra kubja-śaktir apīti tattvam / atha vyakter gav-ādi-padāvācyatve gav-ādi-padād vyakteḥ smaraṇam anubhavo vā na syāt / na ca padāvācyatve 'py anvayasyeva vyakter bhānaṃ sābda-bodhe nānupapannam iti vācyam / tad-dharma-prakāraka-śābda-bodhe tad-dharma-prakāraka-padārthopasthiter hetutayā gotva-prakāraka-buddhau gotvādi-prakāraka-vyakti-smaraṇasyāpekṣitatayā vyakter asmaraṇe vyakteḥ śābdānubhava-viṣayatāyāḥ durupapādatvāt /*, *SV*, p. 206; also: *LM*, p. 1121; *TMT*, Pt.I., pp. 136ff.

Translation [NN.IV.7]

[a] [Objection to the above view of Prābhākaras]: One should accept that the awareness of a primary signification function [ascertained] with respect to only [an individual] qualified [by a generic property] can lead to [a meaning cognition of an individual qualified by that generic property]. Such must be the case, because, if the awareness of a primary signification function [ascertained] with respect to pot-ness alone could lead to a meaning cognition of a pot [i.e. an individual qualified by pot-ness], then one would have to accept that the meaning cognition resulting from the sentence "[a] pot exists" is identical with the meaning cognition derived from "pot-ness exists."

[b] [Response of Prābhākaras to the above objection]: This is a bad argument. This is so, because we accept that the awareness of a primary signification function [ascertained] with respect to pot-ness, unqualified by any other property [like pot-ness-ness], leads to a meaning cognition of [an individual] pot as its qualificandum and of pot-ness as its qualifier.

[c] In this statement, [one must specifically point out that] the word "pot-ness" is used [to refer to pot-ness unqualified by any other property like pot-ness-ness]. Otherwise, it is impossible to speak of anything that is utterly unqualified [by any property].

[d] Thus, we reply to the objection that there is prolixity in considering the awareness of a primary signification function [ascertained] with respect to pot-ness [alone] to be the cause of [a meaning cognition of a qualified individual] because of the introduction of [the additional property of] pot-ness-ness [as a qualifier of pot-ness].

[e] In fact, the awareness of a primary signification function [ascertained] with respect to [an individual] qualified by pot-ness, such that, the qualifier-ness related to [pot-ness] is not limited [by any other property like pot-ness-ness], leads to [a meaning cognition of an individual qualified by pot-ness].

[f] There is no difficulty in construing [the expression] "pot-ness exists," because, here, pot-ness is not a qualifier [of anything, but is a qualificandum in its own right].

Explanation [NN.IV.7.a]: The objector says that it is necessary to have the awareness of a primary signification function ascertained with respect to a qualified individual in order to have a meaning cognition of a qualified individual. If only the awareness of a primary signification function ascertained with respect to pot-ness alone were sufficient to produce a meaning cognition of an individual qualified by pot-ness, then somehow the meaning cognitions resulting from the sentences "a pot exists" and "pot-ness exists" would be identical. According to Prābhākaras, the primary signification functions of the words "pot" and "pot-ness" are equally ascertained with respect to pot-ness. Thus, there would result identical meaning cognitions from the above given sentences. This goes against one's experience.

Explanation [NN.IV.7.b]: The Prābhākara rejects the above objection. Then he presents a more accurate reformulation of his view. To have a meaning cognition of an individual qualified by pot-ness, one must be aware of the primary signification function of the word "pot" ascertained with respect to pot-ness, such that this pot-ness is not further limited or qualified by a property such as pot-ness-ness. This point needs some clarification. Let us say that the primary signification function of the word "pot" could be presented in the following explicit proposition:

[1] "The word 'pot' primarily signifies a pot."

Here, the element which is explicitly verbalized as "a pot" actually represents the cognitive element {an individual pot qualified by pot-ness}. I am using the curley brackets to indicate a cognitive quote. Therefore, in the cognition of this primary signification function, pot-ness figures in as a qualifier of the individual pot, though it is not itself cognized as being qualified by a property like pot-ness-ness. Now let us say that the primary signification function of the word "pot" could be presented in the following explicit proposition...

[2] "The word 'pot' primarily signifies a pot qualified by pot-ness."

Here, the element which is explicitly verbalized by "a pot-qualified by pot-ness" actually represents the cognitive element {an individual pot qualified by pot-ness qualified by pot-ness-ness}. Therefore, pot-ness figuring in the cognition of this primary signification function is qualified by pot-ness-ness.[378] Matilal explains this doctrine in terms of the difference between ordinary language and the Navya-nyāya metalanguage. He says:[379]

> "Thus a cognition that is expressed in ordinary language, as 'this is a pot' is not strictly identical with another cognition that is expressed as 'this has pot-ness,' for their interpretations in the Navya-nyāya metalanguage will differ; the latter contains an additional qualifier (i.e. pot-ness-ness) which is lacking in the former."

In simple terms, according to Navya-nyāya, the use of the word "pot" implies the cognitive presence of the qualifier pot-ness, while the use of the word "pot-ness" implies the cognitive presence of the qualifier pot-ness-ness.

Explanation [NN.IV.7.c]: In the previous section, it is stated that the primary signification function of the word "pot" must be ascertained with respect to "pot-ness which is not further qualified by any property" (*anyāprakāraka-ghaṭatva*). One may object that this is a self-contradictory statement. Once the word "pot-ness" is used, it invariably

---

378 *ghaṭo ghaṭa-pada-śakya ity ākārakam eva ghaṭatvāṃśe anyāprakāraka-ghaṭatva-śakti-jñānam / ayam āśayaḥ / ghaṭatva-viśiṣṭo ghaṭo ghaṭa-pada-śakya ity ākārakaṃ tu ghaṭatvāṃśe 'nyāprakārakaṃ śakti-jñānaṃ na yuktam / ghaṭatva-padasya ghaṭatvatvāvacchinne śaktatvāt /*, *VBS-P*, pp. 242ff.

379 Matilal (1968: 19).

represents the cognitive element {pot-ness qualified by pot-ness-ness}. Thus, it is not possible to speak of "pot-ness which is not qualified by pot-ness-ness." Kauṇḍabhaṭṭa recognizes this technical difficulty, and says that this is a problem with language, and not with the cognitive theory itself. While verbally we cannot have "pot-ness unqualified by pot-ness-ness," cognitively we can have {pot-ness unqualified by pot-ness-ness}. To express the cognitive element {pot-ness unqualified by pot-ness-ness}, one is forced to state explicitly that one means to refer to "pot-ness, not qualified by pot-ness-ness."

Explanation [NN.IV.7.d]: Naiyāyikas object to the Prābhākara view by saying that Prābhākaras are introducing additional elements like pot-ness-ness into the statement of causal relationships.[380] This objection has been already answered above by saying that the word "pot-ness" is used specifically to stand for the cognitive element {pot-ness not qualified by pot-ness-ness}. Such a clarification is the standard defense of Prābhākaras and Bhāṭṭas against this objection.[381]

Explanation [NN.IV.7.e]: The Prābhākara view is restated here again. Earlier we are told that the primary signification function of the word "pot" is ascertained with respect to an individual qualified by pot-ness, such that pot-ness is not further qualified by any property like pot-ness-ness. The same thing is restated by saying that the primary signification function is ascertained with respect to an individual qualified by pot-ness, such that the relation of qualifier-ness pertaining to pot-ness is not limited by pot-ness-ness. The property of pot-ness-ness cannot limit qualifier-ness pertaining to pot-ness, unless it is accepted to be a qualifier of pot-ness. Pot-ness-ness could be a limitor of qualifier-ness (*prakāratāvacchedaka*) pertaining to pot-ness, if and only if, we accept that an individual is qualified by pot-ness, such that, potness is necessarily qualified by pot-ness-ness.

With these clarifications, the Prābhākara asserts that the primary signification function of a word is ascertained only with respect to an individual, while at the same time a generic property such as pot-ness is deemed to be the limitor of cause-ness pertaining to the awareness of the primary signification function (*śakti-jñāna-kāraṇatāvacchedaka*).

Explanation [NN.IV.8.f]: The Prābhākara also asserts that there is no question of the meaning cognitions from the words "pot" and "pot-ness" being identical in his view. In the cognition of meaning derived from the word "pot," the property of pot-ness appears as a qualifier, but it is not qualified in turn by the property of pot-ness-ness. However, in the cognition of meaning derived from the word "pot-ness," the property of pot-ness appears as the qualificandum, and is in turn qualified by the property pot-ness-ness. Thus, in any case, pot-ness-ness does not seem to function as a limitor of qualifier-ness (*viśeṣaṇatāvacchedaka*) pertaining to pot-ness.

---

380 *anvayitāvacchedakatayā gotvatvādi-bhāna-svīkārāpatteḥ / śaktau gotvatvādy-antarbhāvāpatteś ca /*, *SV*, p. 200; also see: **Explanation [NN.IV.7.b-c]**.

381 *yathā vyakti-śakti-mate gotvāṃśe śaktis tad-avacchedakatā vā tad-viśeṣaṇānavacchinnaiva, tathā jāti-śakti-mate 'pi sā tathaiva iti na gotvatvādi-praveśād gaurava-śaṅkāpi / na hi jāti-śakti-mate 'pi śābda-bodhe sā kiñcid-dharma-prakāreṇa bhāsate, yena prakāra-bhānārtham prakāra-viśeṣam antarbhāvya śaktiḥ kalpanīyāpi tu svarūpata eva /*, *SV*, pp. 195-6.

NN.IV.8. (p. 121)

तस्माच्छक्तिर्विशिष्ट एव । कार्यकारणभावः पुनरुपदर्शितरीत्यैवेत्यवधेयम् । उक्तं हि भाष्ये "न ह्याकृतिपदार्थकस्य द्रव्यं न पदार्थ" इति । अत एव द्विकमिति पक्षेणाविरोधः । अन्यथान्यतरस्याप्रामाण्यापत्तेः । विरोधात् । तदाहुः - "को हि मीमांसको ब्रूयाद्विरोधे वाक्ययोर्मिथः । एकं प्रमाणमितरदप्रमाणमितीदृशम् ॥" इति । तथा च द्विकमित्यादेरपि द्विकं शक्यमित्येवार्थो न तथा कार्यकारणभाव इति ध्येयम् ।

Translation [NN.IV.8]

[a] Hence, one should consider [the final conclusion to be that] the primary signification function [of a word is ascertained] with respect to only [an individual] qualified [by a generic property]. However, the causal relationship [between the awareness of a word's primary signification function and a meaning cognition should be explained] in the above discussed manner.

[b] Thus, indeed, it is said in the *Mahābhāṣya*: "It is not the case that one who holds a generic property to be the primary meaning, does not hold an individual [also] to be a primary meaning."

[c] For this very reason, [the view expounded above] is not in opposition with the view that the primary meaning consists of two [elements]. Otherwise, one of the two views [i.e. the primary meaning consists of one element, and that it consists of two elements] would have to be invalid due to their mutual incompatibility. Thus it is said: "Which Mīmāṃsaka would say that when there is opposition between two [authoritative] statements, one of them is valid, while the other one is invalid?"

[d] Similarly, it should be noted that even in the view that [the primary meaning consists of] two [elements], both [the individual and the generic property] are primary meanings, but the cause-effect relationship is not that way [i.e. inclusive of both elements].

Explanation [NN.IV.8.a]: The primary signification function of a word is actually linked with both the individual and the generic property. However, there is a difference between the actual state (*svarūpa*) of the primary signification function, and the cognitive requirements. Cognitively speaking, only the awareness of the primary signification function ascertained with respect to a generic property is necessary and sufficient to cause a meaning cognition of an individual qualified by a generic property. Thus, the Prābhākara, and perhaps Kauṇḍabhaṭṭa himself, can claim that the primary meaning consists of two elements, or an individual qualified by a generic property, and yet the primary signification function needs to be ascertained only with respect to a generic property.

Explanation [NN.IV.8.b]: Kauṇḍabhaṭṭa quotes a passage from the *Mahābhāṣya* in support of this view.[382] Peter Scharf (1990: 98) discusses the passage from the *Mahābhāṣya* at some length and rightly argues that this is Patañjali's compromise solution to the excesses of the two extreme views. However, one must note that Patañjali cleverly uses the term *padārtha* "meaning of a word," without getting entagled here into the question of whether both of these meanings are "primary" meanings for the respective adherents. He uses the terms *pradhāna* "principal" and *guṇa* "subordinate," to indicate the different status of these elements in the respective views, but not anything that would suggest the distinction of primary versus secondary meaning. In my opinion, Patañjali leaves this issue unresolved. Some commentators on Kauṇḍabhaṭṭa's *Vaiyākaraṇa-bhūṣaṇa-sāra* disagree with Kauṇḍabhaṭṭa and point out that the *Mahābhāṣya* passage cannot support the Prābhākara view.[383] There is also another major difference between the *Mahābhāṣya* view and the Prābhākara view. The *Mahābhāṣya* says that for a Jātivādin, the generic property is the principal meaning, while the individual is the subordinate meaning. However, for the Prābhākara, the individual is the principal meaning, and the generic property is only a qualifier.

The unpublished commentary *Kānti* on the *Vaiyākaraṇa-bhūṣaṇa-sāra* disagrees with Kauṇḍabhaṭṭa's presentation for a different reason.[384] According to that commentary, the *Mahābhāṣya* passage merely suggests that an individual and a generic property are inseparable, but it does not support the view that the primary meaning is an individual qualified by a generic property. Even Bhaṭṭojī Dīkṣita takes this *Bhāṣya* passage to mean that either of the two could be the qualificandum and the other could be a qualifier.[385] B.K. Matilal (1985: 386) says:

> "In his conciliatory remarks, Patañjali notes that the meaning of a word has both aspects; it has a universal aspect, a descriptive feature, an adjectival or attributive aspect, and it has a particular aspect, a substantial aspect, or a location. Thus while Vājapyāyana tends to emphasize the first aspect, Vyāḍi tends to emphasize the second."

---

382 *na hy ākṛti-padārthakasya dravyaṃ na padārthaḥ, dravya-padārthakasya vākṛtir na padārthaḥ / ubhayor ubhayam padārthaḥ / kasyacit kiñcit pradhāna-bhūtam, kiñcid guṇa-bhūtam / ākṛti-padārthakasyākṛtiḥ pradhāna-bhūtā, dravyaṃ guṇa-bhūtam / dravya-padārthakasya dravyam pradhāna-bhūtam ākṛtir guṇa-bhūtā /*, *MB*, Vol.I., Sec.II., pp. 98-9. A similar passage also occurs in Śabara: *na hy ākṛti-padārthakasya vyaktir na padārthaḥ, vyakti-padārthakasya vā nākṛtiḥ / ubhayam ubhayasya padārthaḥ / kasyacit kiñcit prādhānyena vivakṣitam bhavati /*, *MS-B(a)*, Pt.I., p. 304.

383 *ubhayor ubhayam padārtha iti bhāṣyāj jātau vyaktau ca gav-ādi-padānāṃ śaktiḥ / paraṃ tu vyakti-śābda-bodhe 'pi jāti-viṣayakatvena jāti-śakti-jñānasyaiva hetutā / ayam eva kubja-śakti-vāda iti vyavahriyate ... ity āhuḥ / tad apy āpāta-manoramam / ... ukte 'rthe bhāṣyopanyasanaṃ tu kasyacit kiñcit pradhāna-bhūtaṃ, kiñcid guṇa-bhūtam iti upasaṃhāra-bhāṣyānālocana-mūlakam eva /*, *VBS-D*, p. 241.

384 *asmāc ca jāti-vyaktyor avyatireko labhyate / na tu viśiṣṭa-pakṣa iti / vakṣyamāṇa-mūlokta-viśiṣṭa-pakṣa-sādhakatā naitad-bhāṣyasyeti sudhiyo vibhāvayantu /*, *Kānti* on *VBS*, quoted in notes on *VB*, p. 670.

385 *yat tu sarūpa-sūtre bhāṣye vakṣyate na hy ākṛti-padārthakasya dravyaṃ na padārtha iti, tat tu jāti-vyaktyor anyatareṇa viśiṣṭasyāparasya vācyatety evaṃrūpam matāntaram /*, *SKB(b)*, Pt.I., p. 22.

It is not certain if the compromise view put forward by Patañjali is shared by Vyāḍi and Vājapyāyana. If Kaiyaṭa is right [cf. Note 311] in claiming that Vyāḍi did not accept the existence of any *jātis*, he could not have accepted the sort of compromise proposed by Patañjali. Therefore, it is appropriate to attribute the compromise view to Patañjali alone.

Explanation [NN.IV.8.c]: This is only a reiteration of the discussion in **NN.IV.5.b**. This argument is refuted by Nāgeśabhaṭṭa who rightly argues that the words *ekam* and *dvikam* both refer to the number of meaning elements in the verbal cognition. Therefore, the *ekam* view can accept either the generic property or the individual to be the primary meaning, but not both. On the other hand, the *dvikam* view accepts both elements to be primary meanings.[386]

Kauṇḍabhaṭṭa explains why he must reconcile these two views, i.e. the *ekam* view and the *dvikam* view. He feels that they must not contradict each other. If there are two incompatible authoritative statements, Mīmāṃsakas believe that both of them must be valid, and there must be an option (*vikalpa*).[387] Thus, one must either reconcile the two views and remove the seeming contradiction, or one must accept them to be incompatible and yet valid alternatives. Kauṇḍabhaṭṭa opts for the first choice.

Explanation [NN.IV.8.d]: Cf. **Explanation [NN.IV.5.b]** and **Explanation [NN.IV.8.c]**.

NN.IV.9. (p. 121)

नन्वत्र पक्षे सर्वशब्दानां त्रैलिङ्ग्यं स्यात् । लिङ्गावाचकत्वस्य सर्वत्र तुल्यत्वादिति चेन्न । पुंलिङ्गाभिधायिप्रत्ययत्वं तत्त्वमित्युपपत्तेः । अत्र ह्युक्तपक्षद्वयेऽपि लिङ्गस्य प्रत्ययार्थत्वात् ।

Translation [NN.IV.9]

[a] [Objection to the *Dvikam* view]: In this view, one would have to accept that all words have three genders, because all words are equal in not denoting gender.

[b] [Refutation of the above objection]: The above [objection] is not valid. It is possible to explain [the gender-difference between words by defining a masculine word as the word that takes] an affix signifying masculine gender. In both of the afore-mentioned views [i.e. the *Ekam* and the *Dvikam* views], gender is [considered to be] a meaning of the affix.

---

386 *ekam prātipadikārtha ity asya jāti-vyaktyor madhye 'nyatarad eva tac-chakyam ity arthah /*, *LM*, p. 1149.

387 *sa ca (vikalpas) tulya-pramāṇa-viśiṣṭānāṃ viruddhānām bhavati / vede yathā - vrīhibhir yajeta, yavair yajeta - iti / vidhi-pratiṣedhayor api tulya-balatve virodhāt vikalpo bhavaty eva / yathā vede - ṣoḍaśinaṃ gṛhṇāti, na gṛhṇāti - iti /*, *VP-P*, p. 161-2; also: *NK*, p. 743.

Explanation [NN.IV.9.a]: In the first two views, i.e. *Ekam* and *Dvikam*, the elements of gender, number, and *kāraka* are signified by the affix and not by the nominal stem. If, in this fashion, all nominal stems are equal in not denoting gender, then either they will have no inherent gender, or may have to be considered to have all three genders. How would one distinguish between nominal stems in terms of gender, if none signifies it?

Explanation [NN.IV.9.b]: The response to the above argument is given in a somewhat circular way. If gender is not signified by the nominal stem, then it must be treated as the meaning of an affix. One could then say that a nominal is termed masculine, if the affix added after it denotes the masculine gender. In my view, this is a circular argument, in the sense that the affixes are prescribed on the prior understanding of the meaning of a nominal stem. One would need to know if a stem is masculine, before adding a gender-specific affix to it. A good answer to such a question perhaps lies in removing gender from the consideration of meaning, and treating it as a feature of the word-form. However, this is not the traditional approach.

NN.IV.10. (p. 121)

प्रकृतिवर्जिते केवलप्रत्ययादेव "स्त्री इयती" इत्यादौ तत्प्रतीतेस्तथैव न्याय्यत्वात् । इदंशब्दात् "किमिदम्भ्यां वो घ" इति वतुपो वकारस्य घकारादेशे, "आयनेयीनीयियः फढखछघां प्रत्ययादीनाम्" इत्यनेन घकारस्येयादेशे, इदम इशादेशे, "यस्येति चे"ति प्रकृतीकारलोपे, "उगितश्चे"ति ङीपि, इयतीति हि रूपम् । अन्वयव्यतिरेकाभ्यां प्रत्ययस्यैव शक्तिसिद्धेश्च । "स्त्रियाम्" इत्यधिकृत्यैव "अजाद्यतष्टाप्" इत्यादिना टाब्ङीबादेर्विधानात् । "तस्माच्छसो नः पुंसी"त्यादेरनुशासनस्यानुरोधाच्च । एवं संख्यादावपि द्रष्टव्यम् ।

Translation [NN.IV.10]

[a] It is justified [to hold that gender is the meaning of an affix, rather than that of a nominal stem], because there is a cognition of [gender] from an affix used by itself, without the stem, in constructions like *strī iyatī* "a woman of this size."

[b] The form *iyatī* is derived, by [applying the affix *-vatUP* to the stem *idam*, *idam + vat*], by substituting *v* of *vatUP* with *gha* by P.5.2.40, [*idam + ghat*], by substituting *gh* with *iy* by P.7.1.2, [*idam + iyat*], by substituting *idam* with *iŚ* by P.5.3.3, [*i + iyat*], by zeroing *i* of the stem by P.6.4.148, [ø + *iyat*], and by adding the affix *-ṄīP* by P.4.1.6, [*iyat + ī*].*

* The upper-case letters in the affixes cited represent metalinguistic markers or *anubandhas* in Pāṇini's grammar.

[c] Certainly, the primary signification function of an affix [with respect to gender] is established by reasoning based on concurrent occurrence and concurrent non-occurrence.

[d] Affixes such as -*ṬāP* and -*ṄīP* are prescribed by rules like P.4.1.4 (*ajādy-ataṣ ṭāp*) which occur under the heading P.4.1.3 (*striyām*) "when feminine gender is to be signified." Similarly, rule P.6.1.103 (*tasmāc chaso naḥ puṃsi*) allows [this interpretation].

[e] Similarly, it should be realized that number etc. [are also meanings of affixes, rather than of the nominal stem].

Explanation [NN.IV.10.a]: A whole usable word, under normal circumstances, has a stem and an affix, and therefore, one could say that a certain meaning is signified by one or the other of these elements. How can we be sure that a certain meaning is signified only by the affix, and not by the stem. A conclusive proof for such a view may come from an example which has no stem, and has only an affix, and yet one has a cognition of gender. Kauṇḍabhaṭṭa attempts to offer such an example. This is the example *iyatī*. Kauṇḍabhaṭṭa argues that in this particular example, no stem is left. The stem is entirely deleted in the process of derivation. Thus, if the remaining word can still denote gender, then one must admit that gender is not the meaning of a stem. The example *iyatī* is found in many other texts.[388]

On the face of it, Kauṇḍabhaṭṭa's argument seems valid. However, one should note that he does not make a crucial distinction between case-affixes and other kinds of affixes. While it is true that in the form *iyatī* the original stem *idam* is completely zeroed, *iyatī* is not a case-affix, but it is a new nominal stem, a *Taddhita* derivation. Thus, while one can make an argument that the gender is denoted here by the *Taddhita* affix, one cannot stretch this to suggest that the form *iyatī* is not a nominal stem. No traditional commentator has pointed out this problem.

However, Nāgeśabhaṭṭa does point out other problems in this argument by offering a counter-example, *vāk* "speech." Here, the case-affix added after the nominal stem is zeroed, and yet gender is signified by the nominal stem.[389] The commentary *Kalā* on Nāgeśa-bhaṭṭa's *Laghu-mañjūṣā* points out that this example is directed against Kauṇḍabhaṭṭa's example *iyatī*.[390]

Explanation [NN.IV.10.b]: There is no separate rule in Pāṇini's grammar prescribing the affix -*vatUP* after the nominal stem *idam*. But such a prescription is inferred on the basis of rule P.5.2.40 (*kim-idambhyāṃ vo ghaḥ*), which prescribes the substitute *gh* for *v* in the affix -*vatUP* after the nominal stems *kim* and *idam*.[391]

---

388 *iyān iti pratyaya-mātram ihāvaśiṣyate* /, *BSS*, Pt.I., p. 1458; *VP-A*, Vol.II., p. 342; also: Puṇyarāja on *VP*, II. 229.

389 *vāg-ādi-śabdebhyo vināpi pratyayaṃ tad-bodhāc ca* /, *LM*, p. 1141.

390 *LM-KL*, p. 1141.

391 *etad eva cādeśa-vidhānaṃ jñāpakaṃ kim-idambhyāṃ vatup-pratyayo bhavatīti* /, *KS*, Vol.IV., p. 157.

Explanation [NN.IV.10.c]: The method of *anvaya* and *vyatireka* is discussed in the Introduction, **B.1-5**. Kauṇḍabhaṭṭa's argument is that even after deleting the nominal stem, one still has a cognition of gender from the affix, and hence gender must be a meaning of the affix. Nāgeśabhaṭṭa's example allows a different analysis. Here, the affix is completely deleted, and yet one has a cognition of gender. This allows one to decide that gender must be the meaning of the stem.

Explanation [NN.IV.10.d]: Kauṇḍabhaṭṭa interprets P.4.1.3 (*striyām*) to mean "when feminine gender is to be signified." Under this heading, Pāṇini gives a number of affixes like *ṬāP*. Kauṇḍabhaṭṭa generalizes this and says that gender is an affix meaning. Again one must note that Kauṇḍabhaṭṭa is conveniently overlooking the distinction between case-affixes, and affixes which produce secondary nominal stems.

P.6.1.103 (*tasmāc chaso naḥ puṃsi*) is interpreted by Kauṇḍabhaṭṭa to mean that, if the affix *Śas* signifies masculine gender, then *s* of *Śas* is replaced by *n*, provided that it is preceded by a long vowel resulting from a sandhi of *a* of *Śas* and the last vowel of the nominal. The semantic condition *puṃsi* is interpreted by Kauṇḍabhaṭṭa to mean "[of *Śas*] which signifies masculine gender," (*puṃsi vartamānasya śasaḥ*).

Nāgeśabhaṭṭa, on the other hand, construes *puṃsi* as a condition on the nominal stem: "if *Śas* occurs after a stem which signifies masculine gender," (*puṃliṅga-śabdasya prakṛtitve*). He also interprets P.4.1.3 (*striyām*) to mean "after a nominal which signifies feminine gender."[392] Nāgeśabhaṭṭa's interpretation is supported by some passages from the *Mahābhāṣya*,[393] and other works.[394]

Explanation [NN.IV.10.e]: This conclusion is also derived by applying the method of *anvaya* and *vyatireka*, and is just mentioned here. This is also the view of Mīmāṃsakas.[395]

---

[392] *tasmāc chasa ity atra puṃsīty asya puṃ-liṅga-śabdasya prakṛtitve ity arthaḥ / striyām ity asya ca tatra vartamānāt prātipadikād ity arthaḥ /*, *LM*, p. 1141.

[393] *siddhaṃ tu striyāḥ prātipadika-viśeṣaṇatvāt svārthe ṭāb-ādaya iti /*, *MB*, Vol.II., pp. 288-298.

[394] *api ca naivātra vivaditavyam, prātipadika-viśeṣaṇaṃ hi strī-śabdaḥ / striyāṃ yat prātipadikaṃ vartate tataş ṭāb-ādaya iti /*, *TT*, Vol.V., p. 1676.

[395] *ekatvādiṣv artheṣu svādayo vidhītante /*, *MB*, Vol.II., p. 280; *anvaya-vyatirekābhyāṃ ... vibhaktyā ca saṃkhyābhidhānāt /*, *TV(b)*, p. 950; *grahaḥ prātipadikārthaḥ, ekatvaṃ vibhakty-arthaḥ /*, *MS-B(a)*, Vol.II., p. 723; Vol.IV., pp. 1203-5; Vol.V., pp. 1751-3; *vibhaktyā hi kārakam pratyāyyate /*, *TV(b)*, p. 503; *api ca vibhakter na vacanam evaikam prayojanam, kiṃ tarhi / kāraka-sambandho 'pi /*, *MS-B(a)*, Vol.II., p. 723.

SECTION FIVE

NN.V.1. (pp. 121-2)

त्रिकमिति जातिव्यक्तिलिङ्गानीत्यर्थः । अयं भावः । "स्तनकेशवती स्त्री स्याद्" इत्यादिना विवक्षितमवयवसंस्थानविशेषवत्त्वमेव स्त्रीत्वपुंस्त्वादिकम् । न चैतन्न शास्त्रीयव्यवहारहेतुः । दारानित्यादौ नत्वाभावप्रसङ्गात् । तटस्तटी तटमित्यादौ यथायथं लिङ्गत्रितयनिबन्धनकार्याणामसिद्धिप्रसङ्गाच्चेति वाच्यम् । आरोपादेव निर्वाहसम्भवात् । लिङ्गानुशासनस्य "रात्राह्नाहाः पुंसि" इत्यादेश्च तत्र मानत्वादित्येके ।

Translation [NN.V.1]

[a] [The primary meaning of a noun consists of] three elements, i.e. a generic property, an individual, and gender. This is how the argument goes.

[b] [First view of gender as physical sex]: Some say that femininity (*strītva*) and masculinity (*puṃstva*) represent the possession of specific configurations intended in statements such as: "a female is one who has breasts and long hair [or female sex organ], ..."

[c] [Objection]: [Gender as defined above is] not the basis of any grammatical operations, because [its acceptance] would lead to the absence of [the replacement] *n* [for *s* of the accusative plural affix -*Śas*] in [the form] *dārān*. Also one will not be able to have the appropriate grammatical operations dependent upon all three genders in forms such as *taṭaḥ, taṭī,* and *taṭam.*

[d] [Reply to the above objection]: One should not raise such an objection. [The application of grammatical operations] can still be carried out by superimposing [natural gender on inanimate objects]. The *Liṅgānuśāsana* texts and rules like P.2.4.29 (*rātrāhnāhāḥ puṃsi*) offer a valid basis for this [kind of superimposition].

Explanation [NN.V.1.a]: In **NN.IV.9-10**, Kauṇḍabhaṭṭa offers arguments to support the view that gender is only a meaning of an affix. Here he defends a different alternative, namely that gender is a meaning of a nominal stem. On some occasions, Patañjali also expresses this view.[396] Mīmāṃsakas like Śabara and Kumārilabhaṭṭa also appear to support this view in some places.[397] Kaiyaṭa explains Patañjali's intention by saying that

---

396 See Note 393.

397 *prātipadikārthasya liṅgasya /*, *TT*, Pt.IV., p. 1357; *liṅgam prātipadikenaivocyamānam / ṭāb-ādayaḥ strīliṅgasya dyotakatvān na bhedena vācakā bhavanti / pūrvasya ca śakty-antaram āvirbhāvayanti /*, *TV(b)*, p. 951.

feminine gender is not principally signified by affixes such as *-ṬāP*, but that these affixes are added after a nominal stem which signifies an individual qualified by feminine gender. These affixes are said to co-signify feminine gender.[398] Nāgeśabhaṭṭa also supports this view [cf. **Explanation (NN.IV.10.d)**].

Explanation [NN.V.1.b]: Cf. Introduction, **D.4.iii**.

Explanation [NN.V.1.c]: The objector points out that gender as physical sex cannot explain a number of usages in language, and it cannot become a consistent basis for grammatical operations.

For instance, the nominal *dāra* "wife" is a masculine word and always takes plural endings. Thus, the accusative plural form is *dārān*. To obtain this form, the *s* of the accusative plural affix *-Śas* needs to be replaced with *n*. This replacement takes place by rule P.6.1.103 (*tasmāc chaso naḥ puṃsi*). The condition on this replacement is *puṃsi*, which could be rendered as: "if the affix follows a nominal stem signifying masculine gender." If gender represents physical sex of the object, then the word *dāra* would be a feminine word. In that case, the above rule would not function with respect to it, and we will not be able to derive the form *dārān*.

Similarly, the word *taṭa* "river bank" occurs in all three genders, and hence it should be subject to grammatical operations prescribed with respect to all three genders. However, since this word refers to an inanimate thing, there is no possibility of physical sex. Thus, it would be impossible to derive forms of this word in different genders.[399] Patañjali offers some more examples where there would be similar problems.[400]

Explanation [NN.V.1.d]: The upholder of physical sex-genders tries to answer these difficulties by suggesting that physical sex-genders could be superimposed on different animate and inanimate objects. In the case of the word *dāra-* "wife," the object has real physical female sex, but the usage helps us to superimpose masculine sex-gender on this object. This is supposed to explain why the word *dāra-* can be a masculine word. Similarly, one can impose all three physical sex-genders on the river bank signified by the word *taṭa-*.

The *Liṅgānuśāsana* texts are designed to regulate the ascription of different genders to words, and as such represent an authoritative source of information. These texts ascribe different genders to words which refer to entities which have contrary sex-genders, or have no sex-genders. These statements are used deductively to assume that physical sex-genders can be imposed on different objects. Similarly, Pāṇini's rules are taken as an authority to do the same. For instance, rule P.2.4.29 (*rātrāhnāhāḥ puṃsi*) speaks of the masculine gender of words like *rātra* "night" and *ahan* "day." How can Pāṇini ascribe genders to entities which have no signs of physical masculine gender? Since Pāṇini could not have

398 *nātra strītvam prādhānyena pratyayābhidheyam / kiṃ tarhi / strītvavati dravye vartamānāt prātipadikāt svārthe ṭāb-ādaya iti /*, *MB-P*, Vol.II., p. 288.

399 *brāhmaṇī dārety ādau dravya-dvārā jāter liṅgāntareṇa yogo na syāt / taṭas taṭīty ādau ca kasyāpi liṅgasya yogo na syāt /*, *MB-P-U*, Vol.I., Sec.II., p. 97.

400 *liṅgāt strī-puṃsayor jñāne bhrukuṃse ṭāp prasajyate / khaṭvā vṛkṣau na siddhyataḥ /*, *MB*, Vol.II., p. 290.

been wrong, there must be something like imposition of physical sex-gender on these entities. Patañjali offers some more arguments in support of this prima facie view, cf. Introduction, **D.4.iii**.

NN.V.2. (p. 122)

भाष्यकारस्तूक्तानुपपत्त्यैव तन्मतं निरस्य "स्त्रियाम्" इति सूत्रे सत्त्वरजस्तमसां प्राकृतगुणानां वृद्धिः पुंस्त्वमपचयः स्त्रीत्वं स्थितिमात्रं नपुंसकत्वम् । अत एवोत्कर्षापकर्षसत्त्वेऽपि स्थितिमात्रमादाय सामान्ये नपुंसकमिति शास्त्रमुपपद्यते । उत्कर्षापकर्षसाम्यावस्थात्रयसाधारणस्थितिमात्रविवक्षायां नपुंसकं भवतीति तदर्थात् । तच्च केवलान्वय्यर्थनिष्ठं च । अयं पदार्थ इयं व्यक्तिरिदं वस्त्विति सर्वत्र व्यवहारात् । पुंलिङ्गः शब्द इत्यादिप्रयोगस्तूपचारात् । पुमान् लिङ्गमस्मात्प्रतीयत इति वास्य शक्यमिति वा यौगिको वा । "आङो नास्त्रियाम्," "तस्माच्छसो नः पुंसि" इत्यादिशास्त्रीये शाब्दे, लौकिके च व्यवहारेऽप्येतान्येव निमित्तानीत्याहुः ।

Translation [NN.V.2]

[a] [First interpretation of Patañjali's view]: However, Patañjali rejects this view [of natural physical sex gender] on the basis of the difficulties pointed out above.

[b] On P.4.1.3 (*striyām*), Patañjali says: "Masculine gender represents the increase of the elements (*guṇa*) of Primal Matter (*prakṛti*), i.e. good-ness (*sattva*), passion (*rajas*), and dark-ness (*tamas*). Feminine gender represents the decrease [of these elements]. The common stable condition (*sthiti*) [of these elements] is represented by neuter gender."

[c] Hence, there can be neuter gender, if the common stable condition [of these elements] is intended, even though [actually] there may be increase or decrease [in these elements]. On this basis, the following rule is justified: "Neuter gender refers to the common condition," because, this rule means that neuter gender occurs with reference to the common stable condition which is common to the three conditions of increase, decrease, and equillibrium [of the ultimate elements].

[d] The [gender thus defined] is universally present [in every object] and it is located in the [signified] object [and not in the word]. This is justified on the basis of the following usages [with reference to any possible object]: "this (*padārtha*, masc.) object," "this (*vyakti*, fem.) object," and "this (*vastu*, neut.) object."

[e] The usage such as "a masculine word" [suggesting that gender pertains to words] is only metaphorical. Alternatively, such a usage could be in the etymological sense of the word *puṃliṅga*: a) "a word from which the masculine gender is cognized," or b) "a word whose primary meaning is [in part] the masculine gender."

[f] These genders form the basis for grammatical operations such as P.7.3.120 (*āṅo nāstriyām*) and P.6.1.103 (*tasmāc chaso naḥ puṃsi*), as well as for the common talk [about genders of words].

Explanation [NN.V.2.a]: Patañjali's arguments for the prima facie view of gender as physical sex and the final rejection of this view have been discussed in the Introduction, **D.4.iii**, and **Explanation [NN.V.1.c]**.

Explanation [NN.V.2.b]: Cf. Introduction, **D.4.iv-v**.

Explanation [NN.V.2.c]: For a detailed discussion of different interpretations of the maxim *sāmānye napuṃsakam*, see: Introduction, **D.4.v-vi**.

Explanation [NN.V.2.d]: A property which exists everywhere and whose absence anywhere is not known is called *kevalānvayin*. Such a universally present property is an unnegatable qualifier of every possible object in the world. For instance, the properties of expressibility (*abhidheyatva*) and cognizability (*prameyatva*) are universally present unnegatable properties according to Naiyāyikas.[401] Kauṇḍabhaṭṭa says that gender is also a universally present unnegatable property. The words *padārtha, vyakti,* and *vastu,* all of which mean "an object," are respectively masculine, feminine, and neuter words, and all of these words can be used with respect to any possible or conceivable entity. Therefore, any possible or conceivable entity in this or any other world must possess all three genders. A word may signify only one of them, but the existence of other genders is not negatable.

Explanation [NN.V.2.e]: An objector points out that common usages such as "a masculine word" would contradict the view that gender is a property of the signified object, and not of the signifier word. By changing the meaning of these expressions, Kauṇḍabhaṭṭa explains away this objection.

Explanation [NN.V.2.f]: The philosophical-technical conception of gender as expounded by Patañjali is said to be the basis of grammatical operations. On the basis of this conception, we can distinguish between physical sex and gender as intended or signified by words. There may not be any correspondence between physical sex and grammatical gender, and yet the technical conception of gender is supposed to explain how language functions.

Rule P.7.3.120 (*āṅo nāstriyām*) prescribes the replacement *nā* for the instrumental singular affix *āṄ*, if this affix is added to a non-feminine nominal ending in *i* or *u* and, if it belongs to a class of stems termed *ghi* [cf. P.1.4.7 (*śeṣo ghy-asakhi*)]. With this rule, we

---

401 *yo dharmaḥ sarvatra vartate, yasya cātyantābhāvo 'prasiddhaḥ, sa dharmaḥ kevalānvayī / yathābhidheyatvaṃ jñeyatvam /, NK*, pp. 242-3; Matilal (1968: 80); Ingalls (1951: 612).

can derive forms like *bhānunā* and *madhunā*, where the nominal stems *bhānu-* and *madhu-* are respectively masculine and neuter words and refer to the sun and honey. These words can easily have the respective genders following Patañjali's doctrine, if one assumes that the respective objects are supposed to exhibit the intended states of the ultimate elements of Primal Matter. The same is the case with P.6.1.103 (*tasmāc chaso naḥ puṃsi*), cf. **Explanation [NN.V.1.c]**. The physical sex of the person denoted by the word *dāra* "wife" is feminine, and yet the philosophical-technical gender pertaining to the same person, as intended to be signified by the word is the masculine gender.[402]

Kauṇḍabhaṭṭa says that this very conception forms the basis of the daily linguistic usage of people. However, one must note that people are certainly not aware of any such metaphysical features of objects they talk about, and hence they could not consciously intend to speak about such features. Kaiyaṭa admits this problem. He says that people do not think when they use words with specific genders, and the listeners are also unaware of gender in this sense. However, Patañjali is a mystic visionary, and therefore, he has explained the real philosophical basis of the common linguistic usage of gender. Thus, this is a technical conception of gender and it is not the common-place notion of gender. Yet Kaiyaṭa is not willing to call it *alaukika*. He still defends the view that Patañjali's conception is *laukika*.[403] The only way one can make sense of this is that while the common people do not comprehend this specific nature of gender, it is reflected in the usage of the common people. However, only the truly perceptive sages like Patañjali can see it reflected in the usage of the common people.

NN.V.3. (p. 122)

अन्ये तूपचयापचयादेर्विरुद्धस्यैकत्र समावेशायोगात्कथं तटस्तटी तटमित्यादयो व्यवहाराः । गुणानां क्षणिकत्वाभ्युपगमेऽपि युगपत्तथाव्यवहारानापत्तिः । आत्मा ब्रह्मेत्यादावविकारिण्यसम्भवश्च । आरोपादिकं च पूर्ववादिनापि सुवचमेवेति न तन्मतदूषणाभिनिवेशः सङ्गच्छते । तस्मात् -

"तिस्रो जातय एवैताः केषाञ्चित्समवस्थिताः ।
अविरुद्धा विरुद्धाभिर्गोमनुष्यादिजातिभिः॥"

इति वाक्यपदीयाज्जातिरेव स्त्रीत्वादिकमित्याहुः ।

---

402 *dārādi-śabdaiḥ śabda-śakti-svābhāvyāt śāstrīya-puṃstva-viśiṣṭasyaiva strī-rūpārthasyābhidhānam* /, *MB-P-U*, Vol.I., Sec.II., p. 221; *evaṃ dāra-padārthasya strītve 'pi śabdenopacaya-lakṣaṇam puṃ-rūpam eva vyajyate* /, Ibid., p. 65.

403 *yady apy avicārita-ramaṇīyaṃ liṅgam āśritya vaktāraḥ śabdān uccārayanti / śrotāraś ca pratipadyante / tathāpi vastu-tattva-nirṇayo bhāṣyakāreṇa kṛta iti yad anyair abhyadhāyi saṃstyānādi-lakṣaṇam alaukikaṃ liṅgam iti tad apākṛtam bhavati* /, *MB-P*, Vol.II., p. 296; *tasmāt strītvādinā pratīyamānaṃ saṃstyānādikaṃ laukikam / tasyālaukikatve tu khaṭvā strī vṛkṣaḥ pumān ity-ādi-vyavahāro 'nupapanna iti tasyāpi laukikatva-prasādhanenālaukikatvaṃ nirākṛtam iti bhāvaḥ* /, *MB-P-U*, Vol.II., p. 296.

Translation [NN.V.3]

[a] [An objection to Patañjali's view]: However, others say that the contradicting conditions of increase and decrease [of the ultimate elements of Primal Matter] cannot co-exist in one and the same [object]. How can, then, [one explain] usages such as *taṭaḥ, taṭī*, and *taṭam*?

[b] [Objection continued]: One may [perhaps] accept that these ultimate elements [or rather their conditions] are momentary. Yet one would not be able to have these [different] usages [of the same word with different genders referring to the same object] at the same time.

[c] [Objection continued]: Similarly, it would be impossible to have any gender for [entities] such as soul (*ātman*) and Brahman, since these [entities] never undergo a change.

[d] [Objection continued]: Explanations on the basis of superimposition etc. could be offered even by the other party [i.e. by the upholder of natural sex-genders]. Therefore, it is not proper [for a grammarian] to criticize the view of [the upholder of natural sex-genders] with such vigour, [if a grammarian himself accepts superimposition in some cases].

[e] Therefore, feminine gender etc. are [special] generic properties. This is accepted on the basis of the following [verse] from the *Vākya-padīya*: "For some thinkers, these three [genders] are certainly generic properties, which co-exist [in all objects]. They are not opposed to other generic properties such as bull-ness and man-ness, which are opposed [to each other]."

Explanation [NN.V.3.a]: If masculine gender represents the increase of the ultimate elements of Primal Matter in an object like river-bank, then this could very well be expressed by the masculine word *taṭaḥ*. However, in the normal linguistic usage, the same object can be expressed by the feminine word *taṭī*, or the neuter word *taṭam*. How is it possible that the same object exhibits both increase and decrease of the ultimate elements? These conditions are contradictory to each other. The Vaiśeṣika author Padmanābhamiśra offers this very argument against Patañjali.[404] He says that no one really comprehends the increase of the ultimate elements of Primal Matter from the masculine word *vṛkṣa* "tree," or their decrease from the feminine word *gaṅgā* "the river Ganges."

Explanation [NN.V.3.b]: A defender of Patañjali's view could reformulate his argument and say that the conditions of the ultimate elements of Primal Matter in a given

---

404 *nanu mahābhāṣya-sammatim puras-kṛtya prasādakṛtaiva likhitam puṃstvam upacayaḥ strītvam apacayaḥ anayor vivakṣāyām puṃ-liṅga-strī-liṅge, ubhaya-vivakṣāyāṃ napuṃsakam iti, tathā copacayādir eva puṃstvaṃ na tattvāntaram iti cen na, puṃ-liṅgādibhiḥ śabdair ya upacayaḥ pratīyate tat-svarūpā-nirūpaṇāt / na hi vṛkṣo gaṅgety ādau upacayāpacayau utkarṣāpakarṣau kaucid vṛkṣa-gaṅgā-gatau pratīyete / tathātve 'vadhijñānāpekṣā syāt /, PB-S*, p. 84; also: *nanu upacayāpacayāv eva puṃ-liṅga-strī-liṅgārthau, pratīyate hi taṭas taṭīty ābhyāṃ śabdārthābhyām mahāṃs taṭaḥ svalpaś ca taṭaḥ iti cen na / napuṃsake ko 'rtha iti vaktavyatvāt / na tāvad upacayābhāve saty apacayābhāvaḥ, tayoḥ paraspara-viruddhatayā ekatrāsambhavāt /*, ibid., p. 86.

object are in constant flux, and hence any single condition such as increase or decrease is momentary. Patañjali himself says that no object ever remains the same even for a single moment. It either grows or decays. Therefore, the conditions of increase and decrease are common to all objects, cf. Introduction, **D.4.v**. The word *taṭa* in different genders could, then, be said to represent these different conditions of the ultimate elements of Primal Matter in one and the same object.

The objector says that this does not solve the problem. These different conditions may exist in one and the same object at different times, but not at the same moment. Thus, one would not be able to use these three words with different genders with reference to the same object at the same time.

Actually, Patañjali says that different genders are not representations of the actual conditions of the ultimate elements, as much as they are representations of the intention of the speaker to characterize those objects in a certain way. While the object itself may have a certain condition of the ultimate elements, one may wish to characterize it differently while speaking about that object, and thus be able to use different genders.

The problem with this argument is that the speakers are never conscious of these states of the ultimate elements, and therefore, one cannot truly speak of the intention of a speaker as the guiding principle in this context. However, Patañjali would like to have his argument both ways.

Explanation [NN.V.3.c]: How about those entities which are ontologically beyond any possible change and are said to be immutable? Such are the entities expressed by the masculine word *ātman* "soul," and by the neuter word *brahman* "ultimate reality." These entities are not derived from Primal Matter at all, and hence do not have the ultimate elements of Primal Matter as their constituents.

Nāgeśabhaṭṭa recognizes this difficulty, and tries to answer it by saying that genders of these words could be explained through superimposition.[405] For a different explanation, see: Introduction, **D.4.vii**.

Explanation [NN.V.3.d]: If one defends Patañjali's view, as does Nāgeśabhaṭṭa, then there is no reason why we should not accept the view of physical sex-genders. If both views involve the notion of superimposition, there is apparently no reason why we should select one, and reject the other.

Explanation [NN.V.3.e]: The view that genders are generic properties is sometimes ascribed to Vaiśeṣikas, though no Vaiśeṣika author known to me espouses such a view. For a detailed discussion, see: Introduction, **D.4.viii**.

---

[405] *ātmani sarvasyādhyastatvena paramparayā tatrāpi styānādi-sattvāt ātmā brahmeti vyavahāropapattiḥ* /, *LM*, p. 1143.

NN.V.4. (p. 122)

नन्वेवमपि समनियतानां जातीनां सर्वत्र प्रतीतेः केवलान्वयित्वं वाच्यम् । तथा चात्र मते भाष्यमते च "पशुना यजेत" इत्यत्र पशुस्त्रिया यागप्रसङ्गः । विवक्षितेऽपि पुंस्त्वे तस्य केवलान्वयित्वेनाव्यावर्त्तकत्वादिति चेन्न । "छागो वा मन्त्रवर्णाद्" इति षष्ठान्त्याधिकरणन्यायेनैव निर्वाहात् ।

Translation [NN.V.4]

[a] [Objection against the Jāti view of gender and Patañjali's view]: Even [if genders are generic properties], these co-extensive generic properties are found in all objects and hence they are universally present and unnegatable.

[b] [Objection continued]: Thus in this view [of genders as generic properties] and in the view of the *Mahābhāṣya* [of genders as conditions of ultimate elements], one would be forced to accept an undesirable possibility of performing a sacrifice with a female animal on the basis of [the injunction] "one should perform a sacrifice with a *paśu* 'animal'." The reason is that the masculine gender intended to be expressed [by the word *paśunā*] is a universally unnegatable property, and as such it cannot exclude [other genders].

[c] [Reply to the above objection]: [The desired exclusion of the female animal] can still be effected on the basis of the doctrine taught in the Mīmāṃsā rule *chāgo vā mantra-varṇāt* [*MS* 6/8/10/31] which occurs in the last section of the sixth chapter [of the *Mīmāṃsā-sūtras*]: "Only a [male] goat [would be sacrificed, [since that is what we directly learn] from the letters of the injunction."

Explanation [NN.V.4.a]: The generic properties of genders co-exist in all objects, since any object can be referred to by a word in any gender. Thus, these generic properties of genders are co-extensive with each other.[406] Actually, if there are two properties which are co-extensive, then both of them cannot be generic properties. One of them must cancel the other one. Even granting all three co-extensive generic properties, for the sake of argument, the objector says that they are all universally present and unnegatable (*kevalā-nvayin*). For the notion of *samaniyata*, see: B.K. Matilal (1985: 166). For the notion of *kevalānvayin*, see: B.K. Matilal (1985: 128ff).

Explanation [NN.V.4.b]: If two properties, say P and Q, are universally present and unnegatable, then neither P nor Q can limit or exclude the other. One cannot say that there is an x such that x has P, but not Q, or that it has Q, but not P. Thus, one universally

---

[406] *tisro jātaya evaitāḥ keṣāñcit samavasthitāḥ* /, *VP*, III, *Liṅga-samuddeśa*, verse 4; *sarvatrāviruddha-samavāyāḥ* /, *VP-H(b)*, p. 432.

present unnegatable property cannot be totally or partially exclusive of another universally present unnegatable property.

This applies to genders as generic properties, as well as to genders as conditions of the ultimate elements of Primal Matter. The changing conditions of the ultimate elements are also universally present, and hence do not exclude each other. A word may signify an object with one gender, and yet it will not be able to exclude the possibility of that object having another gender. Thus, the masculine gender intended or signified by the word *paśunā*, in the injunction *paśunā yajeta* "one should perform a sacrifice with an animal," will not be able to block other genders from being included in the meaning of the word *paśu* "animal." This would leave open the possibility of performing a sacrifice with a female animal. This is undesirable, since it goes against the established sacrificial practice.

Explanation [NN.V.4.c]: To refute the above objection, Kauṇḍabhaṭṭa relies on a Mīmāṃsā doctrine given in *MS* (6/8/10/31, *chāgo vā mantra-varṇāt*). Śabara elaborates this doctrine in the following way.[407] The injunction *paśum ālabheta* says that a *paśu* "animal" should be sacrificed in the Jyotiṣṭoma sacrifice. Should one sacrifice a particular animal, or just any animal? The prima facie view is that there is no restriction. But the final view says that there is a specific injunction which uses the word *chāga* "goat," and hence only a goat should be sacrificed. What the word actually says is the final decision. This is the doctrine.

Similarly, one should accept that the gender which is directly understood from the word is the intended gender of the signified object. This doctrine is used by Kauṇḍabhaṭṭa to establish that the gender directly expressed by a word excludes other genders, inspite of the accepted view that all genders are universally present unnegatable properties of all objects. The word *paśunā* directly expresses the masculine gender, and hence there is no possibility of performing a sacrifice with a female animal. An injunction with the word *chāga* in masculine gender excludes all not-goats, as well as females.[408]

NN.V.5. (p. 122)

किञ्चोक्तमतद्वयेऽपि कुमारब्राह्मणच्छागादिशब्दानां पुंस्येव प्रयोगव्यवस्थित्यनुरोधेन लौकिकपुंस्त्वविशिष्टे शास्त्रीयपुंस्त्वे शक्तिस्वीकारात् तद्विवक्षयैवानतिप्रसङ्गात् । एवं कुमार्यादिशब्दा लौकिकस्त्रीत्वविशिष्टे शास्त्रीयस्त्रीत्वे शक्ताः । अस्तु वा कुमारशब्द एवोभयत्र शक्तः । ङीबादि स्त्रियां नादि च पुंस्त्वे द्योतकमित्यवधेयम् । एतच्च लिङ्गं केषाञ्चिदुभयं केषाञ्चिदेकं केषाञ्चित्त्रयमपीत्यत्र लिङ्गानुशासनं प्रमाणमिति स्थितं शब्दकौस्तुभे ।

---

407 *MS-B(a)*, Pt.IV, p. 1518; *BC*, pp. 121-2.

408 *chāgo vā mantra-varṇāt iti ṣaṣṭhāntyādhikaraṇa-nyāyena cchāga-rūpa-paśu-viśeṣa-grahaṇa iva mantra-varṇasya laukika-puṃstva-vivakṣāyāṃ tātparya-grāhakasya sattvāc ca / chāgasya vapāyā iti mantre chāga-bhinne iva striyām asambhavāt /*, *LM*, p. 1145.

Translation [NN.V.5]

[a] [In defense of genders as generic properties and genders as states of ultimate elements]: Moreover, in both of the above mentioned views, [one could say that] words like *kumāra-* "boy," *brāhmaṇa-* "a Brahmin male," and *chāga-* "a [male] goat" are always found used with reference to masculine [beings], and hence it is accepted that their primary signification function is [ascertained] with respect to technical masculine gender qualified by physical male sex. Hence, if this is intended, there is no undesired over-extension [of a sacrifice to a female animal].

[b] Similarly, for words like *kumārī* "girl," their primary signification function is [ascertained] with respect to technical feminine gender qualified by physical female sex.

[c] Alternatively, [one may say that] the word *kumāra-* itself has its primary signification function [ascertained] with respect to both [i.e. technical masculine gender qualified by physical male sex, and technical feminine gender qualified by physical female sex]. [In that case], it should be realized that [affixes] like *ṄīP* [applied after words like *kumāra-* to derive feminine forms like *kumārī*] and [the substitute] *n* [for *s* in the accusative plural affix *Śas* in forms like *kumārān*] respectively co-signify the feminine and the masculine genders.

[d] Thus, for some [words], there are two genders, for some there is only one gender, while for others there are all three genders. The authority of *Liṅgānuśāsana* texts in this matter is established in the *Śabda-kaustubha* [by Bhaṭṭojī Dīkṣita].

Explanation [NN.V.5.a]: Here, Kauṇḍabhaṭṭa offers some further arguments in favor of the two views discussed earlier, i.e. the genders are generic properties or they represent different conditions of the ultimate elements of Primal Matter. A word like *kumāra-* "boy" is invariably used with respect to an object with physical masculine sex. Thus, one can decide that its primary signification function is ascertained with respect to technical masculine gender qualified by physical masculine sex. If this is acceptable, then the same holds true for the words *paśu* "animal" and *chāga* "goat." One can say that their primary signification function is also ascertained with respect to technical masculine gender qualified by physical masculine sex. If the physical masculine gender of these words is intended by the speaker, then one can say that the words refer to only masculine animals, and female animals are excluded.

Explanation [NN.V.5.b]: Here, it is assumed that the word *kumāra-* "boy" is different from the word *kumārī-* "girl." Therefore, Kauṇḍabhaṭṭa says that the primary signification function of the word *kumārī-* is ascertained with respect to technical feminine gender qualified by physical female sex. This is exactly parallel to the primary signification function of the word *kumāra-*. The same would be true with the word *chāgī* "female goat." Its primary signification function would be ascertained with respect to technical feminine gender qualified by physical female sex. With such an interpretation, the word *chāga* excludes female animals, and the word *chāgī* excludes male animals.

Explanation [NN.V.5.c]: This view agrees more closely with Pāṇini's rules. For Pāṇini, *kumāra-* is the basic nominal stem (*prātipadika*) capable of signifying both genders, the masculine and the feminine. The word *kumārī* is a derivative and not a basic nominal. It is derived by adding the affix *-ṄīP* [= *ī*] to the basic nominal *kumāra,* if the basic nominal is used to refer to an object with feminine gender. Thus, the affix *ī* does not signify feminine gender, but it only co-signifies it.[409]

Explanation [NN.V.5.d]: Here a passage from Bhaṭṭojī Dīkṣita's *Śabda-kaustubha* is quoted to support the present argument.[410] Bhaṭṭojī Dīkṣita speaks of the *Liṅgānuśāsana* texts as the final authority on decisions concerning different genders. There is an extensive literature which goes under the name of *Liṅgānuśāsana*. We know from different sources that almost 41 writers had written independent works of this title. Several of these works are available in print, while others are still in manuscripts or are not available to us.[411]

NN.V.6. (p. 122)
अत्र प्रथमपक्षे लौकिकलिङ्गे पृथक्शक्तिर्न कल्पनीयेति लाघवम् । आरोपश्च खट्वेत्यादावभ्युपेयः । चरमे गौरवमनारोपश्च । भाष्यमते तूभयं कल्प्य-मिति विवेकः ।

Translation [NN.V.6]

[a] [Evaluation of the three views on gender]: There are the following distinctions [between the three views on gender discussed so far]. In the first view [of gender as physical sex], there is economy [of assumptions] in that one does not have to assume a separate primary signification function with respect to physical sex-genders. [However], one has to accept superimposition [of physical sex-genders on inanimate objects] in the case of words like *khaṭvā* (f.) "bed."

[b] In the last [view of gender as generic properties], there is prolixity [in accepting three co-extensive generic properties as an additional commitment, but] one is not required to take recourse to superimposition [to explain any cases].

---

409 *ṅy-āp-prātipadikāt,* P.4.1.1; *ṅy-antād āb-antāt prātipadikāc ca ... / ... prātipadika-grahaṇe liṅga-viśiṣṭasyāpi grahaṇam ... /, SK*, p. 14; also see: *PS*, p. 355.

410 *SKB(a)*, Pt.I., p. 436; *LM*, p. 1143.

411 Vyākaraṇopādhyāyā (1964: 2-3).

[c] In the view of the *Mahābhāṣya* [that genders are reflections of different conditions of the ultimate elements of Primal Matter], one is required to assume both [i.e. separate primary signification functions for physical sex-genders, and superimposition to explain cases like *ātman*].

Explanation [NN.V.6.a]: In this section, the relative merits and demerits of the three views discussed so far are evaluated. The view of gender as physical sex relies upon a direct relation between a word and physical sex distinctions. In other words, the primary signification function of a word is ascertained directly with respect to physical sex distinctions. For this reason, this view does not need to make any additional effort to deal with physical sex distinctions. In this respect, this view has economy. On the other hand, this view requires an assumption of superimposition of physical sex distinctions on inanimate objects to explain the gender distinctions in words referring to inanimate objects. This is a sign of prolixity.

Explanation [NN.V.6.b]: In the view that genders are co-extensive generic properties, there is another kind of prolixity. The prolixity consists in the very acceptance of co-extensive generic properties. Elsewhere, co-extensive properties cannot be generic properties, and one of them must cancel all others. Another aspect of prolixity is that this adds to the ontological commitment, because the additional generic properties are additional members to the inventory of real external entities. There is, however, an element of economy in the fact that there is no need to assume any kind of superimposition. Each object has all the three generic properties, and hence a word could signify any one of them.

Explanation [NN.V.6.c]: For a discussion of the faults in the first interpretation of Patañjali's view, see: **Explanation [NN.V.3.c-d]** and **Explanation [NN.V.5.a]**. Actually, Kauṇḍabhaṭṭa does not believe that this is the real interpretation of Patañjali's view, and therefore he feels free to criticize it. Kauṇḍabhaṭṭa's final interpretation of Patañjali's opinion is given in the next section.

NN.V.7. (p. 123)

वस्तुतस्तु भाष्यमते लिङ्गं शब्दनिष्ठमेव । पुंलिङ्गः शब्द इति व्यवहारात् । पुंलिङ्गवाचकत्वात्तथेति चेत्तर्हि घटः शब्दे इत्यपि स्यात् । आरोपे निमित्तानुसरणमित्यादेरतिगौरवात् । अर्थनिष्ठत्वे तटस्तटी तटमात्मा ब्रह्मेत्यादेरनुपपत्तेरुक्तत्वाच्च । छाग्या यागप्रसङ्गाच्च ।

Translation [NN.V.7]

[a] [Patañjali's real view according to Kauṇḍabhaṭṭa]: However, the real view of the *Mahābhāṣya* is that gender is located in the word [and not in the signified object]. This is because there are usages such as: "a masculine word."

[b] If one says that this is [so, because a word] primarily signifies masculine gender, [and not because the masculine gender is a feature of the word], then one would have to accept [a usage such as] "a pot is in the word," [on the ground that the word primarily signifies a pot].

[c] Similarly, there is extreme prolixity [in explaining the usage "a masculine word" on the basis of superimposition of gender as a property of meaning on the word], since superimposition needs a [specific] justification.

[d] It was already pointed out that one cannot explain cases like *taṭaḥ, taṭī, taṭam, ātmā,* and *brahma,* if gender [is supposed to be] located in the [signified] object.

[e] Similarly, [in the view of gender as a property of the signified object], there would be an undesired possibility of performing a sacrifice with a female goat.

Explanation [NN.V.7.a]: The interpretation of Patañjali's view presented earlier is only a prima facie interpretation for Kauṇḍabhaṭṭa. According to that prima facie interpretation, gender as a reflection of a particular state of the ultimate elements of Primal Matter is a property of the signified object, rather than that of the word. It is located in the signified object and is a property of that object (*artha-niṣṭha / artha-dharma*).

In the present section, Kauṇḍabhaṭṭa begins to present his final interpretation of Patañjali's view. According to this view, gender is only a property of the signifier word, and not of the signified object. It is located in the word and is a property of the word (*śabda-niṣṭha / śabda-dharma*). Kauṇḍabhaṭṭa simply makes this statement, without going into details of how gender can be a property of the word, and yet fit the Sāṃkhyan conception of gender presented by Patañjali. Some commentators have made attempts to explain this point of view by arguing that a word itself is made up of the ultimate elements of Primal Matter, and hence can have states of increase, decrease etc. Nāgeśabhaṭṭa rejects this interpretation of Patañjali's view given by Kauṇḍabhaṭṭa, and argues that, for Patañjali, gender is a property of the signified object and not of the word, cf. Introduction, **D.4.vii**.

Explanation [NN.V.7.b]: While supporting the prima facie interpretation of Patañjali's view, Kauṇḍabhaṭṭa explains in **NN.V.2.e** that a usage such as "a masculine word" should not be taken to mean that gender pertains to the word and not to the signified object. Here, Kauṇḍabhaṭṭa argues the reverse case and he takes a usage like "a masculine word" as evidence in favor of the view that gender is a feature of the word, rather than that of the object. Kauṇḍabhaṭṭa then gives arguments against the previous view. If we say that a word is called a masculine word because it signifies the masculine gender, there would be a number of problems. One would have to accept a usage like *ghaṭaḥ śabde* "a pot is in the word." If we can say "a masculine word," because a word signifies a masculine object, this implies that we are saying that the gender property is in the word, because it signifies that gender property of the object. If such an implication is valid, we should be able to say "a pot is in the word 'pot'." The word "pot" signifies the object pot, and for this reason we should be able to say that the object pot is in the word "pot." Since, such a usage is unheard of, one cannot accept this argument. Therefore, it is better to accept that gender is a property of the word and not of the signified object. Another likely reading of the passage is *ghaṭaḥ śabdaḥ ity api syāt*. Both a) *ghaṭaḥ śabde ity api*, and b) *ghaṭaḥ śabdaḥ ity api* would be reduced to a common reading *ghaṭaḥ śabda ity api* due to sandhis. For Kauṇḍabhaṭṭa, this is Patañjali's final view. This is rejected by Nāgeśabhaṭṭa who says that, for Patañjali, gender is a property of the signified object and not of the signifier word and this is supported by Bhartṛhari and Kaiyaṭa.[412]

Explanation [NN.V.7.c]: For details, see: **Explanation [NN.V.3.c-d]** and **Explanation [NN.V.6.c]**.

Explanation [NN.V.7.d]: Kauṇḍabhaṭṭa offers some examples which cannot be properly explained if gender were to be a property of the signified objects, cf. **Explanation [NN.V.3.a-d]**.

Explanation [NN.V.7.e]: This argument against the prima facie interpretation of Patañjali's view is explained earlier, cf. **Explanation [NN.V.4.b]**.

NN.V.8. (p. 123)

यत्तु च्छागादिशब्दानां पुंस्येव नियतप्रयोगानुरोधेन लौकिकपुंस्त्वविशिष्टे शास्त्रीये शक्तेस्तद्विवक्षया नातिप्रसङ्ग इति । तन्न । एवमप्यचेतनवाचकानां मध्वादिशब्दानां माक्षिकादौ पुन्नपुंसकत्वं, वसन्तादौ शुद्धपुंस्त्वमिति व्यवस्था न स्यात् । एवं "स्वो ज्ञातावात्मनि स्वं त्रिष्वात्मीये स्वोऽस्त्रियां धने" इत्यादिलिङ्गनियमोच्छेदापत्तिः । अत्र प्रकारान्तरानुसरणे तेनैवोपपत्तेर्लौकिकलिङ्गे वाच्यत्वकल्पनं मुधैव । शब्दनिष्ठत्वे च नानुपपत्तिलेशोऽपि ।

Translation [NN.V.8]

[a] [Refutation of the prima facie interpretation of Patañjali's view]: [A defender of the prima facie interpretation of Patañjali's view says that] words like *chāga* "a [male] goat" are invariably found used with reference to masculine [or rather male] animals, and therefore, their primary signification function is [ascertained] with respect to technical [masculine gender] qualified by physical male sex. This [gender] is intended [in sacrificial injunctions], and hence there is no undesirable over-extension [of a sacrificial injunction to a female animal].

412 *napuṃsakārthābhidhāyitvāt tad-abhedāc ca śabdasya napuṃsakatvam iti kaiyaṭa-harī ity anyatra vistaraḥ* /, *LM*, pp. 1146-7.

[b] [Refutation of the above claim]: That does not stand [as a general principle]. Even if [this explanation in the case of words like *chāga* "a [male] goat" is granted], there can be no exact rule concerning the use of words signifying inanimate things. For instance, the word *madhu-* is either masculine or neuter in the sense of honey, and it is only a masculine word in the sense of the spring season. Similarly, the following gender-restriction [in the *Amarakośa*] would not work: "The word *sva* 'relative, one's own self' is used in masculine; *sva* 'one's own belongings' is used in all three genders, and *sva* 'wealth' is used in masculine and neuter."

[c] If [the defender of the prima facie interpretation of Patañjali's view] would opt to follow a different theory [just] here [to explain these cases], then that other theory [by itself] can explain [all cases]. Therefore, it is naive to accept the assumption of physical sex-genders as primary meanings. If [one accepts the final interpretation of Patañjali's view that] gender is located in the words, then there is no difficulty whatsoever.

Explanation [NN.V.8.a]: This is an old argument reiterated here for refutation, cf. **NN.V.5.a-b**.

Explanation [NN.V.8.b]: In the case of the word *chāga,* one may be able to say that the word always occurs in reference to a male animal, and hence the technical gender signified by the word coincides with the physical sex of the animal. Thus, one may say that the primary signification function of this word is ascertained with respect to technical masculine gender qualified by physical male sex. Thus, physical sex is also held to be a primary meaning for this word. With such a formulation, it is claimed that objects referred to by the word are necessarily male animals.

Such a restriction may not work in the case of words like *madhu* or *sva*, which signify inanimate objects like honey, spring season, wealth, belongings etc. In the case of these words, it may not be possible to establish any restriction on usage, if the primary signification function of a word is to be ascertained with respect to technical gender qualified by physical sex. There is no physical sex for objects referred to by these words, and the technical gender does not have any restrictive force, because each object is said to have different genders. Thus, one will not be able to justify any restrictive statements regarding genders of such words. Therefore, Kauṇḍabhaṭṭa argues that one should accept that genders pertain to words, rather than to signified objects.

Nāgeśabhaṭṭa disagrees with Kauṇḍabhaṭṭa's opinion and says that gender pertains to signified objects, and not to words. Yet it is not impossible to determine specific genders of words signifying inanimate objects. This can be done simply by relying on the usage of the elites and on the *Liṅgānuśāsana* texts.[413] Inanimate objects to not have physical sex, and yet they have technical genders.

The verse quoted by Kauṇḍabhaṭṭa is from Amarasiṃha's *Amarakośa* (3.3.211).

Explanation [NN.V.8.c]: Since inanimate objects like honey and wealth have no physical sex, the upholder of the prima facie interpretation of Patañjali's view would have to adopt some other view for these words. Kauṇḍabhaṭṭa says that that would not be consistent. One should opt for a theory which explains all cases. Kauṇḍabhaṭṭa argues that if genders are properties of words, one can explain all cases without any problem. Therefore, he recommends that the new interpretation be adopted.

NN.V.9. (p. 123)

तथा हि । ह्रस्वत्वदीर्घत्वोदात्तत्वानुदात्तत्ववत् स्त्रीत्वपुंस्त्वादिविरुद्धधर्मवत्त्वाच्छब्दा भिद्यन्ते । आनुपूर्वीसाम्यस्यापि तद्वदेवार्थभेदाच्छब्दभेदवादिनो मत इव चोपपत्तेः । केषाञ्चिल्लिङ्गानुशासनेनैकलिङ्गत्वव्यवहारश्च समानानुपूर्वीकत्वेन तेषां तन्त्रेणानुकरणादुपपद्यते । एवं च तटादिशब्देषु समानानुपूर्वीकेषु लिङ्गत्रयं, छागादिषूभयं, पदार्थादिष्वेकमस्तीति सर्वत्र मुख्य एव लिङ्गयोगः । तत्र पुंस्त्वे नाभावः, स्त्रीत्वे टाबादि च द्योतकम् ।

Translation [NN.V.9]

[a] [Defending genders as properties of words]: Thus, words differ on account of different contrasting properties of feminine, masculine [and neuter genders], just as [they differ on account of contrasting properties of vowels such as] short and long quantity, and high and low pitch.

[b] [In this way, a single phonetic sequence is supposed to represent several different items differing in gender]. It is possible [to explain] the sameness of the phonetic sequence [pertaining to different words differing in gender] in accordance with the view [of some] that there must be a difference in the words, whenever there is a difference in meaning, [though these different words may have the same phonetic shape].

[c] [Though words with the same phonetic shape are treated as separate linguistic items if they differ in gender], in the case of some [words], the *Liṅgānuśāsana* texts speak of [them] as having more than one gender. This can be justified by assuming different imitations [of the same word, each with a different gender] on the basis of identical phonetic shape.

---

413 *evam madhu-śabdena puṃstva-napuṃsakatva-viśiṣṭatayā makarandādikam evocyate puṃstva-mātra-viśiṣṭaṃ tu caitrādikam ity api tata eva nirṇeyam / ... prayogād api nirṇeyam / liṅgānuśāsanādibhyo nirṇeyam /*, *LM*, pp. 1143-4; *yat tu bhūṣaṇakṛtā liṅgasyārtha-niṣṭhatve cetane vakṣyamāṇa-rītyā nirvāhe 'pi acetane madhv-ādau vyavasthā na syād iti śabda-niṣṭham eva tad bhāṣya-sammatam iti tan nety āha - evam iti /*, *LM-KL*, p. 1143; also: *LM*, pp. 1146-7; *LM-KL*, p. 1146; *BSS*, Pt.I., pp. 563-4.

[d] Thus, in the case of words like *taṭaḥ*, [*taṭī* and *taṭam*], which have the same phonetic shape, there are three genders; in the case of [words] like *chāga* [and *chāgī*] there are two [genders], while in the case of [words] like *padārtha* there is only one gender. This way the ascription of gender in all cases is always a direct ascription.

[e] In this matter, the [replacement] *nā* [for the instrumental singular affix *-Ṭā* or *-āṄ* by P.7.3.120 (*āṅo nāstriyām*)] is a co-signifier of the masculine [and neuter genders pertaining to the nominal stem] and [affixes] like *-ṬāP* are [co-signifiers of] the feminine gender [pertaining to the nominal stem].

Explanation [NN.V.9.a]: For details of this argument, see: Introduction, **D.4.ix**.

Explanation [NN.V.9.b]: Here, Kauṇḍabhaṭṭa attempts to establish that gender is a distinctive feature of words. The word *-kāra* "agent, maker" differs from the word *kara* "hand" because of the distinction in vowel length. Similarly, the word *bráhman* "a religious incantation" differs from *brahmán* "a priest" because of the difference in accents. Kauṇḍabhaṭṭa says that the words *taṭa(ḥ)* and *taṭa(m)* differ because they have different gender properties. The first word is a masculine word, while the second one is a neuter word. In short, these words may have the same meaning, and the same phonetic shape, and yet they differ in genders, and hence they must be treated as two separate words.

Kauṇḍabhaṭṭa compares this view with another doctrine held by some thinkers. This doctrine holds that a single word *W* cannot be said to have two different meanings, say M_1 and M_2. We should rather say that the word W_1 denotes the meaning M_1, and that the word W_2 denotes the meaning M_2. The fact that the words W_1 and W_2 have the same phonetic shape does not prevent them from being two separate words. On similar lines, Kauṇḍabhaṭṭa says that one should not say that a single word *W* has two different genders, G_1 and G_2. One should rather say that there are two words, W_1 and W_2, which have the genders G_1 and G_2, respectively. The fact that W_1 and W_2 have the same phonetic shape does not prevent them from being two different words.

Explanation [NN.V.9.c]: The reading of this passage as it stands in the Bombay edition and in V.N. Misra's new edition is *liṅgānuśāsanenaikaliṅgatvavyavahāraḥ*, and a possible way to split it is: *liṅgānuśāsanena eka-liṅgatva-vyavahāraḥ* "the ascription of a single gender [to each word] in the *Liṅgānuśāsana* text." The new edition of *Vaiyākaraṇa-bhūṣaṇa* by Manudeva Bhattacharya (p. 132) explicitly splits the text in this fashion. On the other hand, the reading in the *Vaiyākaraṇa-bhūṣaṇa-sāra* is *liṅgānuśāsane 'neka-liṅgatva-vyavahāraḥ* [*VBS-P*, p. 245]. In accordance with this reading, the reading of the *Vaiyākaraṇa-bhūṣaṇa* could be split in this way: *liṅgānuśāsane naika-liṅgatva-vyavahāraḥ*. The words *aneka* and *naika* have the same meaning. I have chosen the interpretation: *liṅgānuśāsane naika-liṅgatva-vyavahāraḥ* for my translation, since it accords with the reading of the *Vaiyākaraṇa-bhūṣaṇa-sāra*. This is also justified in view of the practice of *Liṅgānuśāsana* texts. However, it is clear that this is a somewhat obscure passage, and has given rise to two opposite readings.

This is the dilemma as I understand it. The *Liṅgānuśāsana* texts ascribe more than one gender to a single word. That is to say, they describe that a single word *W* has three genders, G_1, G_2, and G_3. Apparently, this does not fit Kauṇḍabhaṭṭa's theory of gender being a distinctive property of words. Therefore, he would rather reinterrpret the statements in the *Liṅgānuśāsana* texts by restating them using different homophonic imitations, each imitation being given one distinct gender. Thus, Kauṇḍabhaṭṭa's restatement would look something like this: There are three homophonic words, W_1, W_2, and W_3, and they have the genders G_1, G_2, and G_3, respectively. How does one get three words out of the one mentioned in the *Liṅgānuśāsana* text? Kauṇḍabhaṭṭa's answer is two fold. The single word mentioned in the text needs to be repeated several times. This is called *tantra*. Each repetition is then taken to be an imitation (*anukaraṇa*) of a numerically different word. The device of *tantra* is made possible by the fact that the different words said to have been abbreviated into a single expression are all homophonous.

Explanation [NN.V.9.e]: Kauṇḍabhaṭṭa thus argues that gender is a property of the word. It is neither a property of the signified object, nor is it signified by the affix. Kauṇḍabhaṭṭa says that affixes are co-signifiers (*dyotaka*) of the gender property pertaining to the nominal stem. Consider the form *paśunā*. Rule P.7.3.120 (*āṅo nāstriyām*), in accordance with the present view of gender, is interpreted in the following way. The instrumental case affix *āṄ* is replaced by *nā*, if it is added after a non-feminine nominal stem belonging to the *ghi* class. The fact that the form *paśunā* shows this replacement is an indication that the nominal stem *paśu* has a non-feminine gender. In this specific example, it indicates the masculine gender of the nominal stem.

Similarly, P.4.1.3 (*striyām*) could be interpreted to mean: "[the following affixes are added] when the nominal stem is a feminine stem." Thus, the nominal aja_1 is said to denote a male goat, and another homophonic nominal aja_2 is said to denote a female goat. The first word is a masculine word, while the second one is a feminine word. The affix *-ṬāP*, prescribed under the above rule, occurs after the nominal stem *aja*, and this allows the derivation of the feminine form *ajā*. The fact that the affix is added indicates that the stem was a feminine stem. In this sense, the affix is said to be a co-signifier.

Kauṇḍabhaṭṭa is using the notion of *dyotaka* "co-signifier" in an unusual manner. Normally, an item co-signifies a meaning element which is signified by another element. Here, gender is said to be a feature of the word, and not part of the meaning of the stem, and yet it is said to have been co-signified by the affix. Generally, co-signifiers do not co-signify features of words. Thus, this is not a very cogent argument. This argument points out a significant weakness in Kauṇḍabhaṭṭa's thinking. It implies that even while admitting that gender is just a feature of the word, and that it is not a feature of the signified meaning, his treatment in terms of co-signification of gender by the affix endows a kind of pseudo-meaning status to gender. Generally, the Indian tradition is unable to think of gender in non-semantic terms. This indicates a deeper cultural presupposition.

NN.V.10. (p. 123)

तच्च शब्दनिष्ठमपि शब्दवाच्यमर्थपरिच्छेदकत्वेनान्वेति । लिङ्गविशेषविशिष्टस्यैवार्थविशेषवाचकताया लिङ्गानुशासनशास्त्रसिद्धत्वात्स्वाश्रयवाच्यत्वसम्बन्धेन लिङ्गस्यार्थव्यावर्त्तकत्वोपपत्तेः । अत एव प्रयोगनियमोपपत्तिः ।

Translation [NN.V.10]

[a] The [gender] is located in words [as a word-property] and yet it is signified by words, and as such it is construed with the signified object as its excluder [from certain other objects].

[b] On the authority of the *Liṅgānuśāsana* texts, it is firmly established that a word qualified by a given gender alone signifies a specific meaning. Hence, it is appropriate that gender is an excluder (*vyāvarttaka*) of the signified object [from certain other objects], by a specific relation. [This specific relation of gender to the signified object is such that the object in question is] signified (*vācya*) by [the word which is] the locus (*āśraya*) of that [*sva*, i.e. gender itself].

[c] [Since gender pertaining to the word is still an excluder for the signified objects], the restrictions on the usage of words are justified.

Explanation [NN.V.10.a]: If gender were a property of the signified object, then it could be legitimately regarded to be a meaning of the word, in as much as a generic property and an individual are meanings of a word. However, if gender is a property of a word, then how can one say that it is a meaning of a word? Kauṇḍabhaṭṭa proposes here that a gender is a word-property, and yet it is different from other word-properties such as vowel-length or pitch, in that gender is also signified by the word. For this reason, it could still function as the excluder of the signified object from other objects. This is to say that if a word has the property of masculine gender, then this gender pertaining to the word can limit the significata of the word only to the objects having the corresponding physical sex. This whole argument is unconvincing, and, in my opinion, indicates certain propensities of Indian grammarians as regards the notion of gender. It is close to impossible for them to consider gender in non-semantic formal terms. Thus, even while arguing that gender is a property of the word, Kauṇḍabhaṭṭa argues that it is signified by the word, and then it strangely functions as the excluder of the signified object, as if it were a property of that object. This is very unsatisfactory, and, for this very reason, this view is finally rejected by Nāgeśabhaṭṭa.

Explanation [NN.V.10.b]: How can gender be a word-property and still limit the objects signified by a word? Kauṇḍabhaṭṭa says that a word qualified by a specific gender alone is capable of signifying a specific meaning. In a sense, a specific gender works as a specific condition on the primary signification function of a word, and thereby limits the class of objects signified by that word. The relation of gender with signified objects is through the signifier word. A gender is located in a given word as its property, and this given word *qua* a locus of the specific gender signifies a specific meaning. This is described by the term *svāśraya-vācyatva-sambandha*. Here, *sva* refers to gender, *svāśraya* refers to "the locus of *sva*" or the word, and *svāśraya-vācya* refers to the signified object.[414] This whole argument can perhaps be stated elegantly without considering gender as something signified by the word. But Kauṇḍabhaṭṭa gets himself into a contradiction by saying that gender is a property of a word and that it is still signified by the word.

Explanation [NN.V.10.c]: See: **NN.V.8.b** and **Explanation [NN.V.10.b]**.

NN.V.11. (p. 123)

यद्वा शब्दनिष्ठमेवार्थविशेषनिर्णायकमस्तु । बहुव्रीह्यादिस्वर इवान्यपदार्थादिः । एवं च पशुनेत्यत्रापि पुंस्त्वस्य परिच्छेदकत्वान्न पशुस्त्रिया यागप्रसङ्गः । न वा तेषां विरुद्धत्वेन क्वचिदारोप इत्यभ्युपगमः । न च पशुशब्दस्य नित्यपुंस्त्वात् पदार्थादिशब्दोदितलिङ्गवत् साधारण्यात् कथं स्त्रीपशुव्यावृत्तिरिति वाच्यम् । "पश्वा न पायुं गुहा चरन्तम्" इति ऋग्वेदे (स्त्रीलिङ्गपशुशब्दस्य) दर्शनात् पशुनेति पुंस्त्वस्य परिच्छेदकत्वान्न पशुस्त्रिया याग इति मीमांसायां निर्णीतत्वाच्च तस्य नित्यपुंस्त्वाभावनिर्णयात् ।

Translation [NN.V.11]

[a] [Continuing defense of gender as word-properties]: Alternatively, [one could say that] gender is located in words alone, and [yet] it is a decisive factor with respect to specifics of meaning, similar to vowel pitch in the case of a Bahuvrīhi [being a decisive factor for the determination of the reference of the compound which is] other than the meaning of the [constituent] words.

[b] Hence, there is no undesirable possibility of performing a sacrifice with a female animal on the basis of [the injunction] "one should perform a sacrifice with a *paśu* 'animal'." This is so, because the masculine gender [pertaining to the word *paśu-*] in *paśunā* [in the injunction *paśunā yajeta*] is an excluder [with respect to the signified animals].

414 *svāśraya-vācyatva-sambandhena svam puṃstvam, svāśrayaḥ paśu-śabdaḥ, tad-vācyatvam puṃ-vyaktāv iti, tādṛśa-sambandhena* /, *VBS-S*, p. 226; also: *LM-KL*, p. 11 46.

[c] Nor should [one object by] assuming superimposition [of the masculine gender pertaining to the word *paśu* on female animals, and thus raising the possibility of including them as sacrificial animals], because these [properties of masculine gender and feminine gender are] opposed to each other [and would not permit such superimposition].

[d] [Objection to Kauṇḍabhaṭṭa's view]: The word *paśu* always occurs in the masculine, and hence this [masculine gender of the word] is similar to the [invariable masculine] gender signified by the word *padārtha* "object." It is thus common [to all signified objects irrespective of individual sex distinctions]. This being the case, how could there be any exclusion of female animals [from the objects signified by the word *paśu*]?

[e] [Reply to the above objection]: This [objection] is invalid, since it is decided that the word *paśu* is not a universally masculine [word], on the basis [of the following arguments]: i) This word is found in the *Ṛgveda* [1.65.1, *paśvā na pāyuṃ guhā carantam,* used in the feminine form *paśvā*], and ii) it is finally decided in the Mīmāṃsā system that a sacrifice should not be performed with a female animal, because the masculine gender in the form *paśunā* excludes [female animals].

Explanation [NN.V.11.a]: Kauṇḍabhaṭṭa proposes here that gender is a word-property, not signified by a word, and yet it functions as a decisive factor, as an excluder, with respect to objects signified by a word. He compares this with the accent properties of a word. The accent does indeed belong to the word, and yet it affects the determination of meaning. Especially, the accent pattern is very significant in deciding whether something is a Bahuvrīhi or a Tatpuruṣa compound. By P.6.1.223 (*samāsasya*), the last vowel of a compound in general is high-pitched. However, the exception rule P.6.2.1 (*bahuvrīhau prakṛtyā pūrva-padam*) says that the pitch pattern of the first constituent in a Bahuvrīhi compound remains the same. The most famous example is the compound *indra-śatru.* The word *śatru-* "killer" is compounded with the word *indra,* which is the name of the god Indra. If the compound is accented as *indra-śatrú,* then it is a Tatpuruṣa compound meaning "the killer of Indra." However, if the compound is accented as *índra-śatru,* then it is a Bahuvrīhi compound meaning "one whose killer is Indra." This is a significant distinction.[415]

Explanation [NN.V.11.b]: By applying the above reasoning, Kauṇḍabhaṭṭa explains the Vedic injunction *paśunā yajeta* "one should perform a sacrifice with a [male] animal." Here the word *paśu* is a masculine word, and hence the gender pertaining to the word functions as the excluder with respect to the signified animals. This results in the exclusion

---

415 *tatrendrāmitratve siddhe sati 'indrasya śatrur bhava' ity arthe pratipādye 'ntodātte prayoktavye ādy-udātta ṛtvijā prayuktaḥ / ity arthāntarābhidhānād indra eva vṛtrasya śatruḥ sampannaḥ /, MB-P*, Vol.I., Sec.I., p. 23. Stories relating to this example go back to middle Vedic period and indicate that it was already getting to be very difficult to keep track of proper accents in Sanskrit.

of female animals, and therefore the undesirable possibility of sacrificing a female animal is averted.

Explanation [NN.V.11.c]: This refers to an older interpretation of the *Bhāṣya* view. According to that view, sometimes the masculine gender signified by a word is superimposed on an object which has natural feminine sex, cf. **NN.V.1.d** and **NN.V.3.c**. Kauṇḍabhaṭṭa says that such superimposition is unjustified, because the properties of masculine and feminine gender are contradictory to each other.

Explanation [NN.V.11.d]: The objector says that the word *paśu* occurs universally with masculine gender, like the word *padārtha* "object." If this is the case, then the masculine gender pertaining to this word cannot possibly limit the signified objects to a given natural sex. The word *padārtha* "object" may be a masculine word, and yet the objects signified by it are not limited to any given natural sex. This would ultimately lead to the inclusion of female animals in the objects signified by the word *paśu*, and would lead to the undesired possibility of performing a sacrifice with a female animal.

Explanation [NN.V.11.e]: To refute this objection, Kauṇḍabhaṭṭa first argues that the word *paśu* does not occur universally in the masculine gender, and that there are places where it occurs in the feminine. He quotes a passage from the *Ṛgveda*, where the form *paśvā* occurs. This is an instrumental singular form of the word *paśu-*. P.7.3.120 (*āṅo nāstriyām*) says that the instrumental singular affix *āṄ* is replaced by *nā*, if it is preceded by a non-feminine nominal stem. The form *paśvā* is derived by adding the affix *ā* to the word *paśu*, and the affix *ā* has not been replaced by *nā*. Therefore, one can conclude that the word *paśu* occurs in the feminine gender in this form. This makes the form *paśunā* in the injunction *paśunā yajeta* more explicitly a masculine form, such that its use excludes the female animals from being sacrificed.

Actually, Kauṇḍabhaṭṭa knows full well that this is not a valid argument. In his shorter text, *Vaiyākaraṇa-bhūṣaṇa-sāra*, he shows that forms like *paśvā* are not feminine forms, since rule P.7.3.120 is optional as far as the Vedic language is concerned. One can get this form as a masculine form, and it need not be a feminine form [*VBS-P*, p. 248].

Perhaps for this very reason, he offers a second justification, which remains his final justification throughout the remainder of this section. He relies on the interpretation given in the Mīmāṃsā system, where it is decided that what a word directly says is the final decision to be accepted. Since the word *paśunā* directly speaks of masculine gender, the female animals are excluded. See: **Explanation [NN.V.4.c]**. As the following sections indicate, Kauṇḍabhaṭṭa has not only accepted a Mīmāṃsā conclusion, he also accepts the Mīmāṃsā arguments leading upto such a conclusion. Here, the distinction between exegetical arguments and philosophical arguments is conveniently blurred.

NN.V.12. (p. 123)

तथा निर्णयेऽपि वा नानुपपत्तिः । "छागो वा मन्त्रवर्णाद्" इति षष्ठान्त्याधिकरणन्यायेन च्छागव्यक्तिविशेषस्येव पुंस्त्वस्यापि मन्त्रवर्णत एव लाभात् । "छागस्य वपाया" इति मन्त्रे छागस्येति पठितस्य च्छागभिन्न इव स्त्रियामसम्भवात् ।

Translation [NN.V.12]

[a] Even if it is so decided [that the word *paśu* occurs universally in the masculine], still there is no difficulty, because one can derive the [exclusive] masculine gender, like [the other meaning, i.e.] a specific goat, directly from the words of the injunction. This is done on the basis of the logic expounded in Mīmāṃsā rule *chāgo vā mantra-varṇāt* [*MS*, 6/8/10/31] which occurs in the last section of the sixth chapter of the *Mīmāṃsā-sūtras*.

[b] [The sacrificial operation] prescribed by the word *chāgasya* "of a male goat" in the injunction *chāgasya vapāyā* ... "of the omentum of a [male] goat" cannot possibly apply to a non-goat, as well as to a female goat.

Explanation [NN.V.12.a-b]: The principle advocated in this Mīmāṃsā rule and the injunction quoted above have been discussed before, cf. **Explanation [NN.V.4.c]**. The injunction *chāgasya vapāyā* etc. occurs in Śabara's commentary on the *Mīmāṃsā-sūtras*, *MS-B(b)*, Vol.I., p. 121, and Vol.II., p. 462. Parallel passages are found in *Kāṭhaka-saṃhitā* (16.21), *Taittirīya-brāhmaṇa* (3.6.8.1), and *Āpastamba-śrauta-sūtra* (7.21.1).

NN.V.13. (pp. 123-4)

यत्र तु विधौ सन्दिग्धं तत्रापि "सन्दिग्धे तु वाक्यशेषाद्" [*MS*, 1/4/13/24] इत्यनेनाधिकरणेन निर्णयः । संख्यादिवत् । यथा "सारस्वतौ मेषौ भवत" इत्यत्र तद्धितप्रकृतिः स्त्रीलिङ्गः पुंलिङ्गो वेति "सरस्वत्यै चरुम्," "सरस्वते चरुम्" इति द्वयोरपि दर्शनात् सन्देहे "एतद्वै दैव्यं मिथुनम्" इत्यर्थवादादेकशेषेण द्वयोर्ग्रहणमवधार्यते । "आग्नेयोऽष्टाकपालोऽमावास्यायां पौर्णमास्यां चे"ति वाक्ये तद्धितप्रकृतिरेकवचनान्तो वेति "अग्नये कृत्तिकाभ्यस्ते," "अस्मा अग्नयो द्रविणं दत्त्वे"त्यादौ द्वयोरपि दर्शनात् सन्देहे "सोऽग्नये ध्रियस्वे"ति वाक्यशेषादेकवचननिर्णयः ।

Translation [NN.V.13]

[a] [How to remove doubts?] If in a certain injunction, there is a doubt [concerning gender], a decision should be reached by relying on the

following section [from the *Mīmāṃsā-sūtras*]: "Where there is doubt, [the decision is reached] on the basis of the rest of the discourse," *MS*, 1/4/13/24. [Reaching a decision concerning gender would be] similar to [cases involving decisions concerning] number etc.

[b] [First example]: There is a doubt whether the base form in the Taddhita formation *sārasvata* is masculine or feminine in the following injunction: "There are two rams [to be offered] with respect to the deity *sarasvat(ī?)*" (*sārasvatau meṣau bhavataḥ*). Such [a doubt occurs] because both [the feminine and the masculine forms are] seen in the following two injunctions: i) "Cooked rice is offered to Sarasvatī" and ii) "Cooked rice is offered to Sarasvat" (*sarasvatyai caruṃ, sarasvate carum*). At this point, it is decided that both [the feminine and the masculine forms] are to be included [in the base form for the secondary derivation *sārasvata*] by means of a "single-remainder" (*ekaśeṣa*) complex formation. [This decision is] based on the following propitiatory text: "This is the divine couple" (*etad vai daivyam mithunam*).

[c] [Second example]: There is a doubt whether the base form in the Taddhita formation *āgneya* is a singular or a plural in the following injunction: "[A ball of flour cooked on] eight potsherds is [the oblation to be offered] with respect to the deity Fire(s?) on the full moon day and new moon day" (*āgneyo 'ṣṭākapālo 'māvāsyāyām paurṇamāsyāṃ ca*). This [doubt exists] because both [singular and plural forms] are seen in the following texts: i) "To you O Fire, [you who are] from the Kṛttikās" and ii) "O you Fires, after giving him wealth ..." (*agnaye kṛttikābhyas te, asmā agnayo draviṇaṃ dattvā*). At this point, it is decided that [the base form in the Taddhita formation *āgneya*] is in singular. This [is decided] on the ground that [the singular form occurs] in the propitiatory text: "[O you oblation], you hold on for Fire" (*so 'gnaye dhriyasva*).

Explanation [NN.V.13.a]: Śabara explains the doctrine in Mīmāṃsā rule [1/4/13/24] cited by Kauṇḍabhaṭṭa in the following way.[416] There are two sentences in a single context or in a single discourse. The first sentence is: "one should place wet pebbles" (*aktāḥ śarkarā upadadhāti, Taittirīya-brāhmaṇa*, 3.12.5.12) and the second sentence is: "clarified butter is brilliance" (*tejo vai ghṛtam*). The first sentence does not specifically say as to what is used to soak the pebbles. That doubt is removed by the second sentence in the same context.

---

416 *sandigdheṣu vākya-śeṣāt /, MS*, 1.4.13.24; *aktāḥ śarkarā upadadhāti, tejo vai ghṛtam iti śrūyate / tatra sandehaḥ, kiṃ ghṛta-taila-vasānām anyatamena dravyeṇāñjanīyāḥ śarkarā uta ghṛtenaiveti / ... sandigdheṣv evam prāpte brūmaḥ / ... sāmānya-vacanena viśeṣāpekṣiṇopakramo vākyasya, viśeṣe nigamana-vaśena / tasmād ghṛta-vidhānam /, MS-B(a)*, Vol.I., pp. 365-8; *TV(a)*, Pt.I., p. 367; also: K. Kunjunni Raja (1963), pp. 30-1.

Explanation [NN.V.13.b-c]: Both Taddhita formations, *sārasvata* and *āgneya* are derived by P.4.2.24 (*sāsya devatā*), which prescribes certain affixes after a word denoting a certain deity. The meaning of the whole formation is: "[A *y*, such that] *x* is its deity." Since, the case affixes and the feminine affixes are dropped before a Taddhita affix, there is no way to know, except through a scholastic interpretation, whether the base form is in singular or plural, or whether it is masculine or feminine.

The sentences *sārasvatau meṣau bhavataḥ* and *etad vai daivyam mithunam* are cited in Śabara's commentary [*MS-B(b)*, Vol.I., p. 545]. References to Meṣa offerings to Sarasvat and Sarasvatī are found in many texts, e.g. *Taittirīya-saṃhitā* (1.8.21; 2.1.2), *Maitrāyaṇī-saṃhitā* (2.5.2; 4.7-8; 9.3.5), *Kāṭhaka-saṃhitā* (13.1), and *Śatapatha-brāhmaṇa* (12.7.9; 4.2.5.14). The sentence *āgneyo 'ṣṭākapālaḥ* ... is found in several different Vedic texts, *Taittirīya-Saṃhitā* (7.5.21.1), *Maitrāyaṇī-Saṃhitā* (1.10.1), *Kāṭhaka-Saṃhitā* (9.4-5), and *Taittirīya-Brāhmaṇa* (3.9.17.1)] and it also occurs frequently in Śabara's commentary [*MS-B(b)*, Vol.I., p. 72, 172, and 192]. The sentence *agnaye kṛttikābhyaḥ* is cited in Śabara [*MS-B(b)*, Vol.I., p. 564, and Vol.II., p. 434]. Parallels are found in *Taittirīya-brāhmaṇa* (3.1.4.1). Parallels to *sarasvatyai carum* are found in *Taittirīya-saṃhitā* (3.5.1) and *Gopatha-brāhmaṇa* (2.1.12). However, these passages are not totally identical, cf. *sarasvatyai caruṃ sarasvate dvādaśa-kapālam.*

NN.V.14. (pp. 124)

नन्वस्तु तावदेवं, तथापि सर्वनामनिष्ठलिङ्गस्य चेतनाचेतनस्त्रीपुंससाधारणत्वात् "प्रास्मा अग्निं भरते"त्यध्रिगुप्रैषस्य सारस्वत्यां मेष्यामपि प्रवृत्तिः स्यात् । न चेष्टापत्तिः । "लिङ्गविशेषनिर्देशात् समानविधानेष्वप्राप्ता सारस्वती स्त्रीत्वाद्" इत्यूहलक्षणाधिकरणे "पशूनां समानविधानत्वेऽपि पुंलिङ्गनिर्देशान्न तत्र मन्त्र" इत्युक्तेः । लौकिकलिङ्गवाच्यत्वपक्षे च नानुपपत्तिः । सम्भवति मुख्यत्वे गौणताया अन्याय्यत्वेनारोपस्याप्यसम्भवान्नियमसम्भवात् । न च "सामान्ये नपुंसकम्" इत्यनुशिष्टमस्मा इति मेषीसाधारणमस्त्विति वाच्यम् । "अन्वेनं माता मन्यतामनु पिते"त्यन्वादेशेन पुंस्त्वनिर्णयात् । "अन्वादेशे नपुंसक एनद् वक्तव्य" इति वार्त्तिकादेनदित्यापत्तेः ।

Translation [NN.V.14]

[a] [Controversy with the upholder of physical sex-gender]: Even if all this is granted, still the command of the Adhrigu priest "offer him [her?] unto the fire" [*prāsmā agnim bharata*) would be applicable to the female ram [which is to be dedicated to the deity] Sarasvat(ī?). This would be the case, because

the gender pertaining to a pronoun [such as *asmai* in the above command] is common to both sentient and non-sentient, feminine and masculine objects.

[b] [Objection continued]: The resulting possibility [of performing a sacrifice with a female ram] is not desirable. This contradicts what [the Mīmāṃsakas] say on rule *MS* [9/1/16/45] in the *Ūha-lakṣaṇādhikaraṇa*. [They say that] all animals are equally covered by the injunction, and yet the injunction does not apply to [the female ram dedicated to Sarasvat(ī)], since there is an explicit mention of the masculine gender [by the pronoun *asmai* in the command of the Adhrigu priest].

[c] [In the prima facie interpretation of the *Bhāṣya* view which believes that the primary signification function of words like *chāga* is ascertained with respect to the technical gender qualified by] the physical sex-gender [of the object], there is no difficulty in explaining [this command of the Adhrigu]. There are the following justifications:

i) It is unjust to take recourse to a secondary meaning, while the primary meaning is still applicable; and

ii) for this very reason, it is not justified to take recourse to any [unnecessary] superimposition [of the masculine gender signified by the word on a female ram]. Thus, [this view] can establish the exclusion [of a female ram from the domain of application of Adhrigu's command].

[d] [Counter-objection]: Let us say that there is neuter gender in the pronoun *asmai* [in the Adhrigu's command], which would equally apply to a female ram. Such a neuter gender is prescribed by the rule: "The neuter gender occurs for a general reference."

[e] [Reply to the counter-objection]: One should not say this, because it is firmly decided that [the pronoun *asmai* in the Adhrigu's command] is in the masculine. [This is established] on the basis of the anaphoric reference [*enam* to the referent of *asmai*] in the following text: "let his mother and father permit him (*enam*)." [If *asmai* were a neuter form, then the anaphoric reference to its referent] would have to be *enad* [and not *enam*], by the following *Vārttika* [of Kātyāyana]: "In an anaphoric reference, the form *enad* should be ruled in."

Explanation [NN.V.14.a]: In the previous section, Kauṇḍabhaṭṭa has presented his final interpretation of Patañjali's view that gender is a property of the word and not of the signified object. There he refuted the earlier prima facie interpretation of Patañjali's view that gender is a property of the signified object. From here onwards, Kauṇḍabhaṭṭa presents a debate between these two interpretations. The upholder of the prima facie interpretation of Patañjali's view argues that the primary signification function of words like *kumāra* "boy," *chāga* "a goat," and *brāhmaṇa* "a Brahmin" is ascertained with respect to technical masculine gender qualified by physical male sex. This gender is intended, and hence it excludes the female objects, cf. **Explanation [NN.V.5.a-b]**. The objector in the following sections upholds this view.

Śabara discusses this command of the Adhrigu in his *Bhāṣya* [*MS-B(b)*, Vol.II., pp. 180-1 and 250]. The pronoun *asmai* is a masculine or a neuter dative form of the pronominal stem *idam* "this." The command occurs in the context of a sacrifice called *Sārasvatī Iṣṭi*. In this sacrifice, a *meṣa* "ram" has to be offered. The objector says that the word *asmai* will not be able to exclude a female ram, because the genders of pronouns are universally applicable to animate and inanimate, and male and female objects. The Adhrigu Praiṣa texts are found in *Maitrāyaṇī-saṃhitā* (4.13.4), *Kāṭhaka-saṃhitā* (16.21), *Taittirīya-brāhmaṇa* (3.6.6.1), and *Aitareya-brāhmaṇa* (2.4-7). Specific references to a Meṣī being offered to Sarasvatī are found in *Maitrāyaṇī-saṃhitā* (4.7-8; 2.5.2), *Kāṭhaka-saṃhitā* (13.1), and *Taittirīya-saṃhitā* (2.1.2).

Explanation [NN.V.14.b]: Kauṇḍabhaṭṭa quotes *Mīmāṃsā-sūtra* (9/1/16/45) and a discussion related to it. In the context of the Jyotiṣṭoma ritual, several animals to be sacrificed in sub-rituals are mentioned. For instance, it is said that an animal dedicated to Fire should be sacrificed in the Agniṣṭoma ritual. The animal dedicated to Fire and Indra should be sacrificed in the Uktha ritual. A female ram (*meṣī*) dedicated to Sarasvatī should be sacrificed in the Atirātra ritual. After this comes the order of the Adhrigu priest quoted in **NN.V.14.a**. The pronoun *asmai* in this order is applied by Mīmāṃsakas only to male animals, excluding the female ram dedicated to Sarasvatī.[417] Here, the upholder of the prima facie interpretation of Patañjali's view argues that there will be a problem of inclusion of the female ram, if one accepts Kauṇḍabhaṭṭa's second interpretation of Patañjali. Such inclusion of the female ram is contradicted by the Mīmāṃsā practice and interpretation of texts.

Explanation [NN.V.14.c]: The upholder of the prima facie interpretation of Patañjali's view believes that the primary signification function of a word is ascertained with respect to technical gender qualified by physical sex. Since, the pronoun *asmai* is a masculine form, it refers both to technical masculine gender and to physical male sex, and hence it naturally excludes the female ram. Since, there are male animals available in the context, one cannot extend the coverage of the form *asmai* to the female animal either by a secondary signification function or by superimposition. Thus, the word *asmai* will be properly restricted to male animals.

Explanation [NN.V.14.d]: Kauṇḍabhaṭṭa responds by suggesting that the form *asmai* could also be derived as a neuter form, and hence it will not be limited to male animals. Neuter pronouns can include both male and female objects within their reference. For instance, Patañjali says that when a child is born, one asks *kiṃ jātam* "what (neut.) is

---

417 *samāna-vidhāneṣv eṣu paśuṣv aprāptā sārasvatī meṣy adhrigu-vacanaṃ kutaḥ / liṅga-viśeṣa-nirdeśāt / viśiṣṭa-liṅgo hy adhrigu-vacanena nirdiṣṭaḥ prāsmā agnim bharateti pum-paśuḥ / strītvaṃ cāsyāḥ /, MS-B(a),* Pt.V., p. 1692; also: *TV(a)*, Pt.V., p. 1692.

born?" However, what is born can only be a girl or a boy. Thus, the neuter gender will not exclude the female objects.[418] Thus, even if both the sexes are intended, one can use neuter gender.[419] Thus, Kauṇḍabhaṭṭa argues that there would be a problem of extending the command of the Adhrigu priest to a female animal even in the prima facie interpretation of Patañjali's view.

Explanation [NN.V.14.e]: The objector comes back and points out that the word *asmai* is indeed a masculine word, as is indicated by the anaphoric reference *enam*. If the form *asmai* were a neuter form, the anaphoric form would have been *enad*, and not *enam*. To support this conclusion, the objector quotes a modified form of a *Vārttika* of Kātyāyana: *enad iti napuṃsakaika-vacane* [*Vt.* on P.2.4.34, *MB*, Vol.I., Sec.II., p. 550]. The Vedic passages quoted here are part of the Adhrigu Praiṣa, cf. **Explanation [NN.V.14.a]**.

NN.V.15. (p. 124)

इति चेदुच्यते । पूर्वोपस्थिततत्तद्रूपेणोपस्थापकादस्मै एनमित्यादि-पदाच्छागत्वादिनेव पुंस्त्वेनापि व्यावृत्तपशूनां परामर्शान्न मेष्यां प्रवृत्तिः । तत्रापि बह्वनुग्रहाय पुंस्त्वमेवानूद्यते । युक्तं चैतत् । अन्यथा मतान्तरेऽपि "पुमान् स्त्रिये"ति सूत्रात्, "त्यदादितः शेषे पुन्नपुंसकतो लिङ्गानी"ति वार्त्तिकाद्वैकशेषेण मेष्यां प्रवृत्तिः किं न स्यात् । एकवचनादेकशेषाभावो निर्णीयत इति चेत्तर्हि बहुपशुकेषूक्थादिष्वपि मन्त्रो न स्यात् । तथा च "अध्रिगुप्रैषश्च तद्वत्, समानविधानाश्चेद्" इत्यधिकरणोच्छेदापत्तिः । समानविधाना अपि पशवश्चेत्तथाप्यनेकपशुष्वध्रिगुप्रैषो भवति, द्विबहुपत्नी-केऽप्येकवचनान्तपत्नीमन्त्रवदिति तदर्थात् ।

Translation [NN.V.15]

[a] [Refutation of the prima facie interpretation of Patañjali's view]: If that is the objection, then we reply as follows. Pronouns like *asmai* and *enam* signify objects the way they are previously signified [by nouns]. Hence, from these words, there is a cognition of only those animals which are restricted by masculine gender, as well as the property of goat-ness. Therefore, [the sacrificial command] does not apply to a female ram.

[b] [Pronouns re-signify objects in the same form in which they are previously signified, and] in this case, only the masculine gender is re-signified [by the pronouns *asmai* and *enam*] for the benefit of the majority [of animals prescribed in the preceding injunctions].

---

[418] *evaṃ hi dṛśyate loke 'nirjñātārthe guṇa-sandehe ca napuṃsaka-liṅgam prayujyate / kiṃ jātam ity ucyate / dvayaṃ caiva hi jāyate strī vā pumān vā /*, *MB*, Vol.I., Sec.II., pp. 105-6.

[419] *sthitir napuṃsakaṃ, sā ca sarvatra vidyate iti sthiti-rūpatvenaiva strī-puṃsayor api vivakṣāyāṃ siddho napuṃsaka-śabda-prayogaḥ /*, *MB-P*, Vol.I., Sec.II., pp. 105-6.

[c] This is appropriate. Otherwise, there would be the application [of the sacrificial command] to a female ram, by [considering the forms *asmai* and *enam* to be] single-remainder complex formations (*eka-śeṣa*). [These forms could be considered to be single-remainder complex formations] on the basis of P.1.2.67 (*pumān striyā*) and the [first] *Vārttika* [on P.1.2.72]: *tyad-āditaḥ śeṣe pun-napuṃsakato liṅga-vacanāni.*

[d] [Refutation of the above objection]: Should [the objector] attempt to determine that there is no single-remainder complex formation (*eka-śeṣa*) [in the forms *asmai* and *enam*] on account of [their] singular [number], this injunction would not apply to a sacrifice with many animals, [because these are only singular forms].

[e] Similarly, [if the above contention of the objector is upheld], the section [on the *Mīmāṃsā-sūtra* (9/3/8/22):] *adhrigu-praiṣaś ca tadvat, samāna-vidhānāś cet* would become purposeless. It says that, if there are many animals to whom the injunction is equally applicable, then the [above given] command of the Adhrigu priest applies to all of them. This is similar to a case where an injunction with the word *patnī* "wife" in singular applies to a sacrificer who has two or more wives.

Explanation [NN.V.15.a]: In the earlier injunctions, animals like goats are denoted by masculine words like *chāga* in such a way that they are necessarily qualified by both goat-ness, as well as male-ness. A pronominal reference in a later injunction refers to these animals exactly as they are denoted in the earlier context. For this reason, pronouns like *asmai* and *enam* signify these animals as possessed of properties like goat-ness, as well as male-ness.

Explanation [NN.V.15.b]: In the previous injunctions, there are male animals, as well as a female ram dedicated to the deity Sarasvatī. One may say that the pronouns in the subsequent command may also signify this whole range of animals including the female ram. Kauṇḍabhaṭṭa says that only the masculine gender is continued or re-signified by the pronouns for the benefit of the majority of the sacrificial injunctions.

Explanation [NN.V.15.c]: Now Kauṇḍabhaṭṭa assumes the position that these pronouns like *asmai* are single-remainder complex formations (*eka-śeṣa*) for original masculine and feminine words. Therefore, they would include even female animals within their range of reference. This being the case, the undesirable possibility of applying the command of the Adhrigu priest to a female ram cannot be avoided.

P.1.2.67 (*pumān striyā*) says that given two nominals in a construction, which denote a male and a female of the same species, only the male-denoting nominal remains, when a form is used to signify both. For instance, *brāhmaṇau* can be the single-remainder complex formation (*eka-śeṣa*) for *brāhmaṇaś ca brāhmaṇī ca* "a male Brahmin and a female Brahmin."

Kauṇḍabhaṭṭa also quotes a *Vārttika* to support his argument. This *Vārttika* [*Vt.* 1 on P.1.2.72, *tyad-āditaḥ śeṣe pun-napuṃsakato liṅga-vacanāni*] says that if there is a noun and a pronoun undergoing the single-remainder complex formation, only the pronoun remains. Similarly, if there is a masculine or a neuter word involved in this complex formation, whether it be a noun or a pronoun, that masculine or neuter gender is attributed to the finally retained pronoun.[420] Thus, for example, *sā ca devadattaś ca* "she and Devadatta" is transformed into *tau*, and *sā ca kuṇḍe ca* "she and two pots" is transformed into *tāni*. Here, the single remainder complex formations *tau* and *tāni* are respectively in the masculine and in the neuter, and yet the signified objects include female entities. Thus, even if, in general, the primary signification function of a word is ascertained with technical gender qualified by physical sex, wherever possible, single-remainder complex formations like *tau* and *tāni* would include female objects within their range of reference. The same must be the case with the pronouns *asmai* and *enam*, and hence they must cover the female animal.

Explanation [NN.V.15.d]: The weak point in the argument offered above by Kauṇḍabhaṭṭa is that the forms *asmai* and *enam* are in singular, while usually the single-remainder complex formations are in non-singular number. The instances given in the last section, *tau* and *tāni* are respectively in dual and plural. Thus, the objector exploits this point and claims that there cannot be any single-remainder complex formations in singular. Therefore, the forms *asmai* etc. are not single-remainder complex formations.

Kauṇḍabhaṭṭa argues in response that such singular forms must indeed be treated to be single-remainder complex formations. Otherwise, there will be the difficulties pointed out in this section. An injunction which mentions only one wife for the sacrificer would not apply to a sacrificer with many wives. To include these multiple wives, Kauṇḍabhaṭṭa argues that one must consider these singular forms as single-remainder complex formations. If indeed these words like *asmai* are single-remainder complex formations, then it is difficult to avoid inclusion of the female ram from the range of reference for the command of the Adhrigu priest.

Explanation [NN.V.15.e]: The text of the *Mīmāṃsā-sūtra* (9/3/8/22) as quoted by Kauṇḍabhaṭṭa differs to some extent from the text as found in the Poona edition: *adhrigau savanīyeṣu tadvat, samāna-vidhānāś cet,* [*MS*, Vol.V., p. 1756]. In that section, it is decided that an injunction with the word *patnī* "wife" in singular does apply to a person, even if he has more than one wife. Similarly, the order of the Adhrigu priest does apply to sacrifices with many animals, even if it has only a singular pronoun.[421] Thus,

---

[420] *MB*, Vol.I., Sec.II., p. 107.

[421] *asti some paśur agnī-ṣomīyaḥ / ... tatrādhrigāv idaṃ samāmnāyate / prāsmā agnim bharata ... ity evam ādi / yadā tv agnī-ṣomīyaḥ savanīyāś ca samāna-vidhānāḥ, tatredaṃ vicāryate / kim adhrigau prāsmai ity evam ādi padam ūhitavyam uta neti / kim prāptam / tato 'tideśaḥ kriyate / adhrigau tadvad iti / tatra yaḥ patny-adhikaraṇe pūrva-pakṣaḥ, sa iha pūrva-pakṣaḥ / yaḥ siddhāntaḥ sa iha siddhāntaḥ / ūha iti pūrva-pakṣaḥ, avikāra iti siddhāntaḥ /, MS-B(a)*, Pt.V., p. 1756.

Kauṇḍabhaṭṭa finally attempts to show that, in the prima facie interpretation of Patañjali's view, there will be the problem of inclusion of female animals where it is not desired.

NN.V.16. (p. 124)
यत्तु प्रतिव्यक्तिगतैकत्वान्वयेनैकवचनोपपत्तिरिति । तन्न । प्रत्येकं व्यक्तीनामुपस्थितये एकशेषाभ्युपगमे एकवचनस्यैवासम्भवात् । सम्भवे वोक्तरीत्या मेष्याः संग्रहो दुर्वारः । "जात्याख्यायां तद्" इति त्वेकशेषेणानेकसंग्रहस्यैव साधकम् । अन्यथा बहुष्वेकवचनविधानवैयर्थ्यापत्तेः ।

Translation [NN.V.16]

[a] [Objector's defense]: [Accepting for the sake of argument the view that *asmai* etc. are single-remainder complex formations], the singular affix [at the end of these so-called single-remainder complex formations] could be explained by construing it with the singularity of each of the individuals [rather than with all possible objects including female animals].

[b] [Refutation]: That is not valid, because, if a single-remainder complex formation is adopted for signifying each individual severally, then it would be impossible to obtain the singular ending for [such a single-remainder complex formation].

[c] Even if it were possible [to refer to single individuals severally by a single-remainder complex formation], one would not be able to avoid the [undesirable] inclusion of a female ram, as it has been demonstrated earlier.

[d] Rule P.1.2.58 (*jāty-ākhyāyām ekasmin bahu-vacanam anyatarasyām*) is certainly a proof for establishing that a single-remainder complex formation is intended for inclusion of many [objects within the signification of one word]. Otherwise, this special prescription of a singular ending for [signifying] plurality [of signified objects] would be purposeless.

Explanation [NN.V.16.a]: In the last section, Kauṇḍabhaṭṭa pointed out that the form *asmai* in the command of the Adhrigu priest is a single-remainder complex formation (*eka-śeṣa*), and that it would, therefore, include the female animals within its range of reference.

Here, the opponent tries an unsafe argument. He says the following. Let us accept for the sake of argument that there can be a single-remainder complex formation in singular. By the use of the singular ending, it now refers to the singularity inherent in each single individual, but not necessarily all possible individuals, including female animals. Thus, there is a chance that we may be able to exclude the female animal, because its inclusion is not absolutely necessary to explain the singular of the single-remainder complex formation. This argument, if accepted, would be a way out of the difficulties pointed out by Kauṇḍabhaṭṭa.

Explanation [NN.V.16.b]: Kauṇḍabhaṭṭa rejects this proposal. If a single-remainder complex formation in singular were meant to refer to the singularity of single individuals, then it would not be possible to have the singular ending itself. Singularities of many objects together would produce a plurality. Thus, a single-remainder complex formation in singular can refer to all individuals of a class together, and not to a few selected individuals severally.

Explanation [NN.V.16.c]: Even if the reasoning of the objector is accepted for the sake of argument, still it would not be possible to exclude the female animal. The single-remainder complex formation would also refer to the singularity of each female individual. In the view of the objector, a single-remainder complex formation may not necessarily refer to all individuals of a class together, but it certainly refers to any member or any number of members including both genders. There is no logical reason, why it will exclude a female animal.

Explanation [NN.V.16.d]: P.1.2.58 (*jāty-ākhyāyām ekasmin bahu-vacanam anyatarasyām*) says that in case a singular word signifies a whole class, it may optionally take a plural ending. This means that even in the singular it does signify the whole class. For instance, the expressions *brāhmaṇaḥ pūjyaḥ* "a (=any) Brahmin is to be honored" and *brāhmaṇāḥ pūjyāḥ* "[all] Brahmins are to be honored" are identical in their meaning. Kauṇḍabhaṭṭa believes that this rule lends support to his contention that there can be a single-remainder complex formation in singular, and that it signifies the whole class of objects.

Nāgeśabhaṭṭa holds a very different view. He says that the sentence "one should not kill a Brahmin" should be explained by assuming that the word in singular signifies a generic property. For this reason, the word "Brahmin" covers all individuals having the property of Brahmin-ness. However, it cannot be regarded to be a single-remainder complex formation in singular. To be a single-remainder complex formation, the word in singular must be capable of causing a cognition of all Brahmin individuals directly, and not through the intervention of the generic property.[422] Nāgeśabhaṭṭa rightly points out that the notions of single-remainder complex formation and using a singular to indicate a whole class are two entirely different procedures and they presuppose different philosophical views regarding primary meaning. Kauṇḍabhaṭṭa has apparently confused these issues in the heat of the debate. As I see it, part of the problem lies in going to the exegetical discussions for a resolution of what is essentially a philosophical issue. The Mīmāṃsā system has its canons of textual interpretation, which are not necessarily suitable in the context of a philosophical debate. Thus, there is a mixture here of philosophical and exegetical issues, and Kauṇḍabhaṭṭa is not totally convincing in his argumentation.

422 *na ca brāhmaṇaṃ hanyād ity ādau jāti-padārthāśrayeṇaiva nirvāho bhāṣya uktaḥ / vyakti-pakṣe yaṃ kañcit brāhmaṇam ahatvā kṛtī syāt ity ādi dūṣaṇam uktam / eka-śeṣasya tu nāyaṃ viṣayaḥ / sakala-brāhmaṇa-vyakti-bodhakatāvac-chabdasyātidurghaṭatayā tatraika-śeṣeṇa sādhutvānvākhyānasya kartum aśakyatvāt /*, *BSS*, Pt.I., p. 376.

NN.V.17. (p. 125)

कृत्वाचिन्तयाधिकरणप्रवृत्तिस्तूभयत्र समेति । अत एव गुणिपराणां शुक्लादिशब्दानां गुणांशस्याधिकस्य बोधनेऽपि विशेष्यपदोदितलिङ्गसंख्यांशेऽनुवादत्वेन विशेष्यनिघ्नतोपपत्तिः । अत एव पदार्थमात्रविवक्षायां गुणोत्कर्षापकर्षरूपलिङ्गस्याविवक्षितत्वादवर्जनीयसाम्यावस्थया प्रयोगमभिप्रेत्य "सामान्ये नपुंसकम्" इति विधानं सङ्गच्छते । औत्सर्गिकवचनन्यायात् । अजहल्लिङ्गानां तु दारादिशब्दानां नित्यबहुवचनान्तानामेकस्मिन्निवागत्या तथा प्रयोग इति ध्येयम् । एवं च समनियतजात्यभ्युपगमदोषोऽपि न । लौकिकपुंस्त्वादौ पृथक्शक्त्यस्वीकारेण लाघवं चेति युक्तः पन्थाः प्रतिभाति ।

Translation [NN.V.17]

[a] The application of the *Kṛtvā-cintayā Adhikaraṇa* section [in the *Mahābhāṣya*] is equally justified in both [the views].

[b] For this very reason, it is possible to justify that words like *śukla* "white," which refer to objects possessing [color] qualities and which express the added element of [color] quality, simply copy the gender and the number of the substantive word, and, therefore, are in agreement with the substantive word.

[c] Hence, the following rule is justified: "Neuter gender occurs for a general reference." [This rule] is meant [to take into account] the usage [of words] purely in reference to the unavoidable state of equillibrium. When objects in general are intended, gender in the form of the decrease and increase of the ultimate elements of Primal Matter is not intended. [This can be explained] on the basis of the maxim: "After all exceptions are exhausted, what remains is covered by the general rule."

[d] It should be realized that words like *dārāḥ* "wife" have the [fixed] masculine gender and they occur in plural. Since, there is no [general] explanation, their [plural] usage to signify a single object has to be accepted [as an exception] as it stands.

[e] Similarly, in this view [of gender as a word-property], there is no problem of accepting [three] co-extensive generic properties [as genders]. Also, there is economy [of assumptions] in not accepting a separate primary signification function with respect to physical sex. Hence, this seems to be the appropriate way [of interpreting the concept of gender].

Explanation [NN.V.17.a]: The text referred to here as *Kṛtvā-cintayā Adhikaraṇa* is a section of the *Mahābhāṣya* [*MB*, Vol.I., Sec.I., pp. 49-50]. Here, Patañjali considers a number of alternative views one after the other. He rejects a certain view and accepts a certain view, and later he comes back to the earlier view. For a summary of this section, see: Introduction, **D.2.vi**. Most of the references to *kṛtvā cintā* are found in Mīmāṃsā works. Franklin Edgerton (1929: 284) explains this as: "supposition by making (assuming a thing to be so), an illustration of a hypothetical case, 'play' example of a rule for which no actual instance is known to exist." Referring to a discussion in Śabara, Kumārilabhaṭṭa says: *yas tu bhāṣyakāreṇopanyāsaḥ kṛtaḥ sa kṛtvācintā-nyāyeneti draṣṭavyam, TV(a)*, Vol.III., p. 308. Ganganath Jha (1914: 1269) renders this passage as: "That the Bhāṣya has introduced this question here is simply by way of taking for granted and putting forward something for the purpose of introducing a discussion." Kumārilabhaṭṭa also refers to a discussion in the *Paspaśāhnika* of the *Mahābhāṣya* as being in the mode of *kṛtvā cintā - yathā kṛtvā cintā tathā tayā rītyā ity arthaḥ / yat punaḥ parāvṛtya bhāṣyakāreṇoktam (patañjalinā vyākaraṇe) 'athavā punar astu jñāne dharmaḥ' iti abhyupetya-vādamātraṃ tat pūrvokta-doṣa-parihāra-sāmarthya-pradarśanārthaṃ kṛtvā-cintā-nyāyenoktam /, TV* (1.3.8.27) cited in *MK*, Vol.III, p. 1471. For further discussion of *kṛtvā-cintā-nyāya*, see G.A. Jacob (1907: pp. 21-22).

However, it is not very clear as to why Kauṇḍabhaṭṭa brings in this *Adhikaraṇa* in the present context. It may mean that both the forms, singular and plural, used to signify a class are acceptable. The plural form can be explained by saying that a word primarily signifies an individual. The singular form can be justified by saying that a word primarily signifies a generic property. Perhaps, the intention of Kauṇḍabhaṭṭa in citing this section, is to show that linguistic usage can be accounted for by alternative explanations.

Explanation [NN.V.17.b]: Words like *śukla* "white" are quality words, in as much as they signify a color quality. But they could be used in two ways. Either they signify the color quality as their principal meaning, or this color quality is signified as a qualification of an object. If these words are used in the latter capacity, they are adjectival nominals.

The number and gender of these quality words used as adjectivals are determined by their agreement with the substantive, lit. qualificandum-word. Patañjali says that the gender and number of these words are determined by reference to the locus of these qualities. For instance, *śuklaṃ vastram* "white cloth," *śuklā śāṭī* "white sari," and *śuklaḥ kambalaḥ* "white blanket" show three different kinds of agreement. The method of agreement demonstrated by Patañjali heavily relies on an ontological commitment.[423]

Explanation [NN.V.17.c]: The maxim *sāmānye napuṃsakam* has been discussed in detail in the Introduction, **D.4.vi**. Kauṇḍabhaṭṭa says that his explanation of neuter gender as the generic gender is in line with another maxim. The procedure of *autsargika-vacana-nyāya* is a simple procedure which says that the domain of a general rule is what is left over after applying all exception rules.

---

423 *guṇa-vacanānāṃ ca śabdānām āśrayato liṅga-vacanāni bhavanti / tad yathā - śuklaṃ vastraṃ, śuklā śāṭī, śuklaḥ kambalaḥ, śuklau kambalau, śuklāḥ kambalāḥ, iti yad asau drayaṃ śrito guṇas tasya yal liṅgaṃ vacanaṃ ca tad guṇasyāpi bhavati /, MB*, Vol.I., Sec.II., p. 424.

Patañjali says that the singular affix (*eka-vacana*) is the general affix, while dual and plural affixes are exceptions defined in terms of duality and plurality of the signified objects. The singular is not so defined. The domain left over by applying dual and plural affixes is the domain of the singular affix.[424] Similarly, the neuter gender is considered to be the general domain, and the masculine and the feminine genders are the domains of exceptions. Whatever is left over by these two domains is the domain of the neuter gender.

Explanation [NN.V.17.d]: The word *dārāḥ* "wife" is a masculine word and it is always in plural. The gender signified by a word does not necessarily agree with the physical sex of the object. Similarly, though this word occurs in plural, it signifies a single object. These anomalies of speech are a matter of linguistic reality, and they have to be accepted as such.

Explanation [NN.V.17.e]: Here, Kauṇḍabhaṭṭa again sums up the merits of his view in contrast with the demerits of other views of gender. Genders as co-extensive generic properties involve an additional ontological commitment, as well as a violation of the rule that co-extensive properties cannot all be generic properties, cf. Introduction, **D.4.viii.** Similarly, Kauṇḍabhaṭṭa discards the first interpretation of Patañjali's view, which assumes that gender is a property of the signified object, and that the primary signification function of a word is ascertained with respect to both, the technical gender as well as physical sex. This is also said to involve prolixity. Thus, Kauṇḍabhaṭṭa rejects all other views, and insists on his final interpretation of Patañjali's view that genders are properties of words. The question which has been left unexplained by Kauṇḍabhaṭṭa is how gender can be a property of a word, and yet be explainable in terms of the Sāṃkhyan conception offered by Patañjali. This is a significant gap in his discussion, which ultimately provokes Nāgeśabhaṭṭa into rejecting this view altogether.

---

[424] *ekavacanam utsargaḥ kariṣyate, tasya dvi-bahvor arthayor dvi-vacana-bahu-vacane bādhake bhaviṣyataḥ* /, *MB*, Vol.I., Sec.I., p. 224.

SECTION SIX

NN.VI.1. (p. 125)

चतुष्कमिति संख्यासहितं त्रिकमित्यर्थः ।

Translation [NN.V.1.]

[a] [The meaning of a noun consists of] four [elements, i.e. the earlier] three along with number.

Explanation [NN.VI.1.a]: In this alternative, the case-affix signifies only the *kāraka*, and it may be regarded to be a co-signifier (*dyotaka*) of number and gender. Kaiyaṭa and Nāgeśabhaṭṭa refer to a hypothetical view in which all elements except number are signified by the nominal, and number alone is the meaning of the affix. Though this view has been ascribed to Kauṇḍabhaṭṭa by some sources, this is not his view.[425]

Śabara says that a case affix directly signifies number which resides in the meaning of the nominal stem.[426] He uses the method of *anvaya-vyatireka* to establish that number is signified by the affix.[427] This argument is identical to the one which is used by Patañjali, cf. Introduction, **B.2**. Mīmāṃsakas firmly believe that number and *kāraka* are signified by the case affix according to Kātyāyana and Patañjali.[428] These two grammarians have discussed this question in great detail.[429] For a detailed discussion on the nature of number, see: Introduction, **D.5**.

NN.VI.2. (p. 125)

पञ्चकं कारकसहितं चतुष्कमित्यर्थः । यद्यपि लिङ्गादीनां त्रयाणामन्वय-व्यतिरेकादिभ्यः प्रत्ययवाच्यता युक्ता तथापि प्रत्ययवर्जिते "दधि पश्य" इत्यादौ तत्प्रतीतेर्लिङ्गानुशासनस्य प्रकृतावेव दर्शनाच्च प्रकृतेरपि तत्र शक्तिः कल्प्यते । तथा च यस्यैव वाचकताग्रहस्तत एव तेषामुपस्थितिः । सम्भेदे

---

425 *kecit tu saṃkhyā-mātraṃ vibhakty-arthaḥ, kārakāntaṃ catuṣkaṃ prātipadikārthaḥ ity āhuḥ /*, *LM*, p. 1150; *bhūṣaṇādi-mataṃ āha kecit tv iti /*, *LM-KL*, p. 1150.

426 *vibhaktir hi tarhi śrutyā prātipadikārtha-gataṃ saṃkhyārtham brūte /*, *MS-B(a)*, Pt.IV., p. 1203.

427 *loke paśum ānayety eka-vacane sati eka-paśu-viśiṣṭam ānayanam pratīyate / paśū ānayeti dvitva-viśiṣṭaṃ gamyate / tatra hy ekatvam apaiti / dvitvam upajāyate / ... yasya cāgame yad upajāyate, sa tasyārtha iti gamyate /*, *MS-B(a)*, Pt.IV., p. 1205; also Pt.II., p. 723,; and *TV(b)*, p. 950.

428 *dvābhyām api vākya-kāra-bhāṣya-kārābhyām bahu-vacana-vārttike 'bhihita-vārttike ca dvāv api karmatvādy-ekatvādi-vācyatva-pakṣau dūram anusṛtyānte nirdoṣatayāvadhāritam - karmādi-viśiṣṭā ekatvādayo vibhakty-arthā iti /*, *TV(a)*, Pt.II., p. 926.

429 *MB*, Vol.I., Sec.II., p. 235, 239, 478ff; Vol.II., p. 280.

चोभयतोऽपि । अत एव "वाचिका द्योतिका वा स्युर्द्वित्वादीनां विभक्तय" इति वाक्यपदीयं सङ्गच्छते ।

Translation [NN.VI.2]

[a] [Fifth view: The meaning of a noun consists of] five [elements, i.e. the earlier] four along with *kāraka*.

[b] On the basis of concurrent occurrence and concurrent non-occurrence, it is appropriate to say that the three elements beginning with gender are signified by the affix. Yet the primary signification function of a nominal stem with respect to these [elements] is assumed on the following grounds: a) There is cognition of gender etc. in usages such as "look at the yogurt" (*dadhi paśya*), where the [accusative singular] case affix [after the stem *dadhi*] is deleted, and b) the *Liṅgānuśāsana* texts deal only with stems.

[c] Again, a cognition of certain elements could be derived from a certain [linguistic item], if and only if, the item is firmly ascertained to be a signifier [with respect to those elements]. When [the nominal base and the case affix] occur together, [there is a cognition of gender etc.] from both.

[d] This also agrees with the *Vākyapadīya*: "Case affixes could be either signifiers or co-signifiers of duality etc." [*VP*, II. 164]

Explanation [NN.VI.2.a]: For details on this view, see: Introduction, **H.3**. For details on the notion of *kāraka*, see: Introduction, **D.6**.

Explanation [NN.VI.2.b]: Kauṇḍabhaṭṭa clarifies that he does not accept this *pañcaka* view in all cases. However, in general, gender, number, and *kāraka* are signified by the case affix, and this can be established by the method of *anvaya-vyatireka*. Bhartṛhari and Helārāja also apply this method to establish that a *kāraka* is distinct from the meaning of a nominal, and that it is signified by a case affix.[430]

In certain usages, there is no case affix, and yet the nominal stem itself signifies all the five meanings. The example given by Kauṇḍabhaṭṭa is *dadhi paśya*. Here, the form *dadhi* is an accusative singular form, where the affix *-am* is deleted, and the nominal stem *dadhi* has been retained. Yet this nominal stem signifies all the meaning elements, including the *kāraka*, i.e. *karman* "object." This example is discussed by Kaiyaṭa.[431] He also discusses certain other examples.[432] This argument is given from the point of view of the communicative value of the actual form *dadhi* in the utterance *dadhi paśya*, rather than from

430 *dṛṣṭo hy avyatireke 'pi vyatireko 'nvaye 'sati / vṛkṣādy-arthānvayas tasmāt vibhakty-artho 'nya iṣyate //*, *VP*, III, *Sādhana-samuddeśa*, verse 43; also: *VP-H(p)*, p. 265.

431 *pañcakam prātipadikārthaḥ / tathā hi dadhi paśya ity ādau vibhakti-śravaṇam antareṇāpi pañcāpy arthāḥ pratīyante svārthādayaḥ /*, *MB-P*, Vol.I., Sec.II., p. 235.

432 *yathā payaḥ payo jarayatīty atra vināpi vibhaktyā kartṛ-karma-pratītir bhavati pañcaka-prātipadikārtha-darśane /*, *MB-P*, Vol.I., Sec.II., p. 323; *VBS-P*, p. 252.

the point of view of Pāṇinian derivation. From the analytical point of view of Pāṇinian grammar, the zero replacement for the affix *-am* carries the same semantic and syntactic value as the original *-am*. From this point of view, there is no difference between the derivations *vana + am > vanam* and *dadhi + am > dadhi + Ø > dadhi*. The affix *-am* and its allomorph Ø carry the same semantic and syntactic value. However, Kauṇḍabhaṭṭa assumes a different point of view. From the point of a view of a common listener of language, there is only the form *dadhi*, and yet it is contextually capable of signifying the whole range of meanings including gender, number, and *kāraka*. This is the justification for the *pañcaka* view.

The second reason given by Kauṇḍabhaṭṭa in support of the *pacaka* view is that in the *Liṅgānuśāsana* texts, only nominal stems are given and gender is attached to each of them. However, this applies to gender alone.

Explanation [NN.VI.2.c]: A meaning element *M* can be cognized from a linguistic item *L*, if and only if the item *L* is firmly ascertained to be a signifier with respect to *M*. Thus, if one accepts a particular view of signification, one is bound to a particular way of explaining the process of meaning cognition.

Explanation [NN.VI.2.d]: According to Kauṇḍabhaṭṭa, the verse quoted from the *Vākya-padīya* [II.164] refers to *kāraka* and gender as well. According to the commentary *Prabhā*, this is a reference to number and *kāraka*, but not to gender.[433] This commentary interprets the *Vākya-padīya* verse as an indication that gender is indeed signified by the stem, while there may be a question about number and *kāraka*.

NN.VI.3. (p. 125)

नन्वेवं नामार्थप्रकारकशाब्दबोधं प्रति सुबादिजन्योपस्थितेर्हेतुत्वमित्यादिकं विलीयेतेति चेन्न । विभक्तिद्योत्यार्थमादायोपपत्तेः । नैतत्त्रिमुनिसंमतमिति भ्रमं निराचष्टे । शास्त्र इति । सरूपसूत्रादौ ।

Translation [NN.VI.3]

[a] [Objection to the *Pañcaka* view]: If it is the case [that all five elements are signified by the nominal stem], then the following doctrine will become invalidated: "A [meaning] cognition from a *sup* [= case affix] is a cause of a verbal cognition in which the meaning of the nominal is the qualifier [and the meaning of the affix is the qualificandum]."

[b] [Response to the above objection]: This [objection] is not valid. One could still explain [the above doctrine] by taking recourse to the co-signified meaning of case-affixes.

---

433 *atra dvitvādīnāṃ vibhaktaya ity uktyā saṃkhyā-kārakayor vācakatva eva mata-bhedo darśitaḥ / na tu liṅgāṃśe, iti liṅgam prātipadikārtha eveti dhvanyate /*, *VBS-P*, p. 252.

[c] By saying that [all these five alternatives are found] in grammatical texts, [Bhaṭṭojī Dīkṣita] removes a possible misconception that these [alternatives] are not in accordance with [the teachings of] the three great sages. Here, "grammatical texts" is a reference to [discussions in the *Mahābhāṣya*] on P.1.2.64 etc.

Explanation [NN.VI.3.a]: The objector believes that the meaning of an affix is the qualificandum, and the meaning of the nominal stem is the qualifier. This is the view of Naiyāyikas.[434] This cannot be explained, if all meanings are signified by a nominal. Kauṇḍabhaṭṭa points out that such a qualificative cognition can be explained by referring to the meaning co-signified by the affix.

Explanation [NN.3.b]: As pointed out above, the Naiyāyika view of a qualificative cognition can be explained by taking recourse to meanings co-signified by the affix. Different authorities, however, differ on the nature of such a qualificative cognition. For instance, Nāgeśabhaṭṭa rejects the Nyāya view that the meaning of the nominal is the qualifier, and the meaning of the affix is the qualificandum. For him an individual object is the qualificandum, and all other meanings are qualifiers.[435] Mīmāṃsakas believe that number and *kāraka* qualify the individual object signified by the nominal, but they do not agree with Nāgeśabhaṭṭa in holding the *pañcaka* view to be the final view, **Explanation [NN.VI.1.a]**.[436]

---

434 *itarārthānavacchinne svārthe yo bodhanākṣamaḥ / tiṅ-arthasya nibhādy-anyaḥ sa vā pratyaya ucyate //*, *SSP(b)*, p. 11.

435 *na ca pañcānām api prātipadikārthatve prātipadikārtha-prakāraka-bodhe sub-janyopasthitir hetur ity ādikaṃ vilīyeteti vācyam / iṣṭāpatteḥ / jāti-liṅga-saṃkhyā-kāraka-śakti-viśiṣṭasya dravyasyaiva bodhena sub-artha-viśeṣyaka-bodhasya kha-puṣpāyamāṇatvāt /*, *LM*, pp. 1150-1, and 1210-2; *etena ... bhūṣaṇoktam apāstam /*, *LM-KL*, p. 1151; also: *VBS-K*, p. 449.

436 *guṇaś ca vibhakty-arthaḥ (saṃkhyā) / pradhānam prātipadikārthaḥ / prātipadikārtha-viśeṣo vibhaktyābhidhīyate /*, *MS-B(a)*, Pt. V., p. 1753; *śabdās tāvad dvi-prakārāḥ / kecid vācyaṃ sva-pradhānam āhuḥ / nopasarjanatvena / yathā vṛkṣāv iti vṛkṣa-śabdaḥ svārtha-pradhānaḥ uccāryate / kecid vācyam artham anyatropasarjanībhūtam bruvate / na sva-pradhāna-bhūtam / yathātraiva vṛkṣāv iti dvi-vacanam prātipadikopasarjanam ātmānam bravīti /*, *TT*, Pt. V., p. 1893.

SECTION SEVEN

NN.VII.1. (p. 125)

स्थलविशेषे षोढापि प्रातिपदिकार्थ इत्याह -

"शब्दोऽपि यदि भेदेन विवक्षा स्यात्तदा तथा ।
नो चेच्छ्रोत्रादिभिः सिद्धोऽप्यसावर्थेऽवभासते ॥"

शब्दस्तावच्छाब्दज्ञानविषय इत्यनुभवसिद्धम् । "विषयत्वमनादृत्य शब्दैर्नार्थः प्रकाश्यत" इति वाक्यपदीयेऽनुभवप्रदर्शनात् । "गामुच्चारये"त्यादावर्थोच्चारणासम्भवेन विना शब्दविषयं शाब्दबोधासङ्गतिश्चेति तत्रापि वृत्तिर्वाच्या ।

Translation [NN.VII.1]

[a] In certain cases, the meaning of nominals consists of even six [elements]. Thus, [Bhaṭṭojī Dīkṣita] says: "If the distinction [between an imitation word and an imitated word] is intended, then [an imitated] word becomes [the meaning of the imitation word]. If [the above distinction is] not [intended], then a word cognized even through audition etc. appears in the contents of the verbal cognition [as does its meaning]."

[b] It is a matter of direct experience that a word becomes an object of verbal cognition. The *Vākya-padīya* [I.56] refers to such an experience: "Words do not illuminate [their] meaning, without [themselves becoming] objects [of cognition]."

[c] In a sentence such as "Utter the [word] 'bull'," it is not possible to utter the object. Therefore, the verbal cognition [from such a sentence] cannot be properly explained, unless a word [itself] becomes an object [of the verbal cognition]. Thus, it is necessary that there should be a [primary] signification function [of a word] with respect to itself.

Explanation [NN.VII.1.a]: Bhartṛhari points out that the nature of meaning, i.e. the signified object, is often uncertain, but words invariably signify their own form (*sva-rūpa*).[437] All words signify first the generic property pertaining to their own word-form (*śabda-jāti*), and then they signify the generic property pertaining to the signified object.[438] Helārāja explains that the relation of a word with the signified object may fluctuate, but its

---

437 *artha-mātraṃ viparyastaṃ sva-rūpe tu sthitiḥ sthirā* /, *VP*, II, 256cd; also: *VP-P*, Vol.II., p. 368.

438 *svā jātiḥ prathamaṃ śabdaiḥ sarvair evābhidhīyate* /, *VP*, III, *Jāti-samuddeśa*, verse 6.

relation with the generic property pertaining to its own word-form does not change. Therefore, the generic property pertaining to a word's own form is its primary significatum.[439] For details of the notion of a word-generic-property, see: Introduction, **E.3**. The distinction between an imitation word and an imitated word has also been discussed in the Introduction, **F.5-6**.

Let us say that the word *W* signifies the meaning *M*. Then the imitation (*anukaraṇa*) of the word *W* would be "*W*." If the distinction between *W* and "*W*" is intended, then one can say that "*W*" signifies *W*, and that the primary signification function of "*W*" is ascertained with respect to *W*, while the primary signification function of *W* is ascertained with respect to *M*.

If one does not wish to admit the distinction between the imitation word "*W*" and the imitated word *W*, then there is only the word *W* to deal with. In this alternative, one can say that when the word *W* is heard, there are two cognitions. Along with the cognition of the meaning *M*, there is an auditory perception of the word *W*. In this way, the word *W* itself becomes an object of the cognition resulting from itself. The status of the auditorily perceived word *W* is not exactly identical with that of *M*, but it is <u>like</u> that of *M*.

Explanation [NN.VII.1.b]: Cf. Introduction, **F.4**.

Explanation [NN.VII.1.c]: The word *iti* in Sanskrit performs the same function as a quotation mark does in English, cf. Introduction, **F.1**. In some cases, however, *iti* is not used, and yet one has to understand that a word stands for itself. The example given by Kauṇḍabhaṭṭa speaks for itself. In the sentence *gām uccāraya*, the accusative form *gām* stands for the object of the verb *uccāraya* "pronounce, utter." Normally, the accusative *gām*, referring to the meaning of the word would stand for a cow or a bull. However, in the present utterance, the accusative is intended to refer to the form of the word itself, not as *gām*, but as the original word-stem *go*. This inflected use of imitation words in Sanskrit is somewhat like the English usage: "I will not tolerate any ifs and buts," where the word-imitations for "if" and "but" are inflected with plural affixes.

NN.VII.2. (p. 125)

न च लक्षणया निर्वाहः । निरूढलक्षणायाः शक्त्यनतिरेकात् । "जबगडदश्" इत्यादौ शक्याग्रहेण तत्सम्बन्धरूपलक्षणाया अग्रहाच्च । अगृहीतायाश्च वृत्तेरनुपयोगात् । शक्तिभ्रमस्यापि वक्ष्यमाणरीत्यैवासम्भवात् । एवं भाषा-शब्दानामप्यनुकरणे प्रतीयमानत्वात्तेषां शक्त्यभावेन लक्षणाविरहादनुप-पत्तिश्चेति शक्तिरेव वाच्या ।

---

439 *svā go-śabdatvādikā / evaṃ cāsādhāraṇatvena viśeṣaṇatvāt tayā sambandhāvyabhicāraḥ / śabdasyārtha-jātyā sambandha-vyabhicāre 'pīti svā jātir eva mukhyam abhidheyam ity uktam bhavati /, VP-H(p)*, p. 16.

Translation [NN.VII.2]

[a] [Refutation of possible objections from Naiyāyikas]: A secondary signification function [of a word, as proposed by Naiyāyikas], is not sufficient [to let the word-form appear in the content of the verbal cognition], because a conventional secondary signification function is [virtually] identical with a primary signification function.

[b] In an expression such as [the *Śiva-sūtra*]: *ja-ba-ga-ḍa-da-Ś*, no primary meaning [other than the sounds themselves] is perceived. Hence, it is impossible to ascertain a secondary signification function, which is a relation of [primary meaning to secondary meaning]. If a signification function cannot be ascertained, it is useless.

[c] As it will be pointed out later, one cannot take recourse to a misconstrued primary signification function [to account for the cognition of a word from itself].

[d] Similarly, vernacular expressions are cognized from their imitations. [According to Naiyāyikas], they [= vernacular words] do not have any primary signification function. For this [very] reason, they could not have any secondary signification function [with respect to their own form]. Thus, it would be difficult to explain [a cognition of vernacular words from their imitations]. Therefore, one should accept a primary signification function [of a word with respect to its own form].

Explanation [NN.VII.2.a]: Gaṅgeśa says that a word does not have a primary signification function with respect to its own form (*sva-paratve*), but that it has a secondary signification function to refer to it.[440] Kauṇḍabhaṭṭa presumes that Naiyāyikas are claiming that there is a conventional secondary signification function of a word with respect to its own form, and then he points out that a conventional secondary signification function is virtually identical with a primary signification function, cf. Introduction, **E.5.iii**. While a normal secondary signification function is triggered into operation by the realization that the primary meaning cannot be construed with the meaning of other words, or that it does not conform to the known intention of the speaker, no such realization is necessary to trigger the conventional secondary signification function. Thus, its operation is as automatic as that of the primary signification function. Thus, claiming that a conventional secondary signification function allows a word to refer to its own form is as good as admitting a primary signification function.

Explanation [NN.VII.2.b]: Kauṇḍabhaṭṭa cites the *Śiva-sūtra: ja-ba-ga-ḍa-da-Ś* as an example, where there is no primary meaning. A Naiyāyika, therefore, cannot claim that a word signifies its own form by secondary signification function, since, according to the

---

440 *go-padādeś ca sva-paratve lakṣaṇaiva, na śaktiḥ* /, *TC*, p. 681.

Nyāya system, a secondary signification function is a relation of the primary meaning to the secondary meaning. In the absence of a primary meaning, there cannot exist a relation between a primary meaning and a secondary meaning. Since, a secondary signification function cannot be ascertained, there is no question of using an unascertained signification function. It simply does not exist.[441]

Gaṅgeśa argues that, in the *Śiva-sūtra*: *ja-ba-ga-ḍa-da-Ś*, the entire sequence does not have a primary meaning, but each of the individual sounds, i.e. *j*, *b*, *g*, *ḍ*, and *d*, have a primary meaning of their own. For instance, the sound *a* stands for Vāsudeva. Similarly, each sound of the Sanskrit alphabet has a certain meaning. Therefore, one can certainly have a primary meaning, and then have a secondary signification function as a relation of this primary meaning to the secondary meaning, i.e. the form of the word.[442] Gaṅgeśa cites a sentence *ja-ba-ga-ḍa-da-śam āha* "X said *ja-ba-ga-ḍa-da-Ś*." He says that here the verb "said" applies not to the whole collection of sounds, but to each sound individually. Since each sound has one of these mystical meanings, one can then build a case for a secondary signification function of each sound for its own phonetic form. This argument has been refuted by the commentaries *Prabhā* and *Śāṅkarī* on the *Vaiyākaraṇa-bhūṣaṇa-sāra*. They argue that individual sounds may have meaning, but the sequence as a whole does not have any meaning, besides referring to the sounds themselves. They also point out that one can understand the meaning of the sentence "he said *ja-ba-ga-ḍa-da-Ś*," without ever explicitly being aware of the so-called primary meanings of individual sounds.[443] Therefore, one is urged to accept that a word has a primary signification function with respect to its own form.

Explanation [NN.VII.2.c]: Gaṅgeśa proposes that, in the absence of a real primary signification function of a word with respect to its own form, one may take recourse to a kind of misconstrued primary signification function of a word for itself. It is like saying that a word denotes itself in some unofficial, illegal way. One understands a word's own form from a word, and one thinks that this cognition is a meaning cognition, though it is strictly speaking not a legitimate signification function of a word.[444] This may yield a cognition of a word from itself, and yet would not carry with it the legitimacy of a cognition derived from a signification function of a word. Kauṇḍabhaṭṭa says that he has refuted the notion of *śakti-bhrama* "misconstrued signification function" later in his work, though I have not been able to locate this refutation.

Explanation [NN.VII.2.d]: This refers to the peculiar theological attitude of Naiyāyikas toward Sanskrit. They believe that only Sanskrit words can have real primary

---

441 *tad-dharmāvacchinna-viṣayaka-śābda-buddhitvāvacchinnam prati tad-dharmāvacchinna-nirūpita-vṛtti-viśiṣṭa-jñānaṃ hetuḥ / ata eva nāgṛhīta-vṛttikasya śābdabodhaḥ /*, *PLM*, p. 27.

442 *nanv evam ja-ba-ga-ḍa-da-śam āhety ādau nirarthakeṣu lakṣaṇā na syāt / svārtha-sambandhābhāvād iti cen na / na hi ja-ba-ga-ḍa-da-śam āhety atra samudāye kriyānvayaḥ / samudāyasyoccāraṇāsambhavāt / kiṃ tu dvandvānantara-śruta-kriyā-padena pratyeka-varṇe svārthānvaya-bodhanam / pratyeka-varṇasya ca śaktatvena svārtha-sambandhād eva svasmin lakṣaṇā /*, *TC*, pp. 685-6.

443 *VBS-S*, p. 235; *VBS-P*, p. 256.

444 *svārtha-sambandhāgrahe ca sva-rūpopasthitiḥ śakti-bhramāt /*, *TC*, p. 686.

signification functions, in the form of God's desire that a specific word should signify a specific meaning. Such a desire of God does not exist in the case of Prakrit words, which are supposed to be deformations of proper Sanskrit words at the hands of incapable and deficient people. Thus, the Prakrit languages have no legitimate status, including any legitimate meaningfulness. A Prakrit word has no meaning. It reminds the listener of the proper Sanskrit word, which in turn denotes a certain meaning.[445] Kauṇḍabhaṭṭa says that, if Prakrit words cannot have a primary meaning, they cannot have a secondary signification function either to refer to their own form, or to refer to some other meaning. Thus, a Naiyāyika cannot maintain his position.

NN.VII.3. (p. 126)

तथा च शब्दोऽपि यद्यनुकार्यानुकरणयोर्भेदेन विवक्षा तदा तथेति । अनुकार्यः प्रातिपदिकशक्य इत्यर्थः । अयं भावः । पटदिति कुर्वित्याद्यनुकरणस्थलेऽनुकार्यध्वनीनामनुकरणाद्भेदो ध्वनिमयत्ववर्णमयत्वादिविरुद्धधर्मवत्त्वसिद्धः । तथा च तदुपस्थित्यर्थमुपस्थितस्य तस्य शाब्दज्ञानविषयत्वनिर्वाहार्थं च शक्तिरवश्यमभ्युपेयेति ।

Translation [NN.VII.3]

[a] Thus, a word-form itself is likewise [a meaning of a noun], if the distinction between an imitated word and an imitation word is intended. That is to say, an imitated [word] becomes a primary meaning of an [imitation] nominal stem.

[b] This is what is meant. In imitations such as "make [the sound] *paṭat,*" the distinction between an imitation word and an imitated word is clearly established, because they possess opposing properties such as being composed of physical non-linguistic sounds versus being composed of articulated linguistic sounds, etc.

[c] Thus, one has to accept the primary signification function [of an imitation word] with respect to [an imitated] word, in order to derive its cognition and to explain how it becomes a [legitimate] object of a verbal cognition.

Explanation [NN.VII.3.a]: Cf. **Explanation [NN.VII.1.a]**.
Explanation [NN.VII.3.b]: Cf. Introduction, **F.5**.

---

445 *sā ca śaktiḥ saṃskṛta eva nāpabhraṃśeṣu /*, *TC*, p. 641; *tatra sādhu-śabda-smaraṇād evānvaya-bodha ity eke /*, *MD*, p. 85; *teṣām [prākṛtādīnām] saṃskṛta-śabda-jñāpakatayaivārtha-pratyāyakatvasyānubhava-siddhatvena teṣu śakty-akalpanāt / na caivam apabhraṃśād artha-pratīty-anupapattir iti vācyam / śakti-bhramāt tad-upapatteḥ /*, *MD*, p. 86. For the socio-linguistic implications of such doctrines, see: Madhav Deshpande (1985: 144-146) and (1979-b: 12-13).

Explanation [NN.VII.3.c]: It is necessary to assume the primary signification function of a word to refer to its own form. An *x* can become an object of a verbal cognition, and be accepted as a legitimate primary meaning, if and only if *x* is cognized on the basis of a primary signification function of a word. Otherwise, the form of a word may be cognized in some other way, and yet it cannot be accepted as a legitimate primary meaning.

NN.VII.4. (p. 126)

नो चेद्भेदविवक्षा तदा श्रोत्रादिभिः सिद्ध उपस्थितः । अर्थे व अर्थवत् । भासते । न तु स्वतन्त्रवृत्तिकल्पनेत्यर्थः । अयं भावः । वृत्तिविषय एव च शाब्दबोधविषय इति नियमोऽतिप्रसङ्गनिर्वाहाय कल्प्यते । स च निरूपकताश्रयतान्यतरसम्बन्धेन वृत्तिमान् तद्विषय इति भवति तस्य शाब्दबोधविषयतेति ।

Translation [NN.VII.4]

[a] If the distinction [between an imitated word and an imitation word] is not intended, then a word [is said to be] cognized through auditory perception. [The words] *arthe va* [in verse 26] mean *arthavat* "like a meaning." [Thus a word] cognized [through auditory perception appears in the verbal cognition] just like a meaning; there is, however, no assumption of a separate primary signification function [with respect to the form of a word].

[b] This is what is meant. To avoid an undesirable over-extension, the following rule is assumed: "An *x* can be an object of a verbal cognition, if and only if, that *x* is an object of the primary signification function."

[c] An *x* can be an object of a verbal cognition, if and only if, that *x* is related to the primary signification function, either by the relation of being its describer (*nirūpaka*), or by the relation of being its locus. [A word is the locus of a primary signification function, and] therefore it can become an object of a verbal cognition.

Explanation [NN.VII.4.a]: The view of non-difference between an imitated word and an imitation word has been explained briefly in **Explanation [NN.VII.1.a]**. Here, the distinction between the two is not intended, and the cognition of a word's own form is explained on another basis. The word is cognized through auditory perception, while the meaning is cognized through the primary signification function. Both of these cognitions are said to contribute to the resulting verbal cognition, and hence the word cognized through auditory perception is said to appear in the verbal cognition <u>like</u> a meaning. However, it is not necessary to have a primary signification function of a word with respect to its own form to account for the cognition of the word-form. Here, the original text of the *Kārika*, i.e. *arthe 'vabhāsate*, is split differently, i.e. *arthe va bhāsate*, and the word *va* is taken to be an equivalent of *-vat* "like." The shorter version usually has the reading *artho 'vabhāsate*.

Explanation [NN.VII.4.b]: The rule given by Kauṇḍabhaṭṭa is clear. It is offered to avoid undesirable over-extensions (*ati-prasaṅga*). However, he does not explain as to the kind of over-extension he is trying to avoid. A standard case of such an undesirable over-extension is the notion that one cognizes ether (*ākāśa*) from every word, because, a word being a sound is a quality (*guṇa*) of ether, and is related to ether through the relation of inherence (*samavāya*). When one cognizes one relatum of a relation, there is a recollective cognition of the other relatum. Such a cognition of ether is not generated on the basis of the primary signification function of the word, and hence it is not included in the verbal cognition, and ether is not considered to be a meaning of every word.

Explanation [NN.VII.4.c]: This second formulation is specifically intended for the inclusion of a word itself in the verbal cognition resulting from itself, while one must still keep the cognition of ether out of the verbal cognition. The earlier formulation uses the term *vṛtti-viṣaya* "object of a signification function." This term generally refers only to a meaning element, such that the signification function of a word is ascertained with respect to it. Here, the scope of this term is extended by paraphrasing it with the word *vṛttimat* "possessor of a signification function, something related to a signification function." A signification function is a relation between a word and an object. This relation is said to reside in the word and is said to have been described in terms of the signified object. Kauṇḍabhaṭṭa says that an *x* can be said to possess a signification function, either by being its locus, or by the signification function being described in terms of it. This, formulation allows inclusion of a word itself as an element qualified for being an object of a verbal cognition (*vṛtti-viṣaya*).

It also avoids the undesirable over-extension to ether (*ākāśa*), since ether is neither the locus of the signification function of a word, nor is the signification function of a word described in terms of it.

NN.VII.5. (p. 126)

ननु वृत्तिमत एव शाब्दबोधविषयत्वे प्रत्यक्षादिनोपस्थितघटादेरपि शाब्दबोधविषयतापत्तिरिति विषयतया शाब्दबोधमात्रं प्रति वृत्तिसंस्कारज्ञानान्यतरजन्यपदार्थोपस्थितिर्हेतुरिति निर्णीतमन्यत्र । तथा चात्र वृत्तिमत्त्वे श्रोत्रादुपस्थितौ च सत्यामपि तादृशोपस्थित्यविषयत्वात्कथं शाब्दबोधविषयतेति ।

Translation [NN.VII.5]

[a] [Objection to Kauṇḍabhaṭṭa's formulations in **NN.VII.4**]: If it is the case that only an *x* which possesses the primary signification function becomes an object of a verbal cognition, then even a pot cognized through visual perception would have to be considered to be an object of a verbal cognition [derived from the word "pot"].

[b] Therefore, [to avoid such a situation], the following rule has been determined elsewhere: "An *x* can become an object of a verbal cognition, if and only if *x* is cognized from a word either through a mental impression [of a signification function] or through an awareness of a signification function."

[c] If [such a rule is accepted], then how would it be possible for a word to be an object of a verbal cognition? A word is a possessor of a signification function, and is cognized through auditory perception, but it is not cognized in the manner stipulated [in the above rule].

Explanation [NN.VII.5.a]: The formulation offered by Kauṇḍabhaṭṭa in **NN.VII.4.c** avoids the undesirable over-extension of the notion of "object of a verbal cognition" to ether. However, it creates some other difficulties. The formulation essentially says that an *x* can be an object of a meaning cognition, if *x* is a possessor of a signification function. Apparently, the formulation does not specify the way in which this *x* should be cognized in order for it to be an object of a meaning cognition. Thus an object pot is a possessor of a signification function located in the word "pot." Such an object pot may be cognized through visual perception, and yet being a possessor of a signification function, its visual cognition would have to be treated to be a verbal cognition. This is not desirable.

Explanation [NN.VII.5.b]: To avoid the above difficulty, one has to have some other modification in the formulation. The objector points to a formulation which is accepted by Kauṇḍabhaṭṭa elsewhere, cf. **NN.VII.18.a**. This formulation purports to saying that an *x* can be an object of a verbal cognition, if and only if *x* is cognized through an awareness of a signification function of a word, or through a mental impression of a signification function of a word. The object pot, which is visually perceived, is a possessor of a signification function, and it is cognized, but not in the above required manner. Therefore, it cannot be an object of a verbal cognition in this instance. Here a distinction is made between the notions of *vṛtti-jñāna* and *vṛtti-saṃskāra*. The first term *vṛtti-jñāna* seems to refer to a cognitive event or a resulting cognitive state, occurring when a person becomes aware of the relation of a word to a certain meaning for the first time. Thus, *vṛtti-jñāna* may be said to be the immediate result of what is called *śakti-graha* "ascertainment of a word's signification function." On the other hand, *vṛtti-saṃskāra* seems to refer to the mental impression retained by the individual after he has the *vṛtti-jñāna*. There is no continuing perpetual awareness of the relation of a word with a certain meaning, but there are mental impressions of such relationships stored away, and they are reawakened from time to time as the need arises.

Explanation [NN.VII.5.c]: The objector points out that the same would be the case of a word itself. A word is a possessor of a signification function, since it is a locus of it. It could be cognized through auditory perception. However, it is not cognized either on the basis of an awareness of a signification function, or on the basis of a mental impression of a signification function. Therefore, the auditory perception of a word will not qualify for the status of a meaning cognition or a verbal cognition. The following section deals with this objection.

NN.VII.6. (p. 126)

इति चेदुच्यते । गकारादयः क्वचिच्छक्ता वर्णत्वात्, नलादिपदं क्वचिच्छक्तं साधुत्वादिति सामान्यतः शक्तिग्रह एव "तत्पदवाच्यः कश्चिदर्थोऽस्ति" इत्याकारके वाच्यत्वसम्बन्धेन पदप्रकारकबोधे हेतुरित्यनुभवसिद्धम् । अत एवाज्ञातार्थकेष्विदमेकं पदमिति ज्ञातेषु चैत्रगवयनलादिपदेषु श्रुतेषु क एतदर्थ इति प्रश्न उपमानतल्लक्षणकथनादिना तत्प्रतिवचनानि दृश्यन्ते । अत एव सादृश्याद्युपायेन तद्बोधकत्वेनोपमानादेः, प्रसिद्धपदसामानाधिकरण्यादिना तद्बोधकत्वेन कोशादेश्च प्रामाण्यं व्युत्पादयन्ति ।

Translation [NN.VII.6]

[a] [Reply to the objection in **NN.VII.5.c**]: If that [is the objection], then we respond as follows: [Sounds] *g* etc. have a primary signification function with respect to something, since they are linguistic sounds. Words like *nala* have their primary signification functions with respect to something, since they are correct [Sanskrit] words. Such a general cognition of a primary signification function is the cause of a [general verbal] cognition, where the word appears as a qualifier by the relation of being [a signifier of the] signified [meaning]. Such a general cognition is of the following form: "For a given word, there is some meaning signified by this word." This kind of a general cognition is established by common experience.

[b] For this reason, [the following situations are justified]. Words like *caitra, gavaya,* and *nala* are of unknown meaning [for some people], but they are well known as correct Sanskrit words. When these words are heard, there are questions concerning their [specific] meanings. Such questions are answered by analogy, a description of the characteristics of the object, etc.

[c] Therefore, analogy is called a valid means of knowledge, since it helps the understanding [of the meaning of a word] by means of similarity [with a known object], and a dictionary is also called a valid authority, since it helps

the cognition of meaning by pointing out other familiar co-referential [or synonymous] words.

Explanation [NN.VII.6.a-b]: Tantric texts ascribe specific meanings to each and every Sanskrit sound, and there are dictionaries listing meanings of such single sounds (*ekākṣara-kośa*). Similarly, one accepts that every word that forms part of linguistically correct usage is meaningful by definition. With these two assumptions, Kauṇḍabhaṭṭa presents two inferences:

i) "The sound *g* has some meaning, since it is a linguistic sound."

ii) "The word *nala* has some meaning, since it is a correct word."

According to Kauṇḍabhaṭṭa, this helps us to formulate a notion of a general cognition of primary meaning from all words. Thus, we could say:

"Given a word *W*, there exists some *M*, such that *M* is signified by *W*."

Or,

"Given a word *W*, there exists some *M*, such that the primary signification function of *W* is ascertained with respect to *M*."

In this kind of general cognition, one knows the given *W*, but not what it denotes. The signified meaning could be described only in very general terms such as: "some *M* signified by *W*." Kauṇḍabhaṭṭa says that in such cases, the only qualifier of the meaning signified is the word itself (*pada-prakāraka-bodha*). Such a non-specific cognition of meaning is said to be established by common experience. Only after having such a general cognition, can one attempt to get more specific information about the signified object. Such enquiries are then answered by analogies, by descriptions etc.

Explanation [NN.VII.6.c]: Kauṇḍabhaṭṭa explains how analogy (*upamāna*) and dictionaries help a person determine the specifics of meaning. One hears the word *gavaya*, and knows that there must be something signified by this word, but does not know what it specifically refers to. Someone else tells him that a *gavaya* is similar to a bull (*go-sadṛśo gavayaḥ*). This gives him a clue to identify the specific meaning of the word *gavaya*, on the basis of its similarity with a known animal, a bull.[446] A dictionary gives a number of synonymous words and contexts where the given word can occur. From this, one can make out the specific meaning of the given word.[447]

NN.VII.7. (p. 126)

अन्यथा नलादिपदानामस्मदादीन् प्रत्यबोधकत्वप्रसङ्गश्च । नलत्वादिरूपेण शक्तिग्राहकाभावात्तेन रूपेण बोधकत्वासम्भवात् । न चातीतनलादिभावि-चैत्रादिवर्तमानासंनिकृष्टवस्तुगोचराः संस्कारा अनादयो धारारूपेण वि-

---

[446] *kaścid gavaya-śabdārtham ajānan kutaścid āraṇyaka-puruṣād go-sadṛśo gavaya iti śrutvā vanaṃ gato go-sadṛśa-piṇḍam paśyan vākyārthaṃ smarati / tad-anantaram ayam gavaya-pada-vācya ity upamitir utpadyate /*, *TS*, p. 64.

[447] *LM*, p. 342.

शिष्यबोधान्यथानुपपत्त्या कल्प्यन्त इति नैयायिकनव्यकल्पनं युक्तम् ।
हेत्वसिद्धेः । अन्यथोक्तप्रश्नाद्युच्छेदप्रसङ्गात् ।

Translation [NN.VII.7]

[a] Otherwise, words like *nala* would not signify anything to us. There is no means of ascertaining the primary signification function [of the word *nala*] with respect to [a specific individual] qualified by [specific properties like] *nala*-ness. Hence, [the word *nala*] is incapable of causing a cognition [of a specific individual] qualified by that [specific] property [of *nala*-ness].

[b] Navya-naiyāyikas make the following assumption: "There are continuously persisting mental impressions which have no beginning, and which reflect past objects like Nala, future objects like Caitra, and other present objects which lie beyond the reach of sensory perception. [Without this assumption], one cannot explain the specific cognition [of meaning from words like *nala*]."

[c] This assumption is not valid, because [the very existence of a specific meaning cognition from words like *nala*, which is] the basis [for the above assumption], cannot be established. Otherwise, [if there were such a specific meaning cognition], one cannot explain why there should be any questions [concerning the meaning of such words] as pointed out above.

Explanation [NN.VII.7a]: One must accept that the meaning cognition derived from a word like *nala* is non-specific and is of the nature of "some *x* signified by the word *nala*," where the word-form alone becomes the qualifier of an otherwise unspecified individual. If this is not accepted, then the word would not signify any meaning to us.

One cannot say that the word *nala* signifies a specific meaning, i.e. a specific individual. There is no way a person of our age can ascertain the signification function of the word *nala* with respect to the specific individual possessing the specific property of *nala*-ness, One can grasp a specific meaning from the word "bull," since one can have a direct cognition of an individual qualified by the property of bull-ness. That is not the case with the word *nala*. The external significatum of the word *nala* is as much beyond our perception as the Homeric heroes, or as the characters in Shakespearean plays. Nāgeśabhaṭṭa elaborates this argument in his works.[448]

The text of the Bombay edition of *VB* has the reading *śaktigrāhakabhāvāt*. V.N. Misra's edition (p. 122) contains the same reading. This does not make any sense. The reading in Manudeva Bhattacharya's edition (p. 136) is *śaktigrāhakābhāvāt*. I have followed this reading. I had suggested this emendation in my 1972 dissertation, and later I find it supported by this new edition. However, we do not know at this point whether M.

448 *LM*, p. 342; *LM-KL*, p. 342.

Bhattacharya's change of the reading reflects his new reading of the manuscripts, or whether it is an emendation.

Explanation [NN.VII.7.b]: Kauṇḍabhaṭṭa here explains an assumption of Navya-naiyāyikas. Persons like Nala are past objects. Persons like Caitra may be future objects. There are objects which do exist at present, but are beyond the reach of our perception. However, there are words which signify such objects.

Navya-naiyāyikas are said to have proposed that one may never have any chance to know the specific property of *nala*-ness, and yet one has a meaning cognition from the word *nala*, such that it is a cognition of a specific individual qualified by the specific property of *nala*-ness. To explain such a specific cognition, they assume that there are streamlike or continuously persisting mental impressions of cognitions of these objects innate in one's mind when one is born. Such mental impressions or dispositions continue from life to life. They help a person to have a specific meaning cognition from a word such as *nala*.[449] I have not been able to trace this view in a specific Navya-nyāya text.

Explanation [NN.VII.7.c]: Kauṇḍabhaṭṭa says that the basic assumption of the Navya-naiyāyikas that there is such a specific cognition of meaning from words like *nala* is unfounded. There is no such specific cognition. Nāgeśabhaṭṭa also agrees with Kauṇḍabhaṭṭa's criticism.[450] If there were such specific cognitions from words like *nala*, why would one be required to ask questions concerning the specific meanings of these words? The fact that one asks such questions goes against the assumption of Navya-naiyāyikas.

NN.VII.8. (p. 126)

किञ्च देशान्तरगतं प्रसिद्धं चैत्रं काश्यां शृण्वतां विशिष्यागृहीतसङ्गतिकानामपि नलयुधिष्ठिरादिपदादिव बोधानुभवात्, तदनुरोधेनानादिसंस्काराद्विशिष्यशक्तिग्रहसत्त्वाभ्युपगमे तेषामेव कालान्तरे विश्वेश्वरमन्दिरे तं पश्यतां "चैत्रोऽत्र नास्ति" इति वाक्याद् बोधो न स्यात् । स्याद्वा विशिष्यगृहीतसङ्गतिकानां तत्र पश्यतामन्येषाम् ।

Translation [NN.VII.8]

[a] [Continued criticism of the Navya-nyāya view]: [Let us suppose that] there are people in Banaras who hear of someone named Caitra. He is famous, but belongs to a different province. [These people] have never ascertained the specific relation [of the word "Caitra" with respect to a specific person]. Yet they have some meaning cognitions [from the word "Caitra"], just as

---

449 Nāgeśabhaṭṭa also ascribes this view to Navya-naiyāyikas. See: *LM*, p. 342.

450 *viśiṣya-bodha-rūpa-hetv-asiddheḥ* /, *LM*, p. 342.

they have some meaning cognition from words like "Nala" and "Yudhiṣṭhira."

[b] On the basis of the above mentioned meaning cognition, [and following the above explained assumption of Navya-naiyāyikas], one might accept that [these people do] have a cognition of the specific primary signification function [of the word "Caitra" with respect to the specific person Caitra] on account of the mental impressions which are innate [i.e. exist without beginning].

[c] [Objection against the above assumption]: [If one accepts this assumption], then the very same people would have no [meaning] cognition from the sentence "Caitra is not here," while they are [actually] watching him [without recognizing him] in the Viśveśvara Temple in Banaras.

[d] [Another objection]: On the other hand, those people who have specifically ascertained the relation [of the word "Caitra" with the specific person Caitra] would have to have [a meaning cognition from the sentence "Caitra is not here"], while they [actually] watch [him] there [and recognize him].

Explanation [NN.VII.8.a]: Kauṇḍabhaṭṭa explains a normal situation. This is the way a normal meaning cognition would come about, and not in any other way. The people who have just heard the name "Caitra" can by no chance have a specific and definite meaning cognition from the word "Caitra." They would only assume is that there is some x such that x is called Caitra.

Explanation [NN.VII.8.b]: Navya-naiyāyikas basically alter the account of the facts. They believe that even the people who have never seen Caitra would also have the primary signification function of the word "Caitra" ascertained with respect to the specific person. They believe that every person has a specific meaning cognition from the word "Caitra." This is explained on the basis of the innate mental dispositions.

Explanation [NN.VII.8.c]: Kauṇḍabhaṭṭa points out that one who accepts this position of Navya-naiyāyikas would have to face a paradox. By some chance Caitra visits the city of Banaras. He goes to the Temple of Viśveśvara. While he is standing in the temple, many people see him. Some of them know him personally and recognize him, while others just see him as they see so many other people. At that time someone says: "Caitra is not here." Kauṇḍabhaṭṭa says that if we accept the view of Navya-naiyāyikas, then the people who do not know Caitra and cannot recognize him, would have no cognition from this sentence.

The technicalities of the epistemic situation are as follows. According to Naiyāyikas, a perceptual cognition of the presence of x prohibits a verbal cognition of the absence of x. In the present case, the people who do not know Caitra personally and cannot recognize him do have a specific cognition of the specific Caitra from the word "Caitra" in the sentence, according to the doctrine of Naiyāyikas. However, at the same time, they see the man in the temple, though without recognizing him. This perceptual cognition of Caitra's presence would prohibit the verbal cognition of his absence, and hence these people would not have any cognition from this sentence.

Explanation [NN.VII.8d]: There are other people in the same temple at the same time who know Caitra personally and recognize him. What would be their understanding of the sentence "Caitra is not here"? Kauṇḍabhaṭṭa says that in fact they should not have any cognition from the sentence, since this verbal cognition of Caitra's absence must be prohibited by the actual perceptual cognition of his presence. But, he points out that, according to the view of Naiyāyikas, there would have to be a meaning cognition from this sentence for those people. This is paradoxical.

What Kauṇḍabhaṭṭa says does involve a paradox, but it is difficult to explain the second part of the paradox. How could the people who recognize Caitra have any meaning cognition from the sentence, even if we accept the view of Naiyāyikas? The Naiyāyika assumption would bring two kinds of people, those who know Caitra and those who do not, on an equal par. Yet it is not clear how Kauṇḍabhaṭṭa would justify the paradox in this situation. Nāgeśabhaṭṭa does not refer to this particular discussion in his *Laghu-mañjūṣā* or *Parama-laghu-mañjūṣā*, but his bigger work, *Vaiyākaraṇa-siddhānta-mañjūṣā* does deal with this argument. Interestingly, it cites only the first part of the argument, and omits the second part, [cf. *kiñca deśāntaraprasiddhaṃ caitraṃ kāśyāṃ śṛṇvatām viśiṣyāgṛhīta-saṅgatikānām api nalādipadād iva bodhānubhavāt tad-anurodhenānādi-saṃskārād viśiṣya-śakti-graha-sattvābhyupagame teṣām eva kālāntare gaṅgā-taṭe taṃ paśyatām "caitro 'tra nāsti" iti vākyād bodho na syāt, gaṅgā-taṭatvaṃ dharmitāvacchedakīkṛtya caitratvāvacchinna-pratiyogitākābhāvavattā-jñānaṃ prati tadeva dharmitāvacchedakīkṛtya caitratva-prakāraka-tadvattā-dhiyaḥ pratibandhakatvasya sarva-siddhatvāt /, Vaiyā-karaṇa-siddhānta-mañjūṣā*, ed. by K.P. Shukla, p. 132]. Thus, it seems that the second component of Kauṇḍabhaṭṭa's argument is somewhat unclear. The Bombay edition and V.N. Misra's edition read *nalayudhiṣṭhirādipadādivat*, while M. Bhattacharya's edition reads *nalayudhiśṭhirādipadavad*. Considering Nāgeśabhaṭṭa's version, i.e. *padādiva* = *padād iva*, I have chosen the reading *padādiva*.

NN.VII.9. (p. 126-7)

विश्वेश्वरदेवालयत्वं धर्मितावच्छेदकीकृत्य चैत्रत्वावच्छिन्नप्रतियोगिताकाभाववत्ताज्ञानं प्रति तदेव धर्मितावच्छेदकीकृत्य चैत्रत्वप्रकारकतद्वत्ताधियः प्रतिबन्धकत्वाभ्युपगमस्य सर्वसिद्धत्वात् । विशिष्यगृहीतसङ्गतिकानामिव तद्दर्शनात् पदस्मरणं च स्यात् । तदुक्तं -

"यत् संज्ञास्मरणं तत्र न तदप्यन्यहेतुकम् ।
पिण्ड एव हि दृष्टः सन् संज्ञां स्मारयितुं क्षमः ॥" इति ।

Translation [NN.VII.9]

[a] [Criticism of Navya-naiyāyikas continued]: [The difficulties pointed out in **NN.VII.8.c-d** would arise, because] the following principle is accepted by all: [Let *T* stand for the Viśveśvara temple in Banaras, and *C* for the person Caitra]: "Given *T*-ness, as the limitor of property-possessor-ness [in both clauses], a cognition of a possessor of *C* qualified by *C*-ness prohibits the cognition of a possessor of an absence of *C*, such that the counter-positiveness with respect to it is limited by *C*-ness."

[b] Just as those who specifically know the relation [of the word "Caitra" with the specifically known individual Caitra] remember the word ["Caitra"] at his sight, similarly [those who have not ascertained such a specific relation] would also remember [the word "Caitra," while they watch Caitra without recognizing him].

[c] So it is said: "The recollection of a name [which results after seeing the object possessing that name] has no other cause. The object itself, when seen, is capable of causing a recollection of its name."

Explanation [NN.VII.9.a]: In simple language, the principle given by Kauṇḍabhaṭṭa could be stated as follows: "The cognition of the Viśveśvara temple as characterized by Caitra's presence prohibits the cognition of the same temple as characterized by his absence." All other conditions being equal, a cognition "*x* is in *y*" prohibits the cognition "*x* is not in *y*." Actually, these cognitions are mutually prohibitive. However, the cognition of Caitra's presence is a perceptual cognition, while the cognition of his absence is a verbal cognition. In such a conflict, a verbal cognition is prohibited by a perceptual cognition.[451]

Explanation [NN.VII.9.b-c]: If the relation *R* between a specific word *W* and a specific object *O*, *R(W,O)*, is firmly ascertained, then given a cognition of *W*, there can be a recollection of *O*, or given a cognition of *O*, there can be a recollection of *W*. However, it is possible only if one knows both relata, i.e. *W* and *O* fully. Otherewise, one may have a cognition of one, and yet it may not lead to a recollection of the other.

The people who specifically know the person Caitra would remember the word "Caitra" at the sight of Caitra. But if we accept the assumption of Naiyāyikas, then even those people who do not know Caitra, would have a specific cognition of the signification function of the word "Caitra" due to the innate mental impressions or dispositions. Therefore, even these people would be able to remember the word "Caitra" after seeing him, though they cannot consciously recognize him.

Vācaspatimiśra and Haridīkṣita quote this verse [*yat saṃjñā* ...] as a verse from the *Vākya-padīya*, but it is not found in this text.[452] Its source is not known.

---

[451] *NK*, p. 1006; Matilal (1968: 55).
[452] *VP(p)*, p. 365; *SKB*, Pt.I., p. 4.

NN.VII.10. (p. 127)

चैत्रोऽस्ति न वेति संशयश्च न स्यादित्यादि भावप्रत्ययार्थनिरूपणे वक्ष्यते । तथा च विशेषरूपेण बोधाभावादेव सिद्धा हेत्वसिद्धिः ।

Translation [NN.VII.10]

[a] [Criticism of Navya-naiyāyikas continued]: [If one accepts the position of Navya-naiyāyikas, then] there can be no doubt whether Caitra is or is not there. All this will explained [in detail] in the section of *Bhāva-pratyayārtha-nirūpaṇa* [*VB*, pp. 221ff].

[b] Similarly, due to the absence of a cognition [from a word like "Caitra"] of a [person] in all specificity, the inconclusiveness of the reason [given by Navya-naiyāyikas] is proven.

Explanation [NN.VII.10.a]: Under normal circumstances, if one does not know a person, and if someone says "Person x is not here," one would have a doubt as to the presence or absence of that person. Such an experience disproves the doctrine of Navya-naiyāyikas.

NN.VII.11. (p. 127)

तथा च घटचैत्रादिपदानां घटत्वचैत्रत्वादिजातिवच्छक्तिसम्बन्धेन पदमपि शक्यतावच्छेदकत्वाच्छाब्दबोधे भासते । तत्र घटत्वादिजातिवच्छब्दांशे न वृत्तिविषयत्वं कल्प्यम् । मानाभावात् । आश्रयत्वेनैव तत्कार्यसिद्धेः । तथा च सम्बन्धस्योभयनिरूप्यत्वेन सम्बन्धिद्वयोपस्थापकत्वाविशेषाद् घट-त्वाद्यवच्छिन्नशक्त्यैव घटादिवच्छब्दस्यापि तयैव वृत्त्योपस्थितौ सत्यामर्थबोधनतात्पर्ये सति तत्र विशेषणतया स शब्दो भासते । तत्रापि घटत्वादिरूपेण विशिष्य शक्तिग्रहवतां पदजात्युभयप्रकारको बोधोऽन्येषां पूर्वोक्तप्रकारेणोपस्थितकेवलव्यक्तौ शक्तिग्रहाच्छुद्धतद्व्यक्तिविशेष्यकः केवलपदप्रकारको "घटपदवाच्यः कश्चिदर्थ" इत्याकारको बोध इति विशेषः ।

Translation [NN.VII.11]

[a] Thus, in the case of words like "pot" and "Caitra," a word itself also figures in the verbal cognition through the relation of a primary signification function, since [a word is] a limitor of primary-meaning-ness. This is similar to generic properties of pot-ness, Caitra-ness etc. [which are limitors

of primary-meaning-ness, and therefore figure in the contents of verbal cognitions].

[b] One need not assume a primary signification function of a word with respect to itself, just as [one need not assume it with respect to] generic properties like pot-ness, because there are no reasons [to have such assumptions]. The desired result [that a word also figures in the content of the final verbal cognition] can be explained just on the ground that [a word is] the locus [of the primary signification function].

[c] A relation is described in terms of both [relata], and hence it can cause a cognition of both in an identical way. Thus, on the basis of the same primary signification function [of the word "pot"] limited by the property pot-ness, there is a cognition of the word "pot," as well as the cognition of the object pot. Then, if communicating meaning is the [principal] intention, the [cognized] word appears as a qualifier [of meaning].

[d] For those people who have ascertained the primary signification function of a word specifically with respect to pot-ness etc., there is a meaning cognition with both the generic property of pot-ness and the word "pot" as its qualifiers.

[e] For other people, the primary signification function of a word is ascertained simply with respect to an unspecified or unqualified individual as pointed out earlier. Hence, there is a meaning cognition with an otherwise unspecified individual as its qualificandum and the word itself as its qualifier. This cognition is of the form: "There is some object *x*, such that *x* is signified by the word 'pot'." This is the difference [between words whose meaning is specifically known and those whose meaning is not specifically known].

Explanation [NN.VII.11.a]: Just as pot-ness is the limitor of primary-meaning-ness in the case of the word "pot," similarly the word "pot" itself is also a limitor of primary-meaning-ness. A necessary condition for an object to be signified by the word "pot" is that it must possess the generic property pot-ness. But this is not a sufficient condition. There are some other necessary conditions as well. The other necessary condition for an object to be signified by the word "pot" is its relation with the word "pot." An object can become a primary meaning of the word "pot," only if the word "pot" is related to the object by the relation of primary signification function.

Pot-ness can figure in the content of the verbal cognition just by virtue of its being a limitor of primary-meaning-ness. Similarly, the word "pot" can figure in the content of the verbal cognition just by virtue of its being a limitor of primary-meaning-ness, cf. **Explanation [NN.III.9.c]** and **Explanation [NN.III.10.a]**.

Explanation [NN.VII.11.b]: In this section, Kauṇḍabhaṭṭa points out that the word figures in the content of the verbal cognition, and yet it is not necessary to assume the signification function of a word with respect to itself. This could be supported by the arguments already given in sections **NN.III.9-12**. Kauṇḍabhaṭṭa says that a word can figure in the content of the meaning cognition just by being a locus (*āśraya*) of the primary signification function, cf. **Explanation [NN.VII.4.c]**.

Explanation [NN.VII.4.c]: The primary signification function of a word is a relation between a word and its meaning. It is a relation which is described in terms of both the relata. In this sense, the word and the object have the same status. They are both describers of the relation of primary signification function.[453]

Given this situation, just as a word's primary signification function causes a cognition of meaning, similarly it can cause a cognition of a word. If the speaker intends to convey meaning, then the signified word becomes its qualifier, and if the speaker intends just to refer to the word, then the signified meaning appears as its qualifier.

Explanation [NN.VII.11.d-e]: If the primary signification function of a word is ascertained with respect to a specific meaning, i.e. an object as qualified by a specific generic property, then that individual object appears in the content of the verbal cognition as qualified by both the specific generic property and the word. Thus, the individual signified by the word "bull" is cognized as qualified by bull-ness, as well as by the word "bull."

However, if the primary signification function of a word is not specifically ascertained with respect to an individual object as qualified by a specific property, as in the case of words like *nala*, then in the content of the meaning cognition, that individual is unspecified except that it appears as qualified by the word *nala*. Thus the meaning is: "something which is signified by the word *nala*."

NN.VII.12. (p. 127)

यदा तु "न गिरा गिरेति ब्रूयात्," "कवतीषु रथन्तरं गायति," "अच्छा-वाकीयं साम गायति," "रषाभ्यां नो णः ...," "ससजुषो रुः," "गवित्यय-माह," इत्यादौ ब्रूयाद्, गायति, आहेत्यादिभिः स्थान्यर्थकषष्ठ्यादिभिश्चा-न्वययोग्यताकाङ्क्षादिवशाच्छब्दमात्रे तात्पर्यं गृह्यते तदा "घटो नित्यः," "स्वर्गो ध्वस्त" इत्यादौ विशेषणांशवच्छब्दस्वरूपमात्रं प्राधान्येन तया शक्त्या प्रतिपाद्यते । वृत्तिसत्त्वेऽपि तात्पर्याभावादर्थांशो न बोध्यते । लवण-मात्रतात्पर्यदशायां सैन्धवशब्दादश्ववद् बुद्धो वा त्यज्यते ।

---

453 *VBS-S*, pp. 241-2.

Translation [NN.VII.12]

[a] There are the following usages:

i) "One should not say *girā girā*."

ii) "In the Kavatī sacrifices, one recites the Rathantara Sāman."

iii) "One recites the Acchāvākīya Sāman."

iv) "The sound *n* is replaced by *ṇ*, if, within the same item, *n* is preceded by *r* or *ṣ*."

v) "The sound *s* at the end of an inflected item and the final sound of *sajuṣ* are replaced by *rU*."

vi) "He said 'bull'."

[b] In these usages, the intention of the speaker is ascertained with respect to the word itself, because [a word alone] has expectancy for and a capacity to be construed with verbs like "one should say," "one sings" [or " recites"], and "says," as well as with the genitive case signifying a substituendum etc. [If this intention is understood], then a word-form alone is principally signified [by a word] on the basis of the same primary signification function.

[c] This is similar to the sentences "a pot is eternal" and "heaven is destroyed," where only the qualifying properties such as pot-ness and pleasure [are principally signified by the words "pot" and "heaven"].

[d] There is a primary signification function [of a word like "bull" in the sentence "he said 'bull',"] with respect to meaning and yet this meaning is not signified, because it is not intended.

[e] Alternatively, [one could say that] meaning is cognized and then given up later. For instance, [the meaning] 'a horse' is cognized from the word *saindhava*, and yet [this meaning] is given up later, if only salt [i.e. the other meaning of the word] is intended [by the speaker].

Explanation [NN.VII.12.a]: The first two passages are found in Śabara's *Bhāṣya* [*MS-B(b)*, Vol.II., p. 19, 183, 185, 222, and 434]. Passages 4 and 5 are respectively P.8.4.1, and P.8.2.66. The last passage is an example from common speech. Concerning the passage *na girā gireti brūyāt*, D.V. Garge (1952: 43) says: "Under J[aimini] S[ūtra] 9.1.50ff, Śabara cites *yad girā gireti ... udgeyam* from P[añcaviṃśa] B[rāhmaṇa] 8.6.9-10. It is prefixed by the sentence *na girā gireti brūyāt* which is only an inferred injunction (*anumita-vidhi*) not appearing in the original source text." It is clear that Kauṇḍabhaṭṭa is citing these passages as they appear in Śabara. There is a reference to *Kavatī* in the *Tāṇḍya-mahā-brāhmaṇa* (7.8.3).

Explanation [NN.VII.12.b]: In all these examples, there are overt signs which indicate the intention of the speaker that only the word-form is intended. Either there are verbs such as "one says" or "one sings" etc., or there is a usage of the genitive case which indicates that the item with the genitive case is the substituendum, i.e. the item undergoing substitution, cf. P.1.1.49 (*ṣaṣṭhī sthāne-yogā*).

Expressions like *rathantara* and *acchāvākīya* refer to Vedic hymns with these traditional names. But, here there is still a reference to the mere words of the hymns, and not to their meanings.

Explanation [NN.VII.12.c]: Kauṇḍabhaṭṭa gives two examples where the element which is normally a qualifier becomes the principal qualificandum. In the example "a pot is eternal," it is not possible to construe a pot qualified by the property of pot-ness with the primary meaning of the word "eternal." The object pot is not eternal. However, the property pot-ness is eternal. Therefore, depending upon the intention of the speaker, one interprets the sentence to mean "pot-ness is eternal." Here, pot-ness, which is normally a qualifier, becomes a qualificandum.

The same is the case with the example "heaven is destroyed." The word "heaven" (*svarga*) is interpreted by the Mīmāṃsā system to mean "a place with pleasure." That place cannot be destroyed. Thus, one has to interpret the sentence to mean "pleasure is destroyed."[454] Similarly, if the meaning of a word is not intended, and if only the word itself is intended to be signified, then the word itself is cognized as a qualificandum, and the meaning may be cognized as a qualifier or it may not be cognized at all.

NN.VII.13. (p. 127)

यत्र तूक्तानन्यथासिद्धतात्पर्यग्राहकाभावस्तत्र विशिष्योपदेशेन तथा तात्पर्यमाचार्यैर्बोध्यते । यथा "स्वं रूपं शब्दस्याशब्दसंज्ञे"ति सूत्रेण "भू सत्तायाम्," "अग्नेर्ढक्" इत्यादौ ।

Translation [NN.VII.13]

[a] In those cases, where there is no way of realizing the unconditional intention [of the speaker] as described above, that intention is made known by the teachers through explicit statements. This is the case, when by rule P.1.1.68 (*svaṃ rūpaṃ śabdasyāśabda-saṃjñā*), [the term *agni* in] P.4.2.33 (*agner ḍhak*), and [the term *bhū* in the statement] "*bhū* [occurs in the sense of] existence" [stand for their own word-forms].

Explanation [NN.VII.13.a]: Rule P.1.1.68 says: "a linguistic item [used in grammar] stands for its own word-form, unless it is a technical name of [a class of] linguistic items." This has been discussed in detail in Introduction, **F.3**.

---

454 *NK*, p. 1059.

NN.VII.14. (p. 127-8)

न चार्थशक्त्यैव तात्पर्यवशात् प्राधान्येन शब्दस्यापि प्रतिपादनमित्ययुक्तम् । तत्प्रकारकव्यक्तिविशेष्यकबोधत्वस्यैव तद्वृत्तिज्ञानकार्यतावच्छेदकत्वात् । अन्यथा "घटो नित्य" इत्यादेर्घटत्वे लक्षणा न स्यात् । प्राधान्येन बोधार्थं खलु तत्र लक्षणाश्रयणमिति वाच्यम् । तत्र घटत्वादिरूपेण बोधानुरोधेन लक्षणाभ्युपगमात् । अन्यथा घटत्वनिर्विकल्पापत्तेः ।

Translation [NN.VII.14]

[a] [Objection to the view of grammarians]: It is wrong to say that the primary signification function [of a word] ascertained only with respect to meaning, primarily and principally signifies the word-form depending upon the intention of the speaker.

[b] This is so, because the property of being an awareness in which an individual is the qualificandum and *P* is the qualifier is the limitor of effectness pertaining [to a meaning cognition caused by] the awareness of a primary signification function ascertained with respect to [an individual qualified by a certain property *P*.

[c] [If this is not accepted], then there could be no secondary signification function for pot-ness in the construction "a pot is eternal." One needs to accept the secondary signification function for the cognition [of pot-ness] as the principal element [i.e. principal qualificandum].

[d] [Reply to the above objection]: One should not raise such an objection. One has to accept the secondary signification function [in that construction] because there is a cognition [of pot-ness] qualified by pot-ness-ness. Otherwise, [in the absence of a secondary signification function], the cognition of pot-ness would be without any qualifier.

Explanation [NN.VII.14.a-c]: A word such as "pot" may be accepted to be the limitor of primary-meaning-ness, but then there can be a cognition of the word "pot" only as a qualifier of an individual pot, and never as the qualificandum. The general rule is as follows:

> "Given an awareness of a primary signification function ascertain with respect to the limitor *P*, the resulting meaning cognition can be only a cognition of an individual qualified by *P*."

If one desires to have a cognition of *P* as a qualificandum, and not as a qualifier, then one should take recourse to secondary signification function. For instance, the usual primary meaning of the word "pot" is only an individual qualified by pot-ness, and not pot-ness by itself. In the example "a pot is eternal," only pot-ness could be construed with eternality. Therefore, one needs to take recourse to a secondary signification function.

Similarly, if one wants a cognition of the word "pot" from itself as the principal qualificandum, then one should take recourse to a secondary signification function. If one refuses to do this, then one cannot explain the sentence "a pot is eternal."

Explanation [NN.VII.14.d]: Kauṇḍabhaṭṭa says that this objection is not valid. If one so intends, one can certainly cognize the word-form itself as the qualificandum through the primary signification function. Similarly, one can also cognize pot-ness as a qualificandum from the word "pot," if one so intends. However, the property cognized this way is not further qualified by pot-ness-ness. It would remain unqualified.

When one wishes the property of pot-ness to be the principal qualificandum and expects it to be qualified by pot-ness-ness, one has to take recourse to a secondary signification function. The cognition of a word-form derived from a word is already with a qualifier. To have a qualificative cognition of a word, one does not have to take recourse to a secondary signification function. This argument is explained in the following section.

NN.VII.15. (p. 128)

अत्रानुपूर्वीविशिष्टवर्णानां पदरूपतया केवलतदुपस्थितावप्यानुपूर्व्या अवच्छेदकत्वेन भानान्नोक्तदोषः । विशेष्यव्यक्त्यंशाभानात् । पदस्य विशेषणत्वं नास्तीति कृत्वा प्राधान्यमप्यर्थायातम् । मोषवादिभिर्नैयायिकैः प्रमेयत्वप्रकारकसकलानुभवात् प्रमुष्टविशेषणकव्यक्तिमात्रस्मरणाभ्युपगमवत् प्रमुष्टविशेष्यकस्मरणाभ्युपगमात् । उच्चारयेत्यादिसमभिव्याहारस्य मोष एवोपयोगात् ।

Translation [NN.VII.15]

[a] [Kauṇḍabhaṭṭa's justification of his view]: Here, there is no problem. A word is [nothing but] linguistic sounds qualified by a particular sequence. Hence, though a word-form itself is principally cognized, the sound-sequence appears as its qualifier.

[b] [When a word-form is principally cognized], the individual object which is [normally] the qualificandum is not cognized. Therefore, the word no more remains a qualifier, and it naturally becomes the principal element.

[c] For instance, Naiyāyikas who believe in cognitive loss [of an element previously cognized], would say: "Everything is cognized as qualified by [the universally present] property of cognizability. Later on, there can be a cognition of merely the individual [qualificandum], such that the qualifier [= cognizability] is not recollected."

[d] Similarly, we accept that there is a recollection of [the qualifier] word, such that its qualificandum is not recollected. The contextual use of words like "utter" is [an indication] of the non-recollection [of the qualificandum, i.e. meaning].

Explanation [NN.VII.15.a]: A word is nothing but a series of sounds (*varṇa*). In other words, sounds qualified by a particular sequence constitute a word. Hence, in the cognition of a word as the principal element, the sequence of sounds figures in as a qualifier. Hence, the resulting cognition is not an unqualified cognition. This shows that there is no necessity of resorting to a secondary signification function to explain a qualificative cognition.

Explanation [NN.VII.15.b]: When one says that the word-form is itself principally cognized, and that there is no intention to express the meaning, the meaning is not cognized at all. Thus, only the word-form, which is usually a qualifier, is cognized without its qualificandum. Since the qualificandum is not cognized, the qualifier is no more a qualifier. It naturally becomes a qualificandum itself. Thus, there is no special process involved in making the word a qualificandum, except the non-recollection of meaning.

Explanation [NN.VII.15.c]: The process of *moṣa* or *pramoṣa* refers to a non-recollection or cognitive loss of something which has been cognized previously. This has been used by Naiyāyikas to explain the *nirvikalpaka* "non-qualificative" cognition of generic properties.

Naiyāyikas say that the cognition of a generic property, prior to the cognition of an individual qualified by it, is a non-qualificative cognition in a peculiar way. They say that actually even this cognition of a generic property is a qualificative cognition to begin with. Everything is cognized as qualified by the property of cognizability. Later this qualifying property is not recollected, and hence one has a cognition of just a generic property.[455]

NN.VII.16. (p. 128)

वस्तुतो न पदप्रकारकबोधत्वमर्थशक्तिज्ञानकार्यतावच्छेदकं, किन्तु सामान्यसामग्रीवशाद्विशेषणत्वेन भानम् । न चैवं कदाचिद्विशेष्यताया अप्यापत्तिः । निर्विकल्पोत्तरप्रत्यक्षे जातेरिवोपपत्तेरिति तत्त्वम् ।

Translation [NN.VII.16]

[a] [Kauṇḍabhaṭṭa's justification of his view continued]: The property of being a cognition [of meaning with a word as its qualifier is not really the limitor

---

455 *buddhi-viṣayatāvacchedakatvena anugata-dharmeṇa sakala-dharma-viṣayaka-sāmānya-prattyāsatty-adhīna-śakty-anubhave pramuṣṭa-buddhi-viṣayatāvacchedakatvāṃśaṃ svarūpataś caitratvādi-prakāraka-smaraṇaṃ nirābādham eva* /, *SV*, p. 110; *prameyatvādi-rūpeṇa sarvānubhava-sattvāt tatra prameyatvāṃśasyānudbuddha-saṃskāratvena moṣe prathamatas tat-taj-jāty-ādi-rūpaṃ nirvikalpakaṃ smaraṇam* /, *LM*, p. 345.

of effect-ness [with respect to the cause, i.e.] the awareness of a primary signification function [ascertained] with respect to meaning.

[b] However, since a word-form is cognized by means of the common [=non-special, already given] causal conditions [such as auditory perception etc.], it [accidentally] appears as a qualifier.

[c] Thus, there is no difficulty in [the word-form] becoming the [normal] qualificandum [in the verbal cognition]. This is similar to the explanation that after the [first] unqualified cognition, a generic property [does not appear later as a qualificandum in the cognition of qualified objects].

Explanation [NN.VII.16.a]: The objector [in **NN.VII.14.b**] believes that, according to grammarians, the property of being a cognition of meaning qualified by the word-form is the limitor of effect-ness with respect to the cause, i.e. the awareness of the primary signification function ascertained with respect to meaning. This is to say that, according to grammarians, the awareness of the primary signification function ascertained with respect to meaning is determined to be the cause of a cognition of primary meaning qualified by a word. Kauṇḍabhaṭṭa says that this is not exactly true. Acceptance of a word as the limitor of effect-ness pertaining to the meaning cognition would mean that a word is used with the explicit intention of producing a meaning cognition qualified by a word. This is not what a grammarian wishes to say.

Explanation [NN.VII.16.b]: Kauṇḍabhaṭṭa explains the final position of grammarians as he sees it. A word is first heard. Then one has two cognitions, i.e. an auditory perception of the word and a meaning cognition. Since, hearing the word is the common condition for both of these cognitions, the cognized word appears as a qualifier of the cognized meaning. This means to say that the word which figures in the verbal cognition as a qualifier is not what a word is necessarily meant or intended for. Yet it is a feature which unavoidably occurs in every meaning cognition. It is not possible to have a cognition of meaning from a word in the absence of a cognition of the word-form.

Explanation [NN.VII.16.c]: Kauṇḍabhaṭṭa says that there are some benefits in this interpretation. Since a word is not the limitor of effect-ness pertaining to a meaning cognition, and is cognized on the basis of common, non-special causal conditions, there is no fear of the word itself becoming the normal qualificandum, and the meaning becoming the normal qualifier. In all normal usages, a word remains a qualifier of meaning.

As explained in **Explanation [NN.VII.15]**, a word in some cases becomes the qualificandum simply because of the non-recollection of the normal qualificandum. This is similar to the case of a generic property figuring in the perceptual cognition. According to the Nyāya system, one first has a non-qualificative (*nirvikalpaka*) cognition of a generic property, and then one has the qualificative (*savikalpaka* / *viśiṣṭa*) cognition of an individual qualified by that property. In the first non-qualificative cognition, one might say that the generic property is the qualificandum, but in the normal qualificative cognition that follows, a generic property is always a qualifier, cf. **Explanation [NN.VII.15.c]**.

NN.VII.17. (p. 128)

तदेतत्सर्वमभिप्रेत्योक्तं वाक्यपदीये -

"ग्राह्यत्वं ग्राहकत्वं च द्वे शक्ती तेजसो यथा ।
तथैव सर्वशब्दानामेते पृथगवस्थिते ॥" इति ।

अस्यार्थः । द्रव्यचाक्षुषमात्रे आलोकसंयोगो हेतुः । अन्यथान्धकारेऽपि चक्षुःसंयोगमात्राद् घटचाक्षुषापत्तेरित्यविवादम् । तथा चालोकप्रत्यक्षेऽपि स्वस्मादेवोपपत्तिर्वाच्या । तथा च यथा घटालोकसंयोगादेव घटस्येवालोकस्यापि प्रत्यक्षं, तथार्थगोचरशब्दनिष्ठशक्त्यैव शब्दस्यार्थस्य च भानम् । यथा वा घटचक्षुःसंयोगाभावे तस्मादेवालोकसंयोगादालोकस्यैव भानं, तथार्थे तात्पर्यनिर्वाहे तद्वृत्त्यैव सति शब्दे तात्पर्ये तस्यैव बोध इति ।

Translation [NN.VII.17]

[a] With all this in view, the *Vākya-padīya* says: "Just as light has two properties, i.e. of being cognized and of causing a cognition of something, similarly, all words have these two distinctively established properties."

[b] This is what is meant. Conjunction with light is the cause of every visual cognition of objects. Otherwise, one would have such [a visual cognition] even in the dark, simply by having the conjunction [of the object] with the eye organ. Similarly, a perception of light itself should be explained simply on the basis of its own [conjunction with the eye organ].

[c] Thus, from a conjunction of a pot with light, there is a perception of the pot as well as of light itself. Similarly, there is a cognition of meaning as well as of a word, from the primary signification function which resides in the word and is ascertained with respect to meaning.

[d] In the absence of a conjunction of a pot with the eye organ, there can be a perception of light from the very same conjunction of light [with the eye]. Similarly, when there is no intention to express meaning, and when [a word is] intended, there is a cognition of a word through the same primary signification function.

Explanation [NN.VII.17.a]: The verse is *VP* [I.55]. In the case of visual perception, objects like pot have only the property of *grāhyatva* "being cognized," while the sense organ has only the property of *grāhakatva* "being a cause of the cognition." Objects like a pot do not have the property of causing a cognition, while the sense organs do not have the property of being cognized. However, the light which is involved in visual perception has both the properties. The light cannot cause a perception of objects without itself being cognized. Similar is the case of words. They cannot cause a meaning cognition without themselves being cognized,[456] cf. Introduction, **F.4**.

Explanation [NN.VII.17.b]: In the perception of an object as well as in the perception of light, the perceptive connection between the eye organ and light is the causal condition. One cannot have either of these two perceptions in the absence of this connection. Thus light has both the properties, and hence it is given here as an example to explain the similar case of words.

Explanation [NN.VII.17.c]: If light is perceived and its connection with an object is also perceived, then one has the perception of both light and the object. The perception of light may not be intended by the perceiver, and yet one must have it in order to have a perception of the object.

Similarly, if a word is cognized and if the relation between a word and its meaning is cognized, then one has a cognition of meaning as well as of the word-form. One may not expressly intend to have a cognition of the word-form, and yet one must have it in order to have a cognition of its meaning.

Explanation [NN.VII.17.d]: If there were a perceptive connection between the eye and light, but no connection between light and the object, then one would have only a perception of light, without a perception of the object. Similarly, if a word is cognized and its relation with meaning is not intended, or if the meaning is not cognized for some reason, then there is only a cognition of the word-form.

Kauṇḍabhaṭṭa says that if the meaning is not intended, then the same primary signification function ascertained with respect to meaning causes a cognition of the word. That which is cognized merely through auditory perception cannot be legitimately an object of the verbal cognition. Since a word is regarded as being cognized through the primary signification function, there is no problem. This is supported by Helārāja,[457] cf. Introduction, **F.4**.

NN.VII.18. (p. 128-9)

एवञ्च श्रोत्रादिभिरिति मूलेऽपि श्रोत्रमादिर्यस्येति व्युत्पत्त्या शक्तिज्ञानत-त्संस्कारा गृह्यन्ते । श्रोत्रेणोपस्थिते शक्तिग्रहादित्यवधेयम् । अत एव गामु-

---

[456] *ghaṭādayo hi grāhyatvenaiva vyavasthitā iti ghaṭādīnāṃ grahaṇa-kāle naiva kāñcid upalabdhi-sahakāritvenendriyasya viṣayasya vā svalpām apy anugraha-mātrāṃ kurvanti / tathā grāhytvam apratipadyamānāny eva sarvendriyāṇi grāhyasya viṣayasya grahaṇa-nimittatvāya kalpante / tejas tu tamo-rūpa-virodhinā rūpa-bhedena yuktam avadhāryamāṇa-svarūpam anugrāhakatvenopalabdhau kāraṇa-bhāvam pratipadyate / śabdo 'pi bhāvāntara-virodhinā śabdāntara-virodhinā ca svarūpeṇāvadhriyamāṇa-bhedaḥ parigṛhīta-viśeṣa-śabda-svarūpaḥ pratyāyyam artham prakāśayati /, VP-S*, Pt.I., pp. 115-6.

[457] *tathā ca śabdo 'pi vācako 'rtham abhidhīyamānatayā prakāśayann ātmānam abhidhayā eva prakāśayatīty ucitam, na tu śrotrendriya-bhāvopagamanena /, VP-H(p)*, p. 125; also: p. 127.

च्चारयेत्युक्ते विकृतस्यैवोच्चारणापत्तिः । तादृशस्यैव प्रत्यक्षोपस्थितत्वात् । शब्दस्याप्रकृत्यर्थत्वात्तत्र द्वितीयार्थादेरनन्वयापत्तेश्च । प्रत्ययानां प्रकृत्यर्थगतस्वार्थबोधकत्वव्युत्पत्तेः । स्वस्यैव प्रत्यक्षेण शीघ्रमुपस्थितत्वाद्गौरस्तीत्यादावपि स्वपरत्वापत्तेश्चेत्यादिदूषणाभासाः परास्ताः । उक्ततात्पर्यवशाद् वृत्त्यैवाविकृतस्यैव शब्दादुपस्थितत्वात् । अन्यथार्थपरत्वस्यैव न्याय्यत्वात् । तस्मादुक्ततात्पर्यनिर्णये सति शब्द एव प्राधान्येन भासते, तदभावे त्वर्थविशेषणत्वेनैवेति सिद्धम् ।

Translation [NN.VII.18]

[a] Hence, even the original [i.e. verse 26 of Bhaṭṭojī Dīkṣita's *Vaiyākaraṇamatonmajjana*], the word *śrotrādibhiḥ* refers to an awareness of the primary signification function and its mental impressions. This is possible by the analysis of the word *śrotrādi* as "that which begins with audition." One can ascertain the primary signification function of a word only after its auditory perception.

[b] [There are the following objections to this view]:

i) If somebody says *gām uccāraya* "utter the bull," then one would have to utter the inflected form *gām*, [rather than the stem form *go*-]. This is because, only this inflected form is auditorily cognized.

ii) Since an [auditorily perceived] word is not a meaning of the nominal stem, the meaning of the case-affix of the second triplet [in *gām* < *go* + *am*] could not be construed with it. It is the accepted doctrine that affixes signify their meaning which is embedded in the meaning of the stem.

iii) Since a word itself is directly cognized earlier in the construction *gaur asti* "a bull exists," the word would stand for itself, [rather than for the object bull].

[c] [Refutation of these objections]: All these pseudo-objections are firmly rejected, because it is the non-inflected [word, *go*-] alone that is cognized from the [inflected] word [in *gām uccāraya*], on account of the primary signification function and the intention as explained above.

[d] Otherwise, [a word would] justifiably refer to meaning alone. Hence, it is established that, if there is the above described intention, then a word itself is cognized principally. In its absence, a word is only a qualifier of meaning.

Explanation [NN.VII.18.a]: In the earlier section, Kauṇḍabhaṭṭa has argued that though meaning is not intended to be expressed, a word-form is not cognized through auditory perception alone, but through the primary signification function of the word.

Therefore, he proposes a new interpretation of verse 26 of Bhaṭṭojī Dīkṣita's *Vaiyākaraṇa-matonmajjana*. The verse actually refers only to auditory perception as a means of cognizing a word; however, Kauṇḍabhaṭṭa's interpretation makes it say that a word is cognized either through the awareness of a primary signification function or through a mental impression of this primary signification function.

Explanation [NN.VII.18.b]: The objections mentioned here are raised by Gaṅgeśa against the view of grammarians. Kauṇḍabhaṭṭa does not mention who the objector is. The objector says that, if one were to accept the view of grammarians, then upon hearing the sentence *gām uccāraya*, one would have to utter the word *gām*, and not the stem form *go*. This would be the case, because only the inflected form is auditorily perceived. Actually, one is expected to utter just the stem form *go-*.[458] If a word is only auditorily perceived, and yet figures in the content of the verbal cognition, it cannot be treated as a legitimate meaning. Only that which is cognized from a word on the basis of its primary signification function is a word-meaning. Affixes are said to signify their meaning as related to the meaning of the stem. Thus, one would not be able to construe the meaning of the accusative affix *-am* [in *gām* < *go* + *am*] with the word-form cognized from itself through mere auditory perception.[459] If a word-form is cognized only through auditory perception, then this audition always precedes the meaning cognition. The element which is cognized prior would be the usual significatum, and hence even in the sentence "there is a bull," one would have to construe the word itself, rather than the object bull.[460]

Explanation [NN.VII.18.c]: Kauṇḍabhaṭṭa says that these are pseudo-objections, since they assume that according to the grammarian a word-form is cognized only on the basis of auditory perception. This is not true at all. In the expression *gām uccāraya*, the inflected form *gām* is cognized through auditory perception, but the word-form *go* is cognized through the primary signification function of the word. Thus, there is no chance of one being forced to utter the inflected form *gām*, after hearing the sentence cited above.

Explanation [NN.VII.18.d]: This is slightly different from the view of grammarians as presented by Gaṅgeśa. He says that according to *anye* "others," words generally stand for their meaning, and if meaning is not intended, only then they stand for themselves. For instance, in the example *gām uccāraya* "utter the bull," there is no intention for meaning and hence the word *gām* refers to the word-form *go-*.[461]

---

458 *kiñ caivaṃ gām uccārayety ādau vikṛtaṃ go-padam evoccāraṇa-karma-syāt / tasyaiva śrotra-pratyakṣa-tvāt / na tv avikṛtaṃ go-padam /*, *TC*, p. 683.

459 *kiñ ca vibhakty-upanītānvaya-prakāra-karmatvādinānupasthitasyākāṅkṣā-viraheṇa kriyādy-anvayo na syāt / smṛta-pade dvitīyārtha-karmatvānvaya iti cen na / vibhakteḥ prakṛty-arthānvita-svārtha-bodhakatvasya vyutpatti-siddhatvāt /*, *TC*, pp. 684-5.

460 *kiñ ca gaur astīty ādau ubhaya-paratva-sambhave sva-paratvam eva syāt / svasyaiva pratyakṣeṇa śīghram upasthitatvāt /*, *TC*, p. 684.

461 *anye tu padānām autsargikam artha-paratvam / tad-abhāve sva-paratvam / gām uccārayety ādau vācyā-vivakṣayā padena svānvitābhidhānāt /*, *TC*, p. 681.

NN.VII.19. (p. 129)

अत एव "उद्भिदा यजेत पशुकामः," "अग्निहोत्रं जुहोती"त्यादौ नामधेयत्वं व्यवस्थाप्य तस्यापि विशेषणत्वेनान्वयादुद्भिन्नामकेन यागेन भावयेदिति वाक्यार्थः सम्पन्न इत्युद्भिदधिकरणे मीमांसकैरुक्तं सङ्गच्छते । यत्तु मीमांसकमतेऽपि नाम्नि लक्षणैवान्यथा वृत्त्यानुपस्थितत्वेन शाब्दबोधविषयता न स्यात् । अत एव वाक्यार्थे भट्टपादैर्लक्षणाभ्युपगम्यते, परन्तु नामनामिसम्बन्धे सर्वत्रैव सेति निरूढेति न दोष इति समादधिरे । तन्न साधीयः । उक्तरीत्या क्लृप्तशक्त्यैवोपपत्तौ गौरवग्रस्तलक्षणाकल्पनानौचित्यात् । लक्षणया सर्वत्रानिर्वाहस्य प्रागुक्तत्वाच्च ।

Translation [NN.VII.19]

[a] Certainly, for this reason, the following statement of Mīmāṃsakas in the *Udbhid-adhikaraṇa* is justified: First it is established that [the words *udbhid* and *agnihotra*], in the injunctions *udbhidā yajeta paśu-kāmaḥ* "a person desirous of animals should perform an Udbhid sacrifice" and *agnihotraṃ juhoti* "one should perform a sacrifice called Agnihotra," are names of certain sacrifices. Then, by construing these names as qualifiers [of the named sacrifices], the sentence-meaning of the following form is obtained: "One should produce [the desired result] by means of a sacrifice called Udbhid."

[b] [A view of some Mīmāṃsakas]: However, some [Mīmāṃsakas] explain: Even in the view of Mīmāṃsakas, there is a secondary signification function [to be invoked] for [the cognition of] a name. Otherwise, a name would not be an object of the verbal cognition, on the ground that it is not cognized by means of a signification function. Therefore, Kumārilabhaṭṭa accepts a secondary signification function with respect to sentence-meaning. However, for the relation of a name and a nominatum, there is always a conventional secondary signification function. Hence, there is no difficulty.

[c] [Rejection of this view]: That is not a good explanation. It is not proper to assume a secondary signification function and get involved with the problem of prolixity, when it is possible to give an explanation simply on the basis of the primary signification function of a word. [The primary signification function of a word] could be assumed [with respect to word-form] as shown in detail above. It has already been pointed out that [the acceptance of] a secondary signification function does not solve [all difficulties].

Explanation [NN.VII.19.a]: The *Udbhid-adhikaraṇa* is a section in the *Mīmāṃsā-sūtras* [1/4/1-2]. The injunction *udbhidā yajeta* literally says: "One should perform a sacrifice with *udbhid*." Is *udbhid* a name of the substance with which one should perform the sacrifice, or is it the name of a certain sacrifice? Mīmāṃsakas choose the second alternative. Similarly, the word *agnihotra* is taken as a name of a certain sacrifice.

Kumārilabhaṭṭa says that a name always signifies meaning which is qualified by the name itself.[462] The injunctions quoted here are discussed in Śabara's *Bhāṣya* [*MS-B(b)*, Vol.I., pp. 85-6, 89, 146, 157, 160, 176, and 539, and Vol.II., p. 677]. The injunction *udbhidā yajeta* is found in the *Pañca-viṃśa-brāhmaṇa* (19.7.3), and *agnihotraṃ juhoti* is found in the *Chāndogya Upaniṣad* (5.24.1-2). It is not likely that Kauṇḍabhaṭṭa is quoting these passages directly from Vedic sources. He usually quotes these injunctions as they appear in Śabara's *Bhāṣya*.

Explanation [NN.VII.19.b]: Kauṇḍabhaṭṭa discusses an interpretation of the Mīmāṃsā view by some unidentified Mīmāṃsakas. This view is similar to the view of Naiyāyikas. These Mīmāṃsakas say that *udbhid* is a name of a sacrifice, and yet they believe that a word signifies its own form through its secondary signification function. The word-form as cognized through the secondary signification function becomes a qualifier of the meaning signified by the same word. The secondary signification function of a word with respect to its own form is the conventional secondary signification function.

The view of Kumārilabhaṭṭa, as presented here is slightly different from what one finds in his works. Kumārilabhaṭṭa does propose that the name *udbhid* is a qualification of the sacrifice, but he does not mean that it is cognized from the word through any kind of signification function over and above direct auditory perception.[463] Khaṇḍadeva later criticizes and rejects even this view.[464] He points out that ultimately the view presented by Kumārilabhaṭṭa would force one to accept that there is a signification function of a word with respect to its own form. If such a general view is accepted, then even in cases like *somena yajeta* "one should accomplish the desired result by performing a sacrifice with *soma*," one would have to accept that *soma* is a name of the sacrifice. Mīmāṃsakas, in general, do not construe the injunction *somena yajeta* as an injunction of a name. They interpret it to be an injunction of an accessory (*guṇa-vidhi*).

Explanation [NN.VII.19.c]: Kauṇḍabhaṭṭa points out that, if one accepts *udbhid* to be a name of a sacrifice and yet there is a secondary signification function of the word *udbhid*

---

462 *ātma-rūpa-vyavacchinnam evārthaṃ saṃjñā gamayati* /, *TV(a)*, Pt.I., pp. 325-6.

463 *nanv evaṃ śabda-sva-rūpābhidhānam prasajyeta / pratyakṣāvagata-svarūpa-viśiṣṭārthābhidhānād aprasaṅgaḥ* /, *TV(a)*, Pt.I., p. 326; also: *TV-NS*, pp. 408-9.

464 *yat tu vārttike pakṣāntaram uktam - udbhit-padasyodbhit-saṃjñā-viśiṣṭe vijātīya-yāge śaktiḥ / ... na caivaṃ viśeṣaṇī-bhūtodbhit-padasyāpi vācyatāpattiḥ / śrautopasthitasyaiva tasya vācakatva-sambandhena viśeṣaṇatvopapatteḥ / ... ataś codbhit-padam eva vācakatva-sambandhena viśeṣaṇam / ... udbhit-padasya ca śrautād evopasthitatvāt tad-aṃśe viśeṣaṇa-vidhi-kalpanā-bhāvena nāmadheyatva-pakṣe lāghavam iti / ... tat pada-janya-padārthopasthitir vākyārthe kāraṇam ity asya niyamasya bhaṅgāpattau arthādhyāhārādi-prasaṅgāpatteḥ, yāga-gata-vaijātya-bodhasya ca udbhit-saṃjñādhīnatvena śakyatāvacchedaka-bodhābhāve śakti-grahasyaivānupapatteḥ, kḷptāvayava-yogenāpy upapattau atirikta-śakti-kalpanāyāṃ somādi-padānām api tad-āpatter upekṣitam* /, *MKB*, p. 171.

to refer to its own form, there is the fault of prolixity. As explained in the earlier sections, one could explain the cognition of a word-form from itself simply on the basis of its primary signification function.

NN.VII.20. (p. 129)

किञ्चैवं हि नामतोच्छेदापत्तेर्वृद्धिमिच्छतो मूलनाशन्यायापातः । गुणविधित्वे हि -

"मत्वर्थलक्षणापत्तेर्नामधेयत्वमास्थितम् ।
विशिष्टविधिपक्षे हि भवेन्मत्वर्थलक्षणा ॥
सोमादौ गत्यभावात्सा न त्वत्र गतिसम्भवात् ।"

सा च नामधेयत्वेऽपि समा चेत्कुतो गुणविधित्यागः । सामानाधिकरण्यानुपपत्तेर्गुणविधाविवात्रापि बीजत्वेनापेक्षणात् । न हि बीजं विना लक्षणा । साध्यत्वं द्वितीयार्थ इति सक्त्वधिकरणे व्यवस्थापितत्वेन वाजपेयाधिकरणोक्तन्यायेनैकस्यां क्रियायां साध्यद्वयासमवायात् "काष्ठैस्तण्डुलं पचति" इत्यादावपि मत्वर्थलक्षणाया आवश्यकत्वान्निरूढत्वानिरूढत्वे अपि समे । गुणविधौ सर्वत्र मत्वर्थलक्षणाभ्युपगमस्य मीमांसकप्रसिद्धेश्च ।

Translation [NN.VII.20]

[a] Moreover, this [is unacceptable because it] would lead to the uprooting [of the Mīmāṃsā doctrine that *udbhid* etc. are] names. This would be equivalent to what the following maxim says: "one who desires growth [through interest earnings] loses his capital."

b] It is said [by the eminent Mīmāṃsakas] that if [the injunction *udbhidā yajeta*] were an injunction of accessories, then one would have to accept a secondary signification function in the sense of a possessive affix. Therefore, [*udbhid*] is accepted as a name of a sacrifice. If it were a qualificative injunction [of the sacrifice and the accessory together], then there would have to be a secondary signification function in the sense of a possessive affix. In the case of the injunction *somena yajeta*, that [secondary signification function in the sense of a possessive affix] had to be adopted, since there is no other way of interpreting it. However, it is not adopted here [in the case of *udbhid*], because the injunction can be interpreted [without the assumption of a secondary signification function]."

[c] If that [assumption of a secondary signification function in the sense of a possessive affix] is equally necessary in [the view that *udbhid* is] a name, then why should one abandon the view that it is an accessory-injunction?

[d] The difficulty of justifying co-referentiality [of the words *udbhid* and *yāga*] is required as the basis [for assuming the secondary signification function] in [the alternative view that *udbhidā yajeta* is] an injunction of accessories. Similarly, the same difficulty would be required as the basis [for assuming the secondary signification function] also in this [view that *udbhid* is a name and yet the sacrifice with this name is cognized through a secondary signification function]. There can be no secondary signification function without any [sufficient] reason.

[e] It is established in the *Saktv-adhikaraṇa*, that the meaning of the accusative case-affix is: "the property of being an object to be accomplished [by the given action]." Also according to the doctrine in the *Vājapeyādhikaraṇa*, two objects to be accomplished cannot be construed with one and the same action [at once]. For these [two] reasons, it is necessary to adopt a secondary signification function in the sense of a possessive affix even in the example: "one cooks rice with fuel-sticks." Therefore, there is no difference between conventionality and unconventionality [of the secondary signification function].

[f] Also, it is well known that Mīmāṃsakas universally adopt the secondary signification function in the sense of a possessive affix, in the context of an injunction of accessory.

Explanation [NN.VII.20.a]: If one accepts that the word *udbhid* is a name of a sacrifice, and yet its cognition as a qualifier of a sacrifice is only through a secondary signification function, then this view is not valid. There are better reasons for not accepting the view that *udbhid* is a name. This view also contradicts other commonly accepted Mīmāṃsā doctrines. For the maxim quoted here, see: G.A. Jacob (1907: 47-48).

Explanation [NN.VII.20.b]: This verse reflects the views of Mīmāṃsakas on the injunctions *udbhidā yajeta* and *somena yajeta*. Mīmāṃsakas believe that *udbhid* is a name of a specific sacrifice, while the word *soma* stands for the substance used in the sacrifice, i.e. for an accessory of a sacrifice.

In the case of the first injunction, i.e. *udbhidā yajeta*, there is no separate injunction available for a specific sacrifice. Therefore, this very injunction has to be an injunction for a sacrifice. This is accomplished by interpreting the word *udbhid* to be a name of a specific sacrifice.

In the case of the second example, *somena yajeta*, there already exists a separate injunction for the basic sacrifice, and hence the injunction *somena yajeta* needs to be taken as an accessory-injunction. The expression *soma* is interpreted to mean "a sacrifice with *soma*." Thus, the word *soma* is equal to *somavat* by secondary signification function in the sense of a possessive affix [*matv-artha-lakṣaṇā*]. Accepting such a secondary signification function is a weakness of this explanation, and yet it has been accepted, since there is no other choice.

As explained above, the word *udbhid* is interpreted as a name of the sacrifice, and not as an accessory. This avoids the secondary signification function in the sense of a possessive affix.[465] Thus, the main advantage in this interpretation of *udbhid* is that one can get rid of the secondary signification function, and achieve economy.

Explanation [NN.VII.20.c]: Some Mīmāṃsakas say that *udbhid* is a name and yet there is a secondary signification function. This certainly goes against the normal arguments of Mīmāṃsakas. It would be relatively better to say that *udbhid* is an accessory and then say that there a secondary signification function in the sense of a possessive affix. This would at least fit in the general arguments of Mīmāṃsakas.

Explanation [NN.VII.20.d]: Let us consider a hypothetical case. If the term *udbhid* primarily signifies an accessory of the sacrifice, it will have to be construed with the words *yāgena bhāvayet* [= *yajeta*]. The sentence *udbhidā yāgena bhāvayet* could not be properly construed, since the two instrumentals must be co-referential (*samānādhikaraṇa*); otherwise there would have to be two sentences *udbhidā bhāvayet* and *yāgena bhāvayet*. These would respectively mean "one should accomplish the desired result by means of the accessory *udbhid*" and "one should accomplish the desired result by means of a sacrifice." This kind of sentence-splitting (*vākya-bheda*) is not normally permitted. To avoid this, one must make the two expressions *udbhidā* and *yāgena* co-referential, by means of accepting a secondary signification function in the sense of a possessive affix for the word *udbhid*. Thus, the expression *udbhid* itself comes to mean "a sacrifice with the accessory *udbhid*." This new meaning can be co-referential with the expression *yāga* "sacrifice." Thus the reason for a possible acceptance of a secondary signification function in the sense of a possessive affix is the difficulty in explaining co-referentiality.

The same difficulty would have to be the reason for accepting a conventional secondary signification function in the view that *udbhid* is a name of a sacrifice. The term *udbhid* must mean "a sacrifice with the name *udbhid*" in order to be co-referential with the term *yāga*. One cannot really say that there is a secondary signification function, and that there is no reason for it. There has to be some reason. This being the case, there is no reason to deviate from the standard Mīmāṃsā view.

Explanation [NN.VII.20.e]: This faction of Mīmāṃsakas seems to believe that their conventional secondary signification function is superior to the secondary signification function in the sense of a possessive affix. The latter is not conventional. In the present section, Kauṇḍabhaṭṭa tries to prove that the latter kind is equally frequent, and hence there

---

465 *karaṇaṃ hi yāgaḥ, udbhidādy api tṛtīyā-nirdeśāt karaṇam, tatrodbhidā yāgeneti karma-nāmadheyatvena sāmānādhikaraṇya-sāmañjasyaṃ syāt* /, *MS-B(a)*, Pt.I., p. 324.

is not much difference between a conventional and non-conventional secondary signification function.

The Ānandāśrama edition of *MS* and *MS-B* does not separately list any *Saktv-adhikaraṇa*, but it is a part of the *Sammārgādhikaraṇa* [*MS*, Vol.I., pp. 408-416]. Neither Śabara nor Kumārilabhaṭṭa use the term *sādhyatva* in this section. Śabara says that the accusative case is used in the meaning of "that which is most desired to be reached by the agent's action" or "the principal thing to be accomplished."[466] Kumārilabhaṭṭa also supports this view.[467] Khaṇḍadeva refers to the view of those who hold that the meaning of the accusative case is *sādhyatva* alone.[468] The term *sādhyatva* refers to a property of being an object to be accomplished.

The *Vājapeyādhikaraṇa* [*MS*, Vol.I., pp. 337-9] deals with the injunction *svārājya-kāmo vājapeyena yajeta* which literally means "one who desires his own kingdom should perform a sacrifice with *vājapeya*." The *Taittirīya-brāhmaṇa* (1.3.2.3.7.1) has the passage *yo vājapeyena yajeta, gacchati svārājyam*, and the *Āpastamba-śrauta-sūtra* (18.1.1) reads *vājapeyena svārājya-kāmo yajeta*. The term *vājapeya* primarily refers to a gruel (*yavāgū*).[469] The verb *yajeta* is paraphrased as *yāgena bhāvayet* "one should accomplish the desired result by means of a sacrifice." If the word *vājapeya* stands for the gruel, then it is an accessory of the sacrifice. One cannot, however, have a sentence *vājapeyena yāgena svārājyaṃ bhāvayet*, since the terms *vājapeya* and *yāga* are not co-referential. One might, then, try to construe the sentence as: *vājapeyena yāgaṃ, yāgena [ca] svārājyaṃ bhāvayet*. Apparently, one is trying to construe two objects to be accomplished with one and the same verb. This cannot be done unless one splits the sentence. Finally, the term *vājapeya* is interpreted to be a name of a sacrifice. This avoids the difficulties pointed out above.[470] This discussion is taken to mean that one cannot construe two objects to be accomplished with one and the same verb at once.

Then, Kauṇḍabhaṭṭa takes up a simple sentence *kāṣṭhais taṇḍulam pacati* which literally means "one cooks rice with fuel-sticks." By the usual Mīmāṃsā analysis, the verb *pacati* would be paraphrased as *pākena viklittim bhāvayet* "one should accomplish softening [of grains] by means of cooking." Thus, the original sentence could be paraphrased as *kāṣṭhais taṇḍulam pākena viklittim bhāvayet*. Now there are two accusatives, *taṇḍulam* and *viklittim*. Thus, there are two objects-to-be-accomplished to be construed with the same verb. As shown above, this is not acceptable. Therefore, one of the accusatives has to be interpreted in a different way. One could understand the accusative *taṇḍulaṃ* in the sense of an instrumental *taṇḍulena*, and then by a secondary signification function understand

466 *dvitīyā-vibhaktiḥ kartur īpsitatame vartate / ... dvitīyā-nirdeśāt prādhānyam avagacchāmaḥ /*, *MS-B(a)*, Pt.I., pp. 408-410.

467 *dvitīyā tāvat karmatvam pradhāna-rūpam ātma-śaktyā vadati / ... prādhānyam eva dvitīyārthaḥ /*, *TV(a)*, Pt.I., p. 410.

468 *MKB*, pp. 7607; *VB*, p. 114.

469 *vājapeyaṃ yavāgū syāt /*, *TV(a)*, Pt.I., p. 338.

470 *guṇa-vidhi-pakṣe hi sarva ime vākya-bhedādayo doṣāḥ prādurbhaveyuḥ / tasmāt karma-nāmadheyaṃ vājapeya-śabda iti sthitam /*, *MS-B(a)*, Pt.I., p. 339.

this to mean "by that which involves rice-grains." This can be done by accepting a secondary signification function in the sense of a possessive affix (*matv-artha-lakṣaṇā*). Thus, even a simple sentence such as this would have to be explained by taking recourse to a secondary signification function in the sense of a possessive affix. For this reason, this kind of a secondary signification function is as good as a conventional secondary signification function. Thus, there is no real difference between a conventional and a non-conventional secondary signification function, and hence one should not claim superiority of one over the other.

Explanation [NN.VII.20.f]: Cf. **Explanation [NN.VII.20.b]**.

NN.VII.21. (p. 129-30)

अस्मन्मते च नाम्नः शक्यतावच्छेदकत्वेन विनैव लक्षणां यागत्वादिवदुपस्थितेर्नामधेयत्वं सुसङ्गतमिति विभावयामः । अत एव च "कथितपदत्वं न क्वचिद्दोष" इत्यत्र

"उदेति सविता ताम्रस्ताम्र एवास्तमेति च ।
सम्पत्तौ च विपत्तौ च महतामेकरूपता ॥

अत्र ताम्रपदान्तरं विना न तादृशो बोध" इति काव्यप्रकाशकारेण चोक्तं सङ्गच्छते । अत्र घटकलशपदाभ्यां घटबोधे विशेषाभावात्ताम्रार्थकेन रक्तादिपदेन तादृशबोधसम्भवात् शब्दान्तरात्तादृशबोधासम्भव इत्यादेरलग्नकतापत्तेः ।

Translation [NN.VII.21]

[a] [Restating the position of the grammarians]: In our view, the name is a limitor of primary-meaning-ness. Hence, it is cognized without a secondary signification function with reference to it, just as the property of sacrifice-ness [is cognized from the verb root *yaj*]. Therefore, we believe that [words like *udbhid*] can be legitimately accepted as names, without accepting a secondary signification function.

[b] Therefore, what the author of the *Kāvya-prakāśa* says on the line "repetition of a word, already once used, is not a fault in some cases" is justified. He says: "There cannot be a cognition similar to that [caused by the word *tāmra* 'red'], unless the word *tāmra* is [used again], in the verse: 'The sun is red (*tāmra*) when it rises, and it is also red (*tāmra*) when it sets. Similarly, the noble people remain the same in prosperity and calamity'."

[c] [If] there were no difference in the cognition of a pot from the two [synonymous] words, *ghaṭa* and *kalaśa*, [then] one could certainly get an identical meaning cognition from the word *rakta* [and the word *tāmra*]. For

this reason, [if a word does not figure in the meaning cognition], it would be inappropriate [for Mammaṭa] to say that one cannot have [an identical] meaning cognition from a different [synonymous] word.

Explanation [NN.VII.21.a]: Kauṇḍabhaṭṭa says that in his view the word *udbhid* is a name of a sacrifice. The name itself figures in the cognition of a sacrifice as a qualifier on the basis of the primary signification function of the word. This is possible, since a word is also a limitor of primary-meaning-ness, cf. **Explanation [NN.VII.11.a]**. It is not necessary to ascertain the primary signification function specifically with respect to it; a word does not have to be an object of the primary signification function. This is like cognizing the generic property sacrifice-ness (*yāgatva*) from the verb root *yaj* "to sacrifice." The generic property is the limitor of primary-meaning-ness, and appears in the verbal cognition just by virtue of being the limitor of primary-meaning-ness.

Explanation [NN.VII.21.b]: This is an interesting passage from the *Kāvya-prakāśa* by Mammaṭa [*KP*, pp. 367-8]. The verse speaks of the identical condition of the minds of noble people. This identity is exemplified by saying that the sun is red when it rises, and is also red when it sets. The extreme identity is shown by the use of the word *tāmra* "red" twice. In other places, such a repetition is considered a fault, but not so in the quoted verse. The verse cannot express this extreme identity by using two different synonyms.

Explanation [NN.VII.21.c]: Kauṇḍabhaṭṭa interprets the passage in the *Kāvya-prakāśa* by saying that the word itself figures in the verbal cognition. Hence, the verbal cognition from the so-called synonyms, *rakta* and *tāmra*, cannot be really identical. If the cognition of a pot from the two synonyms, *ghaṭa* and *kalaśa*, were identical, then there is no reason, why the verbal cognition from the synonyms *rakta* and *tāmra* cannot be identical. The difference in the verbal cognition which is accepted by Mammaṭa can be easily explained by accepting Kauṇḍabhaṭṭa's view. This interpretation of Kauṇḍabhaṭṭa is supported by the commentary *Sudhā-sāgara* on the *Kāvya-prakāśa*.[471] The recent editions by V.N. Misra and M. Bhattacharya have the reading *śabdāntarāt tādṛśa-bodha-sambhava*. This does not make sense in the present context.

NN.VII.22. (p. 130)

अस्मद्रीत्या पुनस्ताम्रपदरूपविषयवैलक्षण्याद्वैलक्षण्यमित्यवधेयमिति । यद्वा ज्ञानमात्रे शब्दभानमतेन व्याचक्ष्महे । अनुकार्यानुकरणयोर्भेदेऽनुकार्यस्तथा प्रातिपदिकार्थः । नो चेद्भेदविवक्षा तथापि श्रोत्रेण गृहीतसङ्गतिकघटादिभिर्वोपस्थितेऽर्थे पदार्थे घटादौ व इवार्थाद्विशेषणीभूतघटत्वादिवद् भासत इत्यर्थः । डित्थोऽयं ब्राह्मणोऽयमिति प्रत्यक्ष इव शाब्देऽपि स विषयः ।

---

471 The view of the commentary *Sudhā-sāgara* is quoted in *Bālabodhinī* on *KP*, p. 367.

"न सोऽस्ति प्रत्ययो लोके यः शब्दानुगमादृते ।
अनुविद्धमिव ज्ञानं सर्वं शब्देन भासते ॥"

इति प्रसिद्धेः । तथा च घटपदवाच्यमानयेति शाब्दबोध इति भावः । अनुकरणे तु स्वातन्त्र्येणैव भानमिति विशेष इति ।

Translation [NN.VII.22]

[a] In our view, however, the word-form *tāmra* figures [in the verbal cognition from the word *tāmra*]. Due to this distinctive feature, it is different [from the verbal cognition derived from the word *rakta*, which is a synonym of *tāmra*].

[b] Alternatively, we might explain [the *Kāvya-prakāśa* passage and similar usages] by taking recourse to the view that a word-form figures in every cognition.

[c] When an imitated word and an imitation word are held to be different, then an imitated word is the meaning of an [imitation] word.

[d] [Verse 26 of the *Vaiyākaraṇa-matonmajjana* of Bhaṭṭojī Dīkṣita now has the following] meaning. The word *va* means *iva* "like." Even if the distinction [between an imitated word and an imitation word] is not intended to be expressed by the speaker, nevertheless, [the word] appears as a qualifier [in the cognition], like the other properties such as pot-ness. [Such a cognition of a word takes place] when the meaning, i.e. a pot etc., is cognized either through auditory perception [of the word "pot"], or through [a visual perception of the object] pot with which [a perceptual] connection [of the sensory organ] is established.

[e] The word does appear in the verbal [cognition], just as it appears in the perceptual cognitions "this is Ḍittha," "this is a Brahmin," etc. [The word does appear in the perceptual cognition], since it is well known that "there is no cognition in the world in which a linguistic element does not appear. All cognition appears as if permeated by the word," *VP*, I.132.

[f] Therefore, the intended meaning [of verse 26 of the *Vaiyākaraṇa-matonmajjana* of Bhaṭṭojī Dīkṣita] is that the verbal cognition [from "bring a pot"] is of the following form: {bring something which is signified by the word 'pot'}. In the case of an imitation, [the word] figures in the meaning cognition independently. This is the difference.

Explanation [NN.VII.22.a]: Cf. **Explanation [NN.VII.21.c]**.
Explanation [NN.VII.22.b]: Cf. **Explanation [NN.VII.22.e]**.
Explanation [NN.VII.22.c]: Cf. **Explanation [NN.VII.3.a]**
Explanation [NN.VII.22.d]: Cf. **Explanation [NN.VII.22.e]**.

Explanation [NN.VII.22.e]: If we have a perceptual cognition of the form {this is Ḍittha}* or {this is a Brahmin}, then the words "Ḍittha" and "Brahmin" do figure in the contents of these perceptual cognitions. That is to say, the perceptual cognition {this is Ḍittha} is actually of the form {this is someone named Ḍittha} or more specifically {this is some *x*, such that *x* is qualified by the word Ḍittha}. Thus the word appears as a qualifier of the object of the cognition.

The verse quoted by Kauṇḍabhaṭṭa is *VP*, I.123. Bhaṭṭojī Dīkṣita also quotes this verse.[472] The commentary *Ambākartrī* on the *Vākya-padīya* explains this verse in a different way. It says that, for grammarians, the whole world is a complex formation of the ultimate principle, which is of the nature of Word [*śabda-brahman*]. Just as, while cognizing a clay-pot, one cannot but cognize the clay, similarly, while cognizing any object, one cannot but cognize the ultimate principle of Word.[473]

The commentary *Prabhā* on the *Vaiyākaraṇa-bhūṣaṇa-sāra* says that this verse refers only to a qualificative cognition (*sa-vikalpaka*), but it is not necessarily confined to a verbal cognition. It includes all kinds of verbal and non-verbal qualificative cognitions. A cognition with a word as a qualifier cannot but be a qualificative cognition.[474] For grammarians, the objects of the universe are ultimately identically with Word. The signifier and the signified are identical. Thus, when an object is cognized, the word is also cognized.[475] Nāgeśabhaṭṭa also accepts this view.[476]

The commentary *Darpaṇa* on the *Vaiyākaraṇa-bhūṣaṇa-sāra* says that this verse does not refer to cognition in general, but only to some verbal cognitions. The commentary points out that even according to Patañjali a word figures in only some verbal cognitions. It further says that Bhartṛhari's view concerns only the transcendental identity of Brahman and the mystical sound *OM*. This should not apply to worldly language situations.[477]

Explanation [NN.VII.22.f]: The difference between an imitation word and an imitated word has been discussed in **Explanation [NN.VII.3]**. The sentence "bring a pot" is interpreted to mean "bring something referred to by the word 'pot'." However, here the difference between an imitation and an imitated word is not intended. Therefore, a word is

---

* The curley brackets {} are used to indicate the content of a cognitive state.

472 *SKB(b)*, p. 4.

473 *tac ca brahma śabda-tattvaṃ śabdātmakam ity arthaḥ / ... vikārāṇām prakṛty-anvayāt śabdatvopapatteḥ / ... rūpādayo (vikārāḥ) viṣayāḥ śabda-rūpānugatā eva dṛśyante /*, *VP-A*, Pt.I., p. 4.

474 *sa ca bodho nirvikalpakātirikta eva / tatra śabda-bhāne nirvikalpakatvāsiddheḥ / na tu śabda-janyo bodha eva /*, *VBS-P*, p. 253.

475 *vastutas tu śabdārthayor vāstavika-tādātmyam ādāyārtha-bhāne śabda-bhānam upapādanīyam /*, *VBS-P*, p. 254.

476 *evam arthenāpi svākāra-samarpaṇe tata eva śabdākārasyāpi samarpaṇam iti sarvaṃ jñānaṃ śabdānuviddham / ... ata eva cakṣuṣā dṛśyamānam api ajñāta-bodhakam padārthaṃ kim idam iti na jānāmīti vyavaharanti / tad-upadeśe ca jñātam iti vyavaharanti /*, *LM*, pp. 346-7; *kiṃ ca pratyakṣādāv api pada-bhānam āvaśyakam /*, Ibid., p. 353.

477 *pratyayaḥ śābda-bodhātmakaḥ /*, *VBS-D*, p. 253; *ukta-bhāṣyād api kvacic chābda-bodhe śabdo viṣaya ity arthasyaiva lābhāt / ... hari-vacanāni tu praṇava-brahmaṇor abhedopāsana-śraddhātiśaya-bodhakāni bhavantīti na tair vyāvahārikārthasya siddhiḥ / tasmāc chābda-bodha-mātrasya śabda-viṣayakatvaṃ na vicāra-saham /*, ibid., p. 261.

cognized as a qualifier. If the difference is intended, then a word is cognized as the qualificandum.

NN.VII.23. (p. 130)

अत्रेदं तत्त्वम् । अनियमेन घटादेरपि प्रकारान्तरेणोपस्थितिसम्भवाच्छाब्दबोधविषयतापत्तिवारणाय वृत्त्या शब्दादुपस्थितत्वेनैव शाब्दबोधविषय इति कल्पनीयम् । शब्दस्य च नियमेन तदानीमुपस्थितिसत्त्वात्तस्यास्तादृशतया न शाब्दबोधविषयत्वानुपपत्तिः । एवञ्च यथाभिहितान्वयवादिनां मते वृत्तिं विनैवाकाङ्क्षादिवशाद्वाक्यार्थस्य शाब्दबोधे भानं, कुब्जशक्तिवादिनां वा मते वृत्त्यनुपस्थितस्यैव भानं, तथा वृत्त्यविषयशब्दस्यापि ज्ञानसामान्यसामग्र्या तात्पर्याकाङ्क्षादिवशाद्गौर्नित्या गौरनित्येत्यादौ गोत्वादेरिव स्वातन्त्र्येण विशेषणत्वेन वा भानं भवेत् ।

[a] This is the central idea. One has to avoid the undesired possibility that a pot may be cognized in a different way [e.g. through perceptual cognition], and yet it could become an object of a verbal cognition, [since it is an object of the primary significtion function of the word "pot"]. [To avoid such an over-extension], one should have the following assumption: "An *x* can be an object of a verbal cognition, if and only if, *x* is cognized on the basis of a [primary] signification function."

[b] A word is invariably cognized [when meaning is cognized], and this [cognition of a word] is such that [it is produced on the basis of the primary signification function]. Hence, there is no difficulty in justifying how [a word] becomes an object of the verbal cognition.

[c] In the view of the *Abhihitānvaya-vāda*, the sentence-meaning figures in the [final] verbal cognition on account of expectancy etc., though there is no primary signification function with respect to it. Also in the view of the *Kubja-śakti-vāda*, [an individual] not cognized through the primary signification function becomes an object of a verbal cognition.

[d] Similarly, a word is not an object of the primary signification function, and yet [such a cognition of a word could be derived], on the basis of intention, expectancy etc., from the conditions for cognition in general. There could be a cognition of a word, independently or as a qualifier, like the property of cow-ness in constructions such as: "a cow is eternal" and "a cow is not eternal."

Explanation [NN.VII.23.a]: Cf. **Explanation [NN.VII.11.a-c]**.
Explanation [NN.VII.23.b]: Cf. **Explanation [NN.VII.11.b-c]**.

Explanation [NN.VII.23.c]: The *Abhihitānvaya-vāda* view is held by both Naiyāyikas and Bhāṭṭa Mīmāṃsakas. They say that the sentence-meaning is not just an addition of the meanings of its constituents. The meanings of individual words are interrelated in a specific way in the sentence-meaning. Individual word-meanings are cognized on the basis the primary signification functions of individual words. Interrelations between these word-meanings are cognized on the basis of intention and mutual expectancy among words. Yet these interrelations figure in the final sentential meaning cognition.[478] For the theory of *Kubja-śakti-vāda*, see: **Explanation [NN.IV.6.a]**. This view is held by Prābhākaras.

Explanation [NN.VII.23.d]: The conclusions in this section have been discussed in **Explanation [NN.VII.11.a-c]** and **Explanation [NN.VII.16.a]**. For examples given by Kauṇḍabhaṭṭa, see: **Explanation [NN.VII.12.c]**. In "[a] cow is eternal," the generic property of cow-ness needs to be construed with eternality, while "[a] cow is non-eternal," the individual cow needs to be construed with non-eternality. This is done on the basis of intention.

NN.VII.24. (p. 130)
पर्वतो वह्निमानिति शाब्दानुमित्यादितस्तदैव वह्न्यर्थिप्रवृत्तिदर्शनाज्ज्ञानसामान्यसामग्र्या एवार्थविशेषणतया वर्तमानकालभासकत्वकल्पनवत्, प्रत्यक्षशाब्दादौ सर्वत्र शब्दानुभवाज्ज्ञानसामान्यसामग्र्याः शब्दभासकत्वकल्पनात् । तत्रापि विशिष्य गृहीतशक्तिकेभ्यः पदेभ्योऽर्थविशेषस्येवार्थाच्छब्दविशेषस्य भानम् । अन्यत्र नलपदवाच्यः कश्चिदर्थ इति पदविशेषणकवस्तुसामान्यबोधवद्, अर्थदर्शनादप्येतद्वाचकं किञ्चित् पदमिति पदस्यापि सामान्यत एव बोधः । अत एव तदुत्तरं विशेषजिज्ञासया किमस्य नामेत्यादिप्रश्नप्रतिवचनान्युपपद्यन्ते ।

Translation [NN.VII.24]

[a] When there is a verbal or inferential cognition of the form {the mountain [is] on fire}, then immediately after that, one observes the activity of someone who is [seeking] after fire. Therefore, one assumes that the causal conditions for cognition in general do cause a cognition of the present time as qualifying the meaning [of "the mountain [is] on fire"]. Similarly, in all cognitions like verbal and perceptual cognitions, a word is cognized. Therefore, causal conditions for cognition in general are assumed to cause a cognition of a word-form.

---

[478] *pratyeka-padārtha-śaktyā tat-tat-padārtheṣūpasthiteṣu vṛttiṃ vināpy ākāṅkṣādi-sahakāri-vaśāt tat-tad-arthānvita-svārtha-bodhopapatteḥ / ... tasmāt ghaṭādi-padānāṃ tat-tat-padārtha eva śaktiḥ / ākāṅkṣādi-sahakāri-vaśād itarānvaya-bodha iti dik /*, *MD*, p. 76; *NK*, p. 72.

[b] Further, just as there is a cognition of a specific object from words whose signification function is specifically cognized, there is a cognition of the specific word from the specific object.

[c] In other places, at the sight of an object, there is a general cognition of a word of the form: {there is some word, such that it signifies this object}. This is similar to the general cognition of an object qualified by a word such as: {there is some object, such that it is signified by the word 'Nala'}.

[d] Certainly, it is justified that, after this [type of general cognition], one desires to have a more specific cognition, and hence there are questions and answers such as: "What is its name?"

Explanation [NN.VII.24.a]: Let us suppose that one has a verbal or an inferential cognition of the form {the mountain [is] on fire}, or more specifically {the mountain, the locus of fire}. Let us also suppose that the person who has this cognition is actually seeking after fire. After having this cognition, the person immediately acts accordingly. He goes to the mountain.

For Naiyāyikas, the above mentioned cognition has no time reference. [Grammarians would, however, assume the verb *asti* "is".] Thus a cognition with no time reference does produce an activity of the person as an immediate response. Naiyāyikas think that one must assume that conditions which produce the cognition {the mountain, the locus of fire} also produce a cognition of the present tense. Similar is the claim of grammarians, cf. **Explanation [NN.VII.22.d-e].**

Explanation [NN.VII.24.b]: If the primary signification function of the word "bull" is ascertained specifically with respect to a fully known individual bull, then we can have a cognition of that specific individual bull from the word "bull," as well as a specific cognition of the word "bull" from the specific individual bull. These two specific cognitions can be expressed as:

i) {[Given a cognition of the specific word "bull"], there is a specific individual bull, *B*, such that *B* is denoted by the word "bull"}.

ii) {[Given a cognition of the specific individual bull, *B*], there is a cognition of the specific word "bull," such that the word "bull" signifies *B*"}.

Explanation [NN.VII.24.c]: Opposite is the case with words like "Nala," since their primary signification function is not ascertained with respect to a specific identifiable individual person. The case of objects whose names are not known is also similar. With the word "Nala," we have a general cognition of its signified object of the form: {there exists some object, such that it is signified by the word "Nala"}. Similarly, when we see an object which is not known to us by name, we have a general cognition of the word as: {Given a cognition of an object *O*, there exists some word *W*, such that *W* signifies *O*}.

Explanation {NN.VII.24.d]: Cf. **Explanation [NN.VII.6.a-b].**

NN.VII.25. (p. 130-1)

अत एव वृत्त्यविषयशब्दवद् घटादिपदैः समवायादिसम्बन्धेन सम्बन्धिन आकाशादेरप्युपस्थितस्यान्वयबोधप्रसङ्गः । किञ्च गामुच्चारयेत्युक्ते विकृतस्यैवोच्चारणापत्तिः । तादृशस्यैव प्रत्यक्षोपस्थितत्वात् । शब्दस्याप्रकृत्यर्थत्वाद् द्वितीयार्थादेरनन्वयापत्तेश्च । प्रत्ययानां प्रकृत्यर्थगतस्वार्थबोधकत्वव्युत्पत्तेः । स्वस्यैव प्रत्यक्षेण शीघ्रमुपस्थितत्वाद्, गौरस्तीत्यत्रापि स्वपरत्वापत्तेश्चेति निरस्तम् ।

Translation [NN.VII.25]

[a] Therefore, the following objections are refuted:

i) [Objection 1]: The word becomes an object of a verbal cognition, though it is not the object of the signification function [according to the view of grammarians]. [If this is so, then], in a similar manner, ether would be an object of the verbal cognition, when cognized from a word such as "pot" on the basis of the relation of inherence.

ii) [Objection 2]: Since, the inflected word [*gām*] alone is directly cognized from the sentence "utter the bull" (*gām uccāraya*), one would have to utter the word [as *gām*, and not in its stem form *go-*].

iii) [Objection 3]: Since, the word is not the meaning of the stem, one cannot construe the meaning of the accusative case ending with it [in the sentence *gām uccāraya*]. This difficulty would occur due to the maxim: "the endings signify their meaning as embedded in the meaning of the stem."

iv) [Objection 4]: Since, the word is itself first cognized, [prior to the cognition of meaning], even in the sentence "a bull exists," the word "bull" would have to stand for the word-form, [rather than for the individual bull].

Explanation [NN.VII.25.a.i]: Cf. **Explanation [NN.VII.4.b-c]** and **Explanation [NN.VII.26.a]**.

Explanation [NN.VII.25.a.ii]: Cf. **Explanation [NN.VII.18.b.i]** and **Explanation [NN.VII.26.b]**.

Explanation [NN.VII.25.a.iii]: Cf. **Explanation [NN.VII.18.b.ii]**. There is no difficulty in the view of grammarians, since for them the word-form is signified on the basis of the primary signification function, and whatever is signified by a word on the basis of its primary signification function constitutes its meaning.

Explanation [NN.VII.25.a.iv]: Cf. **Explanation [NN.VII.18.b.iii]**.

NN.VII.26. (p. 131)

घटादिपदादुपस्थितस्याप्याकाशादेः शाब्दज्ञानविषयत्वाभावस्तन्नियामकाभावात् । विकृतादेरपि तात्पर्याभावात् । सति च तस्मिन् लक्षणादिना त्वयापि वाच्यत्वात् । न च तात्पर्येणैव सर्वनिर्वाहे वृत्तिमात्रोच्छेदः । तस्य शाब्दसामान्ये हेतुत्वाभ्युपगमात् । अननुगमात् । शब्दादमुमर्थं प्रत्येमि वक्तुस्तात्पर्यं तु न जानामीति सकलानुभवसिद्धत्वाच्च । किं तु क्वचिच्छब्दजन्यबोधप्रमात्वे नियामकं तद्विषयकतात्पर्यज्ञानं तदन्यगोचरज्ञाने प्रतिबन्धकं वा, नातो नानार्थानुपपत्तिः । इत्थं पदादनेकेषामर्थानामुपस्थितावेकस्यैव वानेकसम्बन्धसम्भवे पदार्थविशेषसम्बन्धविशेषयोरध्यवसानाय तात्पर्यं नियामकं कल्प्यत इति न वृत्तिं विना निर्वाह इत्यादिकमूह्यम् ।

Translation [NN.VII.26]

[a] [The objection raised in **NN.VII.25.a.i** is not valid], because ether may be cognized from the word "pot" [*qua* sound] and yet it would not be treated as an object of the verbal cognition, since there is no regulating factor [like the limitor of primary-meaning-ness possessed by ether].

[b] [The objection raised in **NN.VII.25.a.ii** is not valid], because the inflected word is not intended [to be conveyed]. If there were an intention for it, then even you [= the Naiyāyika] must explain it by taking recourse to a secondary signification function.

[c] [Objection to the grammarian's view]: If intention could explain every problem, the [the whole concept of] primary signification function would have to be abandoned. [Refutation of this objection]: This objection should not be raised. We [= grammarians] do not accept that intention is the cause of meaning cognitions in general, because [a cognition of the intention of a speaker] is not necessarily present [in all meaning cognitions]. It is a common experience that one can claim the following: "I understand this meaning from the word, but I do not understand the speaker's intention."

[d] Intention concerning a meaning cognition sometimes determines the validity of the cognition. It can sometimes prohibit a cognition of some other meaning. For this reason, there is no difficulty in assuming that a word can have many meanings. When there are many meanings cognized from a word, or when one [meaning] could be possibly construed with many [meanings], intention of the speaker is assumed to be the decisive factor concerning the specific meaning and the specific way of construing it. Thus, one should realize that we cannot do away with the primary signification function [of a word for its own form].

Explanation [NN.VII.26.a]: Cf. **Explanation [NN.VII.4.b-c]** and Introduction, **E.4.i.**

Explanation [NN.VII.26.b]: Grammarians say that the inflected form *gām* in the sentence *gām uccāraya* "utter the bull" signifies only the uninflected stem *go*, since that alone is intended.

Explanation [NN.VII.26.c]: Naiyāyikas contend that one cannot take recourse to intention to explain all these problems, since this would make even the primary signification function unnecessary. This is not desirable.[479] Kauṇḍabhaṭṭa points out that this is not true. A signification function and intention have essentially different functions. The speaker's intention is not the cause of a meaning cognition, since one can have a meaning cognition even without realizing the intention.

Explanation [NN.VII.26.d]: This distinguishes between the functions of a signification function and the speaker's intention.

NN.VII.27. (p. 131)

नन्वनुकार्यानुकरणयोर्भेद एव युक्तः । अभेदेऽप्यस्तु स्वस्मिन् स्वस्य शक्तिः । अन्यथानुकरणशब्दानां वृत्तिविषयाप्रतिपादकत्वेनार्थवत्त्वाभावात् प्रातिपदिकसंज्ञा न स्यात् । तथा च "वार्त्रघ्नी पौर्णमास्याम्," "कवतीषु रथन्तरं गायति," "ऐरं कृत्वोद्गेयम्" इत्यादिश्रुतयः, "एरुः," "एचोऽयवायावः," "रषाभ्यां नो णः ...," इत्यादिसूत्राणि च विरुद्ध्येरन् । प्रातिपदिकात् सुबन्ताद्वा तद्धितोत्पत्तेः सिद्धान्तितत्वात् ।

Translation [NN.VII.27]

[a] [Objection to the view of grammarians]: It is proper [to say] that the imitated word and the imitation word are clearly different.

[b] Alternatively, [the objector claims that] even if they are not different, let a word have a primary signification function with respect to itself.

[c] Otherwise, imitation words would not have the class-designation "nominal stem," since they would not signify the object of their primary signification function, and hence would be meaningless.

[d] Similarly, the following Vedic injunctions and Pāṇinian rules would be contradicted:

i) *vārttraghnī paurṇamāsyām* "[Vedic stanzas called] *vārttraghnī* [should be recited in the sacrifice] on the full moon day."

ii) *kavatīṣu rathantaraṃ gāyati* "[The priest] should recite the Rathantara [sāman] in the Kavatī [sacrifice]."

---

479 *vṛttiṃ vinā sva-paratvasyānirvāhāt / anyathā vṛtty-antarocchedaḥ /, TC*, p. 681; also: *vṛtty-antareti / atrāntara-śabdaḥ sampātāyātaḥ / vastutas tātparyānyathā-siddhau śakter apy uccheda-sambhavād iti dhyeyam /, TC-R*, pp. 681-2.

iii) *airaṃ kṛtvodgeyam* "One should recite [a certain Vedic hymn] by making [the replacement of the word *girā*] by *irā*."

iv) *er uḥ*, P.3.4.86, "[The final sound] *i* [of the *tiṄ* replacements of *loṬ*] is substituted with the sound *u*."

v) *eco 'yavāyāvaḥ*, P.6.1.78, "[The sounds denoted by the abbreviation] *eC* [= *e*, *o*, *ai*, and *au*] are substituted [respectively] with *ay*, *av*, *āy*, and *āv*, [if followed by a vowel]."

vi) *ra-ṣābhyāṃ no ṇaḥ samāna-pade*, P.8.4.1, "The sound *n* is replaced by the sound *ṇ*, if preceded immediately by the sounds *r* and *ṣ*, within the same inflected item (*pada*)."

[e] [The Vedic passages would be contradicted], since, according to the final view [of the Pāṇinian school], a Taddhita affix can be applied either after a nominal stem or after an inflected nominal.

Explanation [NN.VII.27.a-b]: This and the next passage are an introductiion to verse 27 of the *Vaiyākaraṇa-matonmajjana* of Bhaṭṭojī Dīkṣita occurring in section **NN.VII.29.** Here Kauṇḍabhaṭṭa mentions some objections to the final view of grammarians.

The objector proposes two alternatives. Either we should clearly distinguish between an imitation word and an imitated word, and accept the primary signification function of an imitation word with respect to an imitated word, or one should say that these two are not different from each other, and yet a word has a primary signification function with respect to itself. In any case, the imitated word must be an object of the signification function, and thus becomes a legitimate object of the verbal cognition. This would make an imitation a meaningful item.

Explanation [NN.VII.27.c]: It is absolutely necessary that an imitation be a meaningful word, because otherwise it would not get the designation "nominal stem" (*prātipadika*) by P.1.2.45. This rule can ascribe this designation only to meaningful linguistic items. Nominal case endings and the Taddhita affixes can be added only after a nominal stem, and only inflected items can be used in a sentence.

Explanation [NN.VII.27.d]: The quotation (i) has the word *vārttraghnī*. The word *vṛttra-han* "killer of Vṛttra" occurs in the list of Vimuktādi Gaṇa in the Pāṇinian system, and by the rule P.5.2.61 (*vimuktādibhyo 'ṇ*), we can add the affix *-aṆ* to the word *vṛttra-han* to derive the word *vārttraghna* "the Vedic section in which the word *vṛttra-han* occurs."[480] The word *vārttraghnī* is just the feminine form derived by adding the affix *-ṄīP* by P.4.1.15. In technical ritual literature, the term *vārttraghnī* refers to two Vedic passages.[481]

---

[480] *SK*, p. 151.

[481] *darśa-pūrṇa-māsayoḥ śrūyate / vārttraghnī paurṇamāsyām anūcyete /*, *MS-B(a)*, Pt.II., p. 738; *agnir vṛtrāṇi jaṅghanat / draviṇasyur vipanyayā ity ādi, evaṃ tvaṃ somāsi saptatiḥ tvaṃ rājota vṛtrahā / ity ādi ca vārttraghnī yugalam /*, editor's note to *MS-B(a)*, Pt.II., p. 738.

The basis of this *taddhita* formation is the imitation word *vṛttra-han* which refers to the word occurring in the Vedic hymns. It has to be a meaningful item in order to get the designation "nominal stem." Only then can we justify the application of the nominal inflections and the *taddhita* affixes.[482] The objector believes that a grammarian cannot comply with this requirement, since according to his view, an imitation does not signify the object of its primary signification function.

Quotation (ii) uses the word *rathantara*. It refers to some particular *sāmans*, i.e. *Sāma-veda* (II.i.i.11).[483] The word occurs in the *Ṛgveda* (I.164.25), and Sāyaṇa interprets it as a name of a *sāman*.[484] The word occurs in the Utsādi Gaṇa in the Pāṇinīya system.[485] Problems concerning the ritual application of the *Rathantara Sāman* are discussed in the *Rathantarādhikaraṇa* of the *Mīmāṃsā-sūtras*.[486] The ritual implications of the injunction quoted here are also discussed in the *Mīmāṃsā-sūtras*.[487]

The word *rathantara* is used with the accusative ending *-am*, indicating that it is a nominal stem. It can be a nominal stem only if it is a meaningful item. It can be meaningful only if it signifies the object of its primary signification function. If the word itself is not regarded to be the object of the primary signification function of itself, then the word *rathantara* cannot be a meaningful item.

Quotation (iii) occurs in the context of the Jyotiṣṭoma sacrifice. One is instructed that he should not utter the words *girā girā,* while reciting the *sāmans*. Instead, one should substitute *girā* by *irā*. This substitution is referred to in the sentence quoted by Kauṇḍabhaṭṭa.[488] The ritual implications of this substitution are discussed by the Mīmāṃsakas.[489] According to Kumārilabhaṭṭa, the word *aira* is derived by adding the Taddhita affix *-aṆ* to the word *irā*. This affix is said to have no special meaning; it is a *svārthika* affix, an affix which occurs in the meaning of the stem. For Kumārilabhaṭṭa, the phrases *airaṃ kṛtvā* and *irāṃ kṛtvā* are identical in meaning.[490] The basis of the Taddhita formation is again an imitation word. It could not be justified in the view of grammarians.

---

482 *athaitat samartha-grahaṇaṃ naiva kartavyam / kartavyaṃ ca / kim prayojanam / samarthād utpattir yathā syād asamarthān mā bhūd iti / kim punaḥ samartham / arthābhidhāne yat samartham / kim punas tat / kṛta-varṇānupūrvīkam padam /, MB*, Vol.II., p. 352; *paripūrṇasyaiva padārthāntareṇa sambandhāt sub-antāt taddhitotpattyā pada-vidhitvaṃ spaṣṭam eva / ... evaṃ ca samartha-padenāpi sub-antād utpattiḥ sūcitā /, MB-P-U*, Vol.II., p. 352.

483 *abhi tvā śūrety etaṃ rāthantaram /, Sāyaṇa-bhāṣya* on *RV*, Max Müller's edition, Vol.IV., p. 34; also: *MS-B(a)*, Pt.V., p. 1700.

484 *rathantare etan-nāmake sāmni /, Sāyaṇa-bhāṣya* on *RV*, Max Müller's edition, Vol.II., p. 268.

485 *SK*, p. 98.

486 *MS-B(a)*, Pt.II., pp. 570-78.

487 *MS-B(a)*, Pt. IV., pp. 1541ff.

488 Śabara has the following comment: *jyotiṣṭome yajñāyajñiyam prakṛtyāmananti, na girā gireti brūyāt, yad girā gireti brūyāt ātmānam eva tad udgātodgiret, airaṃ kṛtvodgeyam iti / jyotiṣṭome girā-padasya sthāne irā-padaṃ kartavyam iti /, MS-B(a)*, Pt.V., p. 1697.

489 *MS-B(a)*, Pt.V., pp. 1694-1700.

490 *tasmād yathā-bhūtam irā-padaṃ tathā-bhūtam eva prayoktavyam / nanu ca airam iti vikāre taddhita utpannaḥ / ... nātra vikāre taddhita utpannaḥ / kiṃ tarhi / svārtha eva / yāvad evoktam irāṃ kṛtvodgeyaṃ tāvad airam iti /, TT,* Pt. V., p. 1697.

After these three Vedic quotations, Kauṇḍabhaṭṭa cites three rules from Pāṇini's grammar. In these rules Pāṇini uses inflected nominal forms such as *eḥ*, genitive singular of the sound *i*. These are all metalinguistic imitations of sounds actually undergoing grammatical operations. If one says that a word itself cannot be an object of its own primary signification function, then in all these cases, the imitating sounds would not get the designation "nominal stem" (*prātipadika*). Thus, one would not be able to explain the use of case endings with imitations of sounds in these rules.

Explanation [NN.VII.27.e]: There are two accepted alternative views in grammar. According to the first view, the Taddhita affixes are directly added after the nominal stem (*prātipadika*), while according to the second view, the Taddhita affixes are added after the inflected nominals.[491] In either of these two alternatives, the argument of the objector stands valid.

NN.VII.28. (p. 131)

न चैवं धातूपसर्गादिगणपठितानामनुकरणानामनुकार्यधात्वाद्यर्थवत्त्वात् प्रातिपदिकत्वापत्तौ विभक्तिश्रवणापत्तिः । अविवक्षयैव "अइउण्" इत्यादौ स्वरसन्ध्यकरणवत् सम्भवात् । तत्रेकारोकारादेस्तत्तत्संज्ञास्वसन्देहसिद्धे-रिव सत्यां विभक्तौ नलोपजश्त्वादेरप्यापत्तावदन्तत्वनान्तत्वधान्तत्वदा-न्तत्वादिनिर्णयानुरोधस्य सत्त्वात् । णोपदेशत्वषोपदेशत्वनिर्णयायेव यत्नान्तरापत्तिगौरवापत्तेश्चानुरोधसत्त्वात् ।

Translation [NN.VII.28]

[a] One should not say that this would result in the hearing [i.e. use] of case-endings after imitation words in the lists of roots, pre-verbs, etc., because they are meaningful by having the imitated roots etc. as their meanings, and are, therefore, nominal stems.

[b] It is possible [not to have case-endings after imitations of roots in the lists], similar to not having the vocalic Sandhi operations in the [*Śiva-sūtra*:] "*a-i-u-Ṇ*," just by not desiring [them].

[c] Just as [there is a strong reason] in the [case of the *Śiva-sūtra*] to establish clarity in the particular designations [in the form of sounds] *i*, *u* etc., similarly there exists a strong necessity of establishing whether the root ends in *a* or *n*, in *dh* or *d* etc. If nominal inflections were added [to imitations], there would be deletion of [the final] *n* [by P.8.2.7 (*nalopaḥ prātipadikāntasya*)] and substitution [of the final *jhaL* sounds] by *jaŚ* sounds [by P.8.4.53 (*jhalāṃ jaś jhaśi*) and P.8.4.54 (*vāvasāne*)].

[d] A separate effort is required for deciding as to which roots have *ṇ* and *ṣ* when they are taught. Similarly, a separate effort would be required here [to

[491] *MB*, Vol.II., pp. 448ff.

clarify the difficulties mentioned in **NN.VII.28.c**]. That would involve the fault of prolixity.

Explanation [NN.VII.28.a]: This is a counter-objection to the view of the objector. The objector believes that all imitations are meaningful items and hence are nominal stems. If that is true, then in all listings of roots etc. one would be forced to have case-endings after imitations of verb roots etc.

Explanation [NN.VII.28.b]: This counters the above counter-objection. In *Śiva-sūtras* like "*a-i-u-Ṇ*," the sounds *a, i,* and *u* are listed. According to the view held by the counter-objector, these sound-imitations are meaningful, since they primarily signify the imitated sounds. This would necessitate the nominal inflections, their deletion, and the application of vocalic Sandhi rules.

The objector says that Sandhi is not applied here, since it is not desirable. Application of Sandhi would result in confusion. In order that the form of the sounds to be mentioned should remain clearly identifiable, Sandhi rules are not applied. Similarly, imitations of verb roots etc. are nominal stems, and yet Sandhi rules or nominal inflections are not added, because they are not desirable.

Explanation [NN.VII.28.c]: In the *Śiva-sūtra* "*a-i-u-Ṇ*," the listed sounds have a capacity to stand for all their homgeneous sounds by rule P.1.1.69 (*aṇ-udit savarṇasya cāpratyayaḥ*). It is necessary that the original designation sound should remain in an absolutely identifiable form. For this reason, Sandhi rules are not applied.[492]

The same problem would result in the case of verb roots. If we apply a nominal inflection to an imitation of a verb root, then all other rules of morpho-phonemics must also apply. If the nominative singular affix *-sU* is added after the imitation *han*, the affix *-sU* is deleted by rule P.6.1.68 (*hal-ṅy-ābbhyo dīrghāt su-ti-sy-apṛktaṃ hal*), and the final *n* should be deleted by rule P.8.2.7 (*na-lopaḥ prātipadikāntasya*). This would transform the imitation of *han* into *ha*. Then it would be impossible for the reader to understand whether the root is *ha* ending in *a*, or *han* ending in *n*. Similarly, if the nominative singular affix *-sU* is applied after the imitation of the root *vidh*, the affix would be deleted by P.6.1.68 and the final sound *dh* would be optionally substituted with *d* by P.8.4.54 (*vāvasāne*). Thus, one would not be able to make out if the root ends in *dh* or in *d*. For this reason, one could say that imitations of verb roots are nominal stems, and yet nominal inflections are not added after them, since they are undesirable.

Explanation [NN.VII.28.d]: Should one insist on applying nominal inflections to imitations of verb roots, one would have to devise means to disentangle different roots from each other. In certain cases, Pāṇini himself has followed such a procedure. Kauṇḍabhaṭṭa refers to the *ṇopadeśa* and *ṣopadeśa* verb roots. For certain metalinguistic purposes, Pāṇini mentions some verb roots as beginning with the sounds *ṇ* and *ṣ*, though

---

492 *eṣu saṃhitāyā avivakṣayā na saṃhitā-kāryam / anukaraṇatvena sautratvāc ca na varṇebhyo vibhakty-utpattiḥ /, LSS*, pp. 12-3.

they actually begin with the sounds *n* and *s*. Such roots are respectively called *ṇopadeśa* and *ṣopadeśa* roots.[493] But this makes it necessary for Pāṇini to restore these roots to their real form in the grammatical process. Pāṇini formulates two rules for this purpose, P.6.1.64 (*dhātv-ādeḥ ṣaḥ saḥ*) and P.6.1.65 (*ṇo naḥ*), which respectively restore *ṣ* and *ṇ* to *s* and *n*, provided they occur at the beginning of a verb root.

However, this kind of adjustment rules would become a matter of prolixity in the case of verb roots discussed above, i.e. *han* and *vidh*. Thus, the objector maintains that imitations of verb roots in the root-list (*dhātu-pāṭha*) are certainly nominal stems, and yet nominal inflections are not applied. They are undesirable.

NN.VII.29. (p. 131-2)

इत्याशङ्कां मनसिकृत्याह -

"अत एव गवित्याह भू सत्तायामितीदृशम् ।
न प्रातिपदिकं नापि पदं साधु तु तत्स्मृतम् ॥ २७॥"

अत एव यतो न भेद उक्तरीत्योपस्थितस्यैव च भानमत एव गवित्ययमाह, भू सत्तायामित्यत्र वृत्तिविषयबोधकत्वरूपार्थवत्त्वाभावादर्थवदधातुरित्यप्रवृत्तेः प्रातिपदिकत्वाभावे गौर्भूरिति विभक्त्यनुत्पत्तिः । तथा च न प्रातिपदिकं नापि पदमेतत्, साधु तु भवत्येवेत्यर्थः ।

Translation [NN.VII.29]

[a] Fearing [the above objections], [Bhaṭṭojī Dīkṣita] says: Therefore, [the words *go* and *bhū*], in *gav ity āha* "he said '*go*'" and *bhū sattāyām* "the root *bhū* occurs in the meaning of existence," are neither nominal stems not inflected items, but they are considered to be correct usages.

[b] There is [actually] no difference [between an imitation word and an imitated word], and the word is cognized [from itself] in the way shown in earlier [sections].

[c] Hence, in the constructions *gav ity ayam āha* and *bhū sattāyām*, [the words *go* and *bhū*] are meaningless, in the sense that they do not signify [the meaning, which is] the object of their signification functions. Therefore, rule P.1.2.45 (*arthavad adhātur apratyayaḥ prātipadikam*, "that which is neither a verb root, nor an affix, and yet is a meaningful linguistic item is named a nominal stem") does not apply to them, and hence they are not nominal stems.

[d] For this reason, there is no application of nominal inflections which would result in [undesired forms] *gauḥ** and *bhūḥ**. Thus, this [form, i.e. *go* or

493 For the lists of *ṇopadeśa* and *ṣopadeśa* verb-roots, see: *SK*, pp. 178, 180.

bhū] is neither a nominal stem, nor an inflected item, and yet it is a correct usage.

Explanation [NN.VII.29]: Keeping in mind the objections raised in sections **NN.VII.27-28**, Kauṇḍabhaṭṭa now presents the verse of Bhaṭṭojī Dīkṣita which explains the view of grammarians. The objector argues that imitations of verb roots in the root-list are, in principle, nominal stems, because they primarily signify the imitated verb roots. Yet nominal inflections are not added for the fear of certain undesirable situations.

Grammarians on the other hand believe that imitations are not nominal stems. They believe that they do cause a cognition of the imitated verb roots, and yet the imitated word cannot be a primary meaning. As far as the word *artha* "meaning" in P.1.2.45 is concerned, it only includes the object of the primary signification function, and not everything that figures in the verbal cognition. A word itself is not an object of the primary signification function of itself.

Hence, imitations of verb roots in the root-list are not nominal stems. Now, grammarians can easily explain the usage in the root-list. Imitations of verb roots are given without any nominal inflections, since they cannot get any nominal inflections. However, these usages have to be accepted as correct usages. One cannot use a nominal stem or a verb root without a nominal or verbal ending. But, if something is neither a nominal stem, nor a verb root, then it must be used by itself.

Explanation [NN.VII.29.b]: The text given in the Bombay edition, and the new editions by V.N. Misra and Manudeva Bhattacharya, says *ukta-rītyopasthitasyaiva vā bhānam*. The reading *vā* is not totally unintelligible, but the reading *ca* mentioned in the Bombay edition as belonging to a manuscript from Tanjore Palace Library [*VB*, p. 132] makes much better sense. Kauṇḍabhaṭṭa is presenting only one view, i.e. the view that an imitation and an imitated word are identical. A cognition of a word is generated not because it is an object of its own primary signification function. The way it is cognized is explained in earlier sections, **NN.VII.17-18, 22-23**. The word forms a part of the verbal cognition, though it is not the object of the signification function. However, it is not regarded to be a meaning (*artha*) as intended in rule P.1.2.45. Thus a word signifies itself, and yet it is not regarded to be a meaningful item (*arthavat*) for the purpose of the designation of a nominal stem.

Explanation [NN.VII.29.c-d]: Cf. **Explanation [NN.VII.29.a-b]**.

NN.VII.30. (p. 132)

अयं भावः । भू सत्तायामित्याद्यर्थनिर्देशसहितेष्वसन्दिग्धेषु विभक्त्यसंवलितनिर्देशः परम्परापठनादिसिद्धो भाष्यकाराद्यभ्युपगतश्च । तस्य चोक्तलाघवानुगृहीताभेदपक्ष एवोपपत्तौ निर्बीजाविवक्षयोपपादनमयुक्तम् ।

सन्दिग्धस्थले तदकरणेऽप्यत्र विभक्तिविवक्षाया दुर्वारत्वात् । "प्रत्ययः,"
"परश्चे"ति नियमाच्च ।

Explanation [NN.VII.30]

[a] This is what is meant. There are usages such as *bhū sattāyām*, incorporating a mention of the meaning and where there is no doubt [what the items are]. In such usages, nominal inflections are not added. [Yet such usages are] well known in the oral tradition and are accepted by the author of the *Mahābhāṣya* and others.

[b] This usage can be justified only in the view of identity [of an imitated and an imitation word], with brevity, as demonstrated earlier. Therefore, it is wrong to attempt to justify [these] usages by taking recourse to the [so called] undesirability of nominal inflections, which has no basis.

[c] One may omit [nominal inflections] in cases [where they would create] uncertainty, and yet [under normal conditions] one must have nominal inflections in these cases.

[d] There is also a rule: "An affix always follows [a stem]."

Explanation [NN.VII.30.a]: The objector in **NN.VII.27** says that the imitations *bhū* etc. are meaningful nominal stems, but nominal inflections are not applied in order to avoid a possible confusion. This is not acceptable to grammarians. This is not true in the present case. Even if we apply a nominal inflection to *bhū*, it would not create any confusion. Moreover, these usages in the root-list are well known in the tradition and are accepted by all authorities. Therefore, one cannot give an arbitrary explanation, which lacks universality.

Explanation [NN.VII.30.b]: The explanations of grammarians given in the section **NN.VII.29** are standard explanations in the sense that they apply evenly to all verb roots in the root list. They also have the merit of economy. They do not require assumptions such as the undesirability of nominal inflections. Such assumptions are unwarranted and involve prolixity.

Explanation [NN.VII.30.c]: Kauṇḍabhaṭṭa points out that the assumption of the undesirability of nominal inflections does not apply to all cases. For instance, in the case of *bhū*, there would not be any confusion even with a nominal inflection. Thus one cannot say that the imitation *bhū* is a nominal stem, and yet the nominal inflection is undesirable. There is no basis for such undesirability. Therefore, the objector would not be able to explain these usages.

Explanation [NN.VII.30.d]: If an imitation is a nominal stem, then as a rule it must be followed by a nominal inflection. Rule P.3.1.1 (*pratyayaḥ*) is an *adhikāra* "heading" rule. The next rule P.3.1.2 (*paraś ca*) says that an affix is always added after a stem.

Patañjali and Kātyāyana have a long discussion on the interpretation of this rule. They conclude that it is a restriction on usage (*prayoga-niyama*) of both the affix and the stem. A stem must always precede an affix, and an affix must always follow a stem.[494] This is brought in here to suggest that one must never use a stem by itself; it must always be followed by an inflection. Thus, one cannot speak of a general undesirability of applying nominal inflections to imitations of verb roots, if one regards them to be meaningful nominal stems.

NN.VII.31. (p. 132)

उक्तश्रुतिषु च वृत्तावयवानां जहत्स्वार्थत्वाभ्युपगमादनुपपत्तिरस्त्येव भेदपक्षाश्रयणेऽपि । सा चावयव्यर्थमवयव आरोप्य समाधेयेति वृत्तिनिर्णये वक्ष्यते । उक्तसूत्रेष्वप्यनुकार्यशब्दानां स्थानित्वादेशत्वबोधनाय "षष्ठी स्थानेयोगे"त्याद्यनुरोधादसमर्थसमासवद्वक्ष्यमाणरीत्या प्रातिपदिकत्वविभक्त्यादिकं सौत्रमेव । "भुवो वुग् लुङ्लिटो"रित्याद्यप्येवमेव । तस्माद्युक्ततरमभेदपक्षं प्रतीमः ।

Translation [NN.VII.31]

[a] In the Vedic injunctions mentioned earlier, there is the difficulty of justifying [the Taddhita formations such as *vārttraghnī* and *aira*] even in the view that [an imitation and an imitated word] are different from each other, because the component parts of a complex formation (*vṛtti*) are considered to abandon their own independent meanings [in favor of the meaning of the new formation].

[b] As it will be explained later in the *Vṛtti-nirṇaya* [*VB*, pp. 144 ff], this difficulty can be explained away by superimposing the meaning of the whole [complex formation] on its parts.

[c] Even in the Pāṇinian rules mentioned earlier, there are nominal inflections [added to imitations of sounds] and the designation "nominal stem" [applied to imitations of sounds], in order to show that the imitated word is a substituendum or a substitute. This is obtained on the basis of rule P.1.1.49 (*ṣaṣṭhī sthāne-yogā*). [Hence, this occurrence of the designation "nominal stem" and nominal inflections] is a technical practice [of Pāṇini], as are the compounds [whose components do] not have a direct semantic-syntactic relationship. Rules like P.6.4.88 (*bhuvo vug luṅ-liṭoḥ*) also belong to this type. Therefore, we find that the view of non-difference is more logical.

[494] *prayoga-niyamārtham eva tarhi para-grahaṇaṃ kartavyam / ... 'siddhaṃ tūbhaya-niyamāt'* [*Vt*. 11 on P.3.1.2] / ... *ubhaya-niyamo 'yam / prakṛti-para eva pratyayaḥ prayoktavyaḥ, pratyaya-paraiva ca prakṛtiḥ iti* /, ***MB***, Vol.II., pp. 12-3.

Explanation [NN.VII.31.a]: Kauṇḍabhaṭṭa discusses the examples which the objector quoted in the section **NN.VII.27.** The objector tried to point out that according to grammarians, an imitation word is a meaningless word, and hence it is not a nominal stem. In such a case, a grammarian would not be able to explain the Taddhita forms in those Vedic injunctions. If the base form *vṛttra-han* is a meaningless imitation, then one cannot justify the Taddhita formation *vārttraghnī*. The objector believes that his view can explain these forms. According to him, an imitation word primarily signifies the imitated word, and hence it is a meaningful nominal stem.

Kauṇḍabhaṭṭa counters that argument. He says that in all complex formations (*vṛtti*), the constituent items abandon their own individual meaning; only the whole is a meaningful unit, with parts having no meaning. In that case, the basic linguistic items such as *vṛttra-han* would abandon their meaning, if at all they have any, and would become meaningless items. Thus, the same difficulty occurs in both views. Once, they are meaningless, how should we account for the Taddhita formation? Thus, these items could be meaningless by being meaningless to start with, or by abandoning their meaning.

Explanation [NN.VII.31.b]: Kauṇḍabhaṭṭa proposes that the constituents of a complex formation could be treated as meaningful items, by superimposing the meaning of the whole complex formation on them. This would have to be accepted even by the objector. Kauṇḍabhaṭṭa says that he has explained this argument in the *Vṛtti-nirṇaya* section of his work. In the *Samāsa-śakti-nirṇaya* section of the *Vaiyākaraṇa-bhūṣaṇa,* we find a statement to this effect, though it is not exactly identical with this argument.[495]

Explanation [NN.VII.31.c]: Pāṇini's rules quoted by the objector in **NN.VII. 27.d** contain nominal forms such as *eḥ*. This is the genitive singular of *i*, and *i* is the imitation of the sound *i* occurring in affixes like *-tiP*. The objector believes that the imitation *i* is a meaningful item, and hence a nominal stem, and thus takes nominal inflections.

Kauṇḍabhaṭṭa says that as a general theory, imitations are not meaningful items, and hence they are not nominal stems. However, Pāṇinian rules are an exception to this general view. Pāṇini uses nominal inflections after meaningless imitations for specific metalinguistic purposes. For instance, P.1.1.49 (*ṣaṣṭhī sthāne-yogā*) says that if an item occurs in the genitive case, then that item should be treated as the substituendum or the item undergoing substitution or replacement. There are other specific rules stating specific significance of other case endings.[496] Such a usage is exceptionally allowed in Pāṇini's rules, and cannot be cited to contradict a general theory.

To show that the Pāṇinian usage is in many cases an exception to general theories, Kauṇḍabhaṭṭa refers to another such case. By P.2.1.1 (*samarthaḥ pada-vidhiḥ*), the constituents of a complex formation (*vṛtti*) must be inflected items having mutual semantic relationship or expectancy (*ākāṅkṣā / vyapekṣā*). In the absence of such a relation, there

---

495 *yady api śabdāntaram eva vṛttir avayavā varṇavad anarthakās tathāpi sādṛśyāt tattvādhyavasānam padānām āśritya pṛthag-arthānām ekārthībhāva ity uktam /*, *VB*, p. 142.

496 For instance, see: P.1.1.66 (*tasminn iti nirdiṣṭe pūrvasya*), and P.1.1.67 (*tasmād ity uttarasya*).

cannot be a complex formation. If the constituents of a compound do not have such mutual expectancy or have mutual expectancy with words outside of the compound, then such compounds are called *asamartha-samāsa*s, and they are, in general, prohibited by P.2.1.1. However, Pāṇini himself uses some of such *asamartha-samāsas*, in certain rules. An example of such a usage is rule P.1.1.43 (*suḍ anapuṃsakasya*). Cardona discusses cases of such *asamartha* compounds in Pāṇini's rules.[497]

NN.VII.32. (p. 132)

अथ "भू सत्ताया"मित्यादावधातुरिति पर्युदासादेव न प्रातिपदिकत्वं न वा पदत्वम् । अन्यथा पर्युदासवैयर्थ्यापत्तिः । किञ्चाधातुरिति पर्युदासादर्थवत्त्वलाभादर्थवद्ग्रहणमुत्तरार्थमिति ग्रन्थानामेवमसामञ्जस्यापत्तिः । "भू सत्ताया"मित्यादेरनर्थकत्वात् । अनर्थकत्वादत्र विभक्तिर्नेत्यादि कृत्तद्धितसमासाश्चेति सूत्रे मनोरमायां स्पष्टत्वात् । अपि च धातुरनर्थक इति व्याहतमित्यर्थवत्सूत्रे मतान्तरदूषणाय मनोरमापि स्ववचनविरुद्धैव स्यात् ।

Translation [NN.VII.32]

[a] [Objection to the view of the grammarians]: [The word *bhū*] in *bhū sattāyām* is neither a nominal stem, nor an inflected nominal, simply because of the exclusion of verb roots [in P.1.2.45, *arthavad adhātur apratyayaḥ prātipadikam*, and not because it is meaningless]. Otherwise, this exclusion [of verb roots stated in the condition *adhātuḥ*] would be purposeless.

[b] Moreover, the statement "meaningfulness [as a condition for the classification of an item as a nominal stem by P.1.2.45] is obtained on the basis of the exclusion of verb roots, and hence [the explicit mention of] meaningfulness [in P.1.2.45] is only for the sake of being carried over into the following rules" would be contradicted, since [the *Prauḍha*]-*manoramā* clearly says: "[the word *bhū* in] *bhū sattāyām* is meaningless. Since it is meaningless, there is no nominal inflection after it."

[c] Even [the *Prauḍha*]-*manoramā* would contradict its own pronouncement, in criticism of some other view, when its states [on P.1.2.46]: "to say that something is a verb root and is meaningless is self-contradictory."

Explanation [NN.VII.32.a]: From this section up to section **NN.VII.35**, Kauṇḍabhaṭṭa presents objections to the view of grammarians. These objections are

497 Cardona (1967-b: 41ff).

directed against both the views of identity and difference between an imitation word and an imitated word. In **NN.VII.35**, the objector clearly rejects both of these alternatives.

The objector, in **NN.VII.27**, argued that an imitation primarily signifies the imitated word and hence is a meaningful item, and also is a nominal stem. Yet nominal affixes are not added in order to avoid confusion. Grammarians on the other hand consider imitations of verb roots etc. to be meaningless, and hence they do not take any nominal inflections, because they are not nominal stems.

The objector in this section takes a quite different position. He says that the imitation *bhū* retains its property of being a verb root. Therefore, though it is meaningful, it cannot get the designation "nominal stem," since verbs roots are excluded from the class of nominal stems by the exclusion stated by the term *adhātuḥ* in P.1.2.45. Since it is not a nominal stem, it cannot take any nominal inflections.

Explanation [NN.VII.32.b]: Both quotations in this section are from Bhaṭṭojī Dīkṣita's *Prauḍha-manoramā*. Let us discuss them separately and then see how they contradict each other according to the objector.

<u>Quotation 1:</u> Rule P.1.2.45 (*arthavad adhātur apratyayaḥ prātipadikam*) has two conditions, one of which, according to later grammarians, makes the other superfluous. The maxim *nañ-iva-yuktam anya-sadṛśādhikaraṇe* [*Paribhāṣā* 74 in *PS*] says that when there is a negative particle construed with a nominal, it denotes objects different from the ones denoted by the nominal, yet similar to the ones denoted by it. For instance, the sentence *abrāhmaṇam ānaya* "bring a non-Brahmin" means "bring someone who is not a Brahmin, but who is similar to a Brahmin in other respects." Patañjali says that after listening to this sentence, if someone were to bring a log of wood, the purpose would not be accomplished.[498]

Similarly, the condition *adhātuḥ* in P.1.2.45 refers that which is not a verb root, but which is similar to a verb root. The factor of similarity is explained by taking recourse to meaningfulness.[499] Thus, Bhaṭṭojī Dīkṣita says in his *Prauḍha-manoramā* that the condition of meaningfulness could be obtained by implication from the exclusion of verb roots, and yet Pāṇini explicitly states it in order that it may be continued in the next rule P.1.2.46.[500] This clearly implies that for Bhaṭṭojī Dīkṣita, all verb roots are meaningful items.

<u>Quotation 2</u>: Bhaṭṭojī Dīkṣita considers the word *bhū* in *bhū sattāyām* to be an imitation of the verb root *bhū*. It is meaningless, though it signifies the imitated verb root. Hence, it cannot get the designation "nominal stem," and consequentially it cannot get

498 *nañ-iva-yuktam anya-sadṛśādhikaraṇe tathā hy artha-gatiḥ / ... abrāhmaṇam ānayety ukte brāhmaṇa-sadṛśa evānīyate, nāsau loṣṭam ānīya kṛtī bhavati /*, *MB*, Vol.II., p. 39.

499 *arthavattvenaiva sādṛśyaṃ nānya-dharmeṇa /*, *BSR*, pp. 256-7; also: *LSR*, p. 257.

500 *adhātur iti paryudāsa-balena yady apy arthavattvaṃ labhyate, tathāpy uttarārthaṃ tad ity uktam / etac ca 'sup-tiṅ-antam padam' iti sūtre bhāṣye dhvanitam /*, *PM*, p. 257.

nominal inflections. However, Bhaṭṭojī Dīkṣita, at the same time, accepts that an imitation is identical with the imitated word.[501]

Apparently, this is contradictory. All verb roots are meaningful, and yet their imitations which are identical with them are not meaningful. This is the contradiction pointed out by the objector.

Explanation [NN.VII.32.c]: Here, the objector quotes another passage from the *Prauḍha-manoramā* which contradicts the above given passages. In this passage, Bhaṭṭojī Dīkṣita is criticizing some thinkers who believe that there are meaningless verb roots, and hence the exclusion of verb roots in P.1.2.45 would not imply the condition of meaningfulness. They point to verb roots like *i* in *adhīte* "studies." By itself, the root *i* does not mean anything, since it cannot be used by itself. It is always used with the preverb *adhi*. Bhaṭṭojī Dīkṣita counters this argument by saying that a verb root cannot be a meaningless item. In the case of *adhīte*, the meaningfulness of the verb root could be explained by imposing the meaning of the whole form on the constituent verb root.[502]

NN.VII.33. (p. 132)

न च "भू सत्ताया"मित्यनुकरणस्य न धातुत्वं, किन्त्वेतदनुकार्यस्य भवतीत्यादौ प्रयुज्यमानस्यैव तत्रैव नामत्वसुबुत्पत्त्योर्वारणाय पर्युदासोऽपीति वाच्यम् । एवं हि "भूवादयो धातव" इति सूत्रस्यानुकरणस्यानर्थकत्वेनानुकार्यस्य गणपाठाभावेनाधातुत्वापत्तावसंभवित्वापत्तेः । तस्य गणपठितत्वगर्भतायाः प्राग्व्युत्पादनात् । घटाभिन्नस्याघटत्ववद्धात्वभिन्नस्याधातुताया असम्भवाच्च ।

Translation [NN.VII.33]

[a] [Counter-objection by the grammarians]: The item *bhū* in *bhū sattāyām* which is an imitation is not itself classed as a root. This classification applies only to the imitated [root denoted by the imitation *bhū*] which is actually used in forms like *bhavati*. The exclusion [of verb roots in P.1.2.45, *arthavad adhātur apratyayaḥ prātipadikam*] also serves to prevent this [imitated root] from being classified as a nominal stem and [hence] receiving nominal inflections.

[b] [Reply of the objector]: One should not claim this. [If this claim were true], then it would be impossible to account for rule P.1.3.1 (*bhūvādayo*

---

501 *anukaraṇeṣu tu anukāryeṇa sahābheda-vivakṣāyām arthavattvābhāvād eva na prātipadikatvam / bhū sattāyām iti yathā /*, *PM*, p. 280.

502 *yat tv āhuḥ - paryudāso nārthavattvaṃ gamayati, anarthakayor api dhātu-pratyayayor darśanāt - 'adhīte,' 'yāvaka' iti / adhi-pūrvasyaiveṅaḥ prayogād viśiṣṭa evārthavān na tu kevalaḥ / 'iṅ adhyayane' ity ādy artha-nirdeśas tu avayave samudāyārthāropāt / ... atredaṃ vaktavyam - dhātur anarthaka iti tāvad vyāhatam / kriyā-vācakatvaṃ vinā dhātutvāyogāt / āropitaṃ tad iti cet satyaṃ, tāvataiveṣṭa-siddheḥ /*, *PM*, pp. 257-8.

dhātavaḥ), because the imitation [i.e. *bhū* in *bhū sattāyām*] is meaningless [for grammarians] and the imitated [verb root *bhū*] does not occur in the [root] list, and hence cannot get the designation of a verb root. However, it has been already pointed out that rule P.1.3.1 is based on items being listed in the [root] list [*VB*, pp. 47ff].

[c] Again, that which is identical with a pot cannot be something other than a pot; similarly the [imitation *bhū*] which is [held by grammarians to be] identical with an [imitated] verb root [*bhū*] could not be anything but a verb root.

Explanation [NN.VII.33.a]: For grammarians, an imitation of a verb root is not a verb root itself, though it is identical with the imitated verb root. The item *bhū* in *bhū sattāyām* is only an imitation, and its denotatum is the verb root *bhū* which occurs in forms like *bhavati*. The grammarian thinks that the exclusion of verb roots [*adhātuḥ*] in P.1.2.45 applies to the denotatum of the imitation *bhū*, but not to the imitation itself, since the imitation itself is not a verb root. This exclusion prevents the item *bhū* in forms like *bhavati* from being classified as a nominal stem, and hence from receiving nominal inflections. It is not meant to stop the classification of the imitation of a verb root as a nominal stem. This classification does not apply to the imitation of a verb root for a different reason, i.e. it is a meaningless item.

Explanation [NN.VII.33.b]: The objector says that the counter-objection of the grammarians should not be accepted as a valid argument. It would create severe problems in the interpretation of Pāṇinian rules. The objector quotes P.1.3.1 (*bhūvādayo dhātavaḥ*). This rule is traditionally interpreted to mean that the designation *dhātu* is given to those items which are listed in the root-list and signify activity.[503] To become a verb root, a linguistic item must fulfil both of these conditions.

The objector says that the view of the grammarians cannot explain this rule. According to them, the item *bhū* occurring in the root-list statement *bhū sattāyām* is an imitation which denotes the item *bhū* occurring in forms like *bhavati*, but does not signify activity. The item *bhū* in forms like *bhavati* signifies activity but is not listed in the root list. By this argument, not a single item would satisfy both conditions. Hence, rule P.1.3.1 would be without any examples.

Explanation [NN.VII.33.c]: Grammarians believe in the identity of an imitation and an imitated item. In that case, how could one say that *bhū* as an imitation of *bhū* in *bhavati* is identical with it, and yet is not a verb root. If x is a pot, and y is identical with x, then y must also be a pot. Similarly, if *bhū* is a verb root, and if its imitation *bhū* is identical with it, then the imitation *bhū* must also be a verb root.

---

503 *kriyā-vācino bhv-ādayo dhātu-saṃjñāḥ syuḥ / SK*, p. 3; *bhūś ca vāś ceti dvandvaḥ / ... bhū-prabhṛtayo vā-sadṛśāḥ / sādṛśyaṃ ca kriyā-vācakatvena /, PM*, p. 61; also: *MB*, Vol.I., Sec.II., p. 114.

NN.VII.34. (p. 132-3)

किञ्च "प्रकृतिवदनुकरण"मित्यतिदेशादेव धातुत्वप्रयुक्तपर्युदासलाभात् प्रातिपदिकत्वाभावसम्भवे कुतस्तत्पक्षाभ्युपगमः । कथमन्यथा "ॠत इद्धातो"रितीत्वं कीरित्याद्यनुकरणे लभ्येत ? न चैवं धातुत्वप्रयुक्तप्रकृतित्वलाभेन "न केवला प्रकृतिः प्रयोज्ये"ति निषेधलाभापत्तिः । "यत्तदेतेभ्यः परिमाणे वतुप्" इति ज्ञापकेन यावत्कार्याप्रवृत्तेर्ज्ञापितत्वात् । अत एव कीरित्यनुकरणे प्रातिपदिकत्वं सङ्गच्छते ।

Translation [NN.VII.34]

[a] [Objections against grammarians' view continued]: Moreover, it is possible to obtain the exclusion of verb roots [for an imitation], since it rests on an item being [considered to be] a verb root. [An imitation of a verb root might be considered to be a verb root] on the basis of the transfer maxim: "an imitation is similar to the imitated word." Hence, it is possible to avoid the classification [of *bhū* in *bhū sattāyām*] as a nominal stem. [If so], then why should one accept the view [of grammarians that an imitation is identical with an imitated word]?

[b] [If the above transfer maxim is not accepted], then how else can one get the substitute *i* [for *ṝ*] in the imitation *kīr* [of the verb root *kṝ*] by rule P.7.1.100 (*ṝta id dhātoḥ*) "final *ṝ* of a root is replaced by *i*."

[c] [Counter-objection by grammarians]: Since [imitations of verb roots are] roots [by being similar to the imitated roots], they would also be bases [for verbal affixes]. Therefore, the following prohibition would apply to them: "One should never use a base by itself."

[d] [Objector's reply to the counter-objection]: [This objection] should not be raised. Rule P.5.2.39 (*yat-tad-etebhyaḥ parimāṇe vatup*) is an indication that not all the operations [of the imitated word] apply [to the imitation]. Therefore, the designation "nominal stem" is in order in the case of the imitation *kīr* [which imitates the verb *kṝ*].

Explanation [NN.VII.34.a]: The objector says that imitations of verb roots could be considered to be verb roots by the maxim *prakṛtivad anukaraṇam bhavati* "imitation words are similar to imitated words." This maxim occurs in the *Paribhāṣenduśekhara* as *Paribhāṣā* 36. It says that an imitation behaves like the imitated word. However, this maxim is not obligatory, and hence in some respects, an imitation may behave differently.[504] By this maxim, the imitation *bhū* can have the property of being a verb root. This would help avoid the classification of the imitation of *bhū* as a nominal stem, and

[504] *PS*, pp. 128-9.

would explain the absence of nominal inflections. On the face of this legitimate explanation, one should not accept the view of grammarians that an imitation is identical with a verb root imitated by it.

Explanation [NN.VII.34.b]: Grammarians might want to accept the view of identity, but not accept the above quoted maxim. Therefore the objector points out the necessity of accepting the maxim. In P.7.2.75 (*kiraś ca pañcabhyaḥ*), Pāṇini uses the ablative singular form *kiraḥ* of the imitation of the verb root *kṝ*. This imitation has undergone the operation prescribed by P.7.1.100 (*ṝta id dhātoḥ*). This rule prescribes that the final *ṝ* of a verb root is replaced by *i*. This applies only to verb roots. But it can apply to an imitation of a verb root only on the basis of the transfer maxim.

Explanation [NN.VII.34.c]: A grammarian assumes here that this transfer maxim is obligatory. Thus an imitation of a verb root would always be a verb root, and therefore, it is a base for verbal affixes. A base cannot be used by itself. Thus, one would have to apply verbal affixes to the imitation *bhū* even in the statement *bhū sattāyām*.

Explanation [NN.VII.34.d]: The objector rejects this counter objection by pointing out that the transfer maxim is not obligatory. He quotes a rule of Pāṇini which indicates the non-obligatory character of this maxim. This is P.5.2.39 (*yat-tad-etebhyaḥ parimāṇe vatup*).

Rule P.7.2.102 (*tyad-ādīnām aḥ*) prescribes that, in the masculine, the final sound of words in the list beginning with the item *tyat* is substituted by the sound *a*. This has been applied in the imitation form *etebhyaḥ* in P.5.2.39.

etad + bhyas	
eta + a + bhyas	by P.7.2.102
eta + bhyas	by P.6.1.97
ete + bhyas	by P.7.3.103
etebhyarU	by P.8.2.66
etebhyaḥ	by P.8.3.15.

This form shows that an imitation of a nominal stem behaves like a nominal stem.

The same rule, P.5.2.39, also points out that an imitation behaves differently. Rule P.1.2.72 (*tyad-ādīni sarvair nityam*) says that if an item in the *tyad-ādi* list and a different item have to be compounded, then there is always a single-remainder (*eka-śeṣa*) complex formation (*vṛtti*), such that only the item in the *tyad-ādi* list is retained. Patañjali further points out that if a single-remainder complex formation is to be effected among two or more items in the *tyad-ādi* list, then the item which is given later in the list is retained.[505] By the application of this rule, only *etebhyaḥ* would be retained from the compound *yat-tad-etebhyaḥ*. However, we do not find this kind of a single-remainder complex formation effected by Pāṇini. This is taken to indicate that the operations which apply to an item do

[505] *MB*, Vol.I., Sec.II., p. 108; *MB-P*, Vol.I., Sec.II., p. 108; *SK*, p. 87.

not necesarily apply to its imitation. This rule, along with P.8.2.64 (*kṣiyo dīrghāt*) has often been cited as an indication that the transfer maxim is not obligatory.[506]

NN.VII.35. (p. 133)

तस्माद् “भू सत्ताया”मित्यभेदपक्षसाधकमयुक्तम् । किञ्चानुकार्यत्वानुकरणत्वधातुत्वाधातुत्वध्वनिमयत्ववर्णमयत्वरूपविरुद्धधर्माध्यासाद् अभेदपक्ष एवानयोर्न युक्तः । “भूवादय” इति सूत्रविरोधात् । गणपठितत्वे सति क्रियावाचित्वं धातुत्वमिति तदर्थः । स चास्मिन्न सम्भावितः । अनुकार्यस्य गणपाठाभावात् । अनुकरणस्यार्थवत्त्वेऽपि क्रियावाचकत्वाभावात् । समानानुपूर्वीकशब्दमात्रतात्पर्यकत्वं तादृशशब्दमात्रवाचकत्वं वात्र मतेऽनुकरणत्वम् । शब्दशब्दवारणाय मात्रपदम् । तस्माद् “भू सत्ताया”मित्युदाहरणं पक्षद्वयं चासङ्गतमेव ।

Explanation [NN.VII.35]

[a] [Objections against grammarian's view continued]: Therefore, the example *bhū sattāyām* is not a valid proof for establishing the view of identity [of an imitation word with the imitated word]. The view of identity is not valid, since one would have to assume superimposition of contradicting properties such as imitated-ness, imitation-ness, root-ness, non-root-ness, being composed of physical [non-linguistic] sounds and being composed of linguistic sounds.

[b] Even the view of difference is not valid, since it contradicts rule P.1.3.1 (*bhūvādayo dhātavaḥ*). This rule says that a verb root is that which is listed in the root-list and signifies action. This is not possible in the view of difference. The imitated words are not cited in the root list. Even if the imitation words [cited in the list] have meaning, yet they do not signify action.

[c] In this view, an imitation word is one which is used with the intention [of referring] only [to] another word of the same phonetic shape, or which only signifies another word with the same phonetic shape. The word "only" is added here to exclude the word "word." Therefore, the example *bhū sattāyām* and both the views [i.e. the views of identity and difference] are inconsistent.

Explanation [NN.VII.35.a]: In **NN.VII.33.c** and **NN.VII.34.a**, the objector has given a number of arguments to show that the example *bhū sattāyām* does not support the

---

[506] *BSS*, Vol.I., p. 518.

view of identity. The view of identity suffers another setback. The imitation words and imitated words have totally different properties, and hence they cannot be identified.

Explanation [NN.VII.35.b]: The view of difference is also not valid. If one accepts this view, then one cannot explain rule P.1.3.1 (*bhūvādayo dhātavaḥ*). For the explanation of these arguments, see: **Explanation [NN.VII.33.b-c]**.

Explanation [NN.VII.35.c]: In the view of difference, an imitated word *x* is different from the imitation word "*x*." However, they have the same phonetic shape (*samānā-nupurvī*). The imitation word "*x*" is different from the imitated word *x* in the sense that "*x*" is used with the intention of referring to or signifying only the word *x*, while *x* is used with the intention of signifying some meaning.

The objector thus discards both the views. He does not wish to commit himself to any one doctrine. However, he accepts the transfer maxim quoted in **NN.VII.34.a** and its non-obligatory character. With the help of this maxim, the objector is able to solve all practical difficulties.

NN.VII.36. (p. 134)

इति चेदत्रोच्यते । आनुपूर्वीभेद एव शब्दभेदे तन्त्रम् । अत एव नानार्थत्व-व्यवस्था । तथा च स्वाभिन्नशब्दमात्रतात्पर्यकोच्चारणविषयत्वार्थतात्पर्य-कोच्चारणविषयत्वरूपेऽनुकार्यत्वानुकरणत्वे कथं विरुद्धे ? कथं वा "भू सत्ताया"मिति शब्दमात्रतात्पर्यकस्य क्रियावाचकत्वरूपं धातुत्वम् । तथा च न पर्युदासवार्त्तापि । किन्त्वनर्थकत्वान्न नामत्वमित्येव युक्तम् । "प्रकृति-वदनुकरण"मित्यतिदेशोऽप्यधातुत्वप्रयुक्तसंज्ञा दुर्वारैव । छान्दसत्वं त्वगति-कगतिर्ज्ञापकमात्रोच्छेदकरश्चेति बोध्यम् ।

Translation [NN.VII.36]

[a] [In defense of grammarians]: If the above objections are posed, then we reply [in the following way]. The only true basis for differentiating words [from one another] is their difference in phonetic shape. For this reason, we can have one word with many meanings. An imitated word is the one uttered with the intention [of signifying] a meaning, and an imitation word is the one uttered with the intention of only [referring to] a word identical with itself. Therefore, how could these two contradict each other?

[b] Similarly, how could [the word *bhū* in] *bhū sattāyām*, which is intended only [to signify] an [imitated] word [*bhū*], become a verb root signifying an action? Therefore, there is no question of exclusion [i.e. *adhātuḥ* in P.1.2.45 applying to *bhū* in *bhū sattāyām*]. It is appropriate to say that it is not a nominal stem, simply because it is meaningless.

[c] Additionally, if the transfer rule, "an imitation is similar to an imitated word," is accepted, it is still difficult to avoid [applying] the class-name ["nominal stem"] consequent on the item not being a root. If one should say that [this absence of the nominal inflection is] typically Vedic, that would be an [acceptable last ditch] explanation, only if there were no other possible explanation. Further, [such a view] would [eventually] ruin [the possibility of] all indications (*jñāpaka*). This should be noted.

Explanation [NN.VII.36.a]: Kauṇḍabhaṭṭa now presents the view of grammarians, keeping in mind the extensive objections in sections **NN.VII.32-35**. In sections **NN.VII.36-37**, he presents justifications for the view of identity, and in section **NN.VII.38**, he offers justification for the view of difference. Kauṇḍabhaṭṭa says that one can differentiate two words from each other, if their phonetic shapes are different. The view of identity rests on this assumption. A word may signify meaning or it may signify itself. If it signifies itself, then it is an imitation. The difference in signification does not differentiate words. The same word can function in different capacities.

Explanation [NN.VII.36.b]: Grammarians accept that an imitation of a verb root and the imitated verb root are identical, and they do not accept that an imitation is a verb root. This can be clarified by saying that one and the same linguistic item gets different designations depending on different functions and capacities in which the item functions. When the item *bhū* functions as an imitation, it does not signify an action, and hence it is not a verb root. If the same item *bhū* is used to signify an action and forms a part of words like *bhavati*, then it is a verb root and not an imitation. Thus, the identity in shape between an imitation and an imitated word does not prevent their functioning differently and having different designations. For this reason, the exclusion of verb roots in P.1.2.45 does not apply to imitations of verb roots.

Explanation [NN.VII.36.c]: Now Kauṇḍabhaṭṭa counters the argument of the objector based on the transfer maxim, cf. **Explanation [NN.VII.34.a]**. The objector says that on the basis of this maxim, an imitation of a verb root can be considered to be a verb root. The grammarian points out that an imitation of a verb root has its natural meaninglessness, while the property of being a verb root is secondary, since it is a transferred property. It is difficult to avoid the classification of an imitation of a verb root as a nominal stem, except by taking recourse to its natural meaninglessness.[507]

As an extreme argument, the objector may say that imitations of verb roots are certainly nominal stems, and yet there are no nominal inflections. This is like Vedic usages where no general rules apply, and where there are more exceptions and variations than general rules.[508]

---

507 *arthavat-sūtre 'rthavattvaṃ vṛtti-viṣaya-bodhakatvam / śabdasya ca na vṛtti-viṣayatvam, mānābhāvāt / āśrayatvenaitad-upasthiteḥ /*, *BSR*, p. 279.

508 *sarve vidhayaś chandasi vaikalpikāḥ / bahulaṃ chandasīty ādir asyaiva prapañcaḥ /*, *SK*, p. 331.

Grammarians say that this is not the proper way. This is just making inconsistency a virtue. If we accept such an explanation, then nowhere can one presume any basic consistent structure of grammatical operations. Only a purposeful variation from the generally assumed consistency can be interpreted as being a special indication (*jñāpaka*). However, the objector seems to discard such a basic consistent structure.

NN.VII.37. (p. 133)

एवञ्च न धातुत्वाधातुत्वयोर्विरोधोऽपि । वर्णनित्यतावादिनामानुपूर्व्या ध्वनिमात्रनिष्ठत्वात्तस्योभयत्र तुल्यत्वात् । अव्यक्तानुकरणस्थले व्यक्ति-भेदेऽपि भेदप्रयोजकानुपूर्वीभेदाभावाद्युक्त एवाभेद इत्यभेदवादिनां मतम् ।

Translation [NN.VII.37]

[a] [In defense of grammarians]: Similarly, there is also contradiction between the properties of being a root and not being a root, because, in the view of [grammarians] who believe in the eternal character of linguistic sounds, a sequence belongs only to physical sounds, and this sequence is common to both [the verb root and its imitation].

[b] In the case of an imitation of inarticulate physical sounds, the individual sounds may differ, and yet, there is no difference in the sequence of sounds to differentiate [an imitation from the imitated sounds]. Hence, it is appropriate to consider them to be identical. This is the view of those who consider [an imitation and an imitated word to be] identical.

Explanation [NN.VII.37.a]: According to grammarian-philosophers, linguistic sounds are eternal, while the physical sounds of the world only help manifest these eternal sounds. This is roughly the doctrine of *Sphoṭa*, as it was later understood. The whole word, an inflected item, or even a sentence, is a structurally indivisible unit.[509] The sequence belongs only to physical sounds of the world which manifest the eternal word. In terms of this doctrine, the word *ghaṭa* and its imitation *ghaṭa* are identical in that it is only one and the same eternal word *GHAṬA* which is manifested by two different groups of perishable sound-instances, i.e. *gh-a-ṭ-a*$_1$ and *gh-a-ṭ-a*$_2$. In one manifestation, the word *GHAṬA* is used to signify a pot, while in a different manifestation, it is used to signify itself.

Explanation [NN.VII.37.b]: It is a somewhat different case with imitations of physical sounds like the sound of a falling object, i.e. *paṭat*. There is a genuine difference of kind between the imitation word and the imitated word. Kauṇḍabhaṭṭa says that there is

---

509 *vākyaṃ padaṃ cākhaṇḍam eva / ananta-varṇa-kalpane mānābhāvāt / ... tathā ca pratyakṣād vācakatvānyathānupapattyā tad evedam padam, tad evedaṃ vākyam iti pratītyā cākhaṇḍa-sphoṭaḥ siddhyati /*, *VB*, p. 249.

no difference in the sequence of manifesting sounds. Therefore, one should consider the imitation to be identical with the imitated word.

NN.VII.38. (p. 133)
अन्ये त्वित एवार्थभेदाच्छब्दभेदश्च मन्वानाः शब्दार्थवाचकत्वाभ्यामनयोर्भेदमिच्छन्ति । अत्र मते गणपठितशब्दवाच्यत्वं गणपठितत्वमतो न भूवादिसूत्रविरोधः । अस्मिन्मते “भू सत्ताया”मित्यत्र विभक्तिर्दुर्वारेत्यभिप्रेत्य पक्षद्वयं लक्ष्यानुसारेण स्वीकृतमाकर इति न कश्चिद्दोष इति ध्येयम् । इति श्रीवैयाकरणभूषणे नामार्थपरिच्छेदः समाप्तः ॥

Translation [NN.VII.38]

[a] [In defense of grammarians]: Others believe that if there is a difference in meaning, then there must be a difference in the words. Hence, [an imitation word and an imitated word] are different, since one signifies meaning, while the other signifies a word.

[b] In this view, "being listed in the list" means "being signified by an item listed in the list." Therefore, this view does not conflict with rule P.1.3.1 (*bhūvādayo dhātavaḥ*).

[c] In this view, a nominal inflection [after the imitation *bhū*] in *bhū sattāyām* is unavoidable. With this in view, both alternatives are adopted in the authoritative texts in grammar, in accordance with examples [at hand]. Therefore, it should be noted that there is no difficulty.

Thus ends the section on the meaning of nouns in the Vaiyākaraṇa-bhūṣaṇa.

Explanation [NN.VII.38.a]: The justification for the view of difference is the principle that where there is a difference in meaning, there must be a corresponding difference in the words, cf. **Explanation [NN.V.9.b]**. How this applies to an imitation word and an imitated word is discussed in detail, cf. **NN.VII.35.c**.

Explanation [NN.VII.38.b]: Here Kauṇḍabhaṭṭa rejects the difficulties pointed out by the objectors in **NN.VII.33.b** and **NN.VII.35.b**, by redefining the term "listed in the list." The objection was that in the view of difference, what is listed in the root list is an imitation which signifies a word, but not an action, while the item that occurs in the verb forms and signifies action is not listed in the root list. Thus, there could be no item which is listed in the root list and signifies action. Kauṇḍabhaṭṭa's restated definitions remove this difficulty. An item can signify action, and be signified by another item listed in the root list. Thus, P.1.3.1 does not become redundant.

Explanation [NN.VII.38.c]: Kauṇḍabhaṭṭa finally admits that in the view of difference one would not be able to explain the absence of nominal inflections in the statement *bhū sattāyām*. The imitation *bhū* primarily signifies the verb root *bhū*. It is thus a meaningful item different from a verb root, and hence it would certainly get the designation of a nominal stem. In that case, it has to take nominal inflections.

For this reason, Kauṇḍabhaṭṭa finally says that grammarians do not insist on any particular view. They should choose the view that suits an interpretation of a given rule, or derivation of a given linguistic formation. The science of grammar is finally concerned with describing and justifying usage as it is established by the people. What is given for grammar is the usage, and all the theories about that usage are subservient to the description of that usage, and are negotiable. Hence, Kauṇḍabhaṭṭa says that there is no problem in accepting both the alternative views, in order to be able to explain the diversified usage of language.

BIBLIOGRAPHY

Primary Sources:

BC *Bhāṭṭa-cintāmaṇi* by Gāgābhaṭṭa. Edited by Suryanarayan Shukla. *Chowkhamba Sanskrit Series* 6. Banaras, 1900.

BSR *Bṛhac-chabda-ratna* by Haridīkṣita; See *PM*.

BSS *Bṛhac-chabdendu-śekhara* by Nāgeśabhaṭṭa. Edited by Sitaram Shastri. In 3 volumes. *Sarasvatī Bhavana Granthamālā* 87. 1960. Banaras: Vārāṇaseya Saṃskṛta Mahāvidyālaya.

KM *Kārikāvalī* with *Muktāvalī* by Viśvanātha Tarkapañcānana. Edited by C. Sankara Rama Sastry. With five commentaries. *Sri Bālamanoramā Series* 6. Madras, 1923.

KP *Kāvya-prakāśa* by Mammaṭa. Edited by Vāmanācārya Jhaḷkīkar with his own commentary *Bālabodhinī*. 7th edition. Edited by R.D. Karmarkar. 1965. Pune: Bhandarkar Oriental Research Institute.

KS *Kāśikā-vṛtti* by Vāmana and Jayāditya. With the commentaries *Nyāsa* by Jinendra-buddhi and *Pada-mañjarī* by Haradatta. Edited by Dvarikadas Shastri and Kalika Prasad Shukla. In six volumes. *Prācya Bhāratī Series* 2. 1965-7. Banaras: Prācya Bhāratī Prakāshan and Tārā Publications.

KS-N *Nyāsa* by Jinendrabuddhi on *KS*, see: *KS*.

KS-P *Pada-mañjarī* by Haradatta on *KS*, see: *KS*.

LM *Vaiyākaraṇa-siddhānta-laghu-mañjūṣā* by Nāgeśabhaṭṭa, with *Kalā* by Bālambhaṭṭa and *Kuñjikā* by Durbalācārya. Edited by Madhava Shastri Bhandari. *Chowkhamba Sanskrit Series* 44. Banaras, 1925.

LM-KK *Kuñjikā* by Durbalācārya on *LM*, see: *LM*.

LM-KL *Kalā* by Bālambhaṭṭa on *LM*.

LSR *Laghu-śabda-ratna* by Nāgeśabhaṭṭa on *PM*, see: *PM*.

LSS *Laghu-śabdendu-śekhara* by Nāgeśabhaṭṭa. With six commentaries. Edited by Guruprasad Shastri. *Rajasthan Sanskrit College Series* 14. Banaras, 1936.

MB *Vyākaraṇa-mahābhāṣya* by Patañjali, with the commentaries *Pradīpa* by Kaiyaṭa, *Uddyota* by Nāgeśabhaṭṭa on *Pradīpa*, and *Chāyā* by Vaidyanātha Pāyaguṇḍe on *Uddyota*. In three volumes, first volumes in two sections. 1967. Delhi: Motilal Banarsidass.

MB-D *Dīpikā* [or *Ṭīkā*] by Bhartṛhari on *MB*. Edited by K.V. Abhyankar and V.P. Limaye. *Post-Graduate and Research Department Series* 8. 1970. Pune: Bhandrkar Oriental Research Institute.

MB-P *Pradīpa* by Kaiyaṭa on *MB*, see: *MB*.

MB-P-U *Uddyota* by Nāgeśabhaṭṭa on *MB-P*, see: *MB*.

MD *Maṇi-darpaṇa* by Rājacūḍāmaṇimakhin. Edited by T. Ganapati Sastri. *Trivandrum Sanskrit Series* XXXIV. Trivandrum, 1913.

MK *Mīmāṃsā-kośa*. Edited by Kevalānanda Sarasvatī. In 7 volumes. 1960-63. Vai: Prājña Pāṭhaśālā.

MKB *Mīmāṃsā-kaustubha* by Khaṇḍadeva. Edited by Chinna Swami Sastri. *Chowkhamba Sanskrit Series* 58. Banaras, 1923-33.

MS *Mīmāṃsā-sūtras* by Jaimini, with *Bhāṣya* by Śabara, and *Tantra-vārttika* and *Ṭup-ṭīkā* by Kumārila. In six volumes. Edited by Subba Sastri. *Ānandāśrama Sanskrit Series* 97. Pune, 1929.

MS-B(a) *Bhāṣya* by Śabara on *MS*, see: *MS*.

MS-B(b) *Bhāṣya* by Śabara on *MS*. In two volumes. Edited by Mahesachandra Nyāyaratna. 1889. *Bibliotheca Indica Series* 45. Calcutta: Asiatic Society of Bengal.

NK *Nyāya-kośa* by Bhīmācārya Jhaḷkīkar. 3rd revised edition by Vāsudeva Shastri Abhyankar. *Bombay Sanskrit and Prakrit Series* XLIX. 1928. Pune: Bhandarkar Oriental Research Institute.

NM *Nyāya-mañjarī* by Jayantabhaṭṭa. Edited by S.N. Shukla. In two volumes. 2nd edition. *Kashi Sanskrit Series* 106. Banaras, 1969.

NR *Nirukta* by Yāska. With a commentary by Durga. Edited by R.G. Bhadkamkar. *Bombay Sanskrit Series* 73 and 85. Bombay, 1919, 1942.

NR-B *Bhāṣya* by Durga on *NR*, see: *NR*.

NRM *Nyāya-ratna-mālā* by Pārthasārathimiśra. With the commentary *Nāyaka-ratna* by Rāmānujācārya. Edited by K.S. Ramaswami Sastri. *Gaikwad Oriental Series* LXXV. Baroda, 1937.

NS *Nyāya-sūtras* by Gautama. With *Bhāṣya* by Vātsyāyana. Edited by Ganganath Jha. *Poona Oriental Series* 58. Pune, 1939.

NS-B *Bhāṣya* by Vātsyāyana on *NS*, see: *NS*.

NV *Nyāya-vārttika* by Uddyotakara. *Nyāya-darśana* of Gautama, with Vātsyāyana's *Bhāṣya*, Uddyotakara's *Nyāya-vārttika*, Vācaspatimiśra's *Nyāya-vārttika-tātparya-ṭīkā*, and Udayana's *Pariśuddhi*. Edited by Anantalal Thakur. *Mithila Institute Series*, Ancient Text No. 20. Darbhanga, 1967.

NV-T *Nyāya-vārttika-tātparya-ṭīkā* by Vācaspatimiśra, see: *NV*.

P *Pāṇini-sūtras*.

PB *Praśastapāda-bhāṣya* by Praśastapāda on the *Vaiśeṣika-sūtra* by Kaṇāda, with Śrīdhara's *Nyāya-kandalī*. Edited by K.C. Chattopadhyaya. *Ganganatha Jha Granthamālā* 1. Banaras, 1963.

PB-K *Nyāya-kandalī* by Śrīdhara on *PB*, see: *PB*.

PB-S *Setu* by Padmanābhamiśra on *PB*. Edited by Gopinath Kaviraj and Dhundhiraj Sastri. *Chowkhamba Sanskrit Series* 61. Banaras, 1924-1931.

PLM *Parama-laghu-mañjūṣā* by Nāgeśabhaṭṭa, with the commentary *Jyotsnā* by Pt. Kalika Prasad Shukla. M.S. University of Baroda Research Series - 7. Baroda, 1961.

PLM(b) *Vaiyākaraṇa-siddhānta-parama-laghu-mañjūṣā* by Nāgeśabhaṭṭa. With a Hindi translation and commentary by Kapil Dev Shastri. 1975. Kurukshetra: Kurukshetra University.

PM *Prauḍha-manoramā* by Bhaṭṭojī Dīkṣita, with *Bṛhac-chabda-ratna* by Haridīkṣita and *Laghu-śabda-ratna* by Nāgeśabhaṭṭa. Upto *Avyayībhāva* section. Edited by Sitaram Shastri. *Nepāla Rājya Hindu Viśvavidyālaya Sanskrit Series* 3. Banaras, 1964.

PS *Paribhāṣenduśekhara* by Nāgeśabhaṭṭa. Edited and translated into Marathi with explanations by N.D. Vadegaonkar. Nagpur, 1936.

PV *Pramāṇa-vārttika* by Dharmakīrti. With *Vṛtti* by Manorathanandin. Edited by Dvarikadas Shastri. *Bauddha Bhāratī Series* 3. Banaras, 1968.

RP *Ṛgveda-prātiśākhya* by Śaunaka. With a commentary by Uvaṭa. Edited with translation and notes by Mangal Dev Shastri. Vol. II. Allahabad, 1931.

SD *Sāhitya-darpaṇa* by Viśvanātha Kavirāja. Edited by P.V. Kane. 3rd edition. Bombay, 1951.

SK *Siddhānta-kaumudī* by Bhaṭṭojī Dīkṣita. Edited by Vasudev Laxman Panshikar. Eleventh edition. 1938. Bombay: Nirnaya Sagar Press.

SKB(a) *Śabda-kaustubha* by Bhaṭṭojī Dīkṣita. In two volumes. Vindhyeshvari Prasad Dvivedi and Ganapati Shastri Mokate. *Chowkhamba Sanskrit Series* 2. Banaras, 1917.

SKB(b) *Śabda-kaustubha* by Bhaṭṭojī Dīkṣita. *Chowkhamba Sanskrit Series* 2, Vol. I. Fac. I-IV. Edited by Gopal Shastri Nene and Mukund Shastri Puntamkar. Revised Edition. Banaras, 1933.

SLV *Śloka-vārttika* by Kumārila, with *Nyāya-nirṇaya* by Pārthasārathimiśra. *Chowkhamba Sanskrit Series* 3. Banaras, 1898.

SLV-N *Nyāya-nirṇaya* by Pārthasārathimiśra on *SLV*, see: *SLV*.

SM *Vaiyākaraṇa-siddhānta-mañjūṣā* by Nāgeśabhaṭṭa. Edited by K.P. Shukla. *M. M. Śivakumāraśāstrī-Granthamālā* 3. 1977. Banaras: Sampurnananda Sanskrit University.

SM(S) *Vaiyākaraṇa-siddhānta-mañjūṣā* by Nāgeśabhaṭṭa. Critically edited by Kapil Dev Shastri. 1985. Kurukshetra: Vishal Publications.

SSP(a) *Śabda-śakti-prakāśikā* by Jagadīśa Bhaṭṭācārya. With two commentaries. Edited by J.S. Bhattacharya. *Kashi Sanskrit Series* 109. Banaras, 1934.

SSP(b) *Śabda-śakti-prakāśikā* by Jagadīśa Bhaṭṭācārya. Edited by Jībānanda Vidyāsāgara Bhaṭṭācārya. 2nd edition. Calcutta, 1904.

SV *Śakti-vāda* by Gadādhara Bhaṭṭācārya. With three commentaries. Edited by Gosvami Damodara Sastri. *Kashi Sanskrit Series* 57, *Nyāya* section 7. Banaras, 1927.

TC *Tattva-cintāmaṇi* by Gaṅgeśa. *Śabda-khaṇḍa* part II. *Bibliotheca Indica* Vol. 98, part IV, vol. II. With the commentary *Rahasya* by Mathurānātha Tarkavāgīśa. Edited by K.N. Tarkavagisa. Calcutta, 1901.

TC-R *Rahasya* by Mathurānātha Tarkavāgīśa on *TC*, see: *TC*.

TMT *Tautātika-mata-tilaka* by Bhavadevamiśra. In three volumes. Edited by Mangal Deva Shastri. *The Princess of Wales, Sarasvatī Bhavana Texts* 79. Banaras, 1944.

TS *Tarka-saṃgraha* by Annambhaṭṭa, with the auto-commentary *Dīpikā* and eight other commentaries. Edited by Satkari Sharma Vangiya. *Kāshi Sanskrit Series* 187. Banaras, 1969.

TS-D *Dīpikā* by Annambhaṭṭa on his own *TS*, see: *TS*.

TT *Ṭup-Ṭīkā* by Kumārila on *MS-B*, see: *MS-B(a)*.

TTS *Tattva-saṃgraha* by Śāntarakṣita, with *Pañjikā* by Kamalaśīla. Edited by Dvarikadas Shastri. *Bauddhabhāratī Series* 1-2. Banaras, 1968.

TV(a) *Tantra-vārttika* by Kumārila on *MS-B*, see: *MS-B(a)*.

TV(b) *Tantra-vārttika* by Kumārila on *MS-B*. Edited by Gangadhara Sastri. *Banaras Sanskrit Series* 3. Banaras, 1903.

TV-NS *Nyāya-sudhā* by Someśvarabhaṭṭa on *TV*. Edited by Mukunda Sastri. *Chowkhamba Sanskrit Series* 14. Banaras, 1901-9.

VB *Vaiyākaraṇa-bhūṣaṇa* by Kauṇḍabhaṭṭa with *VBS* and *VBS-K*. Edited by K.P. Tripathi. *Bombay Sanskrit and Prakrit Series* LXX. Bombay, 1915.

VB(M) *Vaiyākaraṇa-bhūṣaṇa* by Kauṇḍabhaṭṭa. Edited by Vidya Nivas Misra. Vol. I. 1987. Banaras: Bharatiya Vidya Prakashan.

VB(B) *Bṛhad-vaiyākaraṇa-bhūṣaṇa* by Kauṇḍabhaṭṭa. With the commentary *Rūpālī* by Manudeva Bhattacharya. *Harjīvandas Prācyavidyā Granthamālā* 2. 1985. Banaras: Chowkhamba Amarabharati Prakashan.

VBS *Vaiyākaraṇa-bhūṣaṇa-sāra* by Kauṇḍabhaṭṭa. For various editions, see: *VB*, *VBS-D*, *VBS-K*, *VBS-P*, *VBS-S*, *VBS-SV*, and *VBS-T*.

VBS-D *Darpaṇa* commentary by Harivallabha Sastri on *VBS*. With the text of *VBS*, and the commentary *Prabhā* by Bālkṛṣṇa Pañcolī on *VBS*. *Ādarśa Granthamālā* 2. Banaras, 1947.

VBS-K *Kāśikā* commentary by Harirāma Kale on *VBS*, see: *VB*.

VBS-P *Prabhā* commentary by Bālkṛṣṇa Pañcolī on *VBS*, see: *VBS-D*.

VBS-S *Śāṅkarī* commentary by Śaṅkaraśāstrī Mārulkar on *VBS*. *Ānandāśrama Sanskrit Series* 135. Pune, 1957

VBS-SV *Sāvitrī*, a commentary in Hindi by Adya Prasad Mishra on *VBS*. *Gangānātha Jhā Granthamālā* 11. 1988. Banaras: Sampurnananda Sanskrit University.

VBS-T *Tattva-darśanī* by Peri Suryanarayana Sastry on *VBS*. Vizianagaram, 1978.
VP *Vākya-padīya* by Bhartṛhari.
VP(P) *Vākya-padīya* by Bhartṛhari. Edited by K.V. Abhyankar and V.P. Limaye. *University of Poona Sanskrit and Prakrit Series* 2. Pune, 1965.
VP-A *Ambākartrī* commentary on *VP kāṇḍas* I and II by Raghunātha Śarmā. *Sarasvatī Bhavana Granthamālā* 91. Vol. I published in 1963 and vol. II published in 1968. Volume I with *Svopajña-ṭīkā*, and volume II with *Svopajña-ṭīkā* and Puṇyarāja's *Ṭīkā* on *VP kāṇḍa* II. Banaras.
VPB *Vedānta-paribhāṣā* by Dharmarājādhvarīndra. Translated and annotated by Svami Madhavananda. 3rd edition. 1963. Howrah: Ramakrishna Belur Matha.
VP-H(p) *Prakīrṇaka-prakāśa* commentary by Helārāja on *VP kāṇḍa* III. Edited by K.A. Subramania Iyer. *Deccan College Monograph Series* 21, vol. I. Pune, 1963.
VP-H(b) *Prakīrṇaka-prakāśa* by Helārāja on *VP kāṇḍa* III. Edited by Gangadhara Sastri and Ramachandra Sastri. *Banaras Sanskrit Series* 5, vol. II. Banaras, 1905.
VP-P *Ṭīkā* by Puṇyarāja on *VP kāṇḍa* II, see: *VP-A*.
VP-S *Svopajña-ṭīkā* on *VP kāṇḍas* I and II, see: *VP-A*.
VV *Vyutpatti-vāda* by Gadādharabhaṭṭa, with commentary *Jayā* by Jayadevamiśra. 3rd edition. Allahabad, 1953.

Secondary Sources:

Alston, W.P. 1964. *Philosophy of Language. Foundation of Philosophy Series.* 2nd edition. Engelwood Cliffs, N.J.: Princeton-Hall Inc.
Arora, Sudesh. 1969. *Ācārya Kauṇḍabhaṭṭa viracita Vaiyākaraṇa-bhūṣaṇa-sāra kā Dhātvartha-prakaraṇa*. In Hindi. Delhi: Nirman Prakashan.
Bali, Suryakant. 1976. *Bhaṭṭojī Dīkṣita: His contribution to Sanskrit Grammar*. Delhi: Munshiram Manoharlal Publishers, Pvt. Ltd.
Biardeau, M. 1967. *Théorie de la Connaissance et Philosophie de la Parole dans le Brahmanisme Classique*. Paris: Mouton and Co.
Brugmann, Karl. 1897. *Nature and Origin of Noun Genders in the Indo-European Languages*. Translated from German by E.Y. Robbins. New York.
Buyssens, Eric. 1970. "The Common Name and the Proper Name." In *Studies in General and Oriental Linguistics*, presented to Shiro Hattori. Tokyo, 1970.
Cardona, George. 1965. "On Pāṇini's Morphophonemic Principles." *Language*, vol. 41.
----------. 1967-a. "Pāṇini's Syntactic Categories." *Journal of Oriental Institute*, Baroda, vol. XVI.
----------. 1967-b. "Negation in Pāṇini's Rules." *Language*, vol. 43.
----------. 1967-8. "Anvaya and Vyatireka in Indian Grammar." *Adyar Library Bulletin*, vol. 31-2.

----------. 1968. Review of *Sphoṭa-nirṇaya* by S.D. Joshi. *Journal of Oriental Institute*, Baroda, vol. XVII.

----------. 1970. "Some Principles of Pāṇini's Grammar." In *Journal of Indian Philosophy*, Vol.1, pp. 40-74.

----------. 1971. "Cause and Causal Agent: The Pāṇinian View." In *Journal of the Oriental Institute*, Baroda, Vol. 21, pp. 20-40.

----------. 1974. "Pāṇini's Kārakas: Agency, Animation and Identity." In *Journal of Indian Philosophy*, Vol.2, pp. 231-306.

Coward, Harold G., and K. Kunjunni Raja. 1990. *The Philosophy of the Grammarians, Encyclopedia of Indian Philosophies*, vol. 5. Princeton: Princeton University Press.

Deshpande, Madhav M. 1975. *Critical Studies in Indian Grammarians I: The Theory of Homogeneity [Sāvarṇya]*. The Michigan Series in South and Southeast Asian Languages and Linguistics, No. 2. Ann Arbor: Center for South and Southeast Asian Studies, The University of Michigan.

----------. 1979. "Candragomin's Syntactic Rules: Some Misconceptions." In *Indian Linguistics*, Vol.40, pp. 133-145.

----------. 1979-b. *Sociolinguistic Attitudes in India: An Historical Reconstruction. Linguistica Extranea, Studia 5*. Ann Arbor: Karoma Publishers, Inc.

----------. 1980. *Evolution of Syntactic Theory in Indian Grammar: Syntax of the Sanskrit Infinitive -tumUN*. Ann Arbor: Karoma Publishers, Inc.

----------. 1985. "Historical Change and the Theology of Eternal Sanskrit." In *Zeitschrift für vergleichende Sprachforschung*, Vol. 98, pp. 122-149.

----------. 1985-b. *Ellipsis and Syntactic Overlapping: Current Issues in Pāṇinian Syntactic Theory*. Post Graduate and Research Department Series No. 24. Pune: Bhandarkar Oriental Research Institute.

----------. 1991. "Prototypes in Pāṇinian Syntax." In *Journal of the American Oriental Society*, Vol. 111, pp. 465-480.

Devasthali, G.V. 1948. "Śabara and Nyāya-Vaiśeṣika." *Journal of Oriental Research*, Madras, vol. XVIII.

----------. 1959. *Mīmāṃsā, the Vākya-śāstra of Ancient India*. Bombay: Booksellers' Publishing Company.

D'sa, Francis X. 1980. *Śabdaprāmāṇyam in Śabara and Kumārila: Towards a Study of the Mīmāṃsā Experience of Language*. Publications of the de Nobili Research Library. Vienna: Institut für Indologie der Universität Wien.

Edgerton, Franklin. 1929. *Āpadeva's Mīmāṃsā-nyāya-prakāśa*, with English translation and annotations. New Haven: Yale University Press.

Faddegon, B. 1936. "Studies on Pāṇini's Grammar. *Verhandeling der Koninklijke Akademie van Wetenschappen te Amsterdam*, vol. 38, no. 1. Amsterdam.

Frauwallner, Erich. 1960. "Sprachtheorie und Philosophie im Mahābhāṣya des Patañjali." *Wiener Zeitschrift für die Kunde Süd und Ostasiens*, band IV.

Gächter, Othmar. 1983. *Hermeneutics and Language in Pūrvamīmāṃsā*. Delhi: Motilal Banarsidass.

Garge, Damodar Vishnu. 1952. *Citations in Śabara-Bhāṣya: A Study*. Deccan College Dissertation Series: 8. Pune: Deccan College.

Gune, Jayashree A. 1978. *The Meaning of Tenses and Moods, the text of Kauṇḍabhaṭṭa's Lakārārthanirṇaya with introduction, English translation and explanatory notes*. Pune: Deccan College.

Ingalls, D.H.H. 1951. *Materials for the Study of Navya-Nyāya Logic. Harvard Oriental Series* 40. Cambridge: Harvard University Press.

Iyer, K.A. Subramania. 1969. *Bhartṛhari, A Study of the Vākya-padīya in the Light of the Ancient Commentaries*. Pune: Deccan College.

Jacob, G.A. 1907. *Laukikanyāyāñjali*. Part I. 2nd revised edition. Bombay: Nirnaya Sagara Press.

Jha, Ganganath. 1914. *English Translation of Kumārilabhaṭṭa's Tantra-vārttika*. Bibliotheca Indica. Calcutta: Asiatic Society.

Joshi, S.D. 1960. *Kauṇḍabhaṭṭa on the Meaning of Sanskrit Verb-roots*. Ph.D. dissertation. Harvard University, Department of Sanskrit and Indian Studies.

----------. 1967. *Sphoṭa-nirṇaya of Kauṇḍabhaṭṭa*. Edited with translation, notes and introduction. Pune: University of Poona, Centre of Advanced Study in Sanskrit.

----------. 1968. *Samarthāhnika, Patañjali's Vyākaraṇa-Mahābhāṣya*. Edited with translation and notes. Pune: University of Poona, Centre of Advanced Study in Sanskrit.

Joshi, S.D. and J.A.F. Roodbergen. 1975. *Kārakāhnika, Patañjali's Vyākaraṇa-Mahābhāṣya*. Edited with translation and notes. Pune: University of Poona, Centre of Advanced Study in Sanskrit.

----------. 1986. *Paspaśāhnika, Patañjali's Vyākaraṇa-Mahābhāṣya*. Edited with translation and notes. Pune: University of Poona, Centre of Advanced Study in Sanskrit.

Kiparsky, Paul. 1982. *Some Theoretical Problems in Pāṇini's Grammar*. Post-Graduate and Research Department Series, No. 16. Pune: Bhandarkar Oriental Research Institute.

Lewis, C.I. 1944. "The Modes of Meaning." In *Semantics and Philosophy of Language*, a collection of readings edited by L. Linsky. Urbana: University of Illinois Press.

Liebich, Bruno. 1923. "Über den Sphoṭa." In *Zeitschrift der Deutschen Morgenländischen Gesellschaft*, vol. 77.

Loux, Michael J. 1970. "The Problem of Universals." In *Universals and Particulars*, edited by M.J. Loux. New York: Anchor Books.

Matilal, Bimal Krishna. 1968. *Navya-Nyāya Doctrine of Negation. Harvard Oriental Series* 46. Cambridge: Harvard University Press.

----------. 1971. *Epistemology, Logic and Grammar in Indian Philosophical Analysis.* The Hague/Paris: Mouton.

----------. 1985. *Logic, Language and Reality: an introduction to Indian philosophical studies.* Delhi: Motilal Banarsidass.

----------. 1986. *Perception: An Essay on Classical Indian Theories of Knowledge.* London: Oxford University Press.

----------. 1991. "Bhavānanda on 'What is Kāraka?'." In *Pāṇinian Studies: Professor S.D. Joshi Felicitation Volume.* Edited by Madhav M. Deshpande and Saroja Bhate. Pp. 263-282.

Mazumdar, Pradip Kumar. 1977. *The Philosophy of Language, in the light of Pāṇinian and the Mīmāṃsaka schools of Indian Philosophy.* Calcutta: Sanskrit Pustak Bhandar.

Mishra, Radheshyam. 1970. *Vyākaraṇaśāstradṛṣṭyā jātisvarūpavimarśaḥ.* Khajurhara, Uttar Pradesh: Śrīśivasaṃkaṭaharaṇādarśasaṃskṛtamahāvidyālayaḥ.

Misra, Ramamanohar. 1983. *Bhūṣaṇa-sāra-parama-laghu-mañjūṣayoḥ siddhāntānāṃ samīkṣā.* Sarasvatī Bhavana Studies, Vol. XXXII. Banaras: Sampurnananda Sanskrit Vishvavidyalaya.

Quine, W.V. 1940. *Mathematical Logic.* Reprinted as a Harper Torchbook in 1962. New York: Harper.

Raja, Kunjunni. 1963. *Indian Theories of Meaning, The Adyar Library Series* 91. Madras: Adyar Library and Research Centre.

Rocher, Rosane. 1966. "*Bhāva* 'état' et *kriyā* 'action' chez Pāṇini." In *Researches Linguistiques en Belgique*, edited by Yvan Lebrun. Universa Wetteren, Belgium.

Russell, Bertrand. 1940. *An Inquiry into Meaning and Truth.* Reprinted in 1967. London: Penguin Books Ltd.

Sarma, Sreekrishna. 1957. "The words Ākṛti and Jāti in the Mahābhāṣya." *Adyar Library Bulletin*, vol. XXI.

Sastri, Bhimasen. 1969. *Vaiyākaraṇa-bhūṣaṇa-sāra* with a Hindi commentary called *Bhaimī*. Delhi.

Scharf, Peter M. 1990. *The denotation of generic terms in ancient Indian grammar, Nyāya, and Mīmāṃsā.* University of Pennsylvania Ph.D. dissertation. Philadelphia.

Scharfe, Hartmut. 1961. *Die Logik im Mahābhāṣya.* Deutsche Akademie der Wissenschaften zu Berlin. Institut für Orientforschung. Veröffentlichung, Nr. 50. Berlin: Akademie Verlag.

Sharma, Dhirendra. 1970. *The Negative Dialectics of India: A Study of the negative dialecticism in Indian Philosophy*. East Lansing, Michigan.

Shastri, Ashutosh Bhattacharya. 1936. *Studies in Post-Śaṃkara Dialectics*. Calcutta: University of Calcutta.

Specht, Ernst Konrad. 1969. *The Foundations of Wittgenstein's Late Philosophy*, translated from German by D.E. Walford. NewYork: Barnes and Noble Inc.

Staal, J.F. 1966. "Indian Semantics I." *Journal of the American Oriental Society*, vol. 86.

----------. With Paul Kiparsky. 1969. "Syntactic and Semantic Relations in Pāṇini." *Foundations of Language*.

Stcherbatsky, Theodor. 1930. *Buddhist Logic*. Originally published in Leningrad in 1930. Reprinted in Dover Paperbacks, 1962.

Strauss, Otto. 1927. "Altindische Speculationen über die Sprache und ihre Probleme." *Zeitschrift der Deutschen Morgenländischen Gesellschaft*.

Tripathi, Ramanarayan. 1970. "Śabdārtha-niṣṭha-liṅga-vimarśaḥ." In *Ṛtam, Journal of Akhil Bharatiya Sanskrit Parishad*, vol. I.

Vyākaraṇopādhyāyā, Vedavatī. 1964. Introduction to her edition of the *Vāmanīya-liṅgānuśāsana*. Ajmer: Bharatiya Prachya Vidya Pratishthan.

INDEX